Climate Change and Sustainable Development

Climate Change and Sustainable Development covers the climatic and atmospheric changes, greenhouse gases and their impact on ecosystem, biodiversity, water resources, agriculture and food security, human health, extreme weather, and environment across two sections. The mitigation and adaptation strategies involving sustainable development is also illustrated, including efficient technology, renewable energy, developmental activities control, and so forth. Nanotechnology for sustainable development, forest protection, environment, social and economic sustainability, and climate change policy planning of international bodies like UNFCC, UNDP, Kyoto Protocol is also included.

FEATURES

- Covers climate change fundamentals and its impact on different ecosystems and natural disasters
- Describes nonrenewable energy aspects like fossil fuel, coal, oil, natural gas, and so forth
- Explores sustainable development in terms of environment, social, and economic aspects
- Includes species diversity and loss, agriculture productivity, water resources scarcity, health and environmental, rise in sea level, and coastal area submergence
- Illustrates scientific hybridization of traditional ecological knowledge for enhancing climate change adaptation

This book is aimed at graduate students and researchers in engineering and public policy, engineering management, sustainable engineering, renewable energy engineering, environmental engineering, and sustainability.

Climate Change and Sustainable Development

Edited by
M. H. Fulekar and
Rama Shanker Dubey

Boca Raton London New York

CRC Press is an imprint of the
Taylor & Francis Group, an **informa** business

First edition published 2023
by CRC Press
6000 Broken Sound Parkway NW, Suite 300, Boca Raton, FL 33487–2742

and by CRC Press
4 Park Square, Milton Park, Abingdon, Oxon, OX14 4RN

CRC Press is an imprint of Taylor & Francis Group, LLC

© 2023 selection and editorial matter, M. H. Fulekar and Rama Shanker Dubey; individual chapters, the contributors

Reasonable efforts have been made to publish reliable data and information, but the author and publisher cannot assume responsibility for the validity of all materials or the consequences of their use. The authors and publishers have attempted to trace the copyright holders of all material reproduced in this publication and apologize to copyright holders if permission to publish in this form has not been obtained. If any copyright material has not been acknowledged please write and let us know so we may rectify in any future reprint.

Except as permitted under U.S. Copyright Law, no part of this book may be reprinted, reproduced, transmitted, or utilized in any form by any electronic, mechanical, or other means, now known or hereafter invented, including photocopying, microfilming, and recording, or in any information storage or retrieval system, without written permission from the publishers.

For permission to photocopy or use material electronically from this work, access www. copyright.com or contact the Copyright Clearance Center, Inc. (CCC), 222 Rosewood Drive, Danvers, MA 01923, 978–750–8400. For works that are not available on CCC please contact mpkbookspermissions@tandf.co.uk

Trademark notice: Product or corporate names may be trademarks or registered trademarks and are used only for identification and explanation without intent to infringe.

ISBN: 978-1-032-07139-8 (hbk)
ISBN: 978-1-032-07140-4 (pbk)
ISBN: 978-1-003-20554-8 (ebk)

DOI: 10.1201/9781003205548

Typeset in Times
by Apex CoVantage, LLC

Dedication

To
Ashita Rai
My best student
for her dedication, devotion, and invaluable
contribution in editing the book
M. H. Fulekar

To
Late Smt. Shanti Devi and Sri Tribhuwan Nath Dubey
My beloved parents
for their unconditional love on me throughout my life
Rama Shanker Dubey

Dedication

Contents

About the Editors ix
List of Contributors xi
Foreword xiii
Smt. Manisha Rajiv Vakil
Preface xv
Acknowledgements xvii

Chapter 1 Climate Change—Global Environmental Concern 1

Ashita Rai and M. H. Fulekar

Chapter 2 Climate Change and Planetary Sustainability 11

Ram Boojh

Chapter 3 Carbon Dioxide Refineries, Hydrogen Economy, and
the Net Zero Goal 31

Ganapati D. Yadav

Chapter 4 Climate Change Impacts on Agriculture: Crop Productivity
and Food Security 61

Pratibha Singh, Shivani Singh, and Rama Shanker Dubey

Chapter 5 Climate Change–Induced Soil Drought and Its Implication
on Phytoremediation of Heavy Metal–Contaminated Soil 87

*Pallavi Sharma, Ambuj Bhushan Jha, and
Rama Shanker Dubey*

Chapter 6 The Impact of Climate Change on Crop Production and
Combat Strategies 103

*Akansha Singh, Esha Rami, Priti Upadhyay, and
Ajit K. Gangawane*

Chapter 7 Environment and Sustainable Development 117

Ashita Rai and M. H. Fulekar

Chapter 8 Thermal Comfort in Informal Settlements: Case Studies in Sub-Saharan Africa... 129

Manuel Correia Guedes, Gonçalo Araújo, and Nádia Albuquerque

Chapter 9 Endorsing Scientific Hybridization of Traditional Ecological Knowledge (TEK) for Enhancing Climate Change Adaptation (CCA) Across Diverse Sectors 149

Suvha Lama, Shalini Dhyani, Atya Kapley, and Rakesh Kumar

Chapter 10 Eco-Hydrology: Conservation of Water Resources 171

Ashita Rai and M. H. Fulekar

Chapter 11 Algae as a Biomarker Using the Free Air Carbon Dioxide Enrichment (FACE) System 181

Khushboo Iqbal, Sanskriti Singh, Behnam Asgari Lajayer, Smriti Shukla, Kartikeya Shukla, Ajit Varma, and Arti Mishra

Chapter 12 Wind Power 199

Dr. Anwesha M. Bhaduri

Chapter 13 Climate Change—International Policies 211

Ashita Rai, M. H. Fulekar, and Rama Shankar Dubey

Chapter 14 Climate Change—National Action Plan 223

Ashita Rai and M. H. Fulekar

Glossary 239
Index 249

About the Editors

M.H. Fulekar is Senior Professor, Environmental Sciences and Joint Director (R&D), Center of Research for Development, Parul University, Gujarat, India. He worked as Professor and Head, Life Sciences (Environmental Biotechnology), University of Mumbai (2002–2011); Senior Professor and Dean, School of Environment and Sustainable Development, Central University of Gujarat (2011–2019); and Director, Central University of Gujarat. He also served as Vice Chancellor (I/C), Central University of Gujarat, Gandhinagar. Fulekar possesses over 38 years of experience in research and teaching. He has published 350 research papers and articles in international and national journals of repute and has two patents in his credit. He is also an author of 15 books published by CRC, Springer, IK International, Oxford, etc. He has guided 32 PhD and 22 MPhil students in environmental biotechnology and environmental nanotechnology. As Principal Investigator, he has completed research projects for UGC, CSIR, BRNS, DBT R&D and industrial projects. He has been awarded ILO fellowship ILO/UNDP1985; ILO/FINNIDA; ILO/JAPAN. UGC-awarded BSR fellow (2018). He has achieved "Who's Who" in science and engineering USA in 1998 and "Outstanding Scientist of the 20th Century" in 2000, from International Biographical Centre, Cambridge, England. He is also a member of New York Academy of Sciences, USA. He is a recipient of Education Leadership Award and International award for Environmental Biotechnology. Recently he has been awarded as Eminent Educationist. He has worked in various capacities in university administration. Areas of research interest are as follows: environmental science, environmental biotechnology, environmental nanotechnology. As an expert, he visited USA, Australia, Singapore, Thailand, Hong Kong, Nepal, etc.

Dr. Rama Shanker Dubey (born 23 December 1955) is serving as Vice Chancellor of the Central University of Gujarat at Gandhinagar, India. He has also served as Vice Chancellor of Tilka Manjhi Bhagalpur University, Bihar, and Guru Ghasidas University, Bilaspur in India. He holds MSc and PhD degrees in biochemistry from Banaras Hindu University. For over 45 years he has conducted pioneering research on environmental issues focusing on soil salinity, water stress, and metal toxicity effects on key metabolic alterations in plants and has characterized many novel proteins/enzymes associated with stress tolerance. His work on the role of antioxidative defence mechanisms in combating drought and metals-induced oxidative damage in crop plants has been well recognized. He has over 173 scientific publications with 18,000+ citations, h-Index 47 and i10-Index 113. He has guided 32 doctoral students and has worked as a visiting scientist in reputed laboratories of Sweden, Germany, and Japan. He is the recipient of several national and international awards in environmental biochemistry and biotechnology, like the BHU Medal in 1976; Young Scientist Award in 1982; Swedish Institute Fellowship in 1989; Japan Society for Promotion of Science Fellowships in 1998, 2005; INSA-German Academy of Science Exchange Program Nominations in 1997, 2003, 2007. He is a fellow of the Indian Society of Agricultural Biochemists, Biotech Research Society of India, and Bio-Ved Research Society of India. He is serving on the editorial board of the Journal of Agronomy and Crop Science and the Indian Journal of Agricultural Biochemistry.

Contributors

Albuquerque, Nádia
Instituto Superior Tecnico, University of Lisbon, Portugal

Araújo, Gonçalo
Instituto Superior Tecnico, University of Lisbon, Portugal

Bhaduri, Anwesha M.
North East Scotland College, Aberdeen, United Kingdom

Boojh, Ram
Mobius Foundation, Laxmi Nagar, Vikas Marg, Delhi, India and Ex-expert, United Nations Educational, Scientific and Cultural Organization

Dhyani, Shalini
Water Technology and Management Division, CSIR-National Environmental Engineering Research Institute, Nagpur, India

Dubey, Rama Shanker
Central University of Gujarat, Sector-29, Gandhinagar, Gujarat, India

Fulekar, M. H.
Center of Research for Development, Parul University, Vadodara, Gujarat, India

Gangawane, Ajit K.
Department of Biochemistry, Parul Institute of Applied Science, Parul University, Vadodara, Gujarat, India

Guedes, Manuel Correia
Instituto Superior Técnico, University of Lisbon, Portugal

Iqbal, Khushboo
Amity Institute of Microbial Technology, Amity University, Noida, Uttar Pradesh, India

Jha, Ambuj Bhushan
Crop Development Centre/Department of Plant Sciences, University of Saskatchewan, 51 Campus Drive, Saskatoon, SK S7N 5A8, Canada

Kapley, Atya
Environmental Biotechnology and Genomics Division, CSIR-National Environmental Engineering Research Institute, Nagpur, India

Kumar, Rakesh
Council for Scientific and Industrial Research (CSIR), New Delhi, India

Lajayer, Behnam Asgari
Department of Soil Science, Faculty of Agriculture, University of Tabriz, Tabriz, Iran

Lama, Suvha
Environmental Material Division, CSIR-National Environmental Engineering Research Institute, Nagpur, India

Mishra, Arti
Amity Institute of Microbial Technology, Amity University, Noida, Uttar Pradesh, India

Rai, Ashita
School of Environment and Sustainable Development, Central University of Gujarat, Gandhinagar, Gujarat, India

Rami, Esha
Department of Biotechnology, Parul Institute of Applied Science, Parul University, Vadodara, Gujarat, India

Sharma, Pallavi
School of Environment and Sustainable Development, Central University of Gujarat, Sector-30, Gandhinagar, Gujarat, India

Shukla, Kartikeya
Amity Institute of Environmental Sciences, Amity University, Noida, India

Shukla, Smriti
Amity Institute of Environmental Toxicology, Safety and Management, Amity University, Noida, India

Singh, Akansha
Department of Genetics and Plant Breeding, Institute of Agricultural Sciences, Banaras Hindu University, Varanasi, India

Singh, Pratibha
Department of Biochemistry, Institute of Science, Banaras Hindu University, Varanasi, India

Singh, Sanskriti
Amity Institute of Microbial Technology, Amity University, Noida, Uttar Pradesh, India

Singh, Shivani
Department of Biochemistry, Institute of Science, Banaras Hindu University, Varanasi, India

Upadhyay, Priti
Department of Botany, University of Delhi, Delhi, India

Varma, Ajit
Amity Institute of Microbial Technology, Amity University, Noida, Uttar Pradesh, India

Yadav, Ganapati D.
Department of Chemical Engineering, Institute of Chemical Technology, Mumbai, India

Foreword

Smt. Manisha Rajiv Vakil
Women and Child Welfare (Independent Charge), Social Justice and Empowerment (Welfare of Schedule Castes)
(State Minister), Government of Gujarat

Parul University, established under Gujarat Private Universities Act 2009, has made long strides in the field of education in Gujarat. The Parul University offers undergraduate, postgraduate, and doctoral degree programmes in wide-ranging faculties. I feel proud to be a chief guest of the international conference "Climate Change Global Scenario" organized by the Center of Research for Development, Parul University, under the leadership of Dr. Devanshu Patel, president of Parul University, and Dr. Geetika Madan Patel, chairman of the Center of Research for Development and medical director and trustee of Parul University. CLIMATE CHANGE is one of the most important global environmental challenges; organizing such an eminent programme on climate change and sustainable development, educating academicians, researchers, and industrial personnel, is a leading step in educational institutes.

Climate change requires a good scientific understanding as well as coordinated action at national and global level. The projected climate change under various scenarios is likely to have an impact on the following: glacial recession, sea level rise, extreme weather—global warming, storm, cyclone and leading to impact on natural resources, water bodies, agriculture, forest, biodiversity, desertification, human health, etc. The Indian government introduced the National Action Plan on Climate Change on 30 June 2008, with achieving sustainable development goals.

The prime minister's Council on Climate Change was constituted in June 2007 to develop the first ever National Action Plan on Climate Change. Honourable Prime Minister attended the Paris Agreement on Climate Change in Paris. Recently, Prime Minister Narendra Modi participated in the Conference of Parties (COP) 26 and addressed how in India we are making every effort with determination, working hard and showing results. Today India ranks fourth in the world with installed renewable energy capacity. India's non-fossil energy has increased by more than 25% in the last seven years. And now it has reached 40% of our energy mix.

In today's international conference, the guest of honour, Prof. B. J. Rao, vice chancellor, Central University of Hyderabad, addressed the various issues of climate change. The international expert Dr. Ram Bhuj, UNESCO expert, highlighted the climate change global scenario; another expert, Dr. Shwetal Shah, technical advisor, Climate Change Department, Govt. of Gujarat, mentioned the status of the climate change in the State of Gujarat. Prof. M. H. Fulekar, convenor, delivered a talk on the National Action Plan followed by a panel discussion.

The proceedings of the conference published by the Center of Research for Development, Parul University, is highly appreciated. This document will be beneficial to academicians, researchers, and experts of climate change.

Preface

"Climate" refers to long-term changes in environmental conditions worldwide, resulting from natural and anthropogenic activities. Changes in average weather conditions or in the time variation of weather within the context of long-term average conditions is referred to as climate change, which exacerbates the depletion and degradation of natural resources such as land, soil, forest, biodiversity, and groundwater. Climate change is one of the most important global environmental challenges. Addressing climate change requires a good scientific understanding and knowledge as well as coordinated action plan at national and international level. The United Nations Framework Convention on Climate Change and the Kyoto Protocol made the provisions for adapting adequate protocol and policy development for mitigating the impacts of climate change. The protocol promotes member parties for the eventual stabilization of greenhouse gases in the atmosphere, recognizing the common but differentiated responsibilities and respective capabilities, based on social and economic conditions of the countries. The effective measures for climate change need to adapt a sustainable development pathway by shifting to environmentally sustainable technologies and promoting energy-efficient technology for mitigation and adaption of climate change. The Intergovernmental Panel on Climate Change was created to provide policymakers with regular scientific assessment on climate change, its implication and potential future risk, as well as to put forward adaptation and mitigation options. India and other developing countries are facing the challenges of promoting mitigation and adaptation of climate change.

Sustainable development emphasizes the use of natural resources in a suitable manner to conserve the resources for future generation. Sustainable development has become a part of all climate change policy discussion at the global level, particularly due to adoption of Agenda 21 and various conventions resulting from the United Nations Conference on Environment and Development, 1992. Effective strategies for mitigating the impact of climate change are to adopt and achieve goals of sustainable development.

The book *Climate Change and Sustainable Development* provides first-hand information on the recent topics viz. climate change science and impact, carbon sequestration, energy-efficient technology, green building, national and international polices on climate change, mitigation and adaptation strategies to combat climate change, and sustainable development. This book will be beneficial to academicians, researchers, students, industrialists, environmentalists, and policymakers for development of strategies, knowledge, and understanding for climate change action.

Acknowledgements

"Happiness is achievable if we embrace a sustainable lifestyle, eradicate poverty, protect the environment, and educate all."

Climate change has unleashed its severity and is a challenge to the environmentalist in developing abatement strategies to achieve sustainable development goals. The United Nations Framework Convention of Climate Change and Kyoto Protocol have acknowledged the climate change impediments and their counter measures promoting the preservation of fresh water, forest, land, farming, ecosystem, soil and environmental services. Climate change is ongoing, and within the next few decades, societies and ecosystems will either be committed to a substantially warmer world, or major actions will have to be taken to limit warming which requires a good scientific understanding and action plan at national and international level.

Environmental sustainability focuses on the incorporation of financial, societal, and environmental concerns. *Climate Change and Sustainable Development* provides in-depth knowledge to the academic and research community to understand the climatic changes on the planet and develop strategies for its adaptation and mitigation. The chapters in the book are contributed by leading scientists, academicians, and researchers in the field.

I, Professor M. H. Fulekar express my deepest appreciation to Ms. Ashita Rai whose efforts, dedication, devotion, and invaluable contribution at each stage of book writing and editing has made this book a success.

I duly acknowledge Dr. Geetika Madan Patel, Chairman CR4D & Vice President, Parul University for her motivational and infrastructural support. Dr. Dhaval Bhatt and library staff are also acknowledged for their unwavering support. I am forever grateful to my wife Dr. Kalpana Fulekar, children Jaya-Amit, Jyoti, Vinay-Sanketa, and Grandchildren Shanaya, Smira and Naysa, for their unconditional love and encouragement in all my pursuits.

I, Professor Rama Shanker Dubey, thank my wife Bhagyawati, sons Ashish and Anupam, daughter in laws Anjali and Shubhra, and grandsons Aryan and Kabir who have always stood by my side and supported me throughout the course of completion of this work.

1 Climate Change—Global Environmental Concern

Ashita Rai and M. H. Fulekar

CONTENTS

I. Introduction: The Earth and Climate Change 1
II. Greenhouse Effect and Global Warming 2
III. Climate Change Impacts 2
IV. Climate Change—Adaptation and Mitigation 7
V. Conclusion 8
References 9

I. INTRODUCTION: THE EARTH AND CLIMATE CHANGE

Global climate change is undoubtedly by far the most significant issues affecting the Earth as well as its people. Climate change is defined as variations in mean temperature, rainfall, and wind over time, as well as related changes in Earth's atmosphere, oceans and natural water supplies, snow, landmasses, biodiversity, and living beings (Parry, Canziani, Palutikof, Van der Linden, & Hanson, 2007). According to scientists, the average global surface temperature has risen by around 1°C since 1900, with more than half of the rise happening ever since mid-1970s. Additional data (including reduced Arctic Sea ice cover and increasing ocean specific heat capacity) and natural world indicators (such as high-latitude migrations in thermally sensitive fish and mammals) all add up to unambiguous proof of anthropogenic climate change (National Academy of Sciences & Royal Society, 2020). Findings suggests that human practices seem to be the primary contributor to climate change ever since 1800, owing to the emission of greenhouse gases in the atmosphere from the combustion of fossil fuels such as coal, oil, and gas, that further act as a blanket around the Earth, capturing the solar heat and elevating temperature (United Nations, n.d.). Changing climate and many other environmental challenges, like forest degradation, loss of biological variety, and ozone layer depletion, pose a threat to our capacity to provide essential human necessities like adequate nutrition, fresh water, energy, and also decent housing and a clean environment. United Nations Framework Convention on Climate Change and Kyoto Protocol have acknowledged the climate change impediments and countermeasures promoting the preservation of fresh water, forest lands, farming, ecosystems, soil, and impacts on environmental services. Global warming is projected to exacerbate the reduction and deterioration of natural resources such as land, soil, vegetation, ecosystems, and groundwater as a result of continuous inappropriate utilization patterns.

DOI: 10.1201/9781003205548-1

Solar radiation is the planet's source of energy. Short-wavelength energy, which encompasses the visible spectrum (400 nm–750 nm), is absorbed by the ocean, lakes, and land and used in the photosynthesis. The Earth does not use a large portion of the incoming radiation, which is reflected back to space as long-wavelength infrared radiation (750 nm—25μm). This phenomenon controls the Earth's average surface temperature. Human-induced greenhouse effect, on the other hand, now controls the Earth's temperature.

II. GREENHOUSE EFFECT AND GLOBAL WARMING

The greenhouse effect is necessary for humans to survive on this planet. Gases in the atmosphere have captured plenty of the sun's incoming energy to maintain the Earth warm enough to sustain life, resulting in an average global temperature of 15°C, that might otherwise be roughly −18°C if these natural greenhouse gases were not there (water vapour and carbon dioxide). The natural greenhouse effect is the name given to this phenomenon. Reckless combustion of fossil fuels and deforestation have increased greenhouse gas concentrations ever since Industrial Revolution around 1850. Greenhouse gasses are gaseous substances which can emit UV radiation within a specific thermal infrared range (Johansson, Meyer, Whistance, Thompson, & Debnath, 2020). Water vapour, chlorofluorocarbons (CFCs), hydrofluorocarbons (HFCs), carbon dioxide (CO_2), methane (CH_4), and nitrous oxide (N_2O) are all prominent greenhouse gases found in the environment (Fletcher & Smith, 2020). Greenhouse gases keep temperatures high in the troposphere, enabling lesser heat to exit to space. Carbon dioxide is by far the most released greenhouse gas, despite the fact that water vapour is perhaps the most prevalent greenhouse gas inherently existing in the environment. The highest CO_2 concentration in the atmosphere in May 2021 was 420 ppm, 50% higher from the previous year and continuing to increase (National Oceanic and Atmospheric Administration, 2021). China, the United States, the European Union, India, the Russian Federation, and Japan were the leading CO_2 emitters in 2014 (United States Environmental Protection Agency, 2021). Table 1.1 summarizes the principal greenhouse gases, their sources, and global emissions for the year 2010. Human-induced greenhouse effect causes global warming, wherein the Earth's temperature and the temperature of the atmosphere layers closest to the Earth increase unnaturally due to greenhouse gases emitted by human activities and a decrease in the sink (ocean, atmosphere, soil, and forest) for these gases. Each greenhouse gas has a global warming potential (Table 1.2), which was devised as a measure to assess the capability of each greenhouse gas to capture heat in the atmosphere (in comparison to another gas). To comply with the IPCC recommendations, CO_2 was selected as the reference gas. The most common timeframe for GWPs is 100 years (Durkee, 2006).

III. CLIMATE CHANGE IMPACTS

Extreme weather is becoming more common as a result of climate change, wreaking havoc on nations and communities around the world. The IPCC report reveals that the effects of climate change will be felt in every location, involving substantial human

TABLE 1.1
Greenhouse gases, their sources, and global emission from 2010

Greenhouse gases	Source of emission	Global emission (%)
Carbon dioxide	Hazardous waste, vegetation, biological matter, and chemical reactions, combustion of fossil fuels	65 (fossil fuel burning and industrial activities) 11 (forestry and land use)
Methane	Processing and distribution of coal, natural gas, and oil; livestock and other farming activities, land utilization, and the decomposition of organic waste in municipal solid waste landfills	16
Nitrous oxide	Agriculture, land usage, industrial operations, fossil fuel, and solid waste combustion, as well as wastewater treatment	6
Fluorinated gases	Industrial processes	2

Source: Edenhofer et al., 2014

TABLE 1.2
Gases and their global warming potential

Industrial name or common name	Chemical formula	GWP values for 100-year time horizon
Carbon dioxide	CO_2	1
Methane	CH_4	28
Nitrous oxide	N_2O	265
CFC-11	CCl_3F	4,660
CFC-12	CCl_2F_2	10,200
Halon-1301	$CBrF_3$	6,290
Carbon tetrachloride	CCl_4	1,730
HCFC-21	$CHCl_2F$	148
Sulphur hexafluoride	SF_6	23,500

Source: Edenhofer et al., 2014

and financial consequences, which will exceed the cost of action. The report examines the effect of global warming of 1.5°C, as well as how much worse the repercussions will become if temperature increases by 2°C. Whether it's the severity and recurrence of rainfall patterns, the harshness of dryness and heat waves, or the melting of ice and snow, each fraction of a degree of warming contributes. Some of the effects of climate change, such as melting ice sheets, rising seas, animal extinction, and much more acidic oceans, will become permanent over time. As emissions rise, the consequences will continue to grow and multiply (World Resource Institute, 2021). The most significant consequences of climate change are listed in the next section (Table 1.3)

TABLE 1.3
Climate change factors and their consequences

S.N.	Factors	Consequences
1.	Rising temperature	Since 1880, the Earth's temperatures have increased at a pace of 0.08°C every decade, with the warming trend over the last 40 years being more than double. According to National Oceanic and Atmospheric Administration temperature readings, 2020 was the second-warmest year recorded, with land masses reaching new highs. The surface temperature in 2020 was 0.98°C warmer than the 20th century average of 13.9°C and 1.19°C warmer than the pre-industrial period (1880–1900) (Lindsey & Dahlman, 2021).
2.	Ocean warming and ocean acidification	Since the 1970s, the ocean has absorbed more than 93% of the excess heat from greenhouse gas emissions, causing ocean temperatures to rise, according to the IPCC's fifth assessment report released in 2013. According to NOAA, the average worldwide sea surface temperature—the temperature of the ocean's upper layers—has climbed by 0.13°C every decade over the last 100 years. According to computational studies presented in the IPCC's 2013 report, by 2100, the average global temperature is predicted to rise by 1–4°C. Ocean warming causes deoxygenation, thermal expansion of sea water, sea level rise, and melting of continental glaciers (International Union for Conservation of Nature, 2021). Carbon dioxide levels in the atmosphere have lowered the pH of the ocean by 0.1, which is a 30% rise in acidity on a logarithmic scale. Acidification of the ocean has an effect on marine animals and ecosystems (National Oceanic and Atmospheric Administration, 2020).
3.	Global sea level	Since 1880, the global mean sea level has increased eight to nine inches, with over a third of that occurring in the previous two and a half decades. The rising water level is primarily due to a mix of glacial melt and ice sheets, as well as the thermal expansion of seawater. Global mean sea level was 91.3 millimetres higher in 2020 than it was in 1993, making it the highest annual average in history (1993–present). Rising oceans pose a threat to infrastructure critical to local jobs and regional businesses in metropolitan areas along coasts. Sea level rise threatens roads, bridges, public transit, waterways, oil and gas wells, power facilities, sewage treatment, landfill, and a long list of other structures. Marine regions that provide recreational, coastal protection and habitat for fish and wildlife, including commercially vital fisheries, are under pressure as sea levels rise. Saltwater is infiltrating freshwater aquifers as sea levels rise, threatening municipal and agricultural water sources as well as natural habitats (Lindsey, 2020).

TABLE 1.3 (*Continued*)
Climate change factors and their consequences

S.N.	Factors	Consequences
4.	Agriculture and food security	Climate change will almost certainly have a negative impact on global agriculture. While some areas and crops will benefit, the majority will not. While increased CO_2 levels in the atmosphere are expected to stimulate growth and enhance irrigation efficiency in some crop species, climate impacts, such as heat waves, droughts, and flooding, are expected to reduce crop yield. Enhanced weed infestation, increased infection and insect pest ranges and seasons, and other changes in agricultural agroecosystems are examples of indirect climate impacts (Soil Science Society of America, n.d.). Throughout the last 30 years, precipitation during the rice-growing season in Punjab, India, has declined by 7% yearly. By 2080, significant climate change will reduce rice yields by 8.10% and wheat yields by 6.51% (Kumar & Kaur, 2019). Maize crop yields are expected to fall by 24%, while wheat yields are expected to rise by roughly 17% (National Aeronautics and Space Administration, 2021). Climate change is expected to cause mayhem on the four dimensions of food security—availability, access, utilization, and stability—as well as their interactions (Food and Agriculture Organization, 2018). Due to a lack of resources to undertake in adaptation and diversification initiatives, low-income farmers and consumers are likely to be the most impacted (United Nations Convention to Combat Desertification, 2017). Other noteworthy implications of climate change on food security include a decline in nutritional quality of food owing to enhanced CO_2 concentrations, competitive pressure for land and natural resources, pervasive crop failure contributing to relocation and dispute (Shukla et al., 2019).
5.	Forests	Climate has an impact on the structure and function of forest ecosystems, as well as on forest health. Many hazards to forests, such as pest outbreaks, wildfires, social development, and droughts, may be exacerbated by a warming environment. The duration of the growth season is often extended when temperatures rise. It also causes some tree species' geographical boundaries to alter. Numerous tree species' ecosystems are projected to shift northward or to higher elevations. Droughts will certainly become more common in some areas, while excessive rainfall and floods will come more often in others as a result of climate change. Temperature increase will affect the timing of snowmelt, affecting water availability throughout the year. Wildfires are expected to grow in size, severity, and recurrence in some parts of the country as a result of climate change (United States Environmental Protection Agency, 2016). Warmer spring and summer temperatures, combined with reduced water supply, cause forests to dry out, increasing the likelihood of wildfires. Fires also can influence the climate by releasing enormous amounts of carbon dioxide into the atmosphere quickly (Backlund, Janetos, & Schimel, 2008).

(*Continued*)

TABLE 1.3 (*Continued*)
Climate change factors and their consequences

S.N.	Factors	Consequences
6.	Indian Monsoon	As global warming affects the economy, the Indian monsoon is projected to become substantially more destructive and heavier. As climatic changes take their toll on the Indian subcontinent's system, the rainfall pattern has shifted over time. Monsoon downpours will probably increase by 5% with every degree Celsius of warming (Zhongming, Linong, Xiaona, Wangqiang, & Wei, 2021). Increased rainfall may appear to be beneficial to crops, but too much might reduce productivity for particular plants throughout the growing period (Katzenberger, Schewe, Pongratz, & Levermann, 2021). Heavy precipitation, particularly multiday downpours that result in massive floods, are on the rise in significant portions of India. Warmer temperatures are hastening glacial melting in the Himalayas, which is expected to result in higher flow rates in the Ganga and Brahmaputra Rivers (Roxy et al., 2017). According to a 2017 global estimate by the World Resources Institute, India has the most GDP at risk from river floods ($14.3 billion), a figure that might increase tenfold by 2030 as the economy grows (Luo, Maddocks, Iceland, Ward, & Winsemius, 2015).
7.	Water resources	Access to water has already been impacted by climate change, which is creating increasingly catastrophic floods and droughts around the globe. Climate change has an impact on the water cycle because it changes when, where, and how much rain falls. With time, it also contributes to more severe weather. In the next years, rising global temperatures will cause additional water to evaporate in larger proportions, resulting in increased levels of atmospheric water vapour and more regular, intense, and severe showers. Increased floods are expected as a result of this transition, according to climate experts, because more water will fall than vegetation and soil can store. The remaining water, referred to as runoff, flows into surrounding waterways, picking up pollutants such as fertilizer along the way. Excessive runoff ultimately pollutes the waterways and restricts access to water for humans and environment by draining into larger bodies of water such as lakes, estuary, and the sea. When agricultural fertilizers wash into lakes and the ocean, they stimulate algae to develop quickly. Algal blooms cause masses of green, blue-green, red, or brown algae to block shores and rivers. The blooms prevent sunlight penetration to aquatic life and reduce oxygen levels in the water. Toxicants released by the blooms can harm fish and other aquatic species, as well as make people sick and even kill humans. Freshwater glaciers around the world begin to melt at an astounding rate as the ocean heats, resulting in sea level rise. The melting glacial freshwater finally flows into the ocean. Saltwater can more readily infiltrate subsurface groundwater, known as aquifer, as sea levels rise (National Geographic, 2019).

TABLE 1.3 (*Continued*)
Climate change factors and their consequences

S.N.	Factors	Consequences
8.	Biodiversity	Altered patterns of precipitation, weather extremes, and ocean acidification are exerting pressure on species severely endangered by other anthropogenic activities, whilst increasing temperatures are impacting diversity. Changes in weather variables have caused species to change their morphological, physiological, and behavioural pattern (Lavergne, Mouquet, Thuiller, & Ronce, 2010). In North American migratory birds, rising summer temperatures have been linked to smaller bodies and longer wings (Weeks et al., 2020). With widespread evidence of earlier migrating and nesting response to increased temperatures and changed precipitation patterns, migratory birds provide clear examples of phenological alterations (Lehikoinen et al., 2019). Climate change makes species vulnerable in both terrestrial and marine ecosystems, causing them to die out in their current habitats and colonize new ones. Natural communities will be disrupted and species will suffer extinction as a result of future climate change (Thomas et al., 2004).
9.	Public health	Climate change, along with other natural and man-made health stressors, has a wide range of effects on human health and disease. Climate change–related health problems range from increased risk of vector-borne disease transmission to reduced access to services as a result of natural catastrophes. Hurricanes and floods caused by climate change can potentially ruin or restrict access to healthcare facilities and supplies (Tye, 2021). Climate change is anticipated to result in an additional 250 deaths annually between 2030 and 2050, due to starvation, malaria, diarrhoea, and heat stress. The physical and economic capacity of people and household already suffering with poor health and chronic illness will be disproportionately affected by the increasing frequency, severity, and length of severe weather events (World Health Organization, 2021). In the long run, changing climate has a similar influence on psychological health. According to the findings, increasing temperatures can exacerbate symptoms of anxiety and depression, schizophrenia, and vascular dementia, as well as increasing hospitalization and suicide risk (American Psychological Association, 2021).

IV. CLIMATE CHANGE—ADAPTATION AND MITIGATION

Climate change is among the most challenging problems we're facing. It has several facets—sciences, economy, society, politics, and moral and ethical issues—and is a global issue which will be experienced on local scales for decades or even centuries. Because we've already agreed to a certain degree of global warming, addressing it involves a two-pronged strategy (National Aeronautics and Space Administration, 2022):

A. **Mitigation**—Reduce the flow of heat-trapping greenhouse gases into the atmosphere, either through lowering sources of these gases or by improving the sinks that accumulate and store these gases. Mitigation seeks to prevent substantial anthropogenic interference with the climate system and stabilise greenhouse gas levels in a timeline good enough to allow ecosystems to acclimatise inherently to climatic changes, guarantee that food supply is not jeopardised, and facilitate economic growth to proceed in a sustainable manner.

B. **Adaptation**—Adapting to living in a changing environment entail making adjustments to the current or anticipated future climate. The objective is to lessen human exposure to climate change's negative consequences. It also includes making the most of any potentially good climate change possibilities (for example, longer growing seasons or increased yields in some regions). Climate change is a long-term battle, but with our united efforts and appropriate mitigation and adaptation measures, we can reduce the damage it causes. Mentioned are some strategies that may help in climate change adaptation and mitigation:
- Optimizing energy efficiency and choosing renewable power instead of fossil energy
- Promotion of public transportation in urban areas
- Green industry, farming, fisheries, and cattle farming, as well as food sustainability, resource conservation, and the 3Rs (reduce, reuse, recycle) rule to be encouraged
- By imposing a tariff on the use of fossil fuels and creating a market for CO_2 emissions
- Constructing safe and sustainable buildings and infrastructure
- Promoting reforestation and restoration of ecosystem
- Looking to diversify crop production to make them more adaptable to changing climates
- Exploring and creating novel approaches for preventing and controlling natural calamities
- Action plans for climate emergencies may be developed

V. CONCLUSION

Global climate changes, primarily temperature rise, is affecting biological systems across the globe, and these rising temperatures are indeed the result of anthropogenic CO_2 emissions. Even the strictest mitigation initiatives will not be able to prevent a few of the consequences of climate change in the near future. This necessitates flexibility, especially when dealing with immediate consequences. Unabated climate change, on the other hand, is projected to surpass human flexibility to cope in the long run. The establishment of a spectrum or combination of methods that encompasses mitigation, adaptation, technology, and research is therefore critical. Government, community, and every citizen, on the other hand, could make a real difference to a meaningful approach to sustainable development.

REFERENCES

American Psychological Association. (2021). Urgent need to address mental health effects of climate change, says report. Retrieved from www.apa.org/news/press/releases/2021/11/mental-health-effects-climate-change

Backlund, P., Janetos, A., & Schimel, D. (2008). The effects of climate change on agriculture, land resources, water resources, and biodiversity in the United States. In *Synthesis and assessment product 4.3*. Washington, DC: US Environmental Protection Agency, Climate Change Science Program, 240 p.

Durkee, J. (2006). *Management of industrial cleaning technology and processes*. Oxford, United Kingdom: Elsevier.

Edenhofer, O., Pichs-Madruga, R., Sokona, Y., Farahani, E., Kadner, S., Seyboth, K., . . . Savolainen, J. (2014). Contribution of working group III to the fifth assessment report of the intergovernmental panel on climate change. *Climate Change*, 1–11.

Fletcher, W. D., & Smith, C. B. (2020). *Reaching net zero: What it takes to solve the global climate crisis*. Los Angeles, United States: Elsevier.

Food and Agriculture Organization. (2018). *The future of food and agriculture: Alternative pathways to 2050*. Rome, Italy: Food and Agriculture Organization of the United Nations, p. 228.

International Union for Conservation of Nature. (2021). Issues brief: Ocean warming. Retrieved from www.iucn.org/resources/issues-briefs/ocean-warming#:~:text=The%20ocean%20absorbs%20most%20of,for%20marine%20fishes%20and%20mammals

Johansson, R., Meyer, S., Whistance, J., Thompson, W., & Debnath, D. (2020). Greenhouse gas emission reduction and cost from the United States biofuels mandate. *Renewable and Sustainable Energy Reviews*, 119, 109513.

Katzenberger, A., Schewe, J., Pongratz, J., & Levermann, A. (2021). Robust increase of Indian monsoon rainfall and its variability under future warming in CMIP6 models. *Earth System Dynamics*, 12(2), 367–386.

Kumar, S., & Kaur, B. S. (2019). Impact of climate change on the productivity of rice and wheat crops in Punjab. *Economic and Political Weekly*, 54(46), 38–44.

Lavergne, S., Mouquet, N., Thuiller, W., & Ronce, O. (2010). Biodiversity and climate change: Integrating evolutionary and ecological responses of species and communities. *Annual Review of Ecology, Evolution, and Systematics*, 41, 321–350.

Lehikoinen, A., Lindén, A., Karlsson, M., Andersson, A., Crewe, T. L., Dunn, E. H., . . . Tjørnløv, R. S. (2019). Phenology of the avian spring migratory passage in Europe and North America: Asymmetric advancement in time and increase in duration. *Ecological Indicators*, 101, 985–991.

Lindsey, R. (2020). Climate change: Global sea level. Retrieved from www.climate.gov/news-features/understanding-climate/climate-change-global-sea-level

Lindsey, R., & Dahlman, L. (2021). Climate change: Global temperature. Retrieved from www.climate.gov/news-features/understanding-climate/climate-change-global-temperature#:~:text=August%2012%2C%202021-,Highlights,land%20areas%20were%20record%20warm

Luo, T., Maddocks, A., Iceland, C., Ward, P., & Winsemius, H. (2015). *World's 15 countries with the most people exposed to river floods*. Washington, DC: World Resource Institute.

National Academy of Sciences (US), & Royal Society (Great Britain). (2020). *Climate change: Evidence & causes: Update 2020*. Washington, DC: National Academies Press.

National Aeronautics and Space Administration. (2021). Global climate change impact on crops expected within 10 years, NASA study finds. Retrieved from https://climate.nasa.

gov/news/3124/global-climate-change-impact-on-crops-expected-within-10-years-nasa-study-finds/

National Aeronautics and Space Administration. (2022). Responding to climate change. Retrieved from https://climate.nasa.gov/solutions/adaptation-mitigation/

National Geographic. (2019). How climate change impacts water access. Retrieved from www.nationalgeographic.org/article/how-climate-change-impacts-water-access/

National Oceanic and Atmospheric Administration. (2020). Ocean acidification. Retrieved from www.noaa.gov/education/resource-collections/ocean-coasts/ocean-acidification

National Oceanic and Atmospheric Administration. (2021). Carbon dioxide peaks near 420 parts per million at Mauna Loa observatory. Retrieved from https://research.noaa.gov/article/ArtMID/587/ArticleID/2764/Coronavirus-response-barely-slows-rising-carbon-dioxide

Parry, M. L., Canziani, O., Palutikof, J., Van der Linden, P., & Hanson, C. (Eds.). (2007). *Climate change 2007-impacts, adaptation and vulnerability: Working group II contribution to the fourth assessment report of the IPCC* (Vol. 4). Cambridge: Cambridge University Press.

Roxy, M. K., Ghosh, S., Pathak, A., Athulya, R., Mujumdar, M., Murtugudde, R., ... Rajeevan, M. (2017). A threefold rise in widespread extreme rain events over central India. *Nature Communications*, 8(1), 1–11.

Shukla, P. R., Skeg, J., Buendia, E. C., Masson-Delmotte, V., Pörtner, H. O., Roberts, D. C., . . . Malley, J. (2019). Climate change and land: An IPCC special report on climate change, desertification, land degradation, sustainable land management, food security, and greenhouse gas fluxes in terrestrial ecosystems.

Soil Science Society of America. (n.d.). How will climate change affect agriculture? Retrieved from www.soils.org/files/science-policy/caucus/briefings/climate-change.pdf

Thomas, C. D., Cameron, A., Green, R. E., Bakkenes, M., Beaumont, L. J., Collingham, Y. C., ... Williams, S. E. (2004). Extinction risk from climate change. *Nature*, 427 (6970), 145–148.

Tye, S. (2021). How climate change affects health and how countries can respond.

United Nations. (n.d.). What is climate change? Retrieved from www.un.org/en/climatechange/what-is-climate-change#:~:text=Climate%20change%20refers%20to%20long,variations%20in%20the%20solar%20cycle.&text=Burning%20fossil%20fuels%20generates%20greenhouse,sun's%20heat%20and%20raising%20temperatures

United Nations Convention to Combat Desertification. (2017). *Global land outlook*. Bonn, Germany, 340 pp. Retrieved from https://www.unccd.int/sites/default/files/documents/2017-09/GLO_Full_Report_low_res.pdf

United States Environmental Protection Agency. (2016). Climate impacts on forests. Retrieved from https://19january2017snapshot.epa.gov/climate-impacts/climate-impacts-forests_.html#:~:text=Climate%20change%20could%20alter%20the,can%20recover%20from%20a%20disturbance

United States Environmental Protection Agency. (2021). Global greenhouse gas emissions data. Retrieved from www.epa.gov/ghgemissions/global-greenhouse-gas-emissions-data

Weeks, B. C., Willard, D. E., Zimova, M., Ellis, A. A., Witynski, M. L., Hennen, M., & Winger, B. M. (2020). Shared morphological consequences of global warming in North American migratory birds. *Ecology Letters*, 23(2), 316–325.

World Health Organization. (2021). Climate change and health. Retrieved from www.who.int/news-room/fact-sheets/detail/climate-change-and-health

World Resource Institute. (2021). 5 big findings from the IPCC's 2021 climate report. Retrieved from www.wri.org/insights/ipcc-climate-report

Zhongming, Z., Linong, L., Xiaona, Y., Wangqiang, Z., & Wei, L. (2021). *Climate change is making Indian monsoon seasons more chaotic*. New York: Lamont-Doherty Earth Observatory.

2 Climate Change and Planetary Sustainability

Ram Boojh

CONTENTS

1.1 Introduction: Background and Driving Forces 11
1.2 Climate Change Impacts 12
1.3 COVID-19 Pandemic 13
2.1 Climate Crisis to Climate Emergency 14
2.2 Global Climate Agreements 14
2.3 Conference of Parties (COP) 15
2.4 Emissions Gap Report 16
3.1 Climate Change and Biodiversity 16
3.2 Ecosystem Services and Nature-Based Solutions 18
4.1 Internationally Designated Sites as Climate Observatories 20
4.2 Wetlands as Carbon Sinks 21
5.1 Climate Change Education and Awareness 22
5.2 Climate Literacy and Capacity Building 22
5.3 Climate Justice: Reaching Out to the Unreachable 23
6.1 Conclusions and Recommendations 25
References 27

1.1 INTRODUCTION: BACKGROUND AND DRIVING FORCES

Climate change is the most serious global challenge and the defining crisis of our time. It is happening at an extraordinarily fast pace and frequency exemplified by many incidences of extreme weather events, rising sea level, melting of glaciers, changes in plant and animal behaviour, etc. The extreme weather events coming with greater intensity and frequency year on year, such as devastating floods in China, Western Europe, and India, and heat waves, droughts, and forest fires in the United States, Australia, Russia, and many other places around the world are bringing the realities of the climate emergency closer to us. Climate change is increasingly impacting our food and water security, health and wellbeing, economic development, jobs and livelihoods and forcing migration and refugee crisis, fuelling instability and conflict in many parts of the world. Human activities are the key driving force for the ever-growing greenhouse gas (GHG) emissions in the atmosphere, as proved by overwhelming scientific and empirical evidence (Boojh 2010a; Boojh et al. 2010; IPCC 2007). The Intergovernmental Panel on Climate Change (IPCC 2021), in its sixth assessment report (AR6) on climate change, reiterates this fact on the basis of voluminous scientific data and observations of more than 2,000 scientists from all over the world. The report categorically states that the observed increases in GHG concentrations in the atmosphere are unequivocally caused by human activities. The report further emphasizes that mean global temperatures are also on the rise with the rising greenhouse gas (GHG) emissions, mainly the carbon dioxide (CO_2), in the Earth's atmosphere. The report has been termed as the "code red of humanity" by the secretary general of the United Nations, Antonio Guterres (United Nations 2021). The situation is so alarming that the UN, many governments, and scientists are in favour of a global climate emergency declaration (Ripple et al. 2020). However, global response to deal with this global emergency is still slow and tepid.

> **BOX 2.1 CLIMATE CHANGE: SOME FACTS**
>
> 1. Earth's climate system has undergone unprecedented change during the past hundred to thousands of years mainly due to rising greenhouse gas emission, which is linked to temperature rise. Human activities are the main cause for such change, which are causing widespread catastrophes and disasters at a huge cost.
> 2. Scientific analyses predict that global surface temperature will continue to increase until at least the middle of the century. Unless we make sharp reductions in greenhouse gas emissions in coming decades, global warming will exceed 1.5°C; after which, climate consequences will be even more severe.
> 3. Extreme weather events such as heatwaves, floods, droughts, cyclones, etc. are all induced by factors linked to climate change.
> 4. The climate system is changing at an unprecedented rate, causing more extreme weather events, including frequent and intense hot extremes, heatwaves, droughts, heavy rainfall, flooding, cyclones, and melting and reductions in snow cover and permafrost.
> 5. The Earth has warmed by 1°C since the pre-industrial era, and two-thirds of this rise has occurred since 1986. The 20 warmest years on record have occurred over the past 22 years.
> 6. The oceans have also warmed considerably over the past few years. Further, oceans are getting acidified due to rising CO_2 levels thus becoming less effective at absorbing CO_2.

1.2 CLIMATE CHANGE IMPACTS

The Earth is warming at an unprecedented rate, and 2021 was again the hottest year on record as per the observations of NOVA and NASA. The year was also the Earth's forty-fourth consecutive year with global land and ocean temperatures, at least nominally, above the 20th-century average (NOAA 2021a). The observations further show that the world's seven warmest years have all been recorded since 2014, with ten of the warmest years occurring since 2005. The global temperature for July 2021 was the highest for July in the 142-year NOAA record, which dates back to

Climate Change and Planetary Sustainability

1880 (NOAA 2021b). According to the NOAA-NCEI's Global Annual Temperature Rankings Outlook, it is very likely that the year 2021 will rank among the ten warmest years on record.

The IPCC Report 2021 reiterates this fact, that the global climate system is changing at an unprecedented rate, which has not happened in the past thousands of years. Some of these changes, such as continued sea level rise and melting of glaciers are irreversible over hundreds to thousands of years. Apart from rise in temperatures, climate change is bringing changes in the water cycle, impacting rainfall pattern, causing excessive floods in some regions as well as drought in others. The sea level rise is expected to continue throughout the 21st century, causing more frequent and severe coastal flooding and erosion. Extreme sea level events that previously occurred once in 100 years could happen every year by the end of this century. The rising temperature will result in changes in the ocean, resulting into more frequent marine heatwaves, ocean acidification, and reduced oxygen levels, causing bleaching of corals and loss of marine biodiversity and associated livelihoods.

1.3 COVID-19 PANDEMIC

The COVID-19 pandemic came at a time when the world was contemplating accelerated climate action, particularly leading to net zero carbon emission. The world was looking to the year 2020 to be the super year for the environment and sustainability (Froggatt & Townend 2021). However, the pandemic overshadowed and relegated all the environment and climate-related actions to the back seat. There was, however, some reduction in GHG emissions during the pandemic mainly due to the strict lockdown in most parts of the world in 2020 and 2021 (Boojh 2020). According to the estimates, COVID-19 brought the historical decline in global CO_2 emissions almost by 5.8% (around 2 Gt CO_2) for the first time in 2020, which was almost five times greater than the 2009 decline during the global financial crisis (IEA 2021). However, with the resumption of economic activities and lifting of the lockdowns, the emissions resumed rising above the pre-COVID level. The emissions are projected to rebound and grow by 4.8% as demand for coal, oil, and gas will rise with the return to economic recovery. The increase of over 1,500 Mt CO_2 would be the largest single increase since the carbon-intensive economic recovery from the global financial crisis more than a decade ago. It leaves global emissions in 2021 around 400 Mt CO_2, or 1.2%, below the 2019 peak.

The IEA's Global Energy Review 2021 reports that there will be a surge of 1.5 billion tonnes in energy-related carbon dioxide emissions in 2021, reversing most of the 2020 COVID-related decline. This will be the biggest annual rise in emissions since 2010, during the carbon-intensive recovery from the global financial crisis. The key driver for this surge is coal demand for power generation. This rise is projected to be around 4.5%, surpassing the 2019 level and approaching its all-time peak from 2014, with the electricity sector accounting for three quarters of this increase. The economic recovery packages of the COVID crisis announced by many countries seem to be not so green or sustainable for the climate. Almost 80% of the coal demand in 2021 is expected to come from China, U.S., European Union, and India. The year 2021 will also see a rise of over 8% in electricity generation from renewables mostly from solar and wind, which will be around 50% of the increase in overall electricity supply worldwide.

2.1 CLIMATE CRISIS TO CLIMATE EMERGENCY

The word "climate emergency" has recently found global acceptance, and Oxford Dictionary declared it as the word of the year in 2019, a serious and urgent issue or situation that requires immediate action. The Earth's climate is changing, and the scientific consensus is that human activities have contributed to it significantly but that the change is far more rapid and dangerous than thought earlier (IPCC 2007, 2021; Risbey et al. 2018). The global mean temperature of the Earth is rising; it has risen by 0.70°C in the 20th century and reached up to 1.2°C now. The prestigious *Scientific American* magazine along with many major news outlets worldwide has started using the term "climate emergency" in its coverage of climate change (Fischetti 2021). UN Secretary General has also urged governments around the world to declare a state of climate emergency until the world reaches the goal of net zero CO_2 emissions (Climate Ambition Summit 2020).

The Alliance of World Scientists, of more than 11,000 scientists from 153 countries, have also urged the decision-makers and all of humanity to promptly respond to warning signals of climate change and declare a climate emergency and act to sustain life on planet Earth, our only home (Ripple et al. 2020). Many countries and areas globally have already declared climate emergency in their jurisdictions, and many more are coming forward with similar declarations and intents. With scientists coming up with newer evidences to suggest that we have already reached the tipping point, we need for more and more countries to come on board with climate emergency declarations supported by concrete actions to combat climate change.

2.2 GLOBAL CLIMATE AGREEMENTS

The Rio Earth Summit, also known as the UN Conference on Environment and Development, held in 1992 in the Brazilian city of Rio de Janeiro was the first to come out with Agenda 21 as the blueprint for the survival of humanity in the 21st century. The conference also came up with the UNFCC (United Nations Framework Convention on Climate Change), which is the basic international instrument for ensuring climate action at the global level. UNFCCC entered into force on 21 March 1994 and enjoys universal membership with almost all 194 parties (member countries) having ratified it.

The Intergovernmental Panel on Climate Change (IPCC) was set up in 1988 as a scientific intergovernmental body of the United Nations to establish the scientific basis of climate change and address the related policy issues. It provides a periodic assessment report on climate change, which is considered as the most authentic scientific assessment on the magnitude, timing, and impacts of climate change. The IPCC sixth Assessment Report was released in August 2021 just before the COP 26 to set the context for the countries to come out with urgent and decisive decision to tackle climate change impacts. The report has unequivocally held human activities as main cause for dramatic rise in carbon dioxide and other greenhouse emissions. It

Climate Change and Planetary Sustainability

further elaborates the dangerous rise in Earth's temperature and widespread, rapid, and intensifying change in climate system, which is unprecedented in thousands of years. Termed as the CODE RED for humanity, the report calls for an emergency response and urgent action. The 2021 Nobel Prize in Physics awarded to three scientists on 6 October 2021 also links human activities to global warming

2.3 CONFERENCE OF PARTIES (COP)

The Conference of Parties (COP) of the countries (parties) signatory of the UNFCC is held every year to take stock of the progress on various agreements reached upon under the convention. The first COP was held in Berlin in 1995, which emphasized the need for "legally binding" actions on climate change. This was further reiterated in COP 2 in Geneva in 1996. COP 3 in Kyoto in 1997 approved the legally binding targets known as the Kyoto Protocol, which paved the way for further negotiations through legally binding targets for developed countries and establishment of carbon markets. The mechanisms proposed by Kyoto Protocol to reduce emissions included Joint Implementation, Clean Development Mechanisms (CDM), and Emissions Trading.

The Buenos Aires Plan of Action to frame rules for Kyoto Protocol was adopted in COP 4, along with continued negotiation efforts in COP 5. The focus of COP 6 and 7 was mainly on mechanisms for joint implementation, CDM markets, emissions trading, technology transfer, and funding mechanisms. The COP 8 held in New Delhi in 2002 emphasized on adaptation measures and stressed that poverty alleviation and development were the utmost priority of developing countries. Further COPs were mostly discussing for a deal for a legally binding post Kyoto climate regime from 2012 to 2020. The discussions at COPs lost track till something substantial was agreed in COP 15 in Paris in 2015 (SDGs, 2015). The Paris Agreement provided the countries to make their own climate pledges to curb the temperature rise well below 2°C (ideally at 1.5°C). The document of these commitments or climate change pledges has been submitted to the UNFCC in the form of a document called Nationally Determined Contributions (NDCs). The agreement allows a "bottom-up approach," which was critical to enabling the adoption of the agreement. However, the NDCs so for are not ambitious enough to limit the global warming to well below 2°C compared to pre-industrial levels, let alone 1.5°C.

The COP 26 in Glasgow, UK, was held in the background of these alarming findings to accelerate the climate action. It was termed as a "make or break" opportunity for humanity to come out with an urgent and concrete action plan to curb emissions and halt the warming of the planet. The COP 26, for the first time, agreed to a broad consensus on limiting global temperature to 1.5°C, in contrast to the previously stated 2°C target under the Paris Agreement, which mandated to limit global warming to 2°C while making efforts to limit it to 1.5°C by the end of the century. However, the scientific reports, including the IPCC, were unequivocally urged for capping the temperature rise to 1.5°C to save humanity from rising climate catastrophes. The COP 26 also took stock of the state of various scientific findings, which raised alarm that Earth's average surface temperature has already reached to about 1.1°C, hardly leaving any scope to allow more emissions. The countries now need to act fast for deep and drastic reduction in greenhouse gas emissions as their NDCs fall short of such expectations.

The COP 26, unlike previous COPs, for the first time came out with a clear agreement to phase down (not phase out) coal power and fossil fuel subsidies, set out carbon markets, commit on climate finance, reversing deforestation and reducing methane emission. This COP was important from the viewpoint that many countries made commitments for net zero emission goal by 2050 (India by 2070 and China by 2060), which covers about 63% of global emissions. The outcome document of COP 26, known as the Glasgow Climate Pact, calls on 197 participating countries to report their progress towards more climate ambition, at COP 27 in Egypt rather than wait until previous schedule of 2025.

However, these efforts are not sufficient enough to reach the goal of 1.5°C by the end of the century. The world is bracing for a climate emergency situation requiring urgent action to reduce greenhouse gases and halt warming of the planet to avoid potentially irreversible damage. There is a need to act urgently and swiftly to address the crisis by countries raising their global climate ambition and accelerate clean energy transition by curtailing carbon emissions to net zero at the earliest possible time to deal with the climate emergency.

2.4 EMISSIONS GAP REPORT

The Emission Gap Report (UNEP 2021) warns that the combined pledges made under the Nationally Determined Contribution (NDCs) along with other mitigation measures proposed by countries might be able to cap temperature at 2.7°C by the end of the century, which is well above the Paris climate agreement of 2° and now agreed limit of 1.5°C during the current century, the world needs to halve annual greenhouse gas emissions by 2030. The net zero commitments if implemented effectively provide a chance to limit the warming to 2.2°C, closer to the well-below 2°C goal of the Paris Agreement. The reduction of methane emissions and Carbon trading could also help slash emissions to some extent.

Transition towards cleaner energy needs a transformative approach towards redesigning our economy towards circularity by sustainably managing waste and pollution, recycling products and materials, and regenerating nature—to reduce emissions and meet the targets set out in the Paris Agreement. We need a circular economy to complete the picture.

3.1 CLIMATE CHANGE AND BIODIVERSITY

Climate change and biodiversity loss are the twin global crises that are inextricably linked. Climate change is one of the key drivers for the rapid loss of biodiversity and ecosystem services, which has been elaborated in numerous scientific reports, including the MEA (Millennium Ecosystem Assessment 2005), IPCC (2007), and IPBES (Intergovernmental Science-Policy Platform on Biodiversity and Ecosystem Services) Report (2019). The IPBES Report warns that humans are driving one million species to extinction, and the global response to halt it is inadequate. The native species in most major land-based habitats have fallen by at least 20% since 1900, and 40% of amphibian species, 33% of corals, and more than a third of all marine mammals and 10% of insects are threatened. The world is losing every three seconds the forest cover the size of a football pitch. We have lost almost half of wetlands that provide the carbon sink and sustainable livelihood to local communities. Our oceans are also in danger, specially its biodiversity hotspots, the coral reefs which provide millions of people with ecosystem services such as food provision, livelihood opportunities, carbon sequestration, and buffering against extreme climate events. As per a study, the global coverage of living corals has declined by half since the 1950s resulting into loss of around 63% of coral-reef-associated biodiversity (Ripple et al. 2020; Wetzel 2021). Rapid loss of biodiversity is too frightening and has been termed as "biological annihilation" and "assault on the foundations of human civilization," which might lead us towards the long-suspected "sixth mass extinction."

Loss of biodiversity is closely related to rapid loss of forest cover particularly biodiversity-rich tropical and subtropical regions. About 8% of global greenhouse gas emissions derive from tropical deforestation. Climate change and biodiversity are currently the most important issues on the global development agenda. With the adoption of the agenda 2030 and the 17 Sustainable Development Goals (SDGs), issues of climate change, biodiversity, and sustainability are now firmly placed on international discourse (Boojh 2013, 2017). Among the SDGs, Goal 13 is directly related to climate change and Goal 15 to biodiversity. While Goal 13 aims mainly to take urgent action to combat climate change and its impacts, Goal 15 aims to, "Protect, restore and promote sustainable use of terrestrial ecosystems, sustainably manage forests, combat desertification, and halt and reverse land degradation and halt biodiversity loss." The global commitment for safeguarding the planet is further strengthened through the Paris Agreement and Sendai Framework for Disaster Risk Reduction (DRR). The initiative of the Megadiverse countries or the Like-Minded Megadiverse Countries (LMMC) with country-focused approach raises national awareness for biodiversity conservation in nations with high biological diversity and endemicity. Internationally designated sites, such as world natural heritage sites, biosphere reserves, global geoparks, and Ramsar sites, play an important role in biodiversity conservation and sustainable development.

The Convention of Biological Diversity (CBD) signed by 150 government leaders at the 1992 Rio Earth Summit is dedicated to promoting conservation of biodiversity, its sustainable use, and equitable sharing of benefits arising out of it. Biological diversity, or biodiversity, consists of the wide variety of plants, animals, and microorganisms, including the genetic diversity and ecosystem diversity. Scientists have been able to identify around 1.75 million species but believe that about 13 million species (estimates range from 3 to 100 million) are yet to be explored (CBD 2018).

The United Nations has declared a Decade on Biodiversity, for the period 2011–2020. The goal of the decade was to support the implementation of the Strategic Plan for Biodiversity and to promote its overall vision of *living in harmony with nature*. With the end of the decade, the world is gearing up to a post-2020 biodiversity framework for 2030. The launch of the UN Decade of Ecosystem Restoration, 2021–2030, provides the opportunity to strengthen ecological restoration programmes including (re)-afforestation and rehabilitation of degraded lands as a response to halt climate change. Ecosystems are the web of life on this planet, providing us with air (oxygen), water, food, materials, and help in climate stabilization while protecting from disasters and diseases.

3.2 ECOSYSTEM SERVICES AND NATURE-BASED SOLUTIONS

Impacts of climate change are most pronounced not only in the unprecedented loss of biodiversity but also in the deterioration of ecosystem services—the goods and services that biodiversity provides (Table 2.1). The landmark IPBES (Intergovernmental Science-Policy Platform on Biodiversity and Ecosystem Services) report (2019) points towards grave threat of warming planet to species and ecosystems, which in turn adversely impacts economy, livelihoods, and resilience. The report further stresses on the need for transformative changes to restore and protect nature, particularly for developing resilience against climate change and for the attainment of global commitments under the Paris Agreement and Sustainable Development Goals (SDGs). The seriousness of climate change can be gauged from the fact that the greenhouse gas emissions are currently around 50% higher than in 1990. There is need to adapt to climate change and invest in low-carbon development to limit the increase in global mean temperature to 1.5°C above pre-industrial levels.

Global warming is likely to adversely impact ecosystem services in climate-sensitive sectors, such as agriculture, forestry, and fishery, depriving millions of their livelihood sources. Developing countries, particularly poorer sections of society, are more vulnerable to climate change with little capacity to withstand adverse conditions (Kelkar & Bhadwal 2007; Boojh 2010a, 2010b; Boojh et al. 2010). The current trend of global warming may put almost 24% of species on the verge of extinction by 2050. The climate change impacts are also very much evident on phenology of the species and ecosystems. Phonological studies, which have been suggested to provide clue to many seasonal and climatic events (Boojh & Ramakrishnan 1983), may become severely affected by global warming. Climate change may also impact the timing of reproduction, length of the growing season, abundance of different species, and frequency of pest and disease outbreaks. Other observed impacts of climate change include changes in the timing of reproduction in certain species, in the length of the growing season in many regions, in the abundance of different species, and in the frequency of pest and disease outbreaks.

Another area which has found significant attention in climate change mitigation and adaptation strategies is the nature-based services (NBS), which has been defined as "actions to protect, sustainably manage, and restore natural or modified ecosystems, that address societal challenges effectively and adaptively, simultaneously providing human wellbeing and biodiversity benefits" (Gowland 2021; IUCN 2021). NBS have the potential to ameliorate impacts of climate change, particularly of extreme climate events such as floods, heat stress or water scarcity, droughts, and other natural disasters (IPCC 2014). NBS also help in reducing vulnerability. Learning from the indigenous knowledge and from historically adapted urban structures and techniques such as urban heat or flood risk reduction practices can help to accelerate local action.

Celebrating nature has been the fundamental value for the humanity. Nature worship is manifested in several forms, such as consideration for sacredness of forest

TABLE 2.1
Ecosystem services for climate stabilization and amelioration

Type of ecosystem services	Contribution to the humanity	Role in climate system
1. Provisioning services	Ecosystems are a source of food, water, medicines, wood, biofuels, etc. Also, they provide conditions for these resources to grow.	Ecosystems provide a sink for sequestration of greenhouse gas emissions and biofuels, a source of renewable energy, reducing dependence on fossil fuels.
2. Regulating services	Ecosystems such as terrestrial, forests, wetlands, marine purify and regulate air quality, prevent soil erosion, and control greenhouse gases. They harbour important species which regulate and controls pests and insects, disease vectors, etc. Climate regulation, floods and other natural disaster regulation, pollination, water purification, and more. Services such as pollination by wind and insects would not be possible without nature.	Regulation of ecological balance, including carbon and other nutrient and elements cycle, reduction of greenhouse gases. Climate change is also impacting pollinators, like bees, for crop pollination.
3. Supporting services	They provide habitat for different life forms, protect biodiversity, help nutrient cycling, and other services for supporting life on Earth.	Protecting and strengthening supporting services of ecosystems help maintain the climate system. Although climate change is impacting most of biodiversity and ecosystems. Ecosystem support services provide resilience for adaptation to climate impacts besides helping in carbon sequestration.
4. Cultural services	Provides nonmaterial benefits such as spiritual enrichment, intellectual development, recreation and aesthetic values, etc. Most natural elements, such as landscapes, mountains, caves, are used as a place for cultural and artistic purposes. Even a few of them are considered sacred. Moreover, ecosystems provide enormous economic benefits in the name of tourism.	Cultural services strengthen human resilience against climate change impacts; particularly, they can provide clues to develop nature-based solutions based on traditional knowledge and systems developed in harmony with nature by local and indigenous communities.

groves, rivers, mountains, and even individual trees, animals, and almost every element of nature. These are prevalent in many traditional societies all over the world. We need to reconnect with nature and live in harmony with it, to succeed in our fight against the current COVID pandemic and many other such calamities. We need to understand that by protecting nature today, we are avoiding the pandemics of tomorrow. The corona crisis therefore should be utilized to reflect and rebuild our relationship with nature, which alone can offer us with the opportunity and solution to "Build Back Better" while we recover from the pandemic. The positive lessons of the corona crisis and the new normal of living in harmony with nature and looking at its invaluable contribution in developing resilience and immunity for better health and wellbeing need to be strengthened and sustained.

4.1 INTERNATIONALLY DESIGNATED SITES AS CLIMATE OBSERVATORIES

Internationally designated sites such as biosphere reserves, world natural heritage sites, Ramsar sites, etc. along with the protected areas are helping in the conservation of biodiversity and sustainable development (Boojh 2008). The world network of Biosphere Reserves designated under UNESCO's Man and the Biosphere (MAB) programme serving as sustainability support sites cover a broad spectrum of ecosystems, ranging from remote mountains, to tropical forests, deserts, to farmland and urban areas all over the globe. Thus, they provide ideal settings for monitoring and implementing climate change and related impacts. As of December 2021, there are 701 biosphere reserves in 124 countries, including 21 transboundary sites. Biosphere reserves have three interrelated zones, namely, the core area, which is strictly protected ecosystem that contributes to the conservation of landscapes, ecosystems, species, and genetic variation; a buffer zone surrounding the core areas used for activities compatible with sound ecological practices that can reinforce scientific research, monitoring, training, and education. The third zone, the transition area, is the part where activities fostering economic and human development that is socioculturally and ecologically sustainable are allowed. The biosphere reserves are being extensively used as learning laboratories for implementing adaptation and mitigation strategies towards climate change. The buffer and transition zones of biosphere reserves in particular are being used for research into innovative combinations of afforestation/reforestation, avoided deforestation, rural energy, and infrastructure development and urban planning (Boojh 2007a, 2007b, 2008).

World Heritage sites are designated by UNESCO under the World Heritage Convention 1972, concerning the protection of the world cultural and natural heritage, which seeks to encourage the identification, protection, and preservation of cultural and natural heritage around the world considered to be of outstanding universal value to humanity. The convention, ratified by 184 parties, recognizes a set of places that are of outstanding universal value, and their deterioration or destruction constitutes a loss to the heritage of all humanity, not just to the country in which they are located. These cultural and natural places make up the world's heritage and are repository of unique biodiversity, specifically the natural and mixed sites. Currently the World

Heritage list contains 1,121 properties, of which 39 are transboundary, 2 delisted, 53 in danger, 869 cultural, 213 natural, 39 mixed in 167 countries.

Climate change is also going to impact some of the pristine world natural heritage sites, putting in danger their outstanding universal value. The UNESCO report (2007) on Climate Change and World Heritage outlines the threats posed by climate change to natural and cultural sites on its World Heritage list. As per the report, the melting of Himalayan glaciers affects the outstanding beauty and destroys the habitat of rare wildlife species, such as the snow leopard, in the Sagarmatha National Park, Nepal. The report examines the effects of climate change on the marine World Heritage sites. Seventy percent of the world's deep-sea corals are expected to be affected by changing conditions related to rising temperatures and increased oceans acidification by the year 2100. The report describes the threat to biodiversity which may lead to changes in the distribution of species, including "invasive species," pathogens and parasites, and on the timing of biological events such as flowering, and the relationships between predator and prey, parasite and host, plant and pollinator, etc. The report recommends several measures to deal with this problem, including the creation of protected areas and relocating particularly endangered species. The real solution lies in the internationally agreed principles of sustainability and creating a fair and equitable world order (WSSD 2002; Boojh 2003).

Global Geoparks are another designation which plays an important role in preservation of habitats and biodiversity apart from preserving the geological heritage. These are designated under the UNESCO's International Geoscience Programme (IGCP) for recognition of the importance of managing outstanding geological sites and landscapes in a holistic concept of protection, education, and sustainable development. At present, there are 169 UNESCO Global Geoparks in 44 countries (UNESCO website 2021, https://en.unesco.org/global-geoparks). Geoparks promote the understanding of climate change and the use of Earth's resources. They hold records of past climate change and are educators on current climate change as well as adopting a best practice approach to utilizing renewable energy and employing the best standards of green tourism and green growth by implementing low-carbon initiatives—adaptation.

4.2 WETLANDS AS CARBON SINKS

The convention on wetlands, called the Ramsar Convention, is an intergovernmental treaty that provides the framework for national action and international cooperation for the conservation and wise use of wetlands and their resources. The countries who have signed the convention (contracting parties) are required to develop and maintain an international network of wetlands, which are important for the conservation of global biological diversity and for sustaining human life through the maintenance of their ecosystem components, processes, and benefits/services. Ramsar sites are designated based on the criteria set for identifying Wetlands of International Importance, specifically sites containing representative, rare, or unique wetland types, and the other eight cover sites of international importance for conserving biological diversity. Currently, the Ramsar List is the world's largest network of protected areas with 2,372 Ramsar sites in 170 countries across the world, covering more than 2.56 million square kilometres (Ramsar 2021). Globally wetlands cover only about 5–8% of the land surface but comprise 20–30% of the world's carbon pool. Wetlands are the most productive systems compared to all terrestrial ecosystems and have the highest carbon density, which makes them play an important role in global biogeochemical and carbon cycles and climate change. They provide valuable ecosystem services such as water purification, flood control, and climate change mitigation.

5.1 CLIMATE CHANGE EDUCATION AND AWARENESS

Education is a critical agent in addressing the issue of climate change (Boojh 2009, 2011, 2017). The UN Framework Convention on Climate Change (UNFCCC) assigns responsibility to Parties of the Convention to undertake educational and public awareness campaigns on climate change and to ensure public participation in programmes and information access on the issue. Climate change education applies systems thinking in order to understand how the world works. It is essential that climate education be based on a scientific understanding of socio-ecological systems and the ethical dimensions of human behaviour. Connections between local and global, between individual behaviour and communitarian practices and climate change need to be identified and illuminated through social experiences. Climate change education should be developed and enriched with contextual, subjective knowing in practice. The resulting dialogical learning situation offers open encounters where adults and young people can learn from each other and together construct pathways for a sustainable future (Lehtonen et al. 2019).

Role of education is also important in addressing linked global challenges of climate change, biodiversity, and the current COVID-19 pandemic. There is a need to reimagine and redesign education in the current context when the pandemic has brought in the great disruption in the formal education setup, forcing some 1.3 million learners out of schools, colleges, and universities all over the world. Educators and learners are looking towards innovative tools and transformative pedagogies, particularly virtual learning spaces and interactive online tools for teaching leaning. In such a situation, ESD, or sustainability education, with its emphasis on learners' transformation process is most appropriate for developing new skills and values for sustainable living and lifestyle. The post-COVID education must provide impetus to more sustainable and nature-positive practices to reduce the individual and community's carbon footprint leading to a low-carbon lifestyle.

5.2 CLIMATE LITERACY AND CAPACITY BUILDING

Considering the seriousness of the issue of climate change and need for emergency action to address it, there is an urgent need to create a mass of climate literate citizenry. Climate literacy will equip citizens with knowledge and skills to take action to resolve climate change related problems at every level. Johnston (2018) has elaborated the concept of climate change literacy as a combination of competencies that can include (1) knowledge of climate system science, (2) understanding of the impacts and threats of climate change, and (3) motivation to make informed decisions to implement mitigative and adaptive solutions to the climate crisis (in short, what causes climate change, what climate change causes, and what can be done about it). UN SDGs provide a good framework for climate literacy specifically in relation to the Goal 13 on "climate action," which requires decision-making at almost every level of the government agencies and functionaries, law makers, businesses, and individual citizens. Policymakers specifically should be equipped with accurate and quality information to propose effective solutions. For policymakers, this is more important considering the global dimension of the climate change issue and its implications at local, national, and regional level. Target 13.3 of the SDG emphasizes on building knowledge and capacity to meet climate challenge, which means "improving education, awareness-raising and human and institutional capacity on climate change mitigation, adaptation, impact reduction and early warning" (UN 2016).

Miler and Sladek (2011) underline the importance of climate change literacy as essential to both mitigation and adaptation specifically for a low-carbon living. The Article 12 of the Paris Agreement also stresses public education, awareness, and participation can help to great extent in bringing about climate action. Youth have come forward in a strong way in spreading climate messages, particularly the campaigns like Fridays for Future, sunrise movement, extinction rebellion, etc., have made their presence felt on major international platforms such as COP and World Economic Forum. Climate literacy can spur millions of green jobs in varied sectors. Education has a crucial role to play in building the workforce for a new, greener economy. There is need to build capacity and create a climate literate population ready to take up green jobs. Climate literacy will also help people finding out climate solutions in their personal and professional life as well through empowerment to take action based on informed decision-making. This will also help them in their personal choices and behaviours in reducing the carbon footprint. New evidence also shows that the combination of women's empowerment and education that includes everyone could result in an 85 gigaton reduction of carbon dioxide by 2050 (Dahan et al. 2021). Quality environmental education is essential for assisting young people in coping with the climate emergency as well as developing critical thinking skills necessary for decision-making.

5.3 CLIMATE JUSTICE: REACHING OUT TO THE UNREACHABLE

Climate change impacts everyone everywhere. However, these impacts are not being felt equally or fairly, between rich and poor, women and men, and older and younger generations. It impacts disproportionately the poor and vulnerable people who already live under precarious conditions. Climate change further increases existing inequalities faced by these vulnerable groups. The concept of climate justice emerged from the idea that historical responsibility for climate change lies primarily with the rich, developed nations, while its consequences are mainly felt by the poorest and most vulnerable (Carbon Brief 2021). The world's rich countries have contributed most to the problem, thus have a greater obligation to take action and to do so more quickly. This also forms the basis for historical burden of emissions as well as common but differentiated responsibilities. **Climate justice** provides the basis for an ethical and social and cultural dimension rather than that of purely environmental or physical nature of the climate crisis. This is done by connecting the concept of justice particularly environmental justice and social justice, equity, equality, human rights and historical rights, and responsibilities to address the climate crisis.

Currently a large number of social and civil society movements are mobilizing people across the world around climate justice agenda. Recent marches, strikes, and protests by hundreds of thousands of schoolchildren, led by Greta Thunberg, points to the intergenerational injustice for climate change. Greta and other climate activists have suggested that a fairer way of assessing emissions would be to look at consumption rather than territorial emissions.

> Climate Justice affirms the rights of communities dependent on natural resources for their livelihood and cultures to own and manage the same in a sustainable manner, and is opposed to the commodification of nature and its resources.
>
> —Bali Principles of Climate Justice, article 18, 29 August 2002, www.corpwatch.org/article/bali-principles-climate-justice

Climate justice is also about reaching out to the unreached regions, people, and communities who are the most vulnerable to climate impacts. The crisis is taking huge toll during pandemics and disasters on the poor and vulnerable communities in developing countries. It is estimated that a mere 2°C warming would put over half of Africa's population at risk of undernourishment. Children are the most vulnerable to diseases that will become more widespread as a result of climate change. Climate crisis is a crisis for children and their rights as well, and some 90% of the burden of disease attributable to climate change is borne by children under the age of 5 (UNICEF 2021).

UNESCO's Declaration of Ethical Principles in relation to Climate Change, adopted in December 2017, provides a number of important ethical principles to guide climate policies (UNESCO 2018). The declaration emphasizes the links between justice, sustainability, and solidarity that could support countries to scale their national commitments and coordinate action across cultures. There are other important international legal instruments containing many well-settled ethical principles which are relevant to national responses to climate change, such as the **"no harm," "precautionary,"** and **"polluter pays"** principles, duties of nations to protect **human rights**, and adopt **emissions reduction targets** at levels to prevent dangerous climate change on the basis of **"equity"** and **common but differentiated responsibilities and respective capabilities**. However, most nations are still ignoring these ethical principles in their national climate change policies, specially the NDCs.

Agenda 2030 and SDGs provide a framework for reaching out to unreached so that no one is left behind. Science, technology, and innovation can play a pivotal role in delivering climate justice, including eradicating poverty, promoting good health, sustainable living and lifestyle, and usher in a just and equitable society. The climate policies must include concerns related to gender, youth and SIDS, LDCs, and Africa while developing pro-poor policies particularly focusing on the COVID stimulus recovery packages. There needs to be a new green deal for ushering in more inclusive and sustainable society.

6.1 CONCLUSIONS AND RECOMMENDATIONS

The climate crisis and its consequences have been well recognized by the world community, which is taking note of the warnings by scientists. Nature is also providing enough red signals about the reality of climate change. However, there is little or no commensurate action to tackle the crisis mainly due to so-called economic reasons. Moving towards accelerated climate action requires transformative changes in the social, ecological, and economic spheres. For which strong social, political, and economic will and measures are needed at a swift speed. While both Agenda 2030 and Paris Climate Agreement provide a global perspective in this direction, the national climate action plans in the form of nationally determined contributions (NDCs) define their policies as the core building blocks of the agreement. NDCs are mostly geared towards target-based mitigation efforts with very little mention of adaptation plans with social or ethical dimensions included in it. Climate crisis needs to be urgently addressed in terms of mitigation of its causes and adaptation to its consequences through sound policies by incorporating environmental, ethical, and social dimensions into climate action plans of nations.

Based on deliberations and recommendations at several forums and meetings, the way forward can be built upon as follows:

i. The world needs to quickly transition towards low-carbon or no-carbon society by abandoning fossil fuels and adopting low-carbon or no-carbon lifestyle. Decarbonization of economy is needed from individual to local to national and global scale at an accelerated pace. There should be an immediate halt to new investments in fossil fuel–based projects to reach net zero carbon emissions by 2050 and to stand any chance of limiting warming to 1.5°C.

ii. The world is rebounding from the COVID pandemic and coming up with green economic recovery packages with a determination to build back better. Climate crisis has deepened over the years and has reached the critical tipping point. The world needs to go into emergency mode and accelerate action to reach net zero for keeping the 1.5° goal alive. Countries need to declare climate emergency and their net zero plan at the earliest possible as there is hardly any time left to wait and watch. Time to act is now.

iii. The planet is in peril. Its fragile climate system is cracking up. The COP and other global platforms, including the COP 26, could not achieve much in terms of the emergency situation which the world is facing. Still, there have been incremental progress, which are building blocks to build upon in the future. There is a need to quickly phase out dirty fuel beginning with coal first and end fossil fuels subsidies altogether for a smooth transition towards renewables.

iv. For realizing the net zero emissions quickly, the world need not transition towards renewables but need transformative changes in their energy and economic systems. The shift from fossil to renewables has to be accelerated to begin with by decarbonizing the electricity sector. Energy efficiency can go a long way in reducing the energy demand. Coal and petroleum must be phased out with a major boost to renewables. Natural carbon sinks, for example, forests, wetlands, oceans, and coastal systems should be conserved and restored.

v. Among the major policy instruments, incentives for low-carbon growth must be promoted. Carbon tax and green investments can spur low-carbon growth and create millions of green jobs. Fossil fuel subsidies should be done away with as quickly as possible.

vi. Going for plant-based foods is another way to reduce our carbon food print and contribute to carbon neutrality. According to the studies, our food systems contribute more than one third of carbon emissions, and animal agriculture accounts for almost 60% of those emissions (Crippa et al. 2021; Xu et al. 2021). These studies point out that reducing meat and animal product consumption might become the biggest climate impact most people can make with their diets.

vii. Transportation is one of the major sources of carbon emissions and also of air pollution killing millions every year (Liu et al. 2019). We must opt for public transportation, walk or bike when possible. Hybrid or electric vehicle instead of one with a typical combustion engine is another smart choice to make for the climate and for air quality.

viii. Nature-based solutions (NBS) are not only important for maintaining the ecosystem health and biodiversity conservation but also in developing resilience to a changing climate. Forests and biodiversity are the most important sink for carbon emissions. Countries must develop strategies for including NBS in their nationally determined contributions (NDCs) based on stewardship of nature. The disruption of ecosystem and nature's processes are also considered to be the reason for COVID and similar infectious diseases (zoonosis).

ix. The new and smart technologies can effectively address global challenges of climate change, biodiversity loss, and overall ecological degradation. The technology has great potential in identifying, measuring, monitoring, and tracking environment and nature for better and sustainable management of these resources. Technologies should help in connecting people with nature since no human technology can fully replace "nature's technology" perfected over hundreds of millions of years. For this, there is a need to educate about the environment and nature, including the intrinsic values of biodiversity through new and innovative methodologies and approaches.

x. Fortunately, teachers and educators all around the world are making serious efforts to create educational materials and methodologies in the area of environment education (EE) in general and education for sustainable development (ESD), climate change education (CCE), and education for biological diversity (EBD) in particular at both formal and non-formal levels apart from creating public awareness about related issues. They take important steps, but unfortunately, the collective political will is not enough to overcome some deep contradictions. Education and awareness to bring positive environment and climate-friendly change, and moving towards green jobs have become even more pronounced with the pandemic as we rethink the way we manufacture, build, transport, or utilize resources.

xi. World's vulnerable groups, communities, and nations need to be helped in building resilience to adapt to climatic catastrophes. There is a need to act on the principle of common but differentiated responsibility and climate justice. Rich nations should come forward to bear the historical burden of emissions on the principle of common but differentiated responsibility and capability by providing already committed $100 billion climate finance to support developing countries.

xii. Young people from vulnerable and marginalized groups who stand to lose the most in the climate crisis should be provided the opportunities of climate literacy, civic participation, and skill development so that they can champion the cause of their communities and lead the change.

REFERENCES

Boojh, R., & Ramakrishnan, P.S. 1983. Phenology of trees in a sub-tropical evergreen montane forest in north-east India. *Geo-Eco-Trop* 5, 189–209.

Boojh, R. 2003. Is a sustainable world possible? *Connect* 28, 7–10, UNESCO, Paris.

Boojh, R. 2007a. Biodiversity conservation through UNESCO's Man and the Biosphere (MAB) and World Heritage programmes. In *Proceedings of the International workshop on "Gulf of Mannar Biosphere Reserve: An Ecological Model for Biodiversity Conservation, Llivelihood and Sustainability"* (Eds. S. Kannaiyan & K. Venkataraman), pp. 131–136. National Biodiversity Authority, Chennai.

Boojh, R. 2007b. SACAM-the regional MAB network for the south and central Asia. *Final Report of the 10th Meeting of UNESCO-MAB East Asian Biosphere Reserve Network (EABRN-10) Protection of Natural Sites: Importance of Biodiversity Conservation, Terelj National Park, Mongolia.* UNESCO, Beijing Office, pp. 216–221.

Boojh, R. 2008. Climate change and past floral succession, survival and migration. *Paper presented in the Conference "Plant Life through the Ages."* Birbal Sahni Institute of Paleobotany, Lucknow, India.

Boojh, R. 2009. Educating about the ecology and environment: Issues, concerns and strategies. *Ecological and Environmental Sciences Education in India 1–18. New Delhi, India.* UNESCO, New Delhi, Peoples Council of Education and Homi Bhabha Centre for Science Education.

Boojh, R., Kipgen, R., Nowroozalizadeh, S., & Giraud, J. 2010. The impact of climate change and the Himalayas in the local context: The case of Nandadevi biosphere reserve. In*Climate Change, Biodiversity and Food Security.* Macmillan, New Delhi, With Ruth Kipgen, Sara.

Boojh, R. 2010a. Addressing climate change and biodiversity issues in the South Asian Region. In *Climate Change, Biodiversity and Food Security in the South Asian Region* (Eds. N. Jerath, R. Boojh, & G. Singh), pp. 3–17. Macmillan, India, New Delhi.

Boojh, R. 2010b. The nagoya biodiversity summit: A new era of living in harmony with the nature. *International Journal of Environmental Consumerism* 6, 8–13.

Boojh, R. 2011. Climate change education for sustainable development. *Technical Proceedings of the International Conclave on Climate Change*, pp. 61–66. Centre for Climate Change, ESCI, Hyderabad, India.

Boojh, R. 2013. Environmental sustainability for the world we want: Moving from the MDGs to post-2015. *Lead Article, Terre Policy Centre Newsletter*, June, pp. 1–3.

Boojh, R. 2017. Climate change and sustainable development. In *Climate Change & Sustainable Agriculture* (Eds. N. Jerath, R. Saluja, P. Bassi, & K.H. Sidhu), pp. 3–15. Desh Bhagat University, Mandi Gobindgarh, India.

Boojh, R. 2020. COVID-19: Through the looking glass. *CSR Mandate*, May. www.csrmandate.org/covid-19-through-the-looking-glass/

Carbon Brief. 2021. What is climate justice? www.carbonbrief.org/in-depth-qa-what-is-climate-justice

CBD-Convention on Biological Diversity. 2018. Biodiversity and 2030 agenda for sustainable development-technical-note. www.cbd.int/development/doc/biodiversity-2030-agenda-technical-note-en.pdf

Climate Ambition Summit. 2020. www.climateambitionsummit2020.org/index.php#programme

Crippa, M., Solazzo, E., Guizzardi, D., Monforti-Ferrario, F., Tubiello, F.N., & Leip, A. 2021. Food systems are responsible for a third of global anthropogenic GHG emissions. *Nat Food* 2, 198–209. www.nature.com/articles/s43016-021-00225-9

Dahan, K.S., Ng, C.C., Baena, D., Gaveta, E., Khatibi, A., Lavalie, E., Nasr, Z., & Seth, A. 2021. Chapter 7: Climate education for women and youth. In *Book: Global Youth Climate Network 2021 Climate Action Position Paper*. www.researchgate.net/publication/356695546_CHAPTER_7_CLIMATE_EDUCATION_FOR_WOMEN_AND_YOUTH

Fischetti, F. 2021. We are living in a climate emergency, and we're going to say so. *Scientific American*, April 12. www.scientificamerican.com/article/we-are-living-in-a-climate-emergency-and-were-going-to-say-so/

Froggatt, A., & Townend, R. 2021. A 'super year' for climate and environment action. *Chathomhouse*. www.chathamhouse.org/2021/03/2021-super-year-climate-and-environment-action

Gowland, S. 2021. What are nature-based solutions and how can they be harnessed to tackle climate change? *World Economic Forum*. www.weforum.org/agenda/2021/12/what-are-nature-based-solutions-tackle-climate-crisis/

IEA-International Energy Agency. 2021. Global energy review 2021, IEA, Paris. www.iea.org/reports/global-energy-review-2021

IPBES-Intergovernmental Science Policy Platform on Biodiversity, & Ecosystem Services. 2019. IPBES assessment report: Summary for policy makers. www.ipbes.net/sites/default/files/inline/files/ipbes_global_assessment_report_summary_for_policymakers.pdf

IPCC-Intergovernmental Panel on Climate Change. 2007. Fourth assessment report climate change 2007: Synthesis report. Intergovernmental Panel on Climate Change, Geneva. www.ipcc.ch/ipccreports/ar4-syr.htm

IPCC. 2014. Climate change 2014: Impacts, adaptation, and vulnerability: Summary for policymakers. *Contribution of Working Group II [WGII] to the Fifth Assessment Report [AR5] of the Intergovernmental Panel on Climate Change*. IPCC, Geneva, Switzerland, p. 44.

IPCC. 2021. Summary for policymakers. In *Climate Change 2021: The Physical Science Basis: Contribution of Working Group I to the Sixth Assessment Report of the Intergovernmental Panel on Climate Change* (Eds. V. MassonDelmotte, P. Zhai, A. Pirani, S.L. Connors, C. Péan, S. Berger, N. Caud, Y. Chen, L. Goldfarb, M.I. Gomis, M. Huang, K. Leitzell, E. Lonnoy, J.B.R. Matthews, T.K. Maycock, T. Waterfield, O. Yelekçi, R. Yu, & B. Zhou). Cambridge University Press. www.ipcc.ch/report/ar6/wg1/downloads/report/IPCC_AR6_WGI_SPM.pdf

IUCN. 2021. The IUCN red list of threatened species, version 2016–1. www.iucnredlist.org

Johnston, J.D. 2018. Climate change literacy to combat climate change and its impacts. In *Encyclopedia of the UN Sustainable Development Goals (Climate Action)* (Eds. Walter Leal Filho, Anabela Marisa Azul, Luciana Brandli, Pinar Gökcin Özuyar, & Tony Wall). | 10.1007/978-3-319-71063-1_31–1 (17) (PDF). www.researchgate.net/publication/331041340_Climate_Change_Literacy_to_Combat_Climate_Change_and_Its_Impacts

Kelkar, U., & Bhadwal, S. 2007. South Asian regional study on climate change: Impacts and adaptation: Implications for human development. *Human Development Occasional Papers (1992–2007)*, HDOCPA-2007-27, Human Development Report Office (HDRO), United Nations Development Programme (UNDP). https://ideas.repec.org/p/hdr/hdocpa/hdocpa-2007-27.html

Lehtonen, A., Salonen, A.O., & Cantell, H. 2019. Climate change education: A new approach for a world of wicked problems. In *Sustainability, Human Well-Being, and the Future of Education* (Ed. J. Cook). Palgrave Macmillan, Cham. https://doi.org/10.1007/978-3-319-78580-6_11

Liu, Q., Baumgartner, J., de Foy, B., & Schauer, J.J. 2019. A global perspective on national climate mitigation priorities in the context of air pollution and sustainable development. *City and Environment Interactions*. https://doi.org/10.1016/j.cacint.2019.100003. www.sciencedirect.com/science/article/pii/S2590252019300030

MEA-Millennium Ecosystem Assessment. 2005. *Ecosystems and Human Well-Being: Biodiversity Synthesis*. World Resources Institute, Washington, DC. www.millenniumassessment.org/documents/document.354.aspx.pdf

Miler, T., & Sladek, P. 2011. The climate literacy challenge. *Procedia—Social and Behavioral Sciences* 12, 150–156. www.sciencedirect.com/science/article/pii/S187704281100111X

NOAA. 2021a. National oceanic and atmospheric administration; 2020 was Earth's 2nd-hottest year, just behind 2016. www.noaa.gov/news/2020-was-earth-s-2nd-hottest-year-just-behind-2016

NOAA. 2021b. National centers for environmental information. *State of the Climate: Global Climate Report for July 2021*, published online August. www.ncdc.noaa.gov/sotc/global/202107/supplemental/page-2, retrieved on August 24, 2021.

Ramsar. 2021. Ramsar sites information service. https://rsis.ramsar.org/

Ripple, W.J., Wolf, C., Newsome, T.M., Barnard, P., & Moomaw, W.R. 2020. World scientists' warning of a climate emergency, 2020. *BioScience* 70(1), January, 8–12. https://doi.org/10.1093/biosci/biz088

Risbey, J.S., Lewandowsky, S., Cowtan, K., Oreskes, N., Rahmstorf, S., Jokimak, A., & Foster, G. 2018. A fluctuation in surface temperature in historical context: Reassessment and retrospective on the evidence. *Environmental Research Letters* 13, 123008. https://doi.org/10.1088/1748-9326/aaf342

SDGs. 2015. Sustainable development goals. www.un.org/sustainabledevelopment/blog/2015/12/sustainable-development-goals-kick-off-with-start-of-new-year/

UNEP. 2021. Emission gap report 2021: The heat is on. www.unep.org/resources/emissions-gap-report-2021

UNESCO. 2007. Case studies on climate change and world heritage. UNESCO, Paris. http://whc.unesco.org/uploads/activities/documents/activity-43-9.pdf

UNESCO. 2018. Declaration of ethical principles in relation to climate change. https://unesdoc.unesco.org/ark:/48223/pf0000260889.page=127

UNICEF. 2021. A year marked by conflict, COVID and climate change: Children are suffering from crises that they cannot control. www.unicef.org/stories/2021-year-marked-conflict-covid-and-climate-change

United Nations. 2016. UN SDG 13. https://sdgs.un.org/goals/goal13

United Nations. 2021. Secretary-general calls latest IPCC climate report 'code red for humanity'. *Stressing 'Irrefutable' Evidence of Human Influence.* www.un.org/press/en/2021/sgsm20847.doc.htm

Wetzel, C. 2021. The planet has lost half of its coral reefs since 1950. *Smithsonian Magazine*, September 17. www.smithsonianmag.com/science-nature/the-planet-has-lost-half-of-coral-reefs-since-1950-180978701/

WSSD. 2002. The Johannesburg plan of implementation of the world summit on sustainable development. www.un.org/esa/sustdev/documents/WSSD_POI_PD/English/WSSD_PlanImpl.pdf

Xu, X., Sharma, P., Shu, S., Shu, S., Lin, T., Ciais, P., Tubiello, F.N., Smith, P., Campbell, N., & Jain, A.K. 2021. Global greenhouse gas emissions from animal-based foods are twice those of plant-based foods. *Nat Food* 2, 724–732. www.nature.com/articles/s43016-021-00358-x

3 Carbon Dioxide Refineries, Hydrogen Economy, and the Net Zero Goal

Ganapati D. Yadav

CONTENTS

1. Introduction 31
2. Carbon-Based Energy and Its Effect 33
3. Energy Demand and CO_2 as Future "Oil" 34
   3.1 Flue Gas as Source of CO_2..35
   3.2 CO_2 and C1 Chemistry 35
4. Hydrogen Economy and Its Role in Decarbonization 36
5. Methanol 39
   5.1 Methanol Uses 41
   5.2 Single-Step Carbon Dioxide Hydrogenation to Methanol 41
      5.2.1 Reaction Pathway 42
   5.3 Catalysts in Methanol Synthesis 42
   5.4 Impact of Methanol Economy on the Environment.........................43
6. Dimethyl Ether 44
   6.1 DME Uses 44
   6.2 DME Properties 45
   6.3 DME Market 45
   6.4 DME Synthesis 47
      6.4.1 Scope for DME 48
7. Biogas as Source of CO_2... 49
8. Hydrocarbon Synthesis 49
9. Plastic Refining: Chemical Recycling 50
10. Future Direction...51
11. Conclusions 53
References 55

1. INTRODUCTION

The 26th Conference of the Parties to the UN Framework Convention on Climate Change, known as COP 26, provided the world leaders with an opportunity to speed up action towards the goals of the Paris Agreement 2015. The four major points discussed there were (1) mitigation—reducing emissions; (2) adaptation—helping those already impacted by climate change; (3) finance—enabling countries to deliver on their climate goals; and (4) collaboration—working together to deliver even greater action. Nationally determined contributions (NDCs) are at the core of the Paris Agreement and the achievement of these long-term goals. NDCs embody efforts by each country to reduce national emissions and adapt to the impacts of climate change. Significantly, under the objective of mitigation, over 90% of world GDP is now covered by net zero commitments, and 153 countries put forward new 2030 emissions targets (NDCs) [1].

Apart from the coal-based power industry, steelmaking releases more than 3 billion metric tons of CO_2 each year, having the biggest climate impact. To help limit global warming, the steel industry will need to shrink its carbon footprint significantly. Much attention has focused on CO_2. But methane is a powerful and dangerous greenhouse gas (GHG), and no other COP in current history has held a major event on methane. At COP 26, over 100 countries signed up to the Global Methane Pledge to reduce global methane emissions by 30% by 2030. This comprises six of the world's top ten methane-emitting countries, such as the United States, Brazil, EU, Indonesia, Pakistan, and Argentina and would account to a potential of 46% of global methane emissions and over 70% of global GDP, playing a critical role in keeping the goal of 1.5°C rise within reach [1]. Among all the anthropogenic greenhouse gases, CO_2 is the most vital as it is largely responsible for global warming and climate change. The focus of this article will thus be more on carbon dioxide since carbon dioxide is such a much-talked-about gas which can be valorized while meeting the net zero goal, and it can be treated as the *"new oil."*

The refiners in the future will use carbon dioxide as a raw material for making fuels, chemicals, and polymers/materials and not the ubiquitous crude oil, which anyway will not be economically extracted and exploited by mid-2050s. Bulk chemicals now produced routinely from CO_2 include urea to make nitrogen fertilizers, salicylic acid as a pharmaceutical ingredient, and polycarbonate-based plastics. CO_2 also could be used more extensively as a solvent; for instance, the use of supercritical CO_2 offers advantages in terms of stereochemical control, product purification, and environmental issues for synthesizing fine chemicals and pharmaceuticals, CO_2 flooding for tertiary oil and gas recovery, enhanced agricultural production, and ponds of genetically modified algae that can translate power plant CO_2 into biodiesel [2]. Important reviews are available on chemical technologies for exploiting and recycling carbon dioxide into the value chain [3,4]. The utilization of CO_2 on massive scale, including that from the atmosphere, is a herculean task, but that dream can be realized by using innovation technologies, process intensification, and reactor design.

Mission Innovation (MI) is a global initiative of 23 countries and the European Union to accelerate the global clean energy innovation. As a part of this initiative, the participating countries have committed to double their government's clean energy research and development (R&D) investments by 2020. Governments participating in Mission Innovation include the United States, China, Japan, the European Union, Saudi Arabia, etc. The increase in R&D budgets from these countries in the next few years offers an important opportunity to scale up government R&D funding for

Carbon Dioxide Refineries, Hydrogen Economy, Net Zero Goal

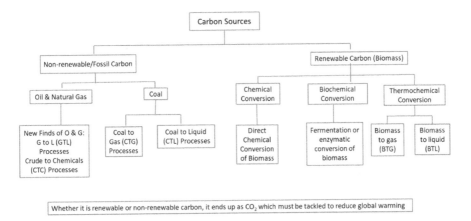

FIGURE 3.1 Carbon conversion processes to manufacture useful products. Carbon has been solely responsible for advancement in lifestyle, comfort, luxury, transport, instant communication, and longevity [6].

CO_2 utilization as Carbon Capture Utilization and Storage is one of the key Mission Innovation Challenge.

Certainly, the year 2020 was horrible for humankind in recent history. Strange it may sound, however, despite the slowdown in economy, the carbon dioxide concentration in the atmosphere went up by 2 ppm to 412 ppm in January 2021 from a year earlier. The annual rate of increase in atmospheric CO_2 over the past 60 years is about 100 times faster than previous natural increases, such as those that happened at the end of the last ice age 11,000–17,000 years ago [5]. We are all used to the carbon-based economy—*luxury, comfort, longevity*—which has revolutionized our lifestyle for more than a century; alas, it has and will bring miseries too if we do not tackle the carbon dioxide emissions through technological interventions. The energy needs of the world are increasing day by day, and the use of carbon-based fuels will continue to rise. To meet the requirements of international treaties, the use of renewable resources is advanced. In fact, during the U.S. presidential election, the issue of the net zero (carbon) economy by 2050 was hotly debated, which subsequently resulted in the Climate Summit in April 2021, in which many countries participated. The European Union revised its 2030 targets of reducing carbon dioxide emissions from 40% to 55% below 1990 level to achieve the net zero carbon goal by 2050. Whether the carbon is coming from fossil fuels, waste biomass, or biofuels, there is a dire need to convert carbon dioxide into fuels, chemicals, and materials to make a net zero economy (**Figure 3.1**) [6].

2. CARBON-BASED ENERGY AND ITS EFFECT

Among all GHGs, carbon dioxide and methane are the principal constituents which contribute the most to the man-made greenhouse effect and climate change. Future processes or concepts that undertake this carbon dioxide reduction must consider the life cycle to guarantee that additional carbon dioxide is not produced beyond what is already being removed from or going into the atmosphere. Carbon dioxide sequestration is widely recognized as an important option to reduce increasing levels of its atmospheric concentrations. However, carbon dioxide storage technology is criticized for permitting continued use of fossil fuels. Carbon dioxide utilization technologies are rapidly emerging as a practical solution that involves recycling of carbon dioxide to various important industrial compounds and feedstock materials bringing to the core the synergism of catalytic chemistry, chemical engineering and technology, and biological sciences to mitigate climate change.

The sustainability of the current generation's lavish lifestyle requires huge amount of energy, which is primarily satisfied by the fossil resources: oil, natural gas, and coal. The concentration of carbon dioxide in the atmosphere has increased from 280 ppm before the Industrial Revolution to 412 ppm in February 2022. The increased atmospheric CO_2 concentration is arguably one of the primary causes of accelerated climate change and global warming. This supply chain from fossil feedstock cannot sustain forever as all these energy sources will diminish within three centuries. From the economic point of view, importing fossil fuel from foreign countries worth billions of dollars is a waste of foreign exchange for the marginal and developing economies having no oil reservoirs or coal deposits. For instance, a fast-growing Indian economy imported 228.6 trillion tons of crude oil at US$ 130 billion in 2020, and the government wants to reduce import of oil by developing new technologies, including renewable resources such as solar, wind, hydro, coal to fuels and chemicals, 2G ethanol, biodiesel, etc. India accounts for more than a quarter of the net global primary energy demand between 2017 and 2040 according to BP Energy [7]; 42% of this new energy demand is met through coal, meaning CO_2 emissions will roughly double by 2040. The Paris Agreement is meant to reduce the risk and impact of global warming by adopting two long-term temperature goals, that is, to check the global average temperature rise well below 2°C above pre-industrial level, and to take more deliberate actions to limit the rise in temperature to 1.5°C above pre-industrial levels. To achieve this goal, a 20/20/20 strategy was adopted, meaning, 20% decrease in CO_2 emission, rise in renewable energy market share by 20%, and 20% increase in efficiency of current technology, which calls for research and innovation. The share of the renewable energy will increase from current ~27% to ~51% by 2035 to ~73% by 2050 totalling 49000 TWh [8].

3. ENERGY DEMAND AND CO₂ AS FUTURE "OIL"

Reducing CO_2 concentration in the atmosphere while meeting the energy demands of an increasing population is a formidable task and requires long-term planning and implementation of CO_2 mitigation strategies. Reduction of CO_2 production by shifting from fossil to renewable fuels, CO_2 capture and storage (CCS), and CO_2 capture and utilization (CCU) are the possible areas for systematic control and reduction of atmospheric CO_2. Carbon Capture and Utilization and Storage (CCUS) is one of the key areas that can achieve CO_2 emission targets while simultaneously contributing to the production of energy, fuels, and chemicals to sustain the increasing demands. In CCU concept, carbon dioxide is captured and separated from emission gases and then converted into valuable products. It is used to produce chemicals such as urea

(75 million tons), salicylic acid, cyclic carbonates, and polycarbonates [2,4,9,10]. As of now, several CO_2 capture technologies based on physisorption, chemisorption, membrane separation, carbamation, amine physical absorption, amine dry scrubbing, and mineral carbonation have been developed. Thus, CO_2 may become the future of oil through the development of synthetic fuels starting from the mixtures of carbon dioxide and hydrogen with specific catalytic chemical reactors. In that way, CO_2 appears as one of the possibilities for high-level energy storage, including the network regulation from renewable energy production. But in every case, new catalytic processes and chemical plants are needed to develop this future industry. Flue gases from fossil fuel–based electricity-generating units are the major concentrated CO_2 sources. If CO_2 is to be separated, as much as 100 MW of a typical 500-MW coal-fired power plant would be necessary for today's CO_2 capture processes based on the alkanolamines absorption technologies [11,12]. Therefore, it would be highly desirable if the flue gas mixtures are used for carbon dioxide conversion but without its pre-separation. Therefore, carbon dioxide conversion and utilization should be an integral part of CO_2 management, although the amount of CO_2 that can be used for making industrial chemicals is small compared to the quantity of flue gas.

3.1 FLUE GAS AS SOURCE OF CO_2

Based on the economic and environmental concerns, there appears to be a unique advantage of directly using flue gases, rather than using pre-separated and purified CO_2 from flue gases. Typical flue gases from natural gas-fired power plants may contain v/v percentages as follows: 8–10 CO_2, 18–20 water, 2–3 oxygen, and 67–72 nitrogen. Whereas a flue gas from coal-fired boilers may contain 12–14 CO_2, 8–10 water, 3–5 oxygen, and 72–77 nitrogen. The furnace outlet temperature of flue gases is usually around 1200°C, which will decrease gradually along the pathway of heat transfer, while the temperature of the flue gases going to the stack is around 150°C. Pollution-control technologies can remove the SO_x, NO_x, and particulate matter effectively, but CO_2 and water as well as oxygen remain largely unchanged [13].

3.2 CO_2 AND C1 CHEMISTRY

As an economical, safe, and renewable carbon source, CO_2 turns out to be an attractive C1 chemical building block for making organic chemicals, materials, and carbohydrates (e.g., foods). The utilization of CO_2 as a feedstock for producing chemicals not only contributes to alleviating global climate changes caused by the increasing CO_2 emissions but also provides a grand challenge in exploring new concepts and opportunities for catalytic and industrial development. CO_2 can be catalytically converted to methane, gaseous hydrocarbons, and higher hydrocarbons useful as solvents and fuels, methanol, dimethyl ether, formic acid, urea, organic carbonates, etc., by thermal catalysis (**Figure 3.2**).

CO_2 conversion into gaseous or liquid hydrocarbon requires high temperature (523–723K) and pressure (20–40 bar), but the conversion is low due to difficulty in the activation of CO_2. Therefore, currently available technologies are not economically suitable for industrial implementation. Efficient heterogeneous catalysts can

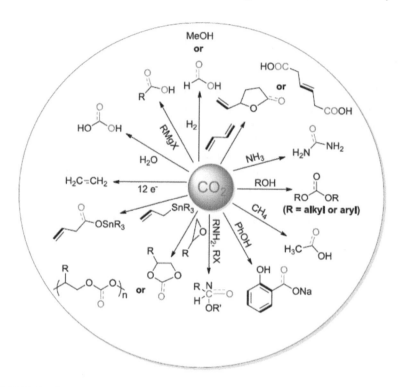

FIGURE 3.2 Schematic representation of possible usage of CO_2 for fuel and chemicals [2,4].

minimize the energy needed for reactions by reducing the activation energy. A lot of literature exists on the utilization of pure CO_2 by different ways, such as using plasma, photocatalytic system, electrochemical reduction, heterogeneous catalysis, etc. [14–18]. A few attempts have been made to develop continuous processes for converting carbon dioxide from flue gas to value-added products that are economical and have the potential to meet energy and material needs of the future. However, hydrogen plays an important part in CO_2 valorization and carbon sequestration.

4. HYDROGEN ECONOMY AND ITS ROLE IN DECARBONIZATION

Hydrogen can be employed as a fuel in many applications, including fuel cell power generation and fuel cell vehicles. It combusts cleanly, producing only water. The coal- and oil-based economy for the manufacture of fuels, chemicals, and materials is not sustainable and has done great harm to the environment. It is predicted that we will run out of oil by the mid-2050s, and new renewable sources of energy and materials are required. As stated earlier, the renewable energy share will rise to ~73% by 2050 in total of 49000 TWh; however, coal will still play a role, thereby the need to hydrogenate CO_2. Thus, hydrogen share could grow from 2% of the global energy mix in 2018 to 13–24% by 2050, at ~ 8% CAGR at the midpoint. An investment of

US$ 150 billion by 2030 is predicted by the International Hydrogen Council and the EU. In the net (carbon) zero economy, green hydrogen will not only achieve the objective of converting CO_2 into fuels and chemicals but also transforming (waste) biomass and waste plastics into fuels and chemicals. Thus, CO_2 and hydrogen are connected in more than one way for protection of environment and provision of future stocks of chemicals and energy.

Hydrogen production technologies cover grey hydrogen, blue hydrogen, and green hydrogen, which are produced using fossil fuels, nonrenewable energy, and renewable energy, respectively (**Figure 3.3**).

Hydrogen is produced as green, blue, and grey hydrogen (**Figure 3.4**). Electrolysis of water using clean electricity from wind, solar, hydro, or nuclear energy sources will give green hydrogen, which produces zero GHG. Steam reforming of biomass, biogas, biooil, or natural gas gives blue hydrogen coupled with CO_2. Blue hydrogen captures up to 90% of the carbon having low to moderate carbon intensity. The steam reforming of fossil fuels, which is the dominant route now, gives grey hydrogen with co-generation of CO_2, which is no longer acceptable. Steelmaking releases more than 3 billion metric tons of carbon dioxide each year, making it the industrial material with the biggest climate impact. To help limit global warming, the steel industry will need to shrink its carbon footprint significantly, and green hydrogen meets that goal. Green hydrogen can be used as a feedstock, a fuel, or an energy carrier and storage and has numerous applications across different industries and in transport, power, and building sectors. It is the key to decarbonize industrial processes [6]. Pyrolysis of methane leading to hydrogen and carbon as co-product is a clean process where no carbon dioxide is generated. The process also produces carbon solids for manufacturing applications. The hydrogen can be used in fuel cells for transportation, including trucks, and large-scale energy storage, while the high-quality carbon products are suitable for a wide range of manufacturing applications, such as electronics, medical devices, aerospace composite materials, and building systems. Commercial sale of the carbon products offsets the cost of hydrogen production—a critical factor for industry.

The reduction of CO_2 emissions of ~35 gigatons in 2020 to ~10 gigatons will contain the global temperature to within 1.5°C by 2050 [7]. For hydrogen to contribute to mitigate climate change and climate neutrality, it must attain much larger scale of production, totally derived from water splitting using green technologies. The hydrogen economy must overcome many challenges, including large-scale infrastructure for refilling stations of hydrogen, akin to those of petrol, diesel, and natural gas, and the cost of hydrogen production, transport, and storage must be low. These challenges can be surmounted collectively by multiple partnerships among companies, nations, and research across institutions and above all local government policies [19]. Green hydrogen must cost below 1.5–2 USD/kg to make the hydrogen economy a reality. Incidentally, the cost of hydrogen production by Institute of Chemical Technology-ONGC Energy Centre (ICT-OEC) hydrogen production technology, developed by this author using water splitting in conjunction with solar energy, is less than USD 1/kg [19].

One of the issues of using carbon-based technology, whether renewable or fossil, is the emission of CO_2, which can be valorized by using hydrogen into a few

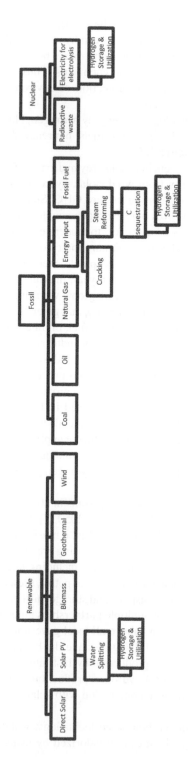

FIGURE 3.3 Hydrogen production from different sources.

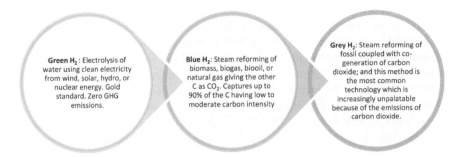

FIGURE 3.4 Types of hydrogen.

chemical products, such as methane and higher hydrocarbons, methanol, dimethyl ether (DME), formic acid, formates, carbonates, ammonia, urea, etc. DME is the cleanest, colourless, non-toxic, non-corrosive, non-carcinogenic, and environmentally friendly replacement of CFC. DME can be effectively used in diesel engines. Like methanol, it is a clean-burning fuel and produces no soot and black smoke. DME is the best substitute for LPG as a cooking fuel, and the well-established LPG industry infrastructure can be used for DME. Hydrogen can serve as a vector for renewable energy storage in conjunction with batteries, guaranteeing as a backup for season variation. Steelmaking releases more than 3 billion metric tons of CO_2 each year, having the biggest climate impact. To help limit global warming, the steel industry will need to shrink its carbon footprint significantly. Thus, hydrogen can substitute fossil fuels in some carbon-intensive industrial processes, such as steel, chemical, and allied industries. It can present solutions for difficult-to-abate parts of the transport system, in addition to what can be accomplished through electrification and other renewable and low-carbon fuels.

5. METHANOL

Net zero demands a radical change across the total economy, abandoning fossil fuels and other sources of emissions wherever possible. For the rest, every ton of CO_2 which is emitted must be met by a ton that should be removed from the atmosphere. Where does the methanol economy fit into this whole game? Due to extreme population rise from the pre-industrial era along with technological advancements, the sustainability of the current high lifestyle entails a large amount of energy. The carbon-based energy has been primarily satisfied by fossil fuels such as oil, natural gas, and coal having limited supply, which will be exhausted in the foreseeable future [18]. Fossil resources also play an essential role as a source of raw materials needed to synthesize a broad array of consumer products. This supply chain can't run for eternity as all these energy sources will diminish within three centuries. From the viewpoint of economics, importing fossil fuel worth billions of dollars is a waste of foreign exchange for all non-oil-producing countries. Carbon dioxide emitted from the energy sources can be converted into different products using hydrogen, the best being the green hydrogen to meet the net zero goal. Hydrogen is viewed as an "energy carrier," and it is only produced by using energy from another source. The green hydrogen produced from a non-carbon source, such as water splitting, will be the best choice. There are some serious limitations of hydrogen utilization as an alternative to conventional fuels, such as the requirement of large infrastructure, as its energy density is low, frequent fluctuation and low controllability, demand for infrastructure modifications over the time. Therefore, the conversion of H_2 and CO_2 into methanol is a better alternative to use hydrogen as energy and CO_2 valorization [20,21]. This approach of recycling captured CO_2 from industrial flue gas into methanol is the heart of the "methanol economy," which was previously proposed by Nobel Laureate George Olah. Methanol as a key commodity has become an important part of the global economy. From building blocks for plastics, paints, and organic solvents to clean fuels applied in fuel cells and combustion engines, 140 million metric tons of methanol were consumed in 2018, and it is predicted to reach 280 million tons in 2030. To reduce CO_2 emissions, production of methanol is an excellent strategy. The life cycle assessment (LCA) of methanol in a circular economy is given in **Figure 3.5**.

Methanol is regarded as an alternative energy carrier because of the higher energy content of 726.3 kJ/mol [22]. The properties of methanol demonstrate its uniqueness as fuel and precursor for different chemicals. In addition, methanol can be used in conventional combustion engines without any major modification. The main idea is to replace gasoline with methanol as a fuel in the combustion engine though gasoline is having a higher energy content of 64,494.5 kJ/kg compared to 31806.7 kJ/kg of methanol. The octane number of methanol is 113, and therefore 10:90 v/v % mixture of methanol: gasoline surges the octane number to 130. However, engines run on pure methanol can achieve efficiency close to 43%. Methanol engines can cover long ranges with a high velocity with 40% efficiency. Moreover, methanol is environment-friendly as its combustion produces almost no harmful by-products like NOx or SOx [22]. Methanol, due to its higher performance, lower emissions, and lower risk of flammability than gasoline, is a better fuel alternative [23].

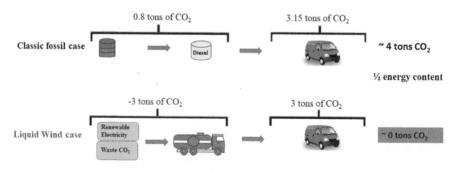

FIGURE 3.5 LCA analysis of renewable methanol economy.

5.1 Methanol Uses

Methanol is being used as a building block material for the commercial production of ethylene, formaldehyde, acetic acid, aromatics, methyl tertiary butyl ether (MTBE), dimethyl carbonate (DMC), biodiesel, and other chemicals. Among the emerging technologies related to gasoline synthesis from renewable sources, a process named "methanol to gasoline (MTG)" is highly appreciated. Methanol has been successfully catalytically converted to aromatics and olefinic hydrocarbons by a number of solid acid catalysts, that is, zeolites, SAPO, etc. These catalysts are continuously perfected to produce a more selective range of alkenes for gasoline synthesis. Therefore, investment in key methanol technologies is essential in the perspective of the global economy. The methanol-derived important bulk chemicals for chemical and energy industries are methylamines (3%), olefins/paraffins (10%), chloromethanes (2%), formaldehyde (29%), MTBE (10%), acetic acid (9%), methyl methacrylate (2%), biodiesel (4%), solvent (5%), gasoline blending (10%), dimethyl ether (10%), and others, including dimethyl terephthalate (6%) [6].

5.2 Single-Step Carbon Dioxide Hydrogenation to Methanol

Although methanol formation from carbon dioxide hydrogenation is an economical and environmentally friendly process, however, this process is thermodynamically limited due to the higher stability and inertness of CO_2. Methanol formation process is given by reaction 1.

$$CO_2 + 3H_2 \leftrightarrow CH_3OH + H_2O, \quad \Delta H_{25°C} = -49.5 \text{ kJ mol}-1 \quad (1)$$

According to the Leshatlier principle, the reaction is thermodynamically favourable at low temperatures and high pressure. By taking into account the higher thermal stability and chemically inertness of CO_2, a high temperature is required to proceed methanol syntheses by this route [24]. Similarly, as methanol synthesis by CO_2 hydrogenation is a molecular reducing reaction, hence it is thermodynamically more favourable at high pressure [25]. As evident from Eq.1, CO_2 hydrogenation to methanol is associated with water formation. Besides, water is a strong oxidant at elevated temperature, oxidizes the active zero-valent form of metal-to-metal oxide (Cu to CuO). Another major obstacle for the lower selectivity of CO_2 hydrogenation of methanol is the reverse water gas shift reaction (RWGS) associated with the process reaction 2.

$$CO_2 + H_2 \leftrightarrow CO + H_2O, \quad \Delta H_{25°C} = 41 \text{ kJ mol}-1 \quad (2)$$

Keeping in mind the stability of CO_2, the activation of CO_2 is more favourable at the higher reaction temperature. However, at higher reaction temperature, RWGS route is more preferred as compared to CO_2 hydrogenation to methanol due to the endothermic nature of the former reaction. Furthermore, the high reaction temperature is generally associated with agglomeration and sintering of active catalyst components during methanol formation at higher temperatures [26].

5.2.1 Reaction Pathway

Generally, two pathways are explained in the literature. The first pathway is the formate formation (*HCOO) by the interaction of surface atomic oxygen with carbon dioxide. This *HCOO intermediate is hydrogenated to dioxymethylene (*HCOOH), which is converted to *H$_2$COOH with further hydrogenation, followed by formation of *H$_2$CO and *OH upon cleavage. The successive hydrogenation of *H$_2$CO leads to the formation of *H$_3$CO, *H$_2$COH, and H3COH as a final product. This route of methanol synthesis by CO$_2$ hydrogenation has been widely reported in the literature. The second reported reaction mechanism is the carboxyl (HOCO) intermediate formation pathway. The HOCO intermediate is converted to the final product of methanol on further hydrogenation.

Arena et al. investigated CO$_2$ hydrogenation on Cu/ZnO and Cu/ZrO$_2$ and reported a similar viewpoint. In dual-site or bifunctional mechanism, H$_2$ is exclusively adsorbed at Cu sites and dissociate to form atomic hydrogen while CO$_2$ adsorption takes place on zirconia. The atomic hydrogen is transported from Cu surface to ZrO$_2$ site by spillover effect, thereby reducing the adsorbed CO$_2$ to formate, methyl, and finally methanol [27].

5.3 Catalysts in Methanol Synthesis

A variety of metal-based catalysts were studied for hydrogenation of carbon dioxide to methanol. The Cu, Zn, Cr, and Pd have been claimed to be the preeminent metals to achieve not only maximum methanol productivity and selectivity but also to minimize the formation of by-products like other hydrocarbons [28]. Based on the previous studies, Sugawa et al. have proposed the following order of activity of different metals for methanol formation from CO$_2$ [29]:

$$Cu \gg Co = Pd = Re > Ni > Fe \gg Ru = Pt > Os > Ir = Ag = Rh > Ru$$

Cu/ZnO is the most extensive catalyst system used for methanol synthesis. Generally, this system is run at a higher temperature (more than 250°C) and a high-pressure range (above 50 bar). Copper-based catalysts have been declared as the most active and selective catalysts for methanol synthesis by hydrogenation of CO$_2$ [30]. Further addition of trivalent ions (M^{3+}) such as Al^{3+} in Cu/ZnO catalyst leads to the enhanced thermal and chemical stability of the catalyst, higher Cu dispersion and metal surface area. Cu/ZnO/Al$_2$O$_3$ is the most extensively studied catalysts for CO$_2$ hydrogenation to methanol. Currently, almost all the entire methanol synthesis is based on Cu/ZnO/Al$_2$O$_3$ catalysts. However, the poor performance of Cu/ZnO/Al$_2$O$_3$ has limited the effective conversion of CO$_2$ to methanol.

Moreover, CO$_2$ hydrogenation was depressed by the strong hydrophilic character of Al$_2$O$_3$ as compared to Cu/ZnO/ZrO$_2$ [31]. Several Ag based catalysts such as Ag/ZrO$_2$, Ag/ZnO, Ag/ZnO/ZrO$_2$ have been utilized for methanol synthesis, and among which Ag/ZrO$_2$ has shown 100% methanol selectivity compared to Cu/ZnO [32]. Ag addition to CuO/ZrO$_2$ catalysts results in enhancing selectivity towards methanol. Pd based catalysts with different supports like SiO$_2$, Al$_2$O$_3$, La$_2$O$_3$, and ThO$_2$ were investigated for carbon dioxide hydrogenation to methanol [33]. Pd/ZnO catalysts with 3.93 wt.% Al doping, where the CO_2 conversion and CH_3OH yield are increased to 2.5 times and 1.7 times that of Pd/ZnO, respectively. However, in comparison to Cu based catalyst, Pd/ZnO catalyst was found less active to methanol synthesis from CO_2 reduction. Higher selectivity of methanol (ca 90%) was recorded at 120 bar pressure and 350°C over Pd/La_2O_3 catalyst [33]. Similarly, PdIn catalysts have also been reported with excellent activity. A 70% higher methanol synthesis rate was recorded with PdIn catalyst as compared to the reference $Cu/ZnO/Al_2O_3$ catalysts. Similarly, Pd based catalysts showed higher selectivity to methane whereby lowering the methanol selectivity [34,35]. A number of metals have been used as promoters such as gallium oxide (Ga_2O_3), niobium oxide (Nb_2O_5), and zinc oxide (ZnO). The introduction of Ga_2O_3 has affected the structural changes in the catalysts and played the role of regulator by keeping the Cu^+/Cu^0 ratio constant throughout the reaction period. Niobia (Nb_2O_5)-supported catalysts have been reported with low acidity and strong metal support interactions.

Similarly, Nb_2O_5 based catalysts exhibited better activity and selectivity in hydrogenation reactions of CO and CO_2. Different supports are also applied to provide the thermal stability to the active phase and avoid sintering of metals particles and include SiO_2, Al_2O_3, ZrO_2, ZnO, carbon nanotubes (CNT). The thermal conductibility associated with CNTs, facilitates it in removing heat generated during the course of the reaction. This ability of CNTs gives an extra advantage in applications of exothermic reactions like CO_2 hydrogenation to methanol [36–42]. Mesoporous manganese-cobalt spinel oxides with different Co/Mn ratios have been utilized for CO_2 hydrogenation to methanol in a fixed bed reactor. The highest methanol selectivity of 29.8% (reaction conditions: 250°C, 10 bar, 44, 400 h^{-1}) was obtained with 20 wt.% manganese with a CO_2 conversion of 49.1%, resulting in a methanol formation rate of 2280 mg/(g_{cat} h) [39]. Among other catalysts studied, only $Cu-ZnO-Ga_2O_3/SiO_2$ and $LaCr_{0.5}Cu_{0.5}O_3$ displayed improved methanol formation rates and high selectivity (up to 99.5%), but their scalability and long-term stability have not been assessed. Experiments on $Cu/CeO_x/TiO_2$ model surfaces [40,41] also showed promising results, but no attempt has been made to translate this material into a practically relevant polycrystalline solid. Martin et al. have studied CO_2 hydrogenation to methanol by using In_2O_3 supported on ZrO_2 catalyst to achieve 100% selectivity and remarkable stability for 1000 h on stream in a fixed bed reactor ($T = 300°C$, $P = 50$ bar, $H_2/CO_2 = 4:1$, and GHSV = 16 000 h^{-1}) [34].

5.4 Impact of Methanol Economy on the Environment

Methanol is a sustainable energy source generated from a variety of traditional (natural gas, coal gasification, biomass) and renewable sources (industrial flue gases, carbon capture, and storage plants). In the molecular structure of methanol, there is no carbon-carbon bond; rather it is full of hydrogen, and therefore it is regarded as a cleaner fuel [18]. Methanol is naturally produced by different natural phenomena, like a volcanic eruption, vegetations, insects, microorganisms, animals, degradation of organic waste, etc. If methanol is accidentally spilled in the environment, it will eventually be degraded naturally by photodegradation or by microorganisms, which can break methanol in CO_2 and H_2O in aerobic or anaerobic conditions. Aquatic species get affected hardly to the exposure of diluted methanol if any accidental release of methanol in water bodies, which is very severe in the case of oil spillage. A concentration of 2,375 mg/mL is a no-observed-effect concentration (NOEC) to freshwater ecosystems.

One of the most important aspects of methanol synthesis is the availability of feedstock at an economic level from cheap sources. Synthesis gas (CO, H_2, and little CO_2) is the most utilized feedstock for methanol synthesis, which is principally produced from reforming of abundantly available natural gas, reforming, or partial oxidation of different carbon-based materials (coal, petroleum coke, heavy oil, petroleum residue, etc.) and biomass-based materials. Therefore, the choice of raw material is not only dependent on the long-term availability but also on the energy consumption, environmental aspect, political influences. The required heat for the whole biomass gasification process is generated via two approaches; the first one is called "allothermal," or indirect process, where heat is provided into the gasifier from an external source. The second process is an autothermal or direct process, where exothermic combustion and partial combustion reactions are responsible for the automatic supply of heat inside the gasifier. There are a hundred types of gasifiers studied and patented to date, though majorly gasifiers can be divided into two groups based on the bed position inside the reactor during gasification, that is (1) fixed bed, (2) fluidized bed gasifier. The third type of gasifier is also developed called entrained flow gasifier, which is designed for finely divided feedstock particles (<0.1–0.4 mm) such as coal particles, but for application in the biomass gasification field, the biomass must be converted into easy-pulverized materials, that is, char, pyrolysis oil, etc. [18].

6. DIMETHYL ETHER

Dimethyl ether (DME) has many fascinating attributes as a fuel which can be produced from carbon dioxide using innovative catalysts, reactors, and separators. The economy of the CCS plant only can be sustainable when it is supported by DME synthesis plant with a capacity of 3000–7500 TPD. DME is the cleanest high-efficiency compression ignition fuel. The reason behind DME's excellent combustion characteristic is its autoignition property. DME is the simplest aliphatic ether and is not toxic, carcinogenic, teratogenic, toxic, mutagenic compound and corrosive. The DME market is projected to grow from $4.364 trillion in 2021 to $8.755 trillion in 2028 at a CAGR of 10.5% during forecast period 2021–2028 [41,42].

6.1 DME Uses

The 1990 Clean Air Act (USA) amendments have put strict emission rules for the industry of the release of volatile organic compounds as it depletes the ozone layer. Though DME is a volatile organic compound, it is not a hazardous. Until recently DME was primarily used as an ozone-friendly aerosol propellant and in the production of ultra-pure glass. However, DME is a favourable transportation fuel because of its many significant benefits: ultra-low exhaust emissions, no particulate matter (PM) emission; very low NOx; no SOx), low engine noise, high fuel economy, high well-to-wheel efficiency and engine thermal efficiency equal to or better than diesel fuel. DME can be employed in diesel engines without engine modification but with minimal modifications to the fuel supply and lubrications. Mixed with propane (30% DME and 70% propane), it can also be used in petrol engines. DME can also be used as fuel for gas turbines for power generation, without modification to turbines or combustors, and as propane blendstock (20% DME aand 80% propane) for cooking and heating, without equipment modifications.

DME is the cleanest high-efficiency compression ignition fuel as a substitute for diesel. DME's autoignition property and high-octane number (55 to 60) are advantageous and allow DME to be used as a propane and butane substitute in LPG as a cooking fuel, and the well-established LPG industry infrastructure can be used for DME market.

DME is considered as the fuel of the future as it can be used in diesel engines with minor modification, its thermal efficiency is higher than traditional fuels, low NO_x emission, and negligible engine noise, and it was critically reviewed by us recently [41,42]. DME is already demonstrated as an efficient fuel for fuel cells. As recommended by World LP Gas Association (WLPGA), DME can be used as a replacement for LPG, and the well-established infrastructure of LPG industry can also be adopted [43]. DME is a clean fuel as it gets depleted very quickly in the atmosphere [44], and it is an intermediate for a variety of chemicals such as acetic acid [45,46], formaldehyde [47], methyl acetate [48], ethanol [49], aromatics [50], gasoline [51], light olefins[51–53], higher ethers, oxygenates, etc. [54,55].

The other major uses of DME, particularly bio-DME, which may contain little methanol and water, are a good alternative to diesel for transportation sector and small-scale power generation industry. Based on LHV (low heating value), 1.2 L of DME is equivalent to 1 litre of diesel. Because of higher octane number (55–60) with a low boiling point (–25°C), it requires little modification of existing diesel engine to carry out its use as a fuel. Inside the diesel engine, DME burns without sooting as similar as an oxygenated fuel additive, and it enhances favorable air/fuel mixture in the engine. DME does not contain sulfur. Thus it does not release any SO_x while burning, and due to unavailability of any C-C bond, it does not produce particulate matter. Due to its high oxygen content (35 wt%), it does not release dark gases while burning and high exhaust gas recycle tolerance. It produces 20–30% reduced NO_x emission compared to other fuels.

6.2 DME Properties

DME is well-known as a higher grade propellant and is used for many healthcare products. Its health and safety properties are better than other conventional petroleum-based fuels. Thus, it can be used as a chemical precursor and multiutility fuel. A comparison of the physical properties of different conventional fuels with DME is shown in Table 3.1. DME outperfoms other fuels.

6.3 DME Market

The substantial DME market is divided in four categories, mainly, (1) LPG blend, (2) diesel replacement as a transportation fuel, (3) gas turbine fuel in power generation

TABLE 3.1
Comparison of properties of different fuels [41,42]

Properties	DME	MeOH	Methane	Propane	Butane	Diesel
Boiling Point (°C)	−25.1	64.6	−161.5	−42	−0.5	180–360
Vapour pressure at 20°C	5.1	—	—	8.4	2.1	—
Liquid density at 20°C gm/cm^3	0.67	0.79	0.42	0.49	0.61	0.84
Specific gravity of gas (vs air)	1.69	—	0.55	1.52	0.6	—
Flammability limits in air, Vol%	3.4–17	5.5–36	5–15	0.94–2.1	1.9–8.4	0.6–7.5
Wobbe Index, kJ/m^3	46198	—	48530	69560	—	—
Cetane No.	55–60	5	0	5	—	40–55
Calorific Value LHV, kcal/Kg	6900	4800	12000	11100	11833	10200
Calorific Value LHV, kcal/nm^3	14200	8600	21800	—	—	—

sector, (4) chemical precursor for different chemicals (olefins and petrochemical). China is the largest DME producer, utilizing 90% of total production for LPG blending. Other countries such as Egypt, Indonesia, South Korea, Vietnam, etc., also started evaluating or establishing manufacturing units to get into this market. According to the World LP Gas Association (WLPGA), DME can be used as a mixture or separately as a substitute in the LPG industry. Other studies suggest that 15–20 volume % of DME blending in LPG is not going to affect the current LPG infrastructure (storage, distribution, and usage). DME gas can be liquefied by pressurized at 5.7 atm at 20°C and by cooling to −25°C at atmospheric pressure. As stated before, the similar physical properties of LPG and DME allow DME to be used as a propane and butane substitute in LPG as a cooking fuel and the well-established LPG industry infrastructure can be used for DME also. Around the world the number of vehicles running on LPG is increasing. Currently, there are more than 10 million LPG operated cars are on the road. But due to the stricter emission guidelines, some new competitors are coming up in the market. DME, especially Bio-DME, can be used as a blending agent with LPG (15–20 volume%) as the solution [41,42].

DME has very low vapour pressure, and it is a chemically and physically stable compound and posses very little toxicity to the human body. Thus, DME can be used as an aerosol propellant and can replace chlorofluorocarbon (CFC), Freon, and R-134, which is one of the reasons behind ozone layer depletion. DME is used as a feedstock for a variety of chemicals such as acetic acid, methyl acetate, aromatics, gasoline, light olefins, higher ethers, oxygenates, etc. As the fuel cell technology matures, the opportunity of bio-DME as fuel in a hybrid vehicle is very high. The DME is a hydrogen carrier, and it can be reformed to produce syngas (H_2+CO) at a lower temperature (120–150°C) when compared with other fuels like diesel, gasoline, and methane (above 650°C). A major portion of produced DME is used to produce dimethyl sulfate by reacting with sulfur trioxide. DME can be catalytically converted to other useful chemicals by reacting with syngas such as formaldehyde, methyl acetate, and ethanol. Other usages of DME include as a solvent a kiln fuel for ceramics, for welding and cutting plus brazing applications [41,42].

6.4 DME Synthesis

Conventionally made from fossil fuels (natural gas and coal), DME can also be produced from renewable materials (biomass, waste—and renewable electricity and carbon dioxide). DME can be synthesized from two processes (1) indirect synthesis or two-step process, (2) direct synthesis or single-step process. The indirect process is a dual-step process in which firstly methanol is synthesized from syngas or CO_2 in the first reactor; then it is dehydrated to produce DME in the second reactor. The direct synthesis process is a single reactor process where both the reactions occur in the presence of a bifunctional catalyst [41,42].

One pot conversion of CO and CO_2 to DME is challenging and energetically unfavorable. Suitable reaction conditions and efficient catalysts are required to carry out such reactions. When direct synthesis of DME is considered, conversion of CO is much easier than CO_2, and therefore the industry prefers CO for DME synthesis. During DME synthesis reaction from CO_2, CO, and water are produced by reverse water gas shift (rWGS) reaction, and other hydrocarbons are also formed from methanol. Formation of a large quantity of water is a big problem during DME synthesis from CO_2 as it creates a thermodynamic limitation for methanol formation and methanol dehydration reactions, and thus, the DME yield is lower when CO_2 is used compared to CO.

DME synthesis was achieved from CO_2 and H_2 in a single step with the combination of methanol synthesis catalyst and methanol dehydration catalyst in a continuous flow reactor. DME synthesis reaction from CO_2 involves a series of reversible reactions Eq. 1 to 3, whereas Eq. 4 is the overall reaction [56–58].

$$2CH_3OH \leftrightarrow CH_3OCH_3 + H_2O + HCs \qquad \Delta H^\circ_{298} = -23.5 \frac{kJ}{mol} \qquad (3)$$

$$CO_2 + 3H_2 \leftrightarrow CH_3OH + H_2O \qquad \Delta H^\circ_{298} = -49.4\, kJ/mol \qquad (4)$$

$$H_2 + CO_2 \leftrightarrow H_2O + CO \qquad \Delta H^\circ_{298} = 41.4\, kJ/mol \qquad (5)$$

Overall, one-pot DME synthesis reaction

$$2CO_2 + 6H_2 \leftrightarrow CH_3OCH_3 + H_2O \qquad \Delta H^\circ_{298} = -122.2\, kJ/mol \qquad (6)$$

DME synthesis from CO_2 is a unique approach as it is a combination of three separate reactions, namely, (1) synthesis of methanol (Eq. 3), (2) dehydration of methanol (Eq. 4), (3) reverse water gas shift reaction (r-WGS) (Eq. 5). There are mainly two strategies of converting H_2 and CO_2 to DME: (a) the two-step strategy involves methanol synthesis on a mixed metal catalyst as a first step and then dehydration of methanol to DME occurred on a solid acid catalyst in the second step (b). In one-step strategy, DME is produced from H_2 and CO_2 on a bifunctional catalyst, which possesses both metal and acid functions. The single-step strategy has significant advantages over the other, such as (1) incorporation of CO_2 as a raw material in DME production, which is advantageous in CO_2 sequestering on a large scale; (2) DME yield is improved as the one-step processes is more thermodynamically favoured and also the equilibrium shifts to the forward direction of DME synthesis (Eq. 2) [59];

(3) in situ methanol dehydration leads to DME synthesis at reduced pressure and higher temperature than the methanol synthesis reaction [60–61]. Over the years, researchers have been at work to convert CO_2 to DME via several catalytic systems, some of them used a bifunctional catalyst, which has both catalyst functions in very close proximity, and others have used a physical mixture of the methanol synthesis catalyst (MSC) and methanol dehydration catalysts (MDC). However, the effectiveness of the bifunctional catalysts is questioned by many scientists as the bifunctional catalysts are very prone to deactivation as coke is formed on the surface of catalyst and inside the pores. A methanol dehydration reaction is accomplished on the solid acid catalyst. The role of Lewis and Bronsted acid sites for DME synthesis from methanol dehydration reaction has been explored by many scientists [62]. Medium acidic Bronsted acid sites are the main contributing sites for methanol dehydration to DME with prolonged reaction rate and without deactivation. Therefore, detailed knowledge of surface acid sites of solid acid catalysts is essential to tweak the acidic property for better results. γ-Alumina, modified γ-alumina, clays, TiO_2-ZrO_2, SO_4-ZrO_2, HZSM-5, HY, SAPO, ion exchange resins, mordenites, M41S mesoporous silica, etc. are among the most used solid-acid catalysts for DME synthesis from methanol [63,64,60–66]. γ-Alumina and modified γ-alumina (with silica, titania) have shown good methanol dehydration properties as they are highly thermally and mechanically stable catalysts possessing very high surface area.

Notwithstanding these advantages, γ-alumina has some disadvantages; most of the acid sites of γ-alumina are Lewis acid type, which is very prone to moisture adsorption and eventually gets deactivated [59]. HZSM-5 has shown better activity than γ-Alumina as it is hydrophobic and active at a moderate temperature range (240–280° C). But the most abundant highly acidic Bronsted acid sites are converting DME further into hydrocarbons. HZSM-5 is microporous and regarded as the most promising catalyst for methanol dehydration. Sometimes these small pores (>1nm) are responsible for blockage of bulky molecules, and therefore, coke formation can deactivate catalysts by blocking the pores [60,61]. M41S mesoporous materials, such as MCM-41 (hexagonal-2D), SBA-15 (hexagonal-2D), SBA-16 (cubic-3D), HMS are getting stupendous attention for their large surface area, defined framework, narrow pore size distribution, and large pore size [62–66]. Al-HMS has been utilized as a solid acid catalyst for DME synthesis from methanol [67]. The effect of Si/Al ratio on the acidity of Al-SBA-15 has been studied for DME synthesis by methanol dehydration reaction [68]. Other catalysts used for catalytic dehydration of methanol to DME include Al-HMS [69], alumina-based catalysts [70].

6.4.1 Scope for DME

Introducing DME as a global fuel is a noble effort taken by many organizations and countries. The production cost of DME is higher with presently available technologies when it is produced from natural gas, coal, and biomass because the conversion of raw materials to syngas is an expensive process. The methanol-based indirect DME synthesis process is a low-risk process as methanol production from syngas is a mature and well-established process. Companies like Linde/Lurgi, Haldor Hospice, Uhde, Toyo Engineering, Mitsubishi Gas Chemical Company hold licenses for the single-step DME synthesis technology. MGC, Toyo, Udhe, and Lurgi are the companies which are developing DME production technology based on indirect synthesis.

7. BIOGAS AS SOURCE OF CO_2

Biogas, typically containing 50–75% methane and 25–50% carbon dioxide, is produced by anaerobic fermentation from almost all types of biomass, including wet biomass (which is not usable for most other biofuels), vegetable and animal livestock waste, manure, harvest surplus, oil residues, municipal solid waste (MSW), etc. It is gaining significant industrial attention as a renewable source of carbon. Conventionally, after purification, biogas can be directly combusted for heat and electricity generation, yet the heat value of such combustion processes is low due to the high concentration of CO_2 in the feed gas. From an efficiency point of view, syngas production by biogas reforming with a H_2/CO ratio close to unity is an appropriate option for the full utilization of both CH_4 and CO_2 in biogas for several industrial applications. Depending on the molar H_2:CO ratio in the reformed bio-syngas, it can be directly applied as a feedstock for the production of methanol, dimethyl ether (DME), long hydrocarbon chains via Fischer-Tropsch (FT) process, or NH_3 synthesis by the Haber route [71–76].

Another incentive for using gaseous biofuels for transport applications is the prospect to diversify feedstock sources. Biomethane, also called renewable natural gas (RNG), or sustainable natural gas (SNG), which is separated from biogas, is the most efficient and clean burning biofuel available today. Biomethane is upgraded to a quality like fossil natural gas, having a methane concentration of 90% or greater, by which it becomes possible to distribute the gas to customers via the existing gas grid within existing appliances. Furthermore, it is very promising to use biogas containing carbon dioxide as the co-reactant for methane conversion in the so-called dry reforming process [77] since carbon dioxide can provide extra carbon atoms for methane conversion, while carbon dioxide also serves as a better oxidant, compared to oxygen or air. The co-feed of carbon dioxide will also increase the methane conversion and the yield of objective product. However, the introduction of carbon dioxide into the feed will lead to a complex product. In addition to syngas, gaseous hydrocarbons (C_2 to C_4), liquid hydrocarbons (C_5 to C_{11+}), and oxygenates can be produced in methane conversion with the co-feed of carbon dioxide. The liquid hydrocarbons are highly branched, representing a high-octane number, while oxygenates mainly consist of series of alcohols and acids. The development of a production technology for direct conversion of methane and carbon dioxide to higher hydrocarbon and oxygenates using novel catalytic system will probably be more economically desired [78–80]. It is also important to note that carbon should not be used as a source of fuel but chemicals and materials and all non-carbon sources of energy such as solar, wind, geothermal, tidal, and nuclear and above all hydrogen from water splitting will meet the requirements of the Paris Agreement [6].

8. HYDROCARBON SYNTHESIS

CO_2 hydrogenation to C_{2+} hydrocarbons can be catalyzed through a modified FT route or methanol-mediated route to promote hydrocarbon chain growth. For the modified FT metal-based catalysts, appropriate active metal should be chosen, such as Fe, to get the best hydrogenation capacity. The support basicity and oxygen vacancies should also be improved to increase CO_2 adsorption and activation. In addition, adding promoters to adjust the surface C/H ratio and reduction capacity of the active metal is another approach to promote hydrocarbon chain growth. For the methanol-mediated route, bifunctional catalysts combining metal oxides and zeolites are crucial for obtaining a higher selectivity of long-chain hydrocarbons. Acid sites are important for the conversion of methanol to hydrocarbons and the channel diameter can influence product selectivity due to the shape-selectivity characteristic SPAO-34 with 8-ring pore structure is beneficial for C_2–C_4 formation [68] and ZSM-5 with 10-ring pore structure will lead to C_5–C_{11} formation. Therefore, tuning acid strength and pore size plays a significant role in the formation of C_{2+} hydrocarbons, and it is a promising direction to promote chain growth [81–83].

9. PLASTIC REFINING: CHEMICAL RECYCLING

Plastics refining is greenhouse-gas intensive. Carbon dioxide emissions from ethylene production are projected to expand by 34% between 2015 and 2030. For instance, polyvinylchloride (PVC) is a widely used thermoplastic polymer due to its stability, affordability, and workability. It is a versatile general plastic widely used in construction, civil material, and many other consumer goods. PVC polymer is highly polar and thus has a good insulation property, but it is inferior to non-polar polymers like polypropylene (PP) and polyethylene (PE). PVC, PE, and PP are commonly used in piping, water sanity, and medical industries, etc., whereas PP is extremely thermal resistant and can tolerate much higher temperatures than PVC. These polymers contribute to carbon footprint and global warming. PVC is shown to have higher energy consumption and CO_2 gas emission that shows its high potential in global warming than other plastics. Likewise, the recycling of PVC has shown substantial contributions in lowering the effect on climate change [84].

PVC can improve its production scale but also reduce global warming. Among all three types of polymers in Table 3.2, PVC has more energy consumption and

TABLE 3.2
Environmental performance of PVC, PP, and PE [84]

Criterion	PVC	PP	PE
Energy consumption	Consumes 223.4 kWh of energy.	Consumes energy of 191 kWh.	Consumes energy of 211 kWh.
Carbon footprint	Emission of 67 kg CO_2.	Emission of 61.5 kg of CO_2.	Emissions of about 58.6 kg of CO_2.
Life cycle impact lower carbon emissions	The recycled polyvinyl chloride has reduced climate impact from 36.21% to 15.53%.	Lower carbon emissions. Better than PE in terms of life cycle impact categories.	Need 22% lesser fossil fuel. It did not work as good in other categories, that is, ozone depletion and eco toxicity impacts.

CO_2 gas emission. Thus, it has more contribution to global warming in comparison to other types of polymers. It was also revealed that recycling and the non-recycling product has the same quality of products.

Worldwide, about 40% of plastics are used as packaging. Typically, packaging is meant for a single use (SUP), so there's a fast turnaround to disposal. The packaging can be handled in three different ways: landfill, incineration, or recycling. Waste incineration has the biggest climate impact of the three options. According to the CIEL report, U.S. emissions from plastics incineration in 2015 were 5.9 million metric tons of CO_2 equivalent. According to the World Energy Council, if plastics production and incineration increase as anticipated, GHG will increase to 49 million metric tons by 2030 and 91 million metric tons by 2050. Landfilling has a much lower climate impact than incineration. But the location of landfills can be associated with similar environmental injustices. Recycling is a different ball game with an entirely different set of problems. Compared to the low costs of virgin materials, recycled plastics are high cost with low commercial value. This makes recycling profitable only rarely, so it requires considerable government subsidies. However, so-called chemical recycling of polymers, including depolymerization and hydrogenation, as I had advocated before, are excellent options. Ellen MacArthur Foundation suggests that only 2% of plastics are recycled into products with the similar functionality. Another 8% are "downcycled" to something of lower quality. The rest of plastic is landfilled, goes into the environment, or incinerated.

Eventually, cutting emissions associated with plastics may require an all-of-the-above strategy: reducing waste, retaining materials by refurbishing or remanufacturing, and recycling. Chemical recycling comprises three mechanisms by which the polymer is purified from plastics without changing its molecular structure, is depolymerised into its monomer building blocks, which in turn can be repolymerised, and is converted into chemical building blocks and can thus be used to produce new polymers. Hydrogen and methane production from Styrofoam waste using an atmospheric-pressure microwave plasma reactor is reported. Polymer upcycling such as SUP conversion into new products is all now worthy of practice. If government-established recycling targets are to be attained, the relationships between consumers, municipalities, and petrochemical production must be enhanced. After all, public opinion is moved by media images of an endangered planet and ecosystem. Only through the collaboration of people, municipalities, and industry—supported by improved technology along the recycled plastics supply chain—a solution for this global crisis can be achieved.

In our laboratory, we thus developed a concept of carbon dioxide refinery using green hydrogen as a solution to the net zero goal (Figure 3.6).

10. FUTURE DIRECTION

Several challenges exist in using/reusing carbon dioxide in an economical way. A major challenge involves determining how best to tap energy sources, since converting carbon dioxide into fuels and chemicals would require substantial energy input. Another challenge is to find new reaction paths, including new heterogeneous catalysts and enzymes, and design and operation of multiphase reactors. This is at the

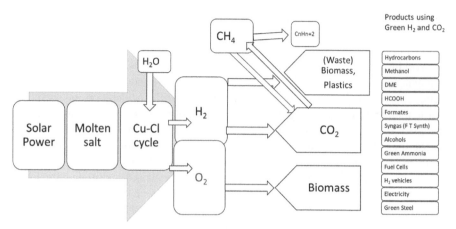

FIGURE 3.6 Carbon dioxide refinery and hydrogen economy.

heart for many approaches in using carbon dioxide to make new products. Presently, only a few developing technologies can find industrial applications. Therefore, there is a need for concerted cutting-edge research to assess the viability of these promising exploratory technologies rationally.

Utilization of pure CO_2 by different ways, such as using plasma, photocatalytic system, electrochemical reduction, heterogeneous catalysis, etc., has been covered in the literature. However, scarce attempts have been made to develop continuous processes for converting carbon dioxide from flue gas to value-added products that are economical and have the potential to meet energy and material needs of the future. Over the next 10 to 20 years, capturing carbon dioxide from fossil fuel–burning power plants, natural gas processing plants, bioethanol plants, and cement plants could become a significant method for mitigating climate change. Most of the captured CO_2 would probably be injected deep into the Earth, a practice known as carbon capture and storage (CCS). One proposed means of reducing the cost of carbon capture is to sell some of the CO_2 for subsequent use. As a result, CO_2 is now considered not just an air pollutant but also a commodity. Among the potential applications outlined the use of CO_2 as a feedstock to produce chemicals, including fuels. In the chemical industry, the greatest use of CO_2 (110–120 million metric tons per year) is to produce urea. Considering that global CO_2 emissions are around 10 billion metric tons per year, converting CO_2 to useful chemicals is not expected to make a big dent in the carbon emissions problem. However, researchers are making progress in developing efficient methods for converting CO_2 into chemicals, so its potential use could be significant.

Decarbonization of the transportation industry is a call of the day. The new setting trend of the mode of transportation is electric cars and hydrogen-driven vehicles, but the question is still unsolved as most of the power plants are using coal and petroleum as the primary source of energy, which releases a huge amount of greenhouse gases (CO_X, SO_X, NO_X) into the environment. Due to these obvious reasons, the lifetime of these natural resources has been reduced dramatically, and their overuse will result in the future generation facing energy supply shortages. It is predicted that by mid-2050s we may not have a viable means of extracting oil from Mother Earth using current technologies. These problems along with GHG emissions, commitment to the Paris Agreement of 2015, aiming at net zero carbon by 2050, and containing global temperature rise to below 1.5°C, have all propelled the development of a new clean energy alternative, which has to be renewable and can be utilized in the industry without any major modification of present infrastructure. For any alternate souce, building new infrastructure in a short period and that too economically, will be horrendous. The three main characteristics of the energy supply chain, which are essential for any type of energy infrastructure, are the energy generation, storage, and distribution are utilization. There are a very few options available which can fulfill all the three criteria.

11. CONCLUSIONS

Net (carbon) Zero is a grand plan of the nations of the World to hold the global temperature rise to less than 1.5°C whereby CO_2 emissions must be reduced from ~35 Gigatons today to less than 10 Gigatons by using non-carbon renewable energy sources. Green hydrogen will play a massive role in converting C1 off gases like CO_2 into valuable chemicals and materials.

The CO_2 conversion into gaseous or liquid hydrocarbon requires high temperature (250–450°C) and pressure (20–40 bar), but the conversion is low due to difficulty in the activation of CO_2. Therefore, currently available technologies are not economically suitable for industrial implementation. Efficient heterogeneous catalysts can minimize the energy needed for reactions by reducing the activation energy. Various catalysts need to be actively investigated to enhance CO_2 conversion and to control selectivity toward specific target products. In fact, hydrogen will play an important role in all these chemicals. Hydrogen is regarded as energy carrier, and it is only produced by using energy from other source.

Sustainable methanol economy refers to the combination of captured CO_2 from various waste sources and cheap hydrogen by using renewable energy to produce methanol. It is also referred to as "liquid sunshine" and has a great potential to resolve the energy crises and mitigate climate change. Throughout the last few decades, there is progressive and competitive development of catalytic technologies in hydrogenation of CO_2 for methanol synthesis, leading to a futuristic carbon-neutral society by scavenging massive CO_2 released into the environment various industries.

The preparation, geometry, chemical composition, and nano-structural characteristics are the deciding factors for the catalyst activity in CO_2 hydrogenation to methanol. The Cu/ZnO-based catalyst is widely accepted because of its optimal activity/cost ratio. Although, the Cu/ZnO catalysts are still not well optimized to answer all the challenges associated with CO_2 hydrogenation reaction, such as low-temperature activity, stability for longer reaction time, and by-product formation. The development of various heterogeneous catalysts (i.e., metals, metal oxides, MOFs, perovskite, alloys, or intermetallic compounds) for methanol synthesis from CO_2 hydrogenation shows that there is a high trend in the use of non-copper-based catalyst, which provides high activity and stability. Much supported metal catalyst (Ga, Au, Pd, Pt, Ag) was highly selective towards methanol at a lower temperature depending on the type of support, preparation methods, and metal precursors. In alloys and IMCs, some advantages like tunable electronic, chemical, and geometric properties make these unique. Still, the drawbacks are related to the ideal and uniform atomic ratios as it is easily affected by the metal composition and reduction conditions.

One of the essential factors for a successful methanol synthesis plant is the expenditure control of the methanol production process to gain maximum profit. The cost of methanol is mainly dependent on the feedstock cost and capital cost. Therefore, mega-scale production of methanol (>3000 MTPD) is the one way to compete with the market. In this regard, reactor design and process optimization are among the significant factors for the industrial implementation of CO_2 to the methanol process.

Biomass, biogas, and industrial flue gas are the potential source of feedstock for the future methanol industry. Therefore, we can imagine the level of variables in the feedstock in terms of composition and the operating conditions also must change accordingly. So future development of reliable and simple dynamic models is necessary for predictive control and dynamic optimization of the methanol synthesis process for a wide variety of feedstock. The CO_2 recycling to methanol synthesis is a great idea but with an expensive energy balance. There is a need for the adoption of renewable energy in this process. Renewable hydrogen is produced electrolytically (water splitting) which accounts for more than 4% of total hydrogen production. Hydrogen demand is continuously rising in methanol manufacturing, especially in countries where methanol is directly blended with fossil fuels, such as South Africa, China, Venezuela, and several Middle Eastern countries.

Most of the hydrogen is produced from hydrocarbon processing in the petrochemical industry, usually by gasification of coal or natural gas reform, which typically costs around at <1 EUR/kg. The cost of hydrogen production mainly comes from the energy (heat and electricity) consumed during the process. Renewable energy is the cheapest option for hydrogen production, including geothermal, wind, hydropower, and solar energy. Therefore, the best approach to consider is to produce hydrogen by renewable energy, preferably solar or wind, and use that hydrogen for CO_2 hydrogenation to methanol synthesis. Several methods of hydrogen production are described in the literature and compared. For sustainable hydrogen production for ammonia synthesis, water electrolysis using wind and solar power is used, which provides a clue for methanol synthesis. In the future, thermochemical water splitting cycles such as Cu—Cl could compete for cheap production of green hydrogen if they are coupled with solar energy, as proved in my lab in the ICT-OEC (Institute of Chemical Technology-ONGC Energy Centre) hydrogen production technology [6,19].

Some strategies have been taken up for direct DME synthesis from syngas and CO_2, but this process remains a two-step process. The main obstacles of the process are the catalyst deactivation due to water generation and coke deposition on the surface of the acid catalyst. The vastly used CO_2 or syngas hydrogenation catalyst is CZA (Cu/ZnO/Al$_2$O$_3$) and for the methanol dehydration reaction. Compared to the syngas to DME (STD) process, DME synthesis from CO_2 is producing more amount of water, and the catalyst got poisoned. A vast array of catalysts have been tested as an acid function for methanol dehydration reaction.

To project DME as a future fuel for our society, new studies encompassing process optimization and scale-up study of one-pot DME synthesis and economic aspects of an efficient and practical DME synthesis plant must be explored. More and more research on the noble metal catalyst development must be taken up, which must tell the most active, reusable, economical in respect of preparation and highly water tolerant. DME is viewed as a "2G fuel/biofuel" and is a powerful, empowering fuel that can range from being ultra-low carbon to carbon-negative. It can significantly reduce the carbon footprint of the transportation sector and beyond (a) as an energy-dense, cost-effective means to move towards renewable hydrogen, (b) as a blending agent for propane, and (c) as a diesel replacement. DME can also be a clean fuel produced from emitted CO_2 captured from flue gases or directly from power plants.

Carbon dioxide refineries are not far away to be seen and to be believed. Thus, hydrogen can substitute fossil fuels in some carbon intensive industrial processes, such as steel, chemical, and allied industries. It can present solutions for difficult-to-abate parts of the transport system, in addition to what can be accomplished through electrification and other renewable and low-carbon fuels. Net zero should happen much before 2050 during the lifetime of many readers.

REFERENCES

[1] COP26 Achievements at a Glance. https://ukcop26.org/wp-content/uploads/2021/11/COP26-Presidency-Outcomes-The-Climate-Pact.pdf.

[2] J. Artz, T.E. Müller, K. Thenert, J. Kleinekorte, R. Meys, A. Sternberg, A. Bardow, W. Leitner, Sustainable conversion of carbon dioxide: An integrated review of catalysis and life cycle assessment, Chem. Rev. 118, 2 (2018) 434–504.

[3] M. Peters, B. Kçhler, W. Kuckshinrichs, W. Leitner, P. Markewitz, T.E. Mller, Chemical technologies for exploiting and recycling carbon dioxide into the value chain, ChemSusChem 4 (2011) 1216–1240.

[4] T. Sakakura, J.-C. Choi, H. Yasuda, Transformation of carbon dioxide, Chem. Rev. 107, 6 (2007) 2365–2387.

[5] www.climate.gov/news-features/understanding-climate/climate-change-atmospheric-carbon-dioxide.

[6] V.G. Yadav, G.D. Yadav, S.C. Patankar, The production of fuels and chemicals in the new world: Critical analysis of the choice between crude oil and biomass vis-à-vis sustainability and the environment, Clean Tech. Environ. Policy, 22 (2020) 1757–1774.

[7] BP Energy Outlook, 2021, www.bp.com/en/global/corporate/energy-economics/energy-outlook.html.

[8] McKinsey, Global Energy Perspective, 2021. www.mckinsey.com.

[9] S. Samanta, R. Srivastava, Atalytic conversion of CO_2 to chemicals and fuels: The collective thermocatalytic/photocatalytic/electrocatalytic approach with graphitic carbon nitride, Mater. Adv. 1 (2020) 1506–1545.

[10] M. Aresta, Carbon dioxide utilization: Chemical, biological and technological applications, in: Greenhouse gases: Mitigation and utilization, CHEMRAWN-XVII and ICCDU-IX, Kingston, Canada, E. Buncel, Ed. Kingston, Canada, 2007: pp. 123–149. (12) (PDF) Carbon Dioxide Utilization: Chemical, Biological and Technological Applications (researchgate.net)

[11] DOE/OS-FE, Carbon Sequestration. State of the Science. Office of Science and Office of Fossil Energy, U.S. DOE, 1999.

[12] T. Weimer, K. Schaber, M. Specht, A. Bandi, Comparison of CO2-sources for fuel synthesis, Am. Chem. Soc. Div. Fuel Chem. Prepr. 41, 4 (1996) 1337–1340.
[13] DOE/FE, Capturing Carbon Dioxide. Office of Fossil Energy, U.S. DOE, 1999.
[14] C. Song, P. Wei, S.T. Srimat, J. Zheng, Y. Li, Y.-H. Wang, B.-Q. Xu, Q.-M. Zhu, Tri-reforming of methane over Ni catalysts for CO_2 conversion to syngas with desired H_2/CO ratios using flue gas of power plants without CO_2 separation, Stu. Surf. Sci. Cat. 153 (2004) 315–322.
[15] S.N. Habisreutinger, L. Schmidt-Mende, J. Stolarczyk, Photocatalytic reduction of CO_2 on TiO_2 and other semiconductors, Angew. Chem. Int. Ed. 52 (2013) 2–39.
[16] B. Hu, C. Guild, S.L. Suib, Thermal, electrochemical, and photochemical conversion of CO_2 to fuels and value-added products, Journal of CO_2 Utilization 1 (2013) 18–27.
[17] C. Costentin, M. Robert, Saveant, catalysis of the electrochemical reduction of carbon dioxide, J. Chem. Soc. Rev. 42 (2013) 2423–2436.
[18] U. Mondal, G.D. Yadav, Methanol economy and net zero emissions: Critical analysis of catalytic processes, reactors and technologies, Green Chem. 23, 21 (2021) 8361–8405.
[19] G.D. Yadav, The case for hydrogen economy, Curr. Sci. 120 (2021) 971–972.
[20] L. Spadaro, M. Santoro, A. Palella, F. Arena, Hydrogen utilization in green fuel synthesis via CO_2 conversion to methanol over new Cu-Based catalysts, ChemEngineering. 1 (2017) 19.
[21] F. Arena, G. Mezzatesta, L. Spadaro, G. Trunfio, Latest advances in the catalytic hydrogenation of carbon dioxide to methanol/dimethylether, in: Transform. Util. Carbon Dioxide, Springer, 2014: pp. 103–130.
[22] S. Zander, T. Ressler, M. Muhler, Preparation and characterization of Cu/ZnO catalysts for methanol synthesis (2012).
[23] A. Bill, B. Eliasson, U. Kogelschatz, L.-M. Zhou, Comparison of CO_2 hydrogenation in a catalytic reactor and in a dielectric-barrier discharge, in: Stud. Surf. Sci. Catal., Elsevier, 1998: pp. 541–544.
[24] S. Saeidi, N.A.S. Amin, M.R. Rahimpour, Hydrogenation of CO2 to value-added products: A review and potential future developments, J. CO_2 Util. 5 (2014) 66–81.
[25] F. Gallucci, L. Paturzo, A. Basile, An experimental study of CO_2 hydrogenation into methanol involving a zeolite membrane reactor, Chem. Eng. Process. Process Intensif. 43 (2004) 1029–1036.
[26] S.G. Jadhav, P.D. Vaidya, B.M. Bhanage, J.B. Joshi, Catalytic carbon dioxide hydrogenation to methanol: A review of recent studies, Chem. Eng. Res. Des. 92 (2014) 2557–2567.
[27] H.-W. Lim, M.-J. Park, S.-H. Kang, H.-J. Chae, J.W. Bae, K.-W. Jun, Modeling of the kinetics for methanol synthesis using Cu/ZnO/Al2O3/ZrO2 catalyst: Influence of carbon dioxide during hydrogenation, Ind. Eng. Chem. Res. 48 (2009) 10448–10455.
[28] S. Sugawa, K. Sayama, K. Okabe, H. Arakawa, Methanol synthesis from CO2 and H2 over silver catalyst, Energy Convers. Manag. 36 (1995) 665–668.
[29] S. Li, Y. Wang, B. Yang, L. Guo, A highly active and selective mesostructured Cu/AlCeO catalyst for CO_2 hydrogenation to methanol, Appl. Catal. A Gen. 571 (2019) 51–60.
[30] S. Ren, W.R. Shoemaker, X. Wang, Z. Shang, N. Klinghoffer, S. Li, M. Yu, X. He, T.A. White, X. Liang, Highly active and selective Cu-ZnO based catalyst for methanol and dimethyl ether synthesis via CO_2 hydrogenation, Fuel. 239 (2019) 1125–1133.
[31] W.H. Chen, B.J. Lin, H.M. Lee, M.H. Huang, One-step synthesis of dimethyl ether from the gas mixture containing CO_2 with high space velocity, Appl. Energy. 98 (2012) 92–101.
[32] S. Tada, S. Satokawa, Effect of Ag loading on CO2-to-methanol hydrogenation over Ag/CuO/ZrO$_2$, Catal. Commun. 113 (2018) 41–45.

[33] X. Jiang, Y. Jiao, C. Moran, X. Nie, Y. Gong, X. Guo, K.S. Walton, C. Song, CO_2 hydrogenation to methanol on PdCu bimetallic catalysts with lower metal loadings, Catal. Commun. 118 (2019) 10–14.

[34] A. García-Trenco, A. Regoutz, E.R. White, D.J. Payne, M.S.P. Shaffer, C.K. Williams, PdIn intermetallic nanoparticles for the hydrogenation of CO_2 to methanol, Appl. Catal. B Environ. 220 (2018) 9–18.

[35] J. Song, S. Liu, C. Yang, G. Wang, H. Tian, Z. Zhao, R. Mu, J. Gong, The role of Al doping in Pd/ZnO catalyst for CO_2 hydrogenation to methanol, Appl. Catal. B Environ. (2019) 118367.

[36] M. Saito, R&D activities in Japan on methanol synthesis from CO_2 and H_2, Catal. Surv. from Asia. 2 (1998) 175–184.

[37] K. Stangeland, D.Y. Kalai, Y. Ding, Z. Yu, Mesoporous manganese-cobalt oxide spinel catalysts for CO_2 hydrogenation to methanol, J. CO_2 Util. 32 (2019) 146–154.

[38] W. Wang, S. Wang, X. Ma, J. Gong, Recent advances in catalytic hydrogenation of carbon dioxide, Chem. Soc. Rev. 40 (2011) 3703–3727.

[39] J. Graciani, K. Mudiyanselage, F. Xu, A.E. Baber, J. Evans, S.D. Senanayake, D.J. Stacchiola, P. Liu, J. Hrbek, J.F. Sanz, Highly active copper-ceria and copper-ceria-titania catalysts for methanol synthesis from CO2, Science (80-.). 345 (2014) 546–550.

[40] O. Martin, A.J. Martín, C. Mondelli, S. Mitchell, T.F. Segawa, R. Hauert, C. Drouilly, D. Curulla-Ferré, J. Pérez-Ramírez, Indium oxide as a superior catalyst for methanol synthesis by CO2 hydrogenation, Angew. Chemie Int. Ed. 55 (2016) 6261–6265.

[41] U. Mondal, G.D. Yadav, Perspective of dimethyl ether as fuel: Part I. Catalysis, J. CO2 Util. 32 (2019) 299–320.

[42] U. Mondal, G.D. Yadav, Perspective of dimethyl ether as fuel: Part II-analysis of reactor systems and industrial processes, J. CO2 Util. 32 (2019) 321–338.

[43] J. Rockall, B. de Calan, DME opportunities in LP gas markets, in: Second Int. DME Conf. London, 2006: pp. 15–17.

[44] D.A. Good, J.S. Francisco, A.K. Jain, D.J. Wuebbles, Lifetimes and global warming potentials for dimethyl ether and for fluorinated ethers: CH_3OCF_3(E143a), CHF_2OCHF_2 (E134), CHF_2OCF_3(E125), J. Geophys. Res. Atmos. 103 (1998) 28181–28186.

[45] S. Clara, D.S. Rice, A. Yamasani, S. Jose, J.B. Parks, S. Clara, E. Millar, M. View, P.C. Richardson, Acetic acid reactive distillation process based on DME/Methanol carbonylation, US 6,175,039 B1, 2012. doi:9168268.

[46] B. Ru, X.B. Li, L.J. Zhu, G.H. Xu, Y.L. Gu, Gas-phase methanol carbonylation for dimethyl ether and acetic acid co-production, Adv. Mater. Res. 554–556 (2012) 760–763.

[47] H. Liu, P. Cheung, E. Iglesia, Structure and support effects on the selective oxidation of dimethyl ether to formaldehyde catalyzed by MoOx domains, J. Catal. 217 (2003) 222–232.

[48] P. Cheung, A. Bhan, G.J. Sunley, E. Iglesia, Selective carbonylation of dimethyl ether to methyl acetate catalyzed by acidic zeolites, Angew. Chemie—Int. Ed. 45 (2006) 1617–1620.

[49] X. Li, X. San, Y. Zhang, T. Ichii, M. Meng, Y. Tan, N. Tsubaki, Direct synthesis of ethanol from dimethyl ether and syngas over combined H-Mordenite and Cu/ZnO catalysts, ChemSusChem. 3 (2010) 1192–1199.

[50] Q. Zhang, Y. Tan, C. Yang, H. Xie, Y. Han, Characterization and catalytic application of MnCl2 modified HZSM-5 zeolites in synthesis of aromatics from syngas via dimethyl ether, J. Ind. Eng. Chem. 19 (2013) 975–980.

[51] Z. Wang, T. He, J. Li, J. Wu, J. Qin, G. Liu, D. Han, Z. Zi, Z. Li, J. Wu, Design and operation of a pilot plant for biomass to liquid fuels by integrating gasification, DME synthesis and DME to gasoline, Fuel. 186 (2016) 587–596.

[52] K.C. Liang, F.M. Yeh, C.G. Wu, H.M. Lee, Gasoline production by dehydration of dimethyl ether with NH4-ZSM-5 catalyst, Energy Procedia. 75 (2015) 554–559.

[53] A.S. Al-Dughaither, H. De Lasa, Neat dimethyl ether conversion to olefins (DTO) over HZSM-5: Effect of SiO_2/Al_2O_3 on porosity, surface chemistry, and reactivity, Fuel. 138 (2014) 52–64.

[54] P. Pérez-Uriarte, A. Ateka, A.G. Gayubo, T. Cordero-Lanzac, A.T. Aguayo, J. Bilbao, Deactivation kinetics for the conversion of dimethyl ether to olefins over a HZSM-5 zeolite catalyst, Chem. Eng. J. 311 (2017) 367–377.

[55] P. Pérez-Uriarte, A. Ateka, A.T. Aguayo, A.G. Gayubo, J. Bilbao, Kinetic model for the reaction of DME to olefins over a HZSM-5 zeolite catalyst, Chem. Eng. J. 302 (2016) 801–810.

[56] K.L. Ng, D. Chadwick, B.A. Toseland, Kinetics and modelling of dimethyl ether synthesis from synthesis gas, Chem. Eng. Sci. 54 (1999) 3587–3592.

[57] Z. Nie, H. Liu, D. Liu, W. Ying, Intrinsic kinetics of dimethyl ether synthesis from syngas, J. Nat. Gas Chem. 14 (2005) 22–28.

[58] X. An, Y.-Z. Zuo, Q. Zhang, D. Wang, J.-F. Wang, Dimethyl ether synthesis from CO 2 hydrogenation on a CuO−ZnO−Al 2 O 3 −ZrO 2/HZSM-5 bifunctional catalyst, Ind. Eng. Chem. Res. 47 (2008) 6547–6554.

[59] X. Zhou, T. Su, Y. Jiang, Z. Qin, H. Ji, Enhanced dimethyl ether synthesis, Chem. Eng. Sci. 153 (2016) 10–20.

[60] R. Liu, Z. Qin, H. Ji, T. Su, Synthesis of dimethyl ether from CO 2 and H 2 using a Cu – Fe – Zr/HZSM - 5 catalyst system (2013).

[61] A. Ateka, J. Ereña, M. Sánchez-Contador, P. Perez-Uriarte, J. Bilbao, A. Aguayo, Capability of the direct dimethyl ether synthesis process for the conversion of carbon dioxide, Appl. Sci. 8 (2018) 677.

[62] Ateka, A., Pérez-Uriarte, P., Gamero, M., Ereña, J., Aguayo, A. T., & Bilbao, J. (2017). A comparative thermodynamic study on the CO_2 conversion in the synthesis of methanol and of DME. Energy, 120, 796–804.

[63] M. Martín, C. Engineering, P. Caídos, Optimal year-round production of DME from CO 2 and water using renewable energy, Biochem. Pharmacol. 13 (2016) 105–113.

[64] X. Guo, D. Mao, G. Lu, S. Wang, G. Wu, Glycine—nitrate combustion synthesis of CuO—ZnO—ZrO_2 catalysts for methanol synthesis from CO_2 hydrogenation, J. Catal. 271 (2010) 178–185.

[65] T. Witoon, P. Kidkhunthod, M. Chareonpanich, J. Limtrakul, Direct synthesis of dimethyl ether from CO_2 and H_2 over novel bifunctional catalysts containing CuO-ZnO-ZrO_2 catalyst admixed with WO_x/ZrO_2 catalysts, Chem. Eng. J. 348 (2018) 713–722.

[66] Z. Azizi, M. Rezaeimanesh, T. Tohidian, M.R. Rahimpour, Dimethyl ether: A review of technologies and production challenges, Chem. Eng. Process. Process Intensif. 82 (2014) 150–172.

[67] S. Hosseini, M. Taghizadeh, A. Eliassi, Optimization of hydrothermal synthesis of H-ZSM-5 zeolite for dehydration of methanol to dimethyl ether using full factorial design, J. Nat. Gas Chem. 21 (2012) 344–351.

[68] S. Xing, P. Lv, J. Fu, J. Wang, P. Fan, Microporous and mesoporous materials direct synthesis and characterization of pore-broadened Al-SBA-15, Microporous Mesoporous Mater. 239 (2017) 316–327.

[69] B. Sabour, M.H. Peyrovi, T. Hamoule, M. Rashidzadeh, Catalytic dehydration of methanol to dimethyl ether (DME) over Al-HMS catalysts, J. Ind. Eng. Chem. 20 (2014) 222–227.

[70] K. Cem, T. Dogu, G. Dogu, Dimethyl ether synthesis over alumina based catalysts, Chem. Eng. J. 184 (2012) 278–285.

[71] W. Li, X. Nie, X. Jiang, A. Zhang, F. Ding, M. Liu, Z. Liu, X. Guo, C. Song, ZrO_2 support imparts superior activity and stability of Co catalysts for CO2 methanation, Appl. Catal. B Environ. 220 (2018) 397–408.

[72] M. Fujiwara, H. Sakurai, K. Shiokawa, Y. Iizuka, Synthesis of C2+ hydrocarbons by CO_2 hydrogenation over the composite catalyst of Cu—Zn—Al oxide and HB zeolite using two-stage reactor system under low pressure, Catal. Today. 242 (2015) 255–260.

[73] F. Jiao, J. Li, X. Pan, J. Xiao, H. Li, H. Ma, M. Wei, Y. Pan, Z. Zhou, M. Li, Selective conversion of syngas to light olefins, Science (80-.). 351 (2016) 1065–1068.

[74] J. Wei, Q. Ge, R. Yao, Z. Wen, C. Fang, L. Guo, H. Xu, J. Sun, Directly converting CO_2 into a gasoline fuel, Nat. Commun. 8 (2017) 15174.

[75] F. Studt, M. Behrens, E.L. Kunkes, N. Thomas, S. Zander, A. Tarasov, J. Schumann, E. Frei, J.B. Varley, F. Abild-Pedersen, The mechanism of CO and CO_2 hydrogenation to methanol over Cu-based catalysts, ChemCatChem. 7 (2015) 1105–1111.

[76] F. Birol, India 2020—Energy Policy Review—NITI Aayog, International Energy Agency, 2020. https://niti.gov.in/sites/default/files/2020-01/IEA-India%202020-In-depthEnergy Policy_0.pdf

[77] A.M. Ranjekar, G.D. Yadav, Dry reforming of methane for syngas production: A review and assessment of catalyst development and efficacy, J. Indian Chem. Soc. 98(1) (2021) 100002.

[78] D. Pakhare, J. Spivey, A review of dry (CO 2) reforming of methane over noble metal catalysts, Chem. Soc. Rev. 43 (2014) 7813–7837.

[79] Y. Gao, J. Jiang, Y. Meng, F. Yan, A. Aihemaiti, A review of recent developments in hydrogen production via biogas dry reforming, Energy Convers. Manag. 171 (2018) 133–155.

[80] J.-L. Liu, X.-S. Li, X. Zhu, K. Li, C. Shi, A.-M. Zhu, Renewable and high-concentration syngas production from oxidative reforming of simulated biogas with low energy cost in a plasma shade, Chem. Eng. J. 234 (2013) 240–246.

[81] M.C.J. Bradford, M.A. Vannice, CO_2 reforming of CH4, Catal. Rev. 41 (1999) 1–42.

[82] H.Y. Kim, J. Park, G. Henkelman, J.M. Kim, Design of a highly nanodispersed Pd—MgO/SiO2 composite catalyst with multi-functional activity for CH4 reforming, ChemSusChem. 5 (2012) 1474–1481.

[83] J.W. Erisman, M.A. Sutton, J. Galloway, Z. Klimont, W. Winiwarter, How a century of ammonia synthesis changed the world, Nat. Geosci. 1 (2008) 636.

[84] A. Alsabri, S.G. Al-Ghamdi, Carbon footprint and embodied energy of PVC, PE, and PP piping: Perspective on environmental performance, Energy Reports 6 (2020) 364–370.

4 Climate Change Impacts on Agriculture
Crop Productivity and Food Security

Pratibha Singh, Shivani Singh, and Rama Shanker Dubey

CONTENTS

1. Introduction 61
2. Impacts of Climate Change on Crop Productivity 63
   - 2.1 Climate Change Impacts on Crop Productivity in Context of India 68
   - 2.2 Climate Change Impacts on Crop Productivity: Global Scenario 70
3. Impact of Climate Change on Food Security 73
   - 3.1 Food Security: India 74
   - 3.2 Food Security: Worldwide 75
   - 3.3 Food Availability 76
     - 3.3.1 Food Availability in India 76
     - 3.3.2 Food Availability in the World 76
   - 3.4 Food Access 77
   - 3.5 Food Utilization 78
   - 3.6 Stability of the Food System 78
4. Conclusions and Future Prospects 79
References 81

1. INTRODUCTION

Climate change refers to any alteration in the long-term shift in the Earth's climate due to human actions, in addition to natural weather variations over time. The factors such as variations in the quantum of solar energy reaching Earth, reflectivity potential of Earth, increasing in greenhouse emissions have all led to global climatic change. Climate change may be caused by natural events, anthropogenic activities, production of greenhouse gases such as carbon dioxide, chlorofluorocarbons (CFCs), methane, etc. Atmospheric level of carbon dioxide has gone up from around 284 ppm during 1832 to 397 ppm in 2013 (Tans and Keeling, 2013) and thereafter to 420 ppm till mid 2021 (Stein, 2021). The increase in the level of atmospheric carbon dioxide as well as other greenhouse gases is specifically related to global warming. CO_2 absorbs heat from the surface of Earth and increases atmospheric temperature, contributing to global warming and other climatic changes. Coal combustion in power plants, land use shifts have direct impacts on global warming (Tans and Keeling, 2013). Climatic change has gained substantial international attention during the recent years due to fears of its long-term adverse effects on global food scarcity, decrease in water availability, increase in global temperatures, public health concerns, etc. Ample evidence indicates that since the mid-19th century, the planet has warmed up (Hansen et al., 2010).

The climate change has drastic impact on agricultural sustainability throughout the world. The prime concern for a growing population in the stressed world during the 21st century is global food security, which includes availability, accessibility, utilization of food as well as sustainability of the food production systems (Firdaus et al., 2019). Climate change will not only have adverse effects on production and consumption of food globally, but it will also affect food production systems locally, as smallholder farmers mostly rely on local as well as on their own food production (Nelson et al., 2012). Climate change will thus possibly facilitate towards a hunger world.

Combating starvation is still a major problem in modern times (Ban, 2012). Starvation has multifarious effects in humans, which triggers nutritional deficiencies, malnutrition, organ damage, and eventually death due to chronic scarcity of food. Starvation occurs due to limitations in availability of food, loss of buying power, poor public policy, food waste, forced migration, etc. Approximately 2 billion people around the world are suffering with micro-nutrient deficiency, besides common important nutritional ailments seen in the developing countries, such as infant underweight, infant mortality, more prone to infection by communicable diseases, etc. Agricultural demand is consistently rising due to increase in world population, prompting a change towards a sustainable production of foods (Garnett et al., 2013). It is imperative that climate change will introduce warmer temperatures, alterations in precipitation trends, extreme climatic conditions, increased CO_2 concentration, and increased incidence of pest and diseases worldwide (Cline, 2007).

The chances of flooding of farmlands in coastal areas would increase due to sea-level rises. Changes in the precipitation patterns, especially on tropical lands, are variable, mainly because the existing models are unable to accurately describe the global hydrological cycle (Lorenz and Kunstmann, 2012). Generally, the Asian monsoon precipitation in summer is predicted to rise, whereas areas of North and South Africa may get dried up (Solomon et al., 2007). In high-yield agriculture areas, climatic erraticism dramatically influences crop production every year. Climatic changes and global warming consequences lead to increased frequencies and severities of adverse weathers. In particular, the effects on developing countries are expected to be more due to climate change as a result of their comparatively low adaptive capacity, higher exposure to environmental hazards, and their limited forecasting systems and strategies (Zhao and Li, 2015). The global average temperature by the end of this century is expected to remain between 1.8°C to 4.0°C higher than the end of the past century (Solomon et al., 2007). During the last 100 years, the world average temperature has increased by about 0.8°C (IPCC, 2014). The average global surface temperatures throughout the past century have increased from 0.55 to 0.8°C and are expected to increase further by 2100 compared to 1980–1999, either from 1.1 to 2.9°C or 2.0 to 5.4°C, depending on greenhouse gases emission, area, and geographic location (IPCC, 2014). High level of CO_2 is a key climate change factor. Current weather reports show that land layer temperatures may increase gradually, possibly as a result of greater CO_2 absorption into deep oceans as anticipated by climate models (Balmaseda et al., 2013). Climate uncertainty and climatic change conditions result in changes in sea levels, precipitation patterns, and severe high- and low-temperature-related events around the world, including floods, water shortages, as well as hurricanes and tornados (Dhillon and Wuehlisch, 2013).

Plants experience numerous biotic and abiotic stresses. The effects of climatic variations result in severity of these stresses, such as temperature extremes like heat and cold, water shortage, salinity build-up in the soil, and higher CO_2 in the atmosphere, which adversely affect plant growth and agricultural productivity at both individual and combined stress levels (Serrano et al., 1999). All such stresses can contribute to substantial losses in crop quality and yield. Farming is perhaps the world's main consumer of freshwater resources and is therefore very susceptible to climate change. High-yielding varieties of food crops consume much more water as irrigation inputs compared to traditional wild varieties. The farming industry provides key livelihoods and job opportunities for a major segment of the population in the developing nations and serves as key contributor to national GDP. Consequently, decline in freshwater resources as a result of global climatic change would adversely affect food production and will impact food safety and livelihood of the poor rural population (Africa Commission, 2005).

One major challenge associated with the climate change is supply of sufficient food for all the time for the rising world population in terms of appropriate quantity and quality in order to achieve food security. Due to climate change, the risk of food security has intensified in many parts of the world. Both food security and nutrition of the people are affected due to climate change. Climate change impacts the availability of food, access of food to the people specially from low-income group, quality of drinking water, incidence of foodborne diseases, causing an overall impact on food security.

The present chapter summarizes our current status of knowledge related to various factors associated with climate changes and their impact on productivity of crops and also analyzes the impacts of climatic change on productivity of major food crops in Indian context and on global scale. Besides, food security issues in relation to climatic change have been elaborately discussed.

2. IMPACTS OF CLIMATE CHANGE ON CROP PRODUCTIVITY

The major factors associated with climatic change which adversely affect crop yield and productivity include irregular rainfall, extremes of temperatures particularly prolonged high temperature spells, increased production of CO_2, soil water availability, soil salinity, etc. (Haokip et al., 2020). The morpho-physiology of plants is greatly affected due to climate change. Variable climatic conditions and climatic change have raised the likelihood of several stresses on plants (Thornton et al., 2014). Crop cultivation is dependent on suitable rainfall and a specific temperature range. Precipitation is the deciding factor for the supply of fresh water and soil humidity as these are essential requirements to achieve optimum productivity of crops. Increasing rainfall improves the yields in rainfed and irrigated farming conditions, but excessive rainfall becomes harmful, and it may result in floods and waterlogging. A detailed account of the consequences of climate disruption and global warming on environmental factors and their effects on growth and productivity of crop plants has been presented in Figure 4.1. The effects of these environmental factors on productivity of crops due to climate change have been described in the following subsections.

i. **Heat:** Temperature as well as soil humidity decide the duration of the crop season and govern the growth and water demand of the crop. High temperature or heat usually reduces the time of frost as well as facilitates farming in the cold-climate conditions. But in arid and semi-arid regions, increasing temperatures reduce the crop lifespan and decrease crop productivity (Parry et al., 2007). In field conditions, heat is one of the most prevalent stresses that has a major effect on existence of plants (Espeland and Kettenring, 2018). Crop plants need an optimum temperature for their growth and productivity. The temperature changes have a major effect on growth and morpho-physiology of plants (Salehi-Lisar and Bakhshayeshan-Agdam, 2016). Heat stress in plants induces morphological, biochemical, and molecular changes, which have adverse effects on plant growth leading to decrease in crop yield. High temperatures reduce plant biomass by causing decline in rate of photosynthesis and increase in transpirational and stomatal conductivity (Jones, 1992). Heat adversely affects the functioning of key enzyme of photosynthetic carbon assimilation in plants ribulose bisphosphate carboxylase (RuBisCO), causing decline in photosynthesis (Crafts-Brandner and Salvucci, 2000). Reproductive stage in plants is greatly affected due to warmer temperatures. Pollination is susceptible to high temperatures. With temperature above 35°C, pollen viability in maize plants decreases (Hatfield and Prueger, 2015). Extreme temperatures trigger flower sterility in plants and disrupt filling of seeds during seed filling phase and thus cause severe loss in yield (Young et al., 2004).

The variation in temperature impacts the seed and grain yields. It has been observed that the severity of heat stress causes significant economic loss to agricultural and horticultural crops, and this phenomenon gets multiplied due to climate change (Beck et al., 2007). It is expected that in future years, climate change will increase more heat, that will in turn cause reduction in global yield of crops by 10% by middle of the present century and up to 25% by end of the century. Such reduction in crop productivity due to heat will ultimately reduce the supply of adequate food to rising world population.

ii. **Precipitation:** Precipitation is a necessary component for agriculture. In rainfed farming, climate variability, including particular shifts in precipitation patterns, adversely affects productivity. Restriction in soil humidity decreases crop yields and enhances the threat for rainfed agriculture. While irrigation reduces the threat of climatic instability, irrigated agriculture systems rely on assured water supplies, hence such systems are affected due to shifts in

Climate Change Impacts on Agriculture

water supply (Molden, 2007). Variability in rainfall affects the productivity of crops, plants become more susceptible to diseases, and soil fertility gets reduced (Kyei-Mensah et al., 2019). Majority of staple food crops on global scale are produced from rainfed agriculture. Specially in rural areas of developing countries and at high altitude regions, large proportion of area represents rainfed region (Kyei-Mensah et al., 2019). It has been generally difficult to forecast local rainfall response in relation to human-induced greenhouse emissions, many ecophysiological and predictive models have been proposed, which make use of rainfall data as well as agronomic information for forecasting rainfall effects on crop productivity (Solomon et al., 2007). Various studies and models related to variable rainfall effects on crop production have always shown that variability in rainfall conditions negatively impacts yield of major food crops (Kyei-Mensah et al., 2019).

iii. **Elevated CO_2 level:** The impact of global warming is being realized since 1950, and due to anthropogenic practices, human and industrial activities, the levels of greenhouse gas emissions, more specially of CO_2, have increased consistently over the years. The impacts, indeed, rely solely on regional differences (Tan and Shibasaki, 2003). After the mid-18th century, atmospheric concentration of CO_2 has risen by around 30% primarily due to fossil fuel combustions, industrial activities, and deforestation (Houghton et al., 2001). Plants are affected primarily by elevated atmospheric CO_2 levels that change the plant's physical structures as well as carbon: nitrogen equilibrium. High CO_2 influences both the quality and quantity of crop production. Enhanced CO_2 levels boost crop growth and biomass through improved photosynthesis and efficiency of water use and reduce transpiration by decreasing stomatal conductivity (Qaderi et al., 2006). The elevated CO_2 level causes increase in CO_2 assimilation, thereby increasing photosynthesis and increasing the capacity of water consumption (Betts et al., 2007). Ainsworth and Rogers (2007) suggested that higher CO_2 levels improve photosynthesis and cause increased production of photosynthetic products such as sugars. A beneficial correlation between growth of wheat leaves and carbon dioxide has been reported by McMaster et al. (1999). Franks and Beerling (2009) found a positive link between stomata size and high CO_2, although there is a negative relationship among both stomata density and higher CO_2. Many other findings have shown that due to the high CO_2 levels, crops become susceptible to various diseases such as wheat stem rust, anthracnose infection on trees and shrubs, and rice sheath blight fungal disease become more intense at high CO_2 levels (Kobayashi et al., 2006). Though increased CO_2 level causes increase in the rate of photosynthesis, plants growing at elevated CO_2 levels show respiratory impairment and decreased production of ATP, which result in decreased nutritional quality (Bhargava and Mitra 2021).

iv. **Drought:** In field conditions, scarcity of water in the soil or drought becomes a crucial factor affecting growth and productivity of crops (Espeland and Kettenring, 2018). Water is an indispensable component for the growth of plants. There has been consistent depletion of water resources in several parts of the world as a result of climatic change. Drought stress causes decline in plant growth, alteration in plant morpho-physiology, and ultimately reduction in yield (Zandalinas et al., 2018). Under severe drought conditions, death of plants may occur. In rainfed conditions, drought is triggered by inadequate precipitation, which results in decrease in crop productivity (Sivakumar et al., 2005). Drought is perhaps the most difficult challenge to world's food safety that specifically diminishes plant growth and productivity by disrupting typical biochemical processes and gene expression. In upland farming, where cultivation depends on rainfed water, long durations without rain may lead to drought conditions in fields. Drought stress restricts seed germination, plant growth, and eventually causes decrease in seed yield in nearly all crops, making it one of the world's biggest threats for agriculture (Mahmood et al., 2013). Due to water shortage, food demand is seriously impacted by drought for rising world populations (Somerville and Briscoe, 2001). Drought intensity relies on precipitation, evaporation, and the soil's ability to retain moisture (Wery et al., 1994). Drought decreases crop yields by three processes: (1) by diminishing the size of canopy, (2) reducing efficiency of radiation usage, and (3) reducing index of harvest (Earl and Davis, 2003). Drought stress induces cell elongation in higher plants by lowering turgor pressure (Farooq et al., 2009). Drought decreases the rate of photosynthesis by reducing leaf expansion (Wahid and Rasul, 2005). Plant water shortage induces alteration in photosynthetic pigment composition, Calvin cycle activity, reducing crop yields (Anjum et al., 2003).

v. **Cold:** Climate change has caused increase in the extremes of weather conditions leading to extreme chilling conditions in many parts of the world (Li et al., 2021). Cold stress or low temperature becomes a key environmental constraint and reduces crop growth and yield. The response of plants to cold depends on the extent of lowering of temperature, such as chilling (0–15°C) and freezing (< 0°C). Chilling stress is encountered by plants when exposed to temperatures below 20°C but above 0°C (Thakur and Nayyar, 2013). Chilling stress affects cellular biomolecules of plants, causes cell bilayer solidification, metabolic processes, and membrane functions are slowed down. Consequences of chilling include wilting, chlorosis, decreased expansion and growth of the leaves, compromised reproductive growth leading to limited seed and pod development that eventually lowers plant yield (Kaur et al., 2008). The production of many important food crops, such as maize, in developing countries gets drastically reduced due to chilling injury (Li et al., 2021).

vi. **Salinity:** Climate change causes increase in root-zone salinity in many parts of the world, more specially in the areas with shallow water table, agricultural land where polluted water is used for irrigation, coastal areas where intrusion of sea water is a common problem (Corwin, 2021). Soil salinity adversely affects agricultural productivity. The problem of salinity in the soil arises from the accumulation of soluble salts of chlorides and sulphates of sodium, magnesium, calcium. A high concentration of soluble salts in the soil makes the soil unsuitable for cultivation. Consistent accumulation of salts in the soil decreases soil fertility. Various approaches have been adopted for soil management in saline regions. In contrast to halophytes, which can grow at high salt levels, the crop plants are sensitive to high salt concentrations. High salinity of the soil causes more uptake of Na^+, Cl^-, induces ion imbalance in the tissues and hyperosmotic stress. These factors taken together adversely affect growth of plants. Certain plant species may become dormant due to salinity stress (Yokoi et al., 2002). The major consequences of salt stress in plants include ion inequalities, osmotic stresses, and ion toxicity to metabolic processes. Salinity stress causes increased production of reactive oxygen species (ROS) in the tissues that causes oxidative damage to cellular biomolecules such as lipids, proteins, nucleic acids, etc.

Besides the factors mentioned previously, the degradation of natural ecosystems and decline in biodiversity appear to be the key negative consequences of the climate change. When Earth's temperature rises, the atmosphere experiences extreme changes, which appear to be abiotically traumatic. Climate change has therefore been regarded as an urgent global problem to be tackled in the 21st century because it reaches across international lines and impacts the entire world population and draws the attention of the scientific community across the world to look for remedial measures. Several countries experience the imminent consequences of climate change distinctly. Developing countries like India are particularly vulnerable to climate-induced tragedies with their poor resilient capacities and strong reliance on climate variables.

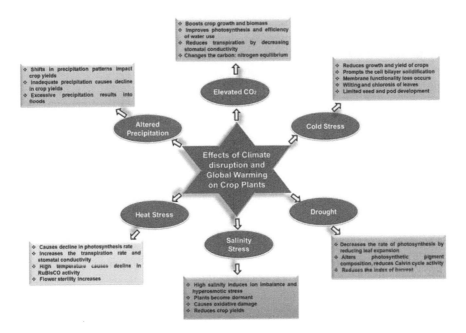

FIGURE 4.1 Effects of climate disruption on growth and productivity of crops. Climate disruption leads to elevated CO_2, temperature shifts, altered precipitation, drought, and salinity stresses, which adversely affect growth, physiology, and productivity of crops.

2.1 CLIMATE CHANGE IMPACTS ON CROP PRODUCTIVITY IN CONTEXT OF INDIA

The consequences of climate change are highly deleterious, which result in increased intensities of flood, drought, erratic rains, woodland burning, intense lake melting, shifting coastline, etc. (IPCC, 2014). Much attention has been paid by Indian scientific community to take stock of global warming effects on the Indian subcontinent. Satellite observations over the last 50 years have shown that average temperature changes across the nation have been around 1°C. Present forecasts predict more changes by the end of the present century, from 2 to 4°C. In fact, forecasts often indicate geographical variability in relation to temperature impacts. It is suggested that increasing global temperature owing to increased greenhouse gas (GHG) is likely to cause changes in the intensity of precipitation cycle in India, specially during summer monsoon, which would adversely affect crop productivity (Katzenberger et al., 2021). During monsoon season, crop cultivation in India is primarily dependent on rain and therefore excessive rain or scarcity of rainfall as a result of global warming will damage the crops (Katzenberger et al., 2021).

The western and southern parts of India are likely to see more increase in temperature rise (Kumar et al., 1994). Changes in the variability of precipitation such as increased incidences of flooding, increasing incidences of extreme drought, shifts in optimum growth seasons, and erratic rainy cycles have caused greater instability for agriculture systems (Misra, 2014). The precipitation decreased in certain parts of the north and northwest India while the precipitation increased over time in the southern, eastern, and northeastern areas. Similarly, the rise in the rate of glaciers melting in the Himalayas has intensified downstream floods, thus affecting lowland crop production (Shrestha et al., 2012). Groundwater levels are perpetually going down due to exhaustive use of groundwater for drinking, irrigation, industrial, and other processes (Gupta et al., 2017).

As a result of green revolution, high yielding varieties (HYV) of important food crops like rice, wheat, pulses are in cultivation since the beginning of the year 1970. These HYVs require much more irrigation water than the traditional wild varieties of crops which were cultivated prior to 1970. To feed the increasing population in India, there is no option other than growing HYVs of crops. Therefore, water management systems need to be worked out, such as water recycling, groundwater recharging, rain water harvesting, etc. Agricultural systems need appropriate groundwater management mechanisms so that required irrigation measures can be assured to tide over shifts in precipitation trends arising from climate change (Misra, 2014). When temperatures remain below 30°C throughout the season, optimum yield can be expected; however when temperatures exceed 30°C, it becomes extremely detrimental to yields for rainfed crops (IPCC, 2014). Climate model predictions indicate that with sufficient irrigation, rice crops may potentially benefit; however, crops like wheat and maize suffer loss in yield due to more irrigation or heavy rainfall due to erratic monsoon (Challinor et al., 2014).

Climate effect forecasts for yields and production have shown variable outcomes and distinct patterns in different regions of India. An estimate for predictions of yields for various crops in India as a result of global climatic change has been presented in

Climate Change Impacts on Agriculture

TABLE 4.1
Future predictions for productivity of major crops up to the year 2080

Crops	Growing season and crop types	Temperature sensitivity	Yield predictions (Yrs. 2050 and 2080)	Regional Disparity	References
Rice	Kharif monsoon season, food crop	Sensitive to low and high temperatures	Decline in yield by 7% and 10% respectively	Decline in yield all over India but mostly in northwest regions like Rajasthan, Gujarat, Punjab, and Haryana	Soora et al. (2013)
Wheat	Ravi crop winter season, food crop	Sensitive above 27°C	Decline in yield by up to 23% by 2050 and up to 25% by 2080	Yield reduction in central and southern region	Kumar et al. (2015)
Sorghum	Kharif crop monsoon season, food crop	Sensitivity increases after increment of every 2°C	Decline in yield by 11% and 32% respectively	Yield reduction in south central, central, and southwest zone	Srivastava et al. (2010)
Cotton	Kharif crop monsoon season, cash crop	Sensitive to local temperature increment	Variable predictions for yield	Yield increment in central, south India, and reduction in northern regions	Hebbar et al. (2013)
Coconut	Kharif monsoon season, plantation crop	Productivity affected above 28°C	5% increase by 2050 and 1% to 4% increase by 2080	Yield increment in south, northeast, and decrease in eastern regions	Kumar and Aggarwal (2013)
Mustard	Ravi crop winter season, cash crop	Decreased yield due to temperature above 25°C	Decline in yield 7.9% and 15% respectively	Yield increment in Punjab and decrease in central and eastern region	Boomiraj et al. (2010)
Potato	Ravi crop winter season, vegetables	Decline in yield due to increase of temperature above 17°C	Decline in yield by 6%, 11% respectively	Yield increment in northwest and decline in eastern region	Kumar et al. (2015)

Table 4.1. By the year 2080, it is expected that yield of most of the staple food crops will decline by 10 to 25% (Soora et al., 2013; Kumar et al., 2015). Since great diversity exists in India in relation to agroclimatic variations, variable predictions are made for different regions and different seasons of crops. With regard to the staple food crops, the probability exists that rice yield would be lower by 7% in the year 2050 in the northwest zones like Punjab, Haryana, and Western Uttar Pradesh because rice production is extremely sensitive to temperature shifts. Currently this region represents highly active rice belt. Experts also forecast that total production of rice will decrease by 10% by 2080 as temperatures will rise. Rice is an important food crop in India, and

its decrease in productivity due to extreme weather conditions will adversely affect food supply for the growing population. Similarly, wheat production is expected to decline by 25% and sorghum production by 32% by the end of 2080 (Srivastava et al., 2010). In horticultural crops, coconut is expected to show nearly 4% increase in yield by 2080 in the south and northeast region of the country (Kumar and Aggarwal, 2013), whereas potato and mustard are expected to face decline in yield due to warmer temperature in the eastern regions of India (Boomiraj et al., 2010; Kumar et al., 2015). For cotton, variable prediction has been made related to its yield depending on different regions. Its yield is expected to increase in central and south India, whereas reduction in yield is expected in northern regions (Hebbar et al., 2013). The output and yield of wheat, maize, and chickpea appears to be quite vulnerable to climate change in rainfed areas (Sharma and Pingali, 2018). Pearls and finger millets, though these are low water requiring crops, appear to face more challenge due to global warming as a result of heat and drought (Sharma and Pingali, 2018).

2.2 Climate Change Impacts on Crop Productivity: Global Scenario

Crop productivity has slowed down steadily during the last 60 years on a global scale as a result of global warming and climate change effects (Ortiz-Bobea et al., 2021). Nearly 21% reduction in yield of crops has been recorded globally since 1961 as a result of climate change, with more reduction in warmer regions like Africa, Caribbean, and Latin America compared to the temperate regions of the world (Ortiz-Bobea et al., 2021). Growth and physiology of crops are affected globally due to climate change (Raza et al., 2019). Weather extremes and changes in climatic conditions have led to increasing risk of environmental stresses (abiotic stresses) on crop plants (Thornton et al., 2014). According to a FAO report of the year 2007, global climatic change has impacted almost all agricultural areas of the world and just nearly 3.5% of agricultural fields remain free from environmental restrictions (van Velthuizen, 2007). Although it is difficult to exactly examine quantitatively the effects of abiotic stresses on crop yields, abiotic stresses due to climatic change have become major challenge to agricultural productivity and the effects of stresses depend on the intensity of stress, duration of its exposure, and the overall area under cultivation. In near future, in several countries of the world, yield of major crops is likely to decline due to global warming, water scarcity, and other environmental implications (Tebaldi and Lobell, 2018).

Based on national yield data as a result of statistical survey conducted in different countries, effect of climate change assessed in southern Europe suggests that low temperature and scanty rainfall are the key reasons for decline in crop productivity, while in northern Europe, low temperature is the main concern hampering crop yield (Olesen et al., 2011; Ray et al., 2019) (Table 4.2). In Hungary, Serbia, Bulgaria, and Romania having continental climate, crop cultivation is greatly affected due to climate change. In northwestern Europe, increase in crop yield is expected due to increment of global warming and greenhouse gas emissions; however in Mediterranean area, a negative effect of climate change on crop yield is expected (Olesen and Bindi, 2002; Raza et al., 2019). In many European countries over the last two decades, a decline in the productivity of cereals has been observed due to climatic change,

TABLE 4.2
Projections in global changes in yields of crops due to climatic change

Crops	Production change (million tons per year)	Percentage change in yield w.r.t current average	Type of stress affecting crop	Affected regions	References
Barley	−10.20	−7.9	Multiple stresses	North and central America; Western and Southern Europe; Eastern and Northern Europe; Northern America; Northern Africa; Sub-Saharan Africa; and Western, Southern, and Southeastern Asia	Ray et al. (2019)
Cassava	−0.92	−0.5	Multiple stresses	North and Central America and Western, Southern, and Southeastern Asia	Ray et al. (2019)
Maize	0.17	0.0	Above 29°C yield decreases	Western and Southern Europe, Eastern and Northern Europe, Northern America, Northern Africa, Sub-Saharan Africa, and Oceania	Raza et al. (2019) and Ray et al. (2019)
Oil palm	−19.79	−13.4	Drought	North and Central America, Caribbean and South America, Sub-Saharan Africa, Central and Eastern Asia and Western, Southern and South-eastern Asia	Raza et al. (2019) and Ray et al. (2019)
Rapeseed	0.21	0.5	Drought and water shortage	North and Central America, Western and Southern Europe, and Northern America	Raza et al. (2019) and Ray et al. (2019)
Rice	−1.62	−0.3	2.6% per degree rise in temperature	North and Central America, Western and Southern Europe, Caribbean and South America, Eastern and Northern Europe, Northern America, Northern Africa, Sub-Saharan Africa, and Western, Southern, and Southeastern Asia	Raza et al. (2019) and Ray et al. (2019)
Sorghum	1.16	2.1	7.8% per degree rise in temperature and drought	Western and Southern Europe, Eastern and Northern Europe, Northern America and Oceania	Ray et al. (2019) and Raza et al. (2019)

(Continued)

TABLE 4.2 *(Continued)*
Projections in global changes in yields of crops due to climatic change

Crops	Production change (million tons per year)	Percentage change in yield w.r.t current average	Type of stress affecting crop	Affected regions	References
Soybean	6.22	3.5	Drought	North and Central America, Western and Southern Europe, Caribbean and South America, Eastern and Northern Europe, Northern America, Northern Africa, Sub-Saharan Africa and Western, Southern and South-eastern Asia	Ray et al. (2019) and Raza et al. (2019)
Sugarcane	11.60	1.0	Rise in ozone and greenhouse gas	Northern America, Northern Africa, Sub-Saharan Africa, and Western and Southern and South-eastern Asia	Raza et al. (2019)
Wheat	−4.95	−0.9	Drought and rise of temperature	North and Central America, Western and Southern Europe, Caribbean and South America, Eastern and Northern Europe, Northern America, Sub-Saharan Africa, Western, Southern, and Southeastern Asia and Oceania	Raza et al. (2019) and Ray et al. (2019)

which has resulted in heat stress and drought, which have adversely affected grain filling and stem elongation (Brission et al., 2010). Yield and productivity of non-tropical crops like wheat, maize, rapeseed, and barley have decreased in western, eastern Europe and in the green belt of western Siberia (Katsov et al., 2014).

In sub-Saharan Africa maize, sorghum, cassava, and sugarcane provide major amount of food calories. Maize and sugarcane yields have increased by 5.8% and 3.9% in provinces of free state and northwest, while sorghum and cassava yields have increased by 0.7% and 1.7% respectively in northeastern Madagascar during the last two decades, whereas cassava yield has decreased in the southern part of Madagascar, Eastern Africa, and Tanzania. Decline in yield of maize has been seen in some southern districts of Togo, but northern part has been benefited from climate change (Ray et al., 2019). In Europe, Southern Africa, and Australia, the impacts of climate change have been positive; however in Asia and Northern and Central America, mixed responses have been observed. An average global food reduction amounting to −3.5 × 10¹³ kcal/year calories reduction has been observed due to decline in production of important food crops (Ray et al., 2019). In Oceania region, the yields of wheat, barley maize, sorghum, and soybean have declined by nearly 9% in Australia (Hochman et al., 2017) due to climate change, but rapeseed, rice, and sugarcane production has increased by 6% (Ray et al., 2019). In north and south America, crops like maize, oil palm, soybean, and sugarcane have been benefitted from climate change. In USA, the yield and productivity of barley, rice, and wheat have decreased, while of maize, sorghum, soybean, and sugarcane have increased (Tack et al., 2015).

In Asia, the effects of climate change on grain yields and consumable calories appear to be diverse. In certain parts of China, overall crop yield has increased over the years, and it has raised consumable food calories by ~2% during the couple of past decades (Ray et al., 2019), while decline in rice yield has been observed in Guangxi and Fujian and decline in wheat yield in Sichuan and Guizhou. Due to climate change, wheat yield has increased in Huang-Huai-Hai plains of China and maize yield has increased in the province of Heilongjiang (Ray et al., 2019). Whereas in many parts of China with high altitude regions, as a result of climate change and extreme weather conditions, maize yield has decreased drastically due to chilling injury (Li et al., 2021). Rice production has declined due to global warming in Vietnam and the Philippines province of Laguna. Similarly, the production of wheat has declined in Turkey. In countries like Bangladesh, Nepal, and Iran, decline in food calories has been observed due to variation in temperature and pattern of rainfall (Ray et al., 2019). The impact of climate change on crop yield has been generally determined by the location of the particular country from the equator. Climate changes induces alteration in yield of major crops. The yield of major crops like wheat, rice, maize, soybeans. and oilseeds is affected almost in every country, but the effect is greater closer to the equator (Cline, 2007).

3. IMPACT OF CLIMATE CHANGE ON FOOD SECURITY

Food security involves sufficient availability of food as well as access, utilization, and stability of food for the population. Over the last 30 years, definitions of food security are changing considering food policy (Myers et al., 2017). The concept of food security emerged as a matter of global concern in the mid-1970s, when World Food Conference (1974) described food security in terms of food protection as follows: "Food protection occurs where all residents having physio-economical exposure to appropriate, secure and nutritious food at all times, satisfying their nutritional requirements and dietary requirements for productive and stable life" (United Nations, 1975; FAO, 2006). Food security has four dimensions: availability, access, utilization, and stability of food. Climate change is influencing food supply by actively and indirectly influencing agricultural production. Climate change causes uncertainty in food production due to its effects leading to decreased crop yield and productivity. Among the four pillars of food security, availability of nutritious food in sufficient quantity for consumption of people is of prime importance. Therefore, food security has been a big challenge due to climate change because climate change directly impacts the total availability of nutrients within a food supply chain. Climate change affects the efficiency of natural resources on which production of food for the consumption of human depends. Degradation of the soil and ocean acidification have reduced nutritional content of grains, safety of livestock and fishery. When production of quality food and nutrient supply declines due to disruption in their production as a result of stressful environmental factors, increasing costs and elevated demand cause uncertainty in their availability for common man. The world's food system is projected to be under increased pressure in future. Furthermore, if food is not properly stored or dispersed during periods of scarcity, this would limit the quality of food products and nutrients. In the following subsections, an account of global climatic change on various dimensions of food security issues has been presented.

3.1 Food Security: India

Agriculture is the backbone of Indian economy. The proportion of agriculture and its related sectors to the GVA (gross value added) of the country at current prices declined from 18.2% in 2014–2015 to 16.5% in 2019–2020 (Sitharaman, 2020). A significant decline in agricultural productivity has been predicted in India due to global climatic change. Due to its tropical location, India will face more warming temperature due to climate change, and it has been estimated that productivity of major crops in India would decline in the years to come, and food security will be at stake due to the twin factors of global warming and increasing population (Hussain, 2019). In India, food security is often correlated with several other considerations, such as socioeconomic conditions, human rights, and the climatic conditions. Indian rural population is more susceptible to global warming as landless labours and small farmers who reside in rural areas are dependent on rainfed mono-cropping systems and therefore typically they are engaged in rainfed cultivation for a few months, and they have to face food security issue for the entire year. Food supplies tend to get used up for such farmers after four to five months of harvest, farm employment becomes scarce, and food shortages escalate to hunger by the next sowing season (Ramachandran, 2014). Environmental changes also have detrimental impacts on fisheries and forestry livelihoods (FAO, 2020).

Farmless field employees, entirely dependent on agricultural income, are more likely to lose access to food (Goyal and Singh, 2002). In areas with high food shortages and inequalities, the rise in the severity of disaster would have a greater effect on children (Parry et al., 2009). Vedeld et al. (2014) surveyed nine settlements in Maharashtra's drought-prone Jalna district and found that in 2012–2013 drought, local farm yields and farmers' annual revenues fell by nearly 60%. Even a significant drop in income is expected to have a major impact on welfare of children, since poor families typically invest most of income on food. Rodriguez-Llanes et al. (2011) observed that vulnerability to floods could be correlated with long term malnutrition in flooded and drought-affected villages in Jagatsingpur district of Orissa state in India. The issue of urban food scarcity is also important as rural and coastal poor households typically move to urban areas for livelihood opportunities (Tacoli, 2013). It is observed that poverty often sparks a surge of relocation to cities and results in creation of slum area. Mostly the labours or marginal farmers who migrate to the cities are those affected by climate disasters (Ramachandran, 2014).

An important aspect of food insecurity can be visualised in many states of India like Uttar Pradesh, Bihar, Madhya Pradesh, and Karnataka, where children below five years suffer from malnutrition and are underweight (Ramachandran, 2014). Mumbai, Chennai, and Kolkata are the metro cities quite vulnerable to climate disasters, as in Kolkata frequent flood during monsoon season exacerbates the life of people living in low tide area (Dasgupta et al., 2012). Because food is a major challenge to poor urban households, relocation, loss of livelihoods, or loss of productive property due to adverse weather conditions would affect household food security (World Bank, 2013). The urban poor were also listed as being the most susceptible category to food price changes as a consequence of demand disruptions and potential climate change conditions.

3.2 Food Security: Worldwide

Though enough food exists in the world to feed the global population, still in many countries people suffer from hunger because they do not have enough food to eat. Due to a steady increase in global population, in the future years demand for food will increase. FAO predicts that if current trend of population growth and consumption pattern continues, agriculture will need considerable transformation in order to feed the growing global population and to provide the basis for economic growth and poverty reduction. But climate change has made the situation more difficult. More than 113 million people from 53 countries do not have enough food to eat and face food insecurity (FAO, 2020). Out of 7.58 billion of world population, about 2 billion people face food insecurity. Most of sub-Saharan and South Asian countries are regarded as "alarming" countries. Climate change affects all four pillars of food security—food availability, access, utilization, and stability. There is large degree of variation in crop yield across the globe (Rosenzweig and Parry, 1994), as yield increases in northern Europe and decline across America and African countries (Rosenzweig and Parry, 1994). Crop yield is much affected in tropical areas than higher latitudes because of its more severe effect. Countries which are under burden of hunger are greatly affected due to food insecurity.

Changes in the yields of major crops grown in Africa and South Asia have shown that average crop yield in both the regions could decline by 8% by 2050 (Knox et al., 2012). In Africa, yields are projected to change by −17.2% (wheat), −5.4% (maize), −14.6% (sorghum), −9.6% (millet), and −17.6% (maize) and −10.8% (sorghum) under climate change throughout South Asia (Knox et al., 2012). The effects of climate change on crop production in African and Asian countries are reliable for millet, sorghum, maize, and wheat but inconclusive and insignificant for sugarcane, cassava, and rice (Knox et al., 2012).

At economic level, the macro-models have been proposed, which are interlinked models which include environment, crop, and economic models. The effects of climate change are easily fed into the models to predict crop yields under different climate scenarios (Wheeler and von Braun, 2013). In these methods, calculated yields are used to forecast the effects of environment, which will affect the capacity to produce such foods globally. Macro-modelling and micro-level study of the linkages between climate change and food security support each other. The effects of global climatic change on the four dimensions of food security have been discussed in the following subsections.

3.3 Food Availability

Food availability is defined as the availability of adequate quantity of food with appropriate quality produced either domestically or imported from elsewhere (FAO, 2006). In order to fulfil global human food needs in the coming years. This is one of the biggest problems of our era to work out how to feed 7.58 billion citizens while simultaneously encouraging sustainable growth, curbing greenhouse gas emissions, and preserving important habitats. The world has already witnessed the threats of climate change, which poses a significant danger to world's existing and potential food systems. Evidence of its threats to health, agriculture, and economic growth suggests that it is necessary to take this challenge seriously when we look to the food systems for the future. Here, we provide a summary of the facts relating to the impact of climate change on global food availability, with special attention given to developing regions of the world. In this segment, we summarize India's and the world's contribution to climate change mitigation and include some suggestions on how climate policy can be based on ensuring sustainable food systems.

3.3.1 Food Availability in India

India accounts for approximately 17% (1.38 billion people) of the world's population. In 2050, the population is projected to grow to 1.6 billion, possibly surpassing China (United Nations, 2017). India has the second-largest proportion of the world's overall arable land area of 159.7 million hectares (Lehane, 2014). It is the largest producer in the world for pulses and second-largest producer of rice, wheat, groundnut, sugarcane, cotton, many fruits and vegetables (FAO in India, 2020). While current food production is more than enough to feed the population of India, still millions are suffering from malnutrition and hunger. So there is need of effective management system and transparency in food delivery system. India had initially PDS (public distribution system), which started to manage food security in India till 1940, later target public distribution system (TPDS) evolved and finally national food security act (NFSA) came into existence, which confers right to food for Indian citizens (Pillay and Kumar, 2018). Targets for reducing malnutrition, ensuring adequate stability, and quality of food are at the core of the sustainable development goals (SDGs).

3.3.2 Food Availability in the World

It is expected that global climatic change will have an overall adverse effect on availability of food due to decline in crop productivity. Increase in global temperature in tropical climates, semi-arid, as well as dry regions of the world will be detrimental for productivity of grain crops, causing their decreased availability for consumption (Firdaus et al., 2019). High temperatures in tropical climates, more specially in developing countries, will cause heat evaporation, thereby inducing water stress on crops, leading to marked decline in productivity (Poudel and Kotani, 2013). Global cereal production has been shown to decline by 14% from 2008 to 2030, in Asian, African, and South and Central American countries due to climate change (Funk and Brown, 2009). For USA it has been predicted that increase in temperature up to 29°C, 30°C, and 32°C respectively for corn, soybeans, and cotton will cause increase in the yield; however, temperatures greater than these will cause decline in productivity (Schlenker and Roberts, 2009).

3.4 FOOD ACCESS

Food access is indirectly related to the climate change. Food access specifically relates to food accessibility and food distribution, according to individual and household priorities (Gregory et al., 2005). To determine the impact of climate change, food access issues have been generally described at both community and household levels. The United States Department of Agriculture (USDA) states that food access should be accessible in socially appropriate forms without, for instance, using emergency food supply, scavenging, theft, or any other survival method. Most of the macro-models consist of interconnected models—such as climate, crops, and economic models. Throughout this way, the results of a climatic model are introduced into the crop model to predict crop production throughout various climatic conditions. The predicted yields are now being used for forecasting the economics on prices, profits, trade, and so on of global climate change. Macro-models can be based on a partial approach to equilibrium, that is, the impacts only on a particular field like agriculture can be examined or generalized equilibrium models aimed at understanding their effects on the entire economy. This approach's drawback is that it does not reflect climate adaptations. Microlevel studies, however, are mostly focused on precise household observations and usually take clearer view of household and community responses to climate change. A prominent example is the IMPACT (International Model for Policy Analysis of Agricultural Commodities and Trade) model, developed by International Food Policy Research Institute (IFPRI), which links climate change possibilities to food supply impacts, market and price results, and the economic implications of food availability factors such as food energy use and children's nutritional conditions for access and utilization of food (Nelson et al., 2010; Ringler et al., 2011).

Specific results depend extensively on assumptions of future incomes and population increase; however, there are clear links between economic development and climate change resilience (Nelson et al., 2010). A number of studies are being conducted to examine how communities and households are vulnerable to climate shocks (Kato et al., 2011; Silvestri et al., 2012). Such strategies aim to capture more capacities to adapt than macro models, including asset recession, work switching, migration, social policy feedback, and joint adaptation and assistance initiatives. Yet the effects of climate change that cross over large regions are difficult to fully understand with micro-level analyses. The capacity to produce several goods at national and global levels could alter by climate change. For instance, if the bio-mass production area changes globally, this will impact the production of all agricultural goods, including food, grain, oils, and fibre, and it will influence food exchange patterns that will impact farm turnover and access to food (Zhao and Running, 2010; Hertel et al.,

2010). Therefore, macro-modelling and micro-level studies are complementary with food security related to climate change.

3.5 FOOD UTILIZATION

The next component of food security is food utilization, which relates to people's metabolism (Tweeten, 1999). The ingested food must be healthy and adequate to fulfil the physiological needs of every person in order to attain food security (Ecker and Breisinger, 2012). Education regarding food processing and nutrition will have an effect on the utilization of food and will strengthen this food security component (Tweeten, 1999). In order to achieve nutritional wellbeing, the utilization of food relies on water and hygiene and is influenced by any effect on health condition caused by climate change. Studies related to this aspect of food and nutritional security are limited. More drinking water connections may be evident if the climatic change inhibits the supply of safe drinking water (Parry et al., 2007; Delpla et al., 2009). Hygiene can also be compromised in areas in which there is no sound sanitation due to extreme weather conditions that cause flooding and drought (Shimi et al., 2010). Furthermore, micronutrient intake can be negatively affected due to the frequency of diarrheal diseases, which are in particular closely linked to temperature (Schmidhuber and Tubiello, 2007). Climate change may also have impact on dietary quality, and rising costs may be due to the measures taken to prevent food contamination caused by ecological pest changes, as well as stored grain diseases (Paterson and Lima, 2010; Tefera, 2012). Further work is needed on vulnerability to food security challenges and approaches to develop adaptive climate change capability, as public policy responses are conditional on these insights (Ziervogel and Ericksen, 2010). New nutritional challenges emerge, and the ongoing "nutrition transition" becomes the most prominent example in which the mechanism of globalization, urbanization, and lifestyle transformation are connected to excessive calories consumption, low-quality diets, and inadequate physical exercise. Along with such factors, the rate of obesity and chronic diseases in developing countries have risen rapidly, also among the poor people (Popkin et al., 2012). The nutrition transition is expected to take place in tandem with climate change in the next decades, yet studies related to the effects of climate change on nutritional events are limiting.

3.6 STABILITY OF THE FOOD SYSTEM

Climate change can adversely affect the stability of entire food systems since the environment is a key factor influencing both future price trends and short-term price fluctuations (Nelson et al., 2010). The stability of food refers to the capacity to get food over a specified period. Insecurity of food may be temporary, periodic, or persistent (FAO, 1997). Food cannot be available for some periods, causing temporary food insecurity (Ecker and Breisinger, 2012). Natural disasters as well as drought contribute to crop destruction and a reduced supply of food at food producing levels (FAO, 1997; Ecker and Breisinger, 2012). Market uncertainty leading to food price increases can lead to temporary food insecurity. The loss of job or performance caused by sickness may temporarily contribute to food insecurity. The regular

Climate Change Impacts on Agriculture

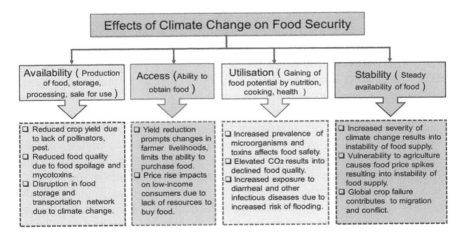

FIGURE 4.2 Observed and projected climate change effects on food security.

patterns of food production during growing seasons may lead to seasonal food insecurity (FAO, 1997). The long-term, continuous shortage of sufficient food is known as persistent food insecurity (Ecker and Breisinger, 2012). In this situation, households are in serious risk of not being able to buy food to fulfil every member's needs. The global food equation seems to have been precariously weak since before 2007, and thus there would be a major effect of prices on the supply and demand side, as was observed in 2008 (von Braun, 2009).

For production as well as for supply, climate change is likely to intensify the uncertainty in the food industry. For example, when strong subsidies for bioenergy and quota policies had been introduced by political system, the stability of food systems might have come at risk through demand shocks (Beckman et al., 2012). As a result of an overall decline in crop yields and acute policy failures contributing to the 2008 global food crisis, the export restrictions imposed by various nations worsened the situation (von Braun and Tadesse, 2012). A diverse range of threats are observed related to food stability, among which climate change is highly crucial, which could lead to destabilization of food system, causing high and unpredictable food prices that could result in financial and economic shocks, losses of jobs, credit constraints, as well as government instability, which ultimately give rise to food insecurity (Arndt et al., 2012; Berazneva and Lee, 2013). A summary of climate change effects on various aspects of food security have been presented in Figure 4.2.

4. CONCLUSIONS AND FUTURE PROSPECTS

Owing to global warming and climate change, plants experience a variety of environmental and climatic conditions which affect their growth, development, and yield. Future climate forecasts point to the global rise in the temperature and CO_2 levels; variability in precipitation; frequent occurrence of heat, cold, drought, salinity; and many more constraints depending on the geographical locations, which would adversely affect crop productivity. The effect of climate change on crop productivity is associated with many factors, amongst which the availability of water in the soil is a crucial component, which is influenced due to global warming. Global warming causes extremities in temperatures leading to cold and heat, irregular precipitation, which directly affect groundwater level and soil moisture, and in turn influence crop yields. The yields of crops are related to types of crop, environmental parameters requirements, accessibility of water throughout the growth period, etc. In future, as a result of global warming, crop productivity will tend to decline due to water supply limitations, temperature rise, fluctuations in precipitation, soil erosion, etc.

Crop productivity as well as food security are vulnerable to climate changes. Sustainability of crop yield and availability of sufficient food across the food chain are important to feed the global population. Decline in agricultural productivity as a consequence of climate change will affect food supplies as well as livelihoods for the people. Indirect impacts of climate change on food, health, employment, and poverty would be more diversified and complicated. Many studies have focused on effects of climate change on crop productivity and to a lesser degree on prices, but the impact of climate change may greatly influence other critical food security issues, like food access, safety, and stability.

Individuals and communities vary greatly in their ability to respond to climate change and reduce greenhouse gas emissions from their living standards and basic necessities. In addition, disparities exist related to national and global concerns to respond to climatic change liabilities and to suggest the governance to take coordinated adaptive measures to tackle food security mitigation options. Strategies need to be prioritized to minimize the unequal prices for the weak producers and consumers across all nations.

A more realistic view of food security needs to be obtained by collecting the data related to the impact of climate change on food availability, access, utilization, and stability. Comprehensive data analysis and advanced modelling, along with the connection with the political economy, is needed for the understanding of indirect effects of climate change on food security. Climate change will have more adverse effects on crop productivity and food security in the nations currently facing hunger, and the situation will worsen with the passage of time. The implications of climate change on world poverty and malnutrition appear to be significant and will grow over time. The impacts of climate change on human beings vary among different regions of the world. Individuals and societies susceptible to severe weather conditions will become more prone and less resistant to changing climatic conditions in future. Greenhouse gas emissions need urgent mitigation steps to tackle global food shortages over the next two to three centuries. Extreme global warming in the future is expected to intensify and will raise risks and uncertainty all over the world's food system. There is a need to invest significantly in improvement and mitigation decisions to avoid the effects of the climate change on worldwide hunger and malnutrition. A variety of adaptability and resilience options are available. Food security should be addressed in the widest possible sense, and global agriculture growth should be ascertained accordingly. Based on technological and management system advancements construction of climate-smart agriculture is an important strategy to adopt, but it is not adequate alone to fulfil acceptable global crop productivity and food security to feed the world population. The entire food supply chain system needs to be adapted to climate change, with a high degree of focus on trade, stocks, food, social and economic policy options as well. We have to focus on climate smart food systems to tackle the effects of climate change on crop productivity as well as food security.

REFERENCES

Africa Commission. 2005. Our Common Interest: Report of the Commission for Africa. Commission for Africa, London. 11 March. www.commissionforafrica.org.

Ainsworth, E.A. and Rogers, A. 2007. The response of photosynthesis and stomatal conductance to rising [CO_2]: Mechanisms and environmental interactions. Plant, Cell and Environment 30, 258–270.

Anjum, F., Yaseen, M., Rasul, E., Wahid, A. and Anjum, S. 2003. Water stress in barley (*Hordeum vulgare* L.). II: Effect on chemical composition and chlorophyll contents. Pak. J. Agric. Sci 40, 45–49.

Arndt, C., Hussain, M.A. and Østerdal, L.P. 2012. Effects of food price shocks on child malnutrition: The Mozambican Experience 2008/09 (No. 2012/89). WIDER Working Paper.

Balmaseda, M.A., Trenberth, K.E. and Källén, E. 2013. Distinctive climate signals in reanalysis of global ocean heat content. Geophysical Research Letters 40, 1754–1759.

Ban, K. 2012. A message from the UN secretary general for the opening session of the 39th session of the committee on world food security, Rome, 15 to 20 October.

Beck, E.H., Fettig, S., Knake, C., Hartig, K. and Bhattarai, T. 2007. Specific and unspecific responses of plants to cold and drought stress. Journal of Biosciences 32, 501–510.

Beckman, J., Hertel, T., Taheripour, F. and Tyner, W. 2012. Structural change in the biofuels era. European Review of Agricultural Economics 39, 137–156.

Berazneva, J. and Lee, D.R. 2013. Explaining the African food riots of 2007–2008: An empirical analysis. Food Policy 39, 28–39.

Betts, R.A., Boucher, O., Collins, M., Cox, P.M., Falloon, P.D., Gedney, N., Hemming, D.L., Huntingford, C., Jones, C.D., Sexton, D.M. and Webb, M.J. 2007. Projected increase in continental runoff due to plant responses to increasing carbon dioxide. Nature 448, 1037–1041.

Bhargava, S. and Mitra, S. 2021. Elevated atmospheric CO_2 and the future of crop plants. Plant Breeding 140, 1–11. https://doi.org/10.1111/pbr.12871.

Boomiraj, K., Chakrabarti, B., Aggarwal, P.K., Choudhary, R. and Chander, S. 2010. Assessing the vulnerability of Indian mustard to climate change. Agriculture, Ecosystems and Environment 138, 265–273.

Brisson, N., Gate, P., Gouache, D., Charmet, G., Oury, F.X. and Huard, F. 2010. Why are wheat yields stagnating in Europe? A comprehensive data analysis for France. Field Crops Research 119(1), 201–212.

Challinor, A.J., Watson, J., Lobell, D.B., Howden, S.M., Smith, D.R. and Chhetri, N. 2014. A meta-analysis of crop yield under climate change and adaptation. Nature Climate Change 4, 287–291.

Cline, W.R. 2007 *Global Warming and Agriculture: Impact Estimates by Country. Centre for Global Development and Peterson Institute for International Economics,* Washington, DC.

Corwin, D.L. 2021. Climate change impacts on soil salinity in agricultural areas. European Journal of Soil Science 72, 842–862.

Crafts-Brandner, S.J. and Salvucci, M.E. 2000. Rubisco activase constrains the photosynthetic potential of leaves at high temperature and CO_2. Proceedings of the National Academy of Sciences 97, 13430–13435.

Dasgupta, S., Roy, S. and Sarraf, M. 2012. Urban flooding in a changing climate: Case study of Kolkata, India. Asian-Afr. J. Econ. Econ. 12, 135–158.

Delpla, I., Jung, A.V., Baures, E., Clement, M. and Thomas, O. 2009. Impacts of climate change on surface water quality in relation to drinking water production. Environment International 35, 1225–1233.

Dhillon, R.S. and von Wuehlisch, G. 2013. Mitigation of global warming through renewable biomass. Biomass and Bioenergy 48, 75–89.

Earl, H.J. and Davis, R.F. 2003. Effect of drought stress on leaf and whole canopy radiation use efficiency and yield of maize. Agronomy Journal 95, 688–696.

Ecker, O. and Breisinger, C. 2012. The food security system: A new conceptual framework (No. 1166). International Food Policy Research Institute (IFPRI).

Espeland, E.K. and Kettenring, K.M. 2018. Strategic plant choices can alleviate climate change impacts: A review. Journal of Environmental Management 222, 316–324.

FAO. 1997. *Agriculture, food and nutrition for Africa: A resource book for teachers of agriculture.* Food and Agriculture Organization, Rome.

FAO. 2006. Policy Brief: Food Security, Rome, June 2.

FAO. 2020. Early Warning Early Action Report on Food Security and Agriculture, Rome, January–March.

FAO in India. 2020. India at a glance. Homepage.

Farooq, M., Wahid, A., Kobayashi, N., Fujita, D.B.S.M.A. and Basra, S.M.A. 2009. Plant drought stress: Effects, mechanisms and management. In: *Sustainable Agriculture* (pp. 153–188). Springer, Dordrecht.

Firdaus, R.B.R., Gunaratne, M.S., Rahmat, S.R. and Kamsi, N.S. 2019. Does climate change only affect food availability? What else matters? Cogent Food and Agriculture 5:1, 1707607. doi.org/10.1080/23311932.2019.1707607.

Franks, P.J. and Beerling, D.J. 2009. Maximum leaf conductance driven by CO2 effects on stomatal size and density over geologic time. Proceedings of the National Academy of Sciences 106, 10343–10347.

Funk, C.C. and Brown, M.E. 2009. Declining global per capita agricultural production and warming oceans threaten food security. Food Security 1, 271–289. doi:10.1007/s12571-009-0026-y.

Garnett, T., Appleby, M.C., Balmford, A., Bateman, I.J., Benton, T.G., Bloomer, P., Burlingame, B., Dawkins, M., Dolan, L., Fraser, D. and Herrero, M. 2013. Sustainable intensification in agriculture: Premises and policies. Science 341, 33–34.

Goyal, S.K. and Singh, J.P. 2002. Demand versus supply of food grains in India: Implications to food security (No. 1026-2016-82014). 13th International Farm Management Congress, Wageningen, The Netherlands, July 7–12.

Gregory, P.J., Ingram, J.S. and Brklacich, M. 2005. Climate change and food security. Philosophical Transactions of the Royal Society B: Biological Sciences 360, 2139–2148.

Gupta, R., Somanathan, E. and Dey, S. 2017. Global warming and local air pollution have reduced wheat yields in India. Climatic Change 140, 593–604.

Hansen, J., Ruedy, R., Sato, M. and Lo, K. 2010. Global surface temperature change. Rev. Geophys. 48, RG4004.

Haokip, S.W., Shankar, K. and Lalrinngheta, J. 2020. Climate change and its impact on fruit crops. Journal of Pharmacognosy and Phytochemistry 9, 435–438.

Hatfield, P.J.L. and Prueger, J.H. 2015. Temperature extremes: Effect on plant growth and development. Weather and Climate Extremes 10, 4–10.

Hebbar, K.B., Venugopalan, M.V., Prakash, A.H. and Aggarwal, P.K. 2013. Simulating the impacts of climate change on cotton production in India. Climatic Change 118, 701–713.

Hertel, T.W., Burke, M.B. and Lobell, D.B. 2010. The poverty implications of climate-induced crop yield changes by 2030. Global Environmental Change 20, 577–585.

Hochman, Z., Gobbett, D.L. and Horan, H. 2017. Climate trends account for stalled wheat yields in Australia since 1990. Global Change Biology 23, 2071–2081.

Houghton, J.T., Ding, Y.D.J.G., Griggs, D.J., Noguer, M., van der Linden, P.J., Dai, X., Maskell, K. and Johnson, C.A. 2001. Climate Change 2001: The Scientific Basis. The Press Syndicate of the University of Cambridge, Cambridge.

Hussain, S. 2019. Climate change poses serious threats to India's food security. The WIRE, September 19.

IPCC, C.C. 2014. Mitigation of climate change. Contribution of Working Group III to the Fifth Assessment Report of the Intergovernmental Panel on Climate Change. www.buildup.eu/en/node/43087.

Jones, H.G. 1992. *Photosynthesis and respiration. In Plants and Microclimate: A Quantitative Approach to Environmental Plant Physiology,* 2nd ed. Cambridge University Press, Cambridge, UK, pp. 163–214.

Kato, E., Ringler, C., Yesuf, M. and Bryan, E. 2011. Soil and water conservation technologies: A buffer against production risk in the face of climate change? Insights from the Nile basin in Ethiopia. Agricultural Economics 42, 593–604.

Katsov, V.M., Semenov, S.M., Alekseev, G.V. and Ananicheva, M.D. 2014. *Second Roshydromet Assessment Report on Climate Change and Its Consequences in the Russian Federation.* Roshydromet, Moscow.

Katzenberger, A., Schewe, J., Pongratz, J. and Levermann, A. 2021. Robust increase of Indian monsoon rainfall and its variability under future warming in CMIP6 models. Earth System Dynamics 12, 367–386.

Kaur, G., Kumar, S., Nayyar, H. and Upadhyaya, H.D. 2008. Cold stress injury during the pod-filling phase in chickpea (*Cicer arietinum* L.): Effects on quantitative and qualitative components of seeds. Journal of Agronomy and Crop Science 194, 457–464.

Knox, J., Hess, T., Daccache, A. and Wheeler, T. 2012. Climate change impacts on crop productivity in Africa and South Asia. Environmental Research Letters 7(3), 034032.

Kobayashi, T., Ishiguro, K., Nakajima, T., Kim, H.Y., Okada, M. and Kobayashi, K. 2006. Effects of elevated atmospheric CO_2 concentration on the infection of rice blast and sheath blight. Phytopathology 96, 425–431.

Kumar, K.R., Kumar, K.K. and Pant, G.B. 1994. Diurnal asymmetry of surface temperature trends over India. Geophysical Research Letters 21, 677–680.

Kumar, S.N. and Aggarwal, P.K. 2013. Climate change and coconut plantations in India: Impacts and potential adaptation gains. Agricultural Systems 117, 45–54.

Kumar, S.N., Govindakrishnan, P.M., Swarooparani, D.N., Nitin, C., Surabhi, J. and Aggarwal, P.K. 2015. Assessment of impact of climate change on potato and potential adaptation gains in the Indo-Gangetic Plains of India. International Journal of Plant Production 9, 151–170.

Kyei-Mensah, C., Kyerematen, R. and Adu-Acheampong, S. 2019. Impact of rainfall variability on crop production within the worobong ecological area of Fanteakwa district. Ghana Article ID 7930127 | 7 pages | https://doi.org/10.1155/2019/7930127.

Lehane, S. 2014. India's Food and Water Security-Future Directions International. 3 June.

Li, Z., Zhang Z., Zhang, J., Luo, Y. and Zhang, L. 2021. A new framework to quantify maize production risk from chilling injury in Northeast China. Climate Risk Management 32, 100299. https://doi.org/10.1016/j.crm.2021.100299.

Lorenz, C. and Kunstmann, H. 2012. The hydrological cycle in three state-of-the-art reanalyses: Intercomparison and performance analysis. Journal of Hydrometeorology 13, 1397–1420.

Mahmood, T., Ali, G.M. and Shehzad, A. 2013. Comprehensive overview for developing drought tolerant transgenic wheat (*Triticum aestivum* L.). Journal of Agrobiology 30, 55–69.

McMaster, G.S., LeCain, D.R., Morgan, J.A., Aiguo, L. and Hendrix, D.L. 1999. Elevated CO2 increases wheat CER, leaf and tiller development, and shoot and root growth. Journal of Agronomy and Crop Science 183, 119–128.

Misra, A.K. 2014. Climate change and challenges of water and food security. International Journal of Sustainable Built Environment 3, 153–165.

Molden, D. 2007. *A Comprehensive Assessment of Water Management in Agriculture: Water for Food, Water for Life*. International Water Management Institute, London.

Myers, S.S., Smith, M.R., Guth, S., Golden, C.D., Vaitla, B., Mueller, N.D., Dangour, A.D. and Huybers, P. 2017. Climate change and global food systems: Potential impacts on food security and undernutrition. Annual Review of Public Health 38, 259–277.

Nelson, G.C., Cai, Z., Godfray, C., Hassan, R., Santos, M. and Swaminathan, H. 2012. Food security and climate change. A report by the High Level Panel of Experts (HLPE) on Food Security and Nutrition of the Committee on World Food Security.

Nelson, G.C., Rosegrant, M.W., Palazzo, A., Gray, I., Ingersoll, C., Robertson, R., Tokgoz, S., Zhu, T., Sulser, T.B., Ringler, C. and Msangi, S. 2010. Food security, farming, and climate change to 2050: Scenarios, results, policy options (Vol. 172). Intl Food Policy Res Inst.

Olesen, J.E. and Bindi, M. 2002. Consequences of climate change for European agricultural productivity, land use and policy. European Journal of Agronomy 16, 239–262.

Olesen, J.E., Trnka, M., Kersebaum, K.C., Skjelvåg, A.O., Seguin, B., Peltonen-Sainio, P., Rossi, F., Kozyra, J. and Micale, F. 2011. Impacts and adaptation of European crop production systems to climate change. European Journal of Agronomy 34, 96–112.

Ortiz-Bobea, A., Ault, T.R., Carrillo, C.M., Chambers, R.G. and Lobell, D.B. 2021. Anthropogenic climate change has slowed global agricultural productivity growth. Nature Climate Change, April 1. doi: 10.1038/s41558-021-01000-1.

Parry, M., Evans, A., Rosegrant, M.W. and Wheeler, T. 2009. *Climate Change and Hunger: Responding to the Challenge*. Intl Food Policy Res Inst., Washington, DC, USA.

Parry, M., Parry, M.L., Canziani, O., Palutikof, J., Van der Linden, P. and Hanson, C., eds. 2007. Climate Change 2007-Impacts, Adaptation and Vulnerability: Working Group II Contribution to the Fourth Assessment Report of the IPCC (Vol. 4). Cambridge University Press, Cambridge.

Paterson, R.R.M. and Lima, N. 2010. How will climate change affect mycotoxins in food?. Food Research International 43, 1902–1914.

Pillay, D.P.K. and Kumar, T.M. 2018. Food security in India: Evolution, efforts and problems. Strategic Analysis 42, 595–611.

Popkin, B.M., Adair, L.S. and Ng, S.W., 2012. Global nutrition transition and the pandemic of obesity in developing countries. Nutrition Reviews 70, 3–21.

Poudel, S. and Kotani, K. 2013. Climatic impacts on crop yield and its variability in Nepal: Do they vary across seasons and altitudes? Climatic Change 116, 327–355. doi: 10.1007/s10584-012-0491-8.

Qaderi, M.M., Kurepin, L.V. and Reid, D.M. 2006. Growth and physiological responses of canola (Brassica napus) to three components of global climate change: Temperature, carbon dioxide and drought. Physiologia Plantarum 128, 710–721.

Ramachandran, N. 2014. Persisting undernutrition in India. In Causes, Consequences and Possible Solutions. Springer Nature e-book, New Delhi. doi: 10.1007/978-81-322-1832-6.

Ray, D.K., West, P.C., Clark, M., Gerber, J.S., Prishchepov, A.V. and Chatterjee, S. 2019. Climate change has likely already affected global food production. PloS One 14(5), e0217148. https://doi.org/10.1371/journal.pone.

Raza, A., Razzaq, A., Mehmood, S.S., Zou, X., Zhang, X., Lv, Y. and Xu, J. 2019. Impact of climate change on crops adaptation and strategies to tackle its outcome: A review. Plants 8, 34. doi: 10.3390/plants8020034.

Ringler, C., Bryan, E., Hassan, H., Alemu, T. and Hillesland, M. 2011. How Can African Agriculture Adapt to Climate Change: Insights from Ethiopia and South Africa. International Food Policy Research Institute, Washington, DC.

Rodriguez-Llanes, J.M., Ranjan-Dash, S., Degomme, O., Mukhopadhyay, A. and Guha-Sapir, D. 2011. Child malnutrition and recurrent flooding in rural eastern India: A community-based survey. BMJ Open, 1(2), e000109.

Rosenzweig, C. and Parry, M.L. 1994. Potential impact of climate change on world food supply. Nature 367, 133–138.

Salehi-Lisar, S.Y. and Bakhshayeshan-Agdam, H. 2016. Drought stress in plants: Causes, consequences, and tolerance. In *Drought Stress Tolerance in Plants* (Vol. 1, pp. 1–16). Springer, Cham.

Schlenker, W. and Roberts, M.J. 2009. Nonlinear temperature effects indicate severe damages to U.S. crop yields under climate change. Proceedings of the National Academy of Sciences of the United States of America 106, 15594–15598. doi: 10.1073/pnas.0906865106.

Schmidhuber, J. and Tubiello, F.N. 2007. Global food security under climate change. Proceedings of the National Academy of Sciences 104, 19703–19708.

Serrano, R., Mulet, J.M., Rios, G., Marquez, J.A., De Larrinoa, I.F., Leube, M.P., Mendizabal, I., Pascual-Ahuir, A., Proft, M., Ros, R. and Montesinos, C. 1999. A glimpse of the mechanisms of ion homeostasis during salt stress. Journal of Experimental Botany 50, 1032–1036.

Sharma, A.N. and Pingali, P. 2018. Looking beyond rice and wheat: Climate change impacts on food systems and food security in India. World Food Policy 4, 153–174.

Shimi, A.C., Parvin, G.A., Biswas, C. and Shaw, R. 2010. Impact and adaptation to flood. Disaster Prevention and Management: An International Journal 19, 298–313.

Shrestha, U.B., Gautam, S. and Bawa, K.S. 2012. Widespread climate change in the Himalayas and associated changes in local ecosystems. PloS One 7(5), e36741. https://doi.org/10.1371/journal.pone.0036741.

Silvestri, S., Bryan, E., Ringler, C., Herrero, M. and Okoba, B. 2012. Climate change perception and adaptation of agro-pastoral communities in Kenya. Regional Environmental Change 12, 791–802.

Sitharaman, N. 2020. Economic survey 2019–20. Report Summary presented by the Finance Minister of India, Ms. Nirmala Sitharaman on January 31.

Sivakumar, M.V.K., Das, H.P. and Brunini, O. 2005. Impacts of present and future climate variability and change on agriculture and forestry in the arid and semi-arid tropics. In *Increasing Climate Variability and Change* (pp. 31–72). Springer, Dordrecht.

Solomon, S., Manning, M., Marquis, M. and Qin, D. 2007. Climate change 2007-the physical science basis: Working group I contribution to the fourth assessment report of the IPCC (Vol. 4). Cambridge University Press, Cambridge.

Somerville, C. and Briscoe, J. 2001. Genetic engineering and water. Science, June 22, 292(5525), 2217. doi: 10.1126/science.292.5525.2217.

Soora, N.K., Aggarwal, P.K., Saxena, R., Rani, S., Jain, S. and Chauhan, N. 2013. An assessment of regional vulnerability of rice to climate change in India. Climatic Change 118, 683–699.

Srivastava, A., Kumar, S.N. and Aggarwal, P.K. 2010. Assessment on vulnerability of sorghum to climate change in India. Agriculture, Ecosystems and Environment 138, 160–169.

Stein Theo 2021. Carbon dioxide peaks near 420 parts per million at Mauna Loa observatory. June 7. NOAA Communications, at theo.stein@noaa.gov.

Tack, J., Barkley, A. and Nalley, L.L. 2015. Effect of warming temperatures on US wheat yields. Proceedings of the National Academy of Sciences (USA) 112, 6931–6936.

Tacoli, C. 2013. Urban poverty, food security and climate change. IIED Briefing Paper-International Institute for Environment and Development, Human Settlements Working Paper No.37.

Tan, G. and Shibasaki, R. 2003. Global estimation of crop productivity and the impacts of global warming by GIS and EPIC integration. Ecological Modelling 168, 357–370.

Tans, P. and Keeling, R. 2013. Trends in Atmospheric Carbon Dioxide: Daily Mean Concentration of Carbon Dioxide for Mauna Loa. National Oceanic and Atmospheric Administration, Earth System Research Laboratory (NOAA/ESRL), Hawaii.

Tebaldi, C. and Lobell, D. 2018. Estimated impacts of emission reductions on wheat and maize crops. Climatic Change 146, 533–545.

Tefera, T. 2012. Post-harvest losses in African maize in the face of increasing food shortage. Food Security 4, 267–277.

Thakur, P. and Nayyar, H. 2013. Facing the cold stress by plants in the changing environment: Sensing, signaling, and defending mechanisms. In *Plant Acclimation to Environmental Stress* (pp. 29–69). Springer, New York, NY.

Thornton, P.K., Ericksen, P.J., Herrero, M. and Challinor, A.J. 2014. Climate variability and vulnerability to climate change: A review. Global Change Biology 20, 3313–3328.

Tweeten, L. 1999. The economics of global food security. Review of Agricultural Economics 21, 473–488.

United Nations. 1975. Report of the World Food Conference, Rome, November 5–16, 1974. New York.

United Nations. 2017. World Population Prospects: The 2017 Revision, Key Findings and Advance Tables. UN Department of Economic and Social Affairs, New York.

van Velthuizen, H. 2007. Mapping biophysical factors that influence agricultural production and rural vulnerability (No. 11). Food and Agriculture Organization.

vedeld, T., Salunke, S.G., Aandahl, G. and Lanjekar, P. 2014. Governing extreme climate events in Maharashtra, India. Final Report on WP3. 2: Extreme Risks, Vulnerabilities and Community-based Adaptation in India (EVA): A Pilot Study. CIENS-TERI.

von Braun, J. 2009. Addressing the food crisis: Governance, market functioning, and investment in public goods. Food Security 1, 9–15.

von Braun, J., Tadesse, G. (2012). Food Security, Commodity Price Volatility, and the Poor. In: Aoki, M., Kuran, T., Roland, G. (eds) Institutions and Comparative Economic Development. International Economic Association Series. Palgrave Macmillan, London.

Wahid, A. and Rasul, E. 2005. Photosynthesis in leaf, stem, flower, and fruit. In *Handbook of Photosynthesis* (Ed. M. Pessarakli) (pp. 479–497). CRC Press, Boca Raton.

Wery, J., Silim, S.N., Knights, E.J., Malhotra, R.S. and Cousin, R. 1994. Screening techniques and sources of tolerance to extremes of moisture and air temperature in cool season food legumes. In *Expanding the Production and Use of Cool Season Food Legumes* (pp. 439–456). Springer, Dordrecht.

Wheeler, T. and von Braun, J. 2013. Climate change impacts on global food security. Science 341(6145), 508–513.

World Bank. 2013. Turn down the heat: Climate extremes, regional impacts, and the case for resilience. A Report for the World Bank by the Potsdam Institute for Climate Impact Research and Climate Analytics.

Yokoi, S., Bressan, R.A. and Hasegawa, P.M. 2002. Salt stress tolerance of plants. JIRCAS Working Report 23, pp. 25–33.

Young, L.W., Wilen, R.W. and Bonham-Smith, P.C. 2004. High temperature stress of Brassica napus during flowering reduces micro-and megagametophyte fertility, induces fruit abortion, and disrupts seed production. Journal of Experimental Botany 55, 485–495.

Zandalinas, S.I., Mittler, R., Balfagón, D., Arbona, V. and Gómez-Cadenas, A. 2018. Plant adaptations to the combination of drought and high temperatures. Physiologia Plantarum 162, 2–12.

Zhao, D. and Li, Y.R. 2015. Climate change and sugarcane production: Potential impact and mitigation strategies. International Journal of Agronomy 2015, Article ID 547386, 10 pages. doi: 10.1155/2015/547386.

Zhao, M. and Running, S.W. 2010. Drought-induced reduction in global terrestrial net primary production from 2000 through 2009. Science 329, 940–943.

Ziervogel, G. and Ericksen, P.J. 2010. Adapting to climate change to sustain food security. Wiley Interdisciplinary Reviews: Climate Change 1, 525–540.

5 Climate Change–Induced Soil Drought and Its Implication on Phytoremediation of Heavy Metal–Contaminated Soil

Pallavi Sharma, Ambuj Bhushan Jha, and Rama Shanker Dubey

CONTENTS

1. Introduction 87
2. Effect of Climate Change on Soil Drought 89
3. Phytoremediation of Heavy Metal–Contaminated Soil 91
4. Impact of Drought on Biomass and Heavy Metal Uptake of Plants 92
5. Effect of Drought on Microbes and Microbe-Assisted Phytoremediation 94
6. Conclusions and Future Prospects 96
References 96

1. INTRODUCTION

Climate change, which the entire world is experiencing, is a great environmental concern mainly due to its threat to all living organisms, including plants. Climate change could be due to natural causes as well as man-made factors. Natural causes include changes in Earth's orbit, volcanic eruptions, intensity of sunlight, circulation of the ocean, etc. (IPCC, 2013). Man-made factors like emissions of carbon dioxide (CO_2) and other greenhouse gases (GHG) such as chlorofluorocarbon, ozone (O_3), methane (CH_4), and nitrous oxides (N_xO) are the main drivers of climate change. Various environmental stresses including drought are known to be induced due to climate change. Although drought occurs naturally, climate change has generally speeded up the hydrological processes, making drought occurrence quicker and with high intensity, leading to adverse consequences and a range of detrimental effect on growing plants (Mukherjee et al., 2018).

DOI: 10.1201/9781003205548-5

Phytoremediation, which utilizes plants to clean up various contaminants, including heavy metals, has received a considerable attention because of its cost-effectiveness, ecofriendly approach, and capability to remediate large contaminated sites (Jha et al., 2017; Yan et al., 2020; Sharma et al., 2021; Singh et al., 2019a, 2019b; Singh et al., 2021a, 2021b, 2021c; Tiwari et al., 2021). Drought and heavy metal stresses individually and in combination can severely impact plant growth and hence can reduce phytoremediation efficiency (Tennant and Wu, 2000; de silva et al., 2012). Plenty of nutrient and water is needed by plants throughout their life cycle. Therefore, reduced soil moisture can disturb various physiological and biochemical processes of plants, ultimately causing reduction in growth and yield. Drought can also reduce phytoremediation efficacy of plants by altering plants' metal uptake and their interaction with beneficial microbes (Figure 5.1). Complex physiological and biochemical adaptations have been evolved in plants to adapt and adjust to abiotic stresses (Sharma et al., 2009, 2010; Sharma and Dubey, 2011; Osakabe et al., 2014). Various stresses, including drought, cause enhanced synthesis of stress proteins, accumulation of osmoprotectants, activation of antioxidant defence system, and activation/deactivation of ion transporters in plants, which play key roles in adaptation to stresses (Sharma and Dubey, 2006, 2007, 2008, 2010, 2011, 2019; Kumar et al., 2008; Sharma et al., 2010, 2012, 2019; Fraire-Velázquez et al., 2011; Rejeb et al., 2014; Huang et al., 2019; Jha and Sharma, 2019; Lamers et al., 2020).

Plants tolerant to one stress can also show promising resistance against other stresses (Bowler and Fluhr, 2000). However, it is difficult to predict plant responses to combination of stresses based on individual stresses since responses to combination of

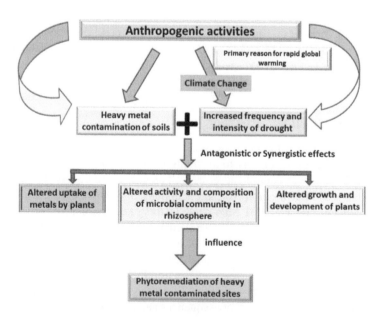

FIGURE 5.1 Effects of combination of drought and heavy metals on phytoremediation of heavy metal–contaminated soil.

stresses can be complex and specific (Atkinson and Urwin, 2012). Scenario associated with climate change suggests enhanced drought frequency and its severity worldwide, which could change the susceptibility of plants to climate change–induced drought (Vicente-Serrano et al., 2020). Drought-tolerant plants can be of more value for phytoremediation under climate change. Thus, efforts are being made to develop plants that can withstand both drought and heavy metals. Investigation of responses of plants against drought and heavy metals individually and in combination can be useful to develop drought and heavy metal–tolerant plants with improved phytoremediation efficiency under drought conditions. This chapter will provide an insight of the climate change–induced drought, effects of drought on growth of plants, metal uptake, microflora in the soil, and microbe-assisted phytoremediation.

2. EFFECT OF CLIMATE CHANGE ON SOIL DROUGHT

Climate change is the global phenomenon of variations of usual climate of the planet. Large alteration in Earth's climate has been shown by geological records. Climate change has occurred slowly and consistently over thousands or millions of years. Many factors, including solar energy variations, volcanic eruptions along with variations in greenhouse gases (GHG) such as CO_2, O_3, CH_4, and N_xO contribute to climate change, but current change is more rapid compared to the changes shown earlier in geological records. Since mid-20th century, anthropogenic activities contribute as primary reason for global warming and thus climate change. Various human activities such as GHG emissions, burning of fossil fuels such as coal, gas and oil, methane production, release of fluorinated gases due to industrial practices, use of fertilizers, and deforestation, etc. contribute to global warming. Warming of Earth's surface is due to absorption of infrared (IR) radiation by GHG, which absorb thermal IR from Earth's surface (Ledley et al., 1999). The concentration of CO_2, major contributor of climate change has increased significantly (> 40%) in the past few years. Increase in CO_2 concentration during 1960s was 0.6 ± 0.1 ppm/year, whereas it increased to 2.3 ppm/year during 2009–2018. It is predicted to reach up to 900 ppm from 409.8 ± 0.1 ppm in 2019 by the end of this century, if energy demand keeps on growing, and it is to be fulfilled mainly with fossil fuels (Lindsey, 2020). Warming due to CO_2 is nearly irreversible for > 1,000 yr. as CO_2 shows exceptional persistence up to millennia. Non-CO_2 GHG such as CH_4 are not irreversible because they can persist only up to decades (Solomon et al., 2010).

There are various ways in which climate alteration can contribute to drought (Figure 5.2). A positive significant correlation has been observed between temperature and CO_2 concentration. Thus, increased concentration of CO_2 can increase air temperature (Liu et al., 2017). Soil water evaporation can be enhanced by higher temperature, which in turn can make low precipitation phases drier. Dry soils and sparse vegetation cover can further suppress precipitation in a previously dry region. Atmospheric rivers, which are responsible for high transport of moisture in atmosphere and cause rainfall on land gradually become devoid of water due to climate change. Fluctuating water levels in atmospheric rivers and higher temperatures can affect snowpack and its melting, which may lead to reduced supply of water (Payne et al., 2020). Although drought occurs naturally, climate change in general

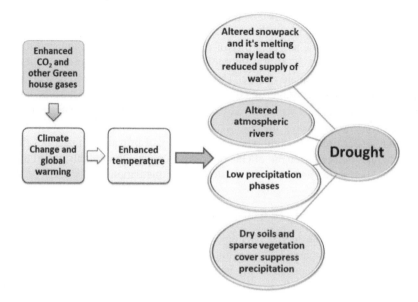

FIGURE 5.2 Various ways by which climate change and enhanced temperature due to global warming contribute to drought.

has augmented the hydrological processes that make them happen quicker and more intense, leading to detrimental effects on plants (Mukherjee et al., 2018).

Increased evaporative demands coupled with comparatively more persistent and frequent dry spells in association with increasing temperatures suggest that drought conditions aggravate plant growth and productivity in many parts of the world. Two thirds of global population suffers a progressive enhancement in drought with warming. Drought durations in dry areas are projected to increase rapidly with increased warming. Averaged globally, it could be from 2 months per °C when warming is below 1.5°C to duration of 4.2 months per °C when warming approaches 3°C. For 30% of global landmass, drought magnitudes are predicted to be doubled (Naumann et al., 2018). Increase in severity of drought and alteration in the mean aridity level of land are the key concerns of global warming (Berg and Sheffield, 2018).

Global climate models (GCMs) predicted increased dryness for the 21st century at global level and reported expansion of dryland owing to increased demand of evaporative and hydrological cycle (Scheff and Frierson, 2015; Zarch et al., 2017; Greve et al., 2019). Temperate drylands are projected to get reduced by one third mainly changing to subtropical drylands. Also deep soil layers are predicted to be drier in the growing season leading to major shifts in vegetation over the 21st century (Schlaepfer et al., 2017). In future, droughts are estimated to be frequent, more severe, and long lasting compared to droughts in recent decades (Ault, 2020), which will create more damage to plants and will alter their phytoremediation capacity (Vicente-Serrano et al., 2020).

3. PHYTOREMEDIATION OF HEAVY METAL–CONTAMINATED SOIL

Remediation of toxic metal contaminated soil is particularly challenging. Since metals are nondegradable, their cleanup generally requires either fixation or removal (Lasat, 2002). Traditional remediation methods of heavy metal–contaminated soil have been in practice for a long time and have yielded promising results, but these methods have their own disadvantages. In general, the contaminants removed using physical techniques such as heat treatment, electro-remediation, soil replacement, and vitrification need extra processing and have comparatively higher cost of application when compared to many other techniques. Chemical treatments such as precipitation, ion exchange, chemical extraction and oxidation, chemical leaching, soil amendments, and nanoremediation are highly effective at field scale, but the by-product formed during the process enhances steps involved in downstream processing (Sharma et al., 2018). Both physical and chemical methods severely affect overall health of soil and environment (Dhaliwal et al., 2020).

Phytoremediation is an alternative process which is economic, environment friendly, and aesthetically pleasing and utilizes microorganism and plants to remediate soils polluted with heavy metals (Salt et al., 1998; Ali et al. 2013; Suman et al., 2018). It includes various approaches such as phytoextraction, phytostabilization, phytovolatilization, phytofiltration, and phytodegradation/rhizodegradation. The removal of heavy metals from soil and accumulation in the aerial tissues of plants grown in heavy metal–polluted sites through absorption, translocation, and accumulation is termed as phytoextraction. The efficiency of this process is determined by selection and performance of plants, characteristics of soils and rhizospheres, and heavy metals bioavailability.

Plants used for phytoextraction should show good biomass yields, better metal hyperaccumulation capability, developed root system, tolerance to high metal concentrations, fast growth in affected areas with greater adaptation to stressed situations and escape mechanism against herbivores to avoid entry into food chain (Seth et al., 2012; Ali et al., 2013). Addition of chelating agents to soil can enhance the bioavailability and induce the hyperaccumulation of heavy metals in normal plants, but there is risk of undesirable impact on environment (Farid et al., 2013). Hyperaccumulator plants concentrate heavy metals in above-ground parts when grown in metal-contaminated soils. Hyperaccumulator plants can accumulate 0.01 to 1% of metals in their biomass (Brooks et al., 1998; Raskin and Ensley, 2000), and this property together with high biomass makes these plants suitable for phytoextraction of metals (Salt et al., 1998). They accumulate high level of metals in above-ground plant parts and cause sequestration and compartmentalization of heavy metals in their tissues (Ali et al., 2013). These heavy metal–laden plants can be removed by harvesting. Both postharvest and preharvest strategies are necessary for evolving a practical and sustainable phytoremediation technology (Mohanty, 2016; Sharma et al., 2021; Sinha et al., 2021). Phytoextraction provides stable answer to eliminate metals from contaminated soils but needs disposal of hazardous biomass (Awa and Hadibarata, 2020). In soils contaminated heavily with heavy metals, use of plants for heavy metal removal is expected to take an impracticable time. As an alternative, phytostabilization should be considered, which focuses on sequestration or immobilization of metals using plants roots. In phytostabilization approach, metal ions bind with the cell walls, form complexes with root exudates/mucilage, or get chelated with molecules like metallothioneins and phytochelatins and thus get sequestrated in the root vacuoles.

Heavy metal precipitation in the rhizosphere and sequestration in root tissues reduces availability of metals and thus avoids risk of metal exposure to livestock, wildlife, human, groundwater contamination from heavy metal and dispersal via wind (Mendez and Maier, 2008). Plants used for phytostabilization should show fast growth, extensive root system, low transportation of pollutants from roots to above-ground portions, non-edible, and greater stress tolerance (Ismail, 2012). Phytostabilization of metal ions can be significantly increased by treatment of contaminated soil with different inorganic and organic amendments, which will alter the properties of soil to increase the plant metal availability. Phytotransformation involves utilization of plants and associated microbes, including fungus and bacteria to transform highly toxic metal species to less toxic metal species (Garbisu and Alkorta, 2001).

Phytovolatilization involves volatilization of heavy metals like Se and Hg from the foliage. In phytovolatilization, the toxic metal species are transformed into less toxic volatile forms. Volatile forms are released through transpiration in the atmosphere (Mendez and Maier, 2008). Advantage of this method is that disposal of harvested plant is not required. However, contaminants can't be removed completely and may cause secondary metal-contamination to the surrounding environments (Sakakibara et al., 2010). Rhizofiltration is used for filtering contaminants from polluted groundwater and surface water (Kristanti et al., 2020). Heavy metals are absorbed, and then either they get sequestered or precipitated in plant roots. Through this approach, water can be treated only up to rooting depth. Limitation of phytoremediation technique includes requirement of more time, labour, and high initial capital investment (McIntyre, 2003).

4. IMPACT OF DROUGHT ON BIOMASS AND HEAVY METAL UPTAKE OF PLANTS

The effects of drought are predicted to increase due to climate change and increasing water scarcity. Climate alteration—induced drought will affect all living beings, including plants. Since plants are sessile and can't change their position, they will especially suffer from water scarcity. Drought is considered as a major environmental stress factor that influences growth and development of plants. Soil moisture reduction affects various metabolic, physiological, and biochemical processes, including photosynthesis, respiration, germination, cell division, etc., and thus, deficit of water leads to adverse effects on plant growth and metabolism that include decreased CO_2 diffusion in leaves, reduced size and number of leaves with less plant height and fruit production (Lange et al., 2012; Alizadeh et al., 2015). High degree of drought stress severely affects plant functions, and the prime consequence is decrease in carbon fixation, which causes decreased plant growth depending on duration of the stress, the stage, and the existence

TABLE 5.1
Effect of drought on metal uptake in different plant species

Plant species	Metal	Metal uptake in presence of drought	References
Triticum aestivum	Cd	Enhanced	Khan et al., 2019
Ricinus communis	Cd	Reduced	Shi et al., 2015
Alyssum murale *Berkheya coddii* *Thlaspi caerulescens*	Ni and Zn	Enhanced	Angle et al., 2003
Ricinus communis Brassica juncea	Cd	Reduced	Bauddh and Singh, 2012
Brassica oxyrrhina	Cu and Zn	Reduced	Ma et al., 2016b
Quercus ilex	As, Cd, Ni, Pb, and Cr	Enhanced	Sardans and Peñuelas, 2007
Festuca arundinacea	Se	Enhanced	Tennant and Wu, 2000
Populus tremula x P. alba	Pb	Enhanced	Samuilov et al., 2016
Beta vulgaris	Cd	Enhanced	Tang et al., 2019

of other stresses. Thus, potential of plants to phytoremediate metal contaminated site can also get affected under drought stress.

Understanding of relation of drought, plant growth, and metal uptake is necessary for phytoremediation under climate change. Effect of drought stress on heavy metal uptake in different plant species is listed in Table 5.1. Both drought and high metal concentrations led to reduced hydraulic conductance and leaf and xylem-specific conductivity in *Acer rubrum* (L.) plants, and additive effect of metal stress and water stress on growth was observed (de Silva et al., 2012). Drought increased the magnitude of oxidative stress in Cd-stressed wheat plants grown for 125 days with significant inhibition in plant biomass (Khan et al., 2019). PEG-induced drought led to repression of root growth, inhibition of leaf gas exchange, and reduction in uptake and Cd accumulation in plants. Accumulation of Cd in the shoots and roots and total Cd in the castor plants showed positive correlation with growth, ratio of root and shoot length, total length of root, surface area, root tips, and diameter and root volume but not with transpiration rate. Therefore, the drought-induced decrease in uptake of Cd by castor plants may be the result of inhibition of growth of roots and changes in root morphology, instead of decreased transpiration (Shi et al., 2015). *Alyssum murale*, *Thlaspi caerulescens*, and *Berkheya coddii* also showed less accumulation of metals (Ni and Zn) *via* decreased uptake and lower plant biomass when grown in low moisture compared to high moisture condition (Angle et al., 2003). In roots of *Lolium multiflorum* Lam., Pascual et al. (2004) witnessed inhibition in the relocation and concentration coefficient of Mn, Ni, Zn, and Cu in sewage-sludge-treated plants under drought conditions. This is due to preservation of these metals in chemical forms and thus lowering their availability. Likewise, Bauddh and Singh (2012) reported reduced uptake of Cd in *Brassica juncea* plants grown for 90 days under water deficit. Conversely, Ma et al. (2016b) did not observe significant alterations in plant growth when they provided metal stress alone and in combination with water stress.

Various reports also suggest that drought enhances accumulation of metals in plants. Drought enhanced Cd concentrations was reported in the roots of dominant tree *Quercus ilex* and in leaves of codominant shrubs *Arbutus unedo* and *Phillyrea latifolia* in Mediterranean *Quercus ilex* forest (Sardans and Peñuelas, 2007). Tennant and Wu (2000) reported increased accumulation of Se in *Festuca arundinacea* with decreased biomass under low soil moisture and thus significantly affected phytoremediation process under drought. Drought led to decreased water content rather than reduced biomass production in wild poplar, while Pb was seen counteracting this decline under combined exposure. It seems Pb provides protection against drought by interacting with abscisic acid (ABA) dependent stomatal closure. Drought enhanced Pb accumulation in roots, but after rewatering, Pb could leak (Samuilov et al., 2016). Tang et al. (2019) reported variable Cd remediation when *Beta vulgaris* at organogenesis stage was grown in soils contaminated with Cd under different deficit irrigation in different blocks (T1: 300 L, T2: 200 L, and T3: 100 L). They observed 39.7% and 61.8% higher Cd remediation efficiency with greater shoot biomass in T2 (5.42 g ha^{-1}) in comparison to T1 and T3, respectively.

5. EFFECT OF DROUGHT ON MICROBES AND MICROBE-ASSISTED PHYTOREMEDIATION

Soil microbes establish complex communication systems with plants by using nutrient and energy sources provided by root exudates. Some of these microbes, which belong to group of plant growth promoting rhizobacteria (PGPR), facilitate adaptation of plants to metal rich environments and are used for microbe-assisted phytoremediation (Rizvi et al., 2020). These microorganisms cause alleviation of metal phytotoxicity and stimulate plant growth directly by solubilizing mineral nutrients and indirectly by inducing production of phytohormones, secretion of specific enzymes (e.g., 1-aminocyclopropane-1-carboxylate deaminase). They can also alter metal bioavailability in soil by various mechanisms, including acidification, precipitation, redox reactions, complexation, and chelation (Ma et al., 2016a).

Phytoremediation assisted by microbes associated with plants such as plant growth-promoting rhizobacteria, endophytes, and arbuscular mycorrhizal fungi is useful for remediation of heavy metals from contaminated sites as it can alleviate the heavy metal toxicity in plants by facilitating and improving growth of host plants under heavy metal stress (Deb et al., 2020). Drought induced by climate change events such as high temperature and less rainfall affects not only metals uptake and growth of plants but also growth and composition of microbial community, which can affect phytoremediation. As water potential of cell drops due to drought, there is loss of cell turgor (Harris, 1981), which can disturb microbial physiological functions and alter metabolic rates eventually leading to loss of cellular functions and death of the microorganisms. Also, drought can change the distribution of photosynthates in the rhizosphere, which in turn can adversely impact microorganism growth and activity and thus plant's health (Compant et al., 2010; Guenet et al., 2012). Drought can also affect composition of microbial community by supporting growth of desiccation-tolerant microbes or altering soil chemistry and diffusion rates (Naylor and Coleman-Derr, 2018).

Actual impact of drought on microbes is dependent on various factors such as strains and types of microbes (Guenet et al., 2012). In general, soil fungal networks are more stable to drought in comparison to bacterial networks due to the presence of exploratory and extended hyphal structures (Barnard et al., 2013; de Vries et al., 2018). Bacterial sensitivity has been attributed to enhanced damages to viable cells leading to decreased activity of microbes (Kieft et al., 1987; Nocker et al., 2012). Some microbial inoculants can alleviate the harmful effects of drought on plants (Augé et al., 2001; Marulanda et al., 2009; Tiwari et al., 2016; Singh et al., 2020). *Pseudomonas putida* adjusted the morphophysiological, molecular, and biochemical responses in *Cicer arietinum* L. during drought stress and thereby promoted plant growth and alleviated stress (Tiwari et al., 2016). Singh et al. (2020) showed that microbial inoculants (*Trichoderma* and *Pseudomonas*) successfully improved intrinsic molecular and biochemical capabilities of rice under stress. They directly led to over-expression of genes associated with defence pathways, including enzymatic and non-enzymatic antioxidants in plants facing drought stress that contributed strongly towards stress mitigation. Likewise, Martins et al. (2018) also showed that under certain conditions, soybean plant associated bacteria can reduce drought stress and may lead to improved water efficiency in soybean. It has been reported that Arbuscular mycorrhizal fungi enhanced water and nutrient absorption, aquaporin expression, root structure, photosynthesis, osmolyte and polyamine accumulation, activation of antioxidative defence systems, and phytohormone balance to resist soil water deficit (Begum et al., 2019; Diagne et al., 2020; Zou et al., 2021).

Under semiarid conditions, inoculation of drought and heavy metal–resistant strains of serpentine rhizobacterial *Pseudomonas libanensis* and *Pseudomonas reactans* has been proved beneficial for improvement of phytoremediation of metal-polluted soils. These strains led to enhanced growth of plants, leaf relative water content (RWC), and pigment content but caused decline in proline and malondialdehyde content in leaves of *B. oxyrrhina* growing under metal stress irrespective of water conditions. Concentrations of metals greatly increased in these plants in presence as well as absence of drought. Accelerated metal phytoremediation and improved growth of *Trifolium arvense* plants under dry conditions were observed in presence of endophyte *Pseudomonas azotoformans* ASS1, which colonized tissue interiors and rhizosphere under drought and metal stresses (Ma et al., 2017). *P. azotoformans* increased growth, chlorophyll and proline content, antioxidant enzyme activities, and uptake of Cu, Zn, Ni, in *T. arvense* but reduced MDA content in leaves of plants.

Integrative PGPR use with salicylic acid is as an efficacious approach for improvement of the heavy metal phytoremediation and growth of plants under drought. Cao et al. (2016) observed improved plant growth (root length, shoot biomass, and plant height), higher Cd accumulation and translocation with greater bioconcentration factor in *Amaranthus hypochondriacus* under drought condition upon inoculation of a drought-tolerant actinomycete strain *Streptomyces pactum* Act12. This strain greatly increased Cd tolerance by inducing the activities of antioxidant enzymes, SOD and CAT, glutathione (GSH) and reducing MDA content.

6. CONCLUSIONS AND FUTURE PROSPECTS

Climate change–induced increase in intensity and duration of drought can have large influence on the phytoremediation process. Drought can affect metal uptake, growth, and biomass of plants and activity and composition of microbial population in rhizosphere. Effect of drought on phytoremediation can vary substantially depending on the type and concentration of heavy metals, microbial diversity, plant species, presence of some other stresses, etc. More studies are needed to understand physiological, biochemical, and molecular mechanisms that plant uses to withstand drought and heavy metal stress. Deeper understanding of these mechanisms and genes associated with tolerance to drought and heavy metals simultaneously will help in developing transgenic plants that can tolerate both drought and heavy metals well.

REFERENCES

Ali, H., Khan, E. and Sajad, M.A., 2013. Phytoremediation of heavy metals—concepts and applications. *Chemosphere*, *91*:869–881.

Alizadeh, V., Shokri, V., Soltani, A. and Yousefi, M.A., 2015. Effects of climate change and drought-stress on plant physiology. *International Journal of Advanced Biological Biomedical Research*, *3*:38–42.

Angle, J.S., Baker, A.J., Whiting, S.N. and Chaney, R.L., 2003. Soil moisture effects on uptake of metals by Thlaspi, Alyssum, and Berkheya. *Plant and Soil*, *256*:325–332.

Atkinson, N. and Urwin, P.E., 2012. The interaction of plant biotic and abiotic stresses: From genes to the field. *Journal of Experimental Botany*, *63*:3523–3544.

Augé, R.M., Stodola, A.J., Tims, J.E. and Saxton, A.M., 2001. Moisture retention properties of a mycorrhizal soil. *Plant and Soil*, *230*:87–97.

Ault, T.R., 2020. On the essentials of drought in a changing climate. *Science*, *368*:256–260.

Awa, S.H. and Hadibarata, T., 2020. Removal of heavy metals in contaminated soil by phytoremediation mechanism: A review. *Water, Air, and Soil Pollution*, *231*:1–15.

Barnard, R.L., Osborne, C.A. and Firestone, M.K., 2013. Responses of soil bacterial and fungal communities to extreme desiccation and rewetting. *The ISME Journal*, *7*:2229–2241.

Bauddh, K. and Singh, R.P., 2012. Growth, tolerance efficiency and phytoremediation potential of *Ricinus communis* (L.) and *Brassica juncea* (L.) in salinity and drought affected cadmium contaminated soil. *Ecotoxicology and Environmental Safety*, *85*:13–22.

Begum, N., Qin, C., Ahanger, M.A., Raza, S., Khan, M.I., Ashraf, M., Ahmed, N. and Zhang, L., 2019. Role of arbuscular mycorrhizal fungi in plant growth regulation: Implications in abiotic stress tolerance. *Frontiers in Plant Science*, *10*:1068. doi: 10.3389/fpls.2019.01068.

Berg, A. and Sheffield, J., 2018. Climate change and drought: The soil moisture perspective. *Current Climate Change Reports*, *4*:180–191.

Bowler, C. and Fluhr, R., 2000. The role of calcium and activated oxygens as signals for controlling cross-tolerance. *Trends in Plant Science*, *5*:241–246.

Brooks, R.R., Chambers, M.F., Nicks, L.J. and Robinson, B.H., 1998. Phytomining. *Trends in Plant Science*, *3*:359–362.

Cao, S., Wang, W., Wang, F., Zhang, J., Wang, Z., Yang, S. and Xue, Q., 2016. Drought-tolerant Streptomyces pactum Act12 assist phytoremediation of cadmium-contaminated soil by Amaranthus hypochondriacus: Great potential application in arid/semi-arid areas. *Environmental Science and Pollution Research, 23*:14898–14907.

Compant, S., Van Der Heijden, M.G. and Sessitsch, A., 2010. Climate change effects on beneficial plant—microorganism interactions. *FEMS Microbiology Ecology, 73*:197–214.

Deb, V.K., Rabbani, A., Upadhyay, S., Bharti, P., Sharma, H., Rawat, D.S. and Saxena, G., 2020. Microbe-assisted phytoremediation in reinstating heavy metal-contaminated sites: Concepts, mechanisms, challenges, and future perspectives. In Arora, P.K. (ed.) *Microbial Technology for Health and Environment* (pp. 161–189). Springer, Singapore.

de Silva, N.D.G., Cholewa, E. and Ryser, P., 2012. Effects of combined drought and heavy metal stresses on xylem structure and hydraulic conductivity in red maple (Acer rubrum L.). *Journal of Experimental Botany, 63*:5957–5966.

de Vries, F.T., Griffiths, R.I., Bailey, M., Craig, H., Girlanda, M., Gweon, H.S., Hallin, S., Kaisermann, A., Keith, A.M., Kretzschmar, M. and Lemanceau, P., 2018. Soil bacterial networks are less stable under drought than fungal networks. *Nature Communications, 9*:1–12.

Dhaliwal, S.S., Singh, J., Taneja, P.K. *et al.*, 2020. Remediation techniques for removal of heavy metals from the soil contaminated through different sources: A review. *Environmental Science and Pollution Research, 27*: 1319–1333.

Diagne, N., Ngom, M., Djighaly, P.I., Fall, D., Hocher, V. and Svistoonoff, S., 2020. Roles of arbuscular mycorrhizal fungi on plant growth and performance: Importance in biotic and abiotic stressed regulation. *Diversity, 12*:370. https://doi.org/10.3390/d12100370.

Farid, M., Ali, S., Shakoor, M.B., Bharwana, S.A., Rizvi, H., Ehsan, S., Tauqeer, H.M., Iftikhar, U. and Hannan, F., 2013. EDTA assisted phytoremediation of cadmium, lead and zinc. *International Journal of Agronomy and Plant Production, 4*:2833–2846.

Fraire-Velázquez, S., Rodríguez-Guerra, R. and Sánchez-Calderón, L., 2011. Abiotic and biotic stress response crosstalk in plants. In Shanker, A. (ed.) *Abiotic and Biotic Stress Response Crosstalk in Plants-Physiological, Biochemical and Genetic Perspectives* (pp. 1–26). InTech Open Access Company, Rijeka, Croatia.

Garbisu, C. and Alkorta, I., 2001. Phytoextraction: A cost-effective plant-based technology for the removal of metals from the environment. *Bioresource Technology, 77*:229–236.

Greve, P., Roderick, M.L., Ukkola, A.M. and Wada, Y., 2019. The aridity index under global warming. *Environmental Research Letters, 14*:124006.

Guenet, B., Lenhart, K., Leloup, J., Giusti-Miller, S., Pouteau, V., Mora, P., Nunan, N. and Abbadie, L., 2012. The impact of long-term CO2 enrichment and moisture levels on soil microbial community structure and enzyme activities. *Geoderma, 170*:331–336.

Harris, R.F., 1981. Effect of water potential on microbial growth and activity. In Parr, J.F., Gardner, W.R. and Elliott, L.F. (eds.) *Water Potential Relations in Soil Microbiology* (pp. 23–95). Soil Science Society of America, Inc., Madison, WI.

Huang, H., Ullah, F., Zhou, D.X., Yi, M. and Zhao, Y., 2019. Mechanisms of ROS regulation of plant development and stress responses. *Frontiers in Plant Science*, 10:800. doi:10.3389/fpls.2019.00800.

IPCC, 2013. Climate change 2013. In Stocker, T.F., Qin, D., Plattner, G.K., Tignor, M., Allen, S.K., Boschung, J., Nauels, A., Xia, Y., Bex, V. and Midgley P.M. (eds.) *The Physical Science Basis: Contribution of Working Group I to the Fifth Assessment Report of the Intergovernmental Panel on Climate Change.* Cambridge University Press, Cambridge, United Kingdom and New York, NY, USA.

Ismail, S., 2012. Phytoremediation: A green technology. *Iranian Journal of Plant Physiology, 3*:567–576.

Jha, A.B., Misra, A.N. and Sharma, P., 2017. Phytoremediation of heavy metal-contaminated soil using bioenergy crops. In Bauddh, K., Singh, B. and Korstad, J. (eds.) *Phytoremediation Potential of Bioenergy Plants* (pp. 63–96). Springer, Singapore.

Jha, A.B. and Sharma, P., 2019. Regulation of osmolytes syntheses and improvement of abiotic stress tolerance in plants. In Hasanuzzaman, M., Nahar, K., Fujita, M., Oku, H. and Islam, T. (eds.) *Approaches for Enhancing Abiotic Stress Tolerance in Plants* (pp. 311–338). CRC Press, Boca Raton, Florida.

Khan, Z.S., Rizwan, M., Hafeez, M. et al., 2019. The accumulation of cadmium in wheat (*Triticum aestivum*) as influenced by zinc oxide nanoparticles and soil moisture conditions. *Environmental Science and Pollution Research*, 26:19859–19870. doi.org/10.1007/s11356-019-05333-5.

Kieft, T.L., Soroker, E. and Firestone, M.K., 1987. Microbial biomass response to a rapid increase in water potential when dry soil is wetted. *Soil Biology and Biochemistry*, 19:119–126. doi: 10.1016/0038-0717(87)90070-8.

Kristanti, R.A., Ngu, W.J., Yuniarto, A. and Hadibarata, T., 2020. Rhizofiltration for removal of inorganic and organic pollutants in groundwater: A review. *Biointerface Research in Applied Chemistry*, 11:12326–12347.

Kumar, K., Rao, K.P., Sharma, P. and Sinha, A.K., 2008. Differential regulation of rice mitogen activated protein kinase kinase (MKK) by abiotic stress. *Plant Physiology and Biochemistry*, 46:891–897.

Lamers, J., Van Der Meer, T. and Testerink, C., 2020. How plants sense and respond to stressful environments. *Plant Physiology*, 182:1624–1635.

Lange, O.L., Kappen, L. and Schulze, E.D. eds., 2012. *Water and Plant Life: Problems and Modern Approaches* (Vol. 19). Springer Science and Business Media, Berlin, Germany.

Lasat, M.M., 2002. Phytoextraction of toxic metals: A review of biological mechanisms. *Journal of Environmental Quality*, 31:109–120.

Ledley, T.S., Sundquist, E.T., Schwartz, S.E., Hall, D.K., Fellows, J.D. and Killeen, T.L., 1999. Climate change and greenhouse gases. *Eos, Transactions American Geophysical Union*, 80:453–458.

Lindsey, R., 2020. *Climate Change: Atmospheric Carbon Dioxide*. www.climate.gov/news-features/understanding-climate/climate-change-atmospheric-carbon-dioxide. Assessed on 19.12.2021.

Liu, S., Waqas, M.A., Wang, S.H., Xiong, X.Y. and Wan, Y.F., 2017. Effects of increased levels of atmospheric CO_2 and high temperatures on rice growth and quality. *PloS One*, 12:e0187724. doi: 10.1371/journal.pone.0187724.

Ma, Y., Oliveira, R.S., Freitas, H. and Zhang, C., 2016a. Biochemical and molecular mechanisms of plant-microbe-metal interactions: Relevance for phytoremediation. *Frontiers in Plant Science*, 7:918. doi: 10.3389/fpls.2016.0091.

Ma, Y., Rajkumar, M., Moreno, A., Zhang, C. and Freitas, H., 2017. Serpentine endophytic bacterium *Pseudomonas azotoformans* ASS1 accelerates phytoremediation of soil metals under drought stress. *Chemosphere*, 185:75–85.

Ma, Y., Rajkumar, M., Zhang, C. and Freitas, H., 2016b. Inoculation of Brassica oxyrrhina with plant growth promoting bacteria for the improvement of heavy metal phytoremediation under drought conditions. *Journal of Hazardous Materials*, 320:36–44.

Martins, S.J., Rocha, G.A., de Melo, H.C., de Castro Georg, R., Ulhôa, C.J., de Campos Dianese, É., Oshiquiri, L.H., da Cunha, M.G., da Rocha, M.R., de Araújo, L.G. and Vaz, K.S., 2018. Plant-associated bacteria mitigate drought stress in soybean. *Environmental Science and Pollution Research*, 25:13676–13686.

Marulanda, A., Barea, J.M. and Azcón, R., 2009. Stimulation of plant growth and drought tolerance by native microorganisms (AM fungi and bacteria) from dry environments: Mechanisms related to bacterial effectiveness. *Journal of Plant Growth Regulation*, 28:115–124.

McIntyre, T., 2003. Phytoremediation of heavy metals from soils. *Phytoremediation*, *78*:97–123.

Mendez, M.O. and Maier, R.M., 2008. Phytostabilization of mine tailings in arid and semiarid environments-an emerging remediation technology. *Environmental Health Perspectives*, *116*:278–283.

Mohanty, M., 2016. Post-harvest management of phytoremediation technology. *Journal of Environmental and Analytical Toxicology*, *6*:398. doi: 10.4172/2161-0525.1000398.

Mukherjee, S., Mishra, A. and Trenberth, K.E., 2018. Climate change and drought: A perspective on drought indices. *Current Climate Change Reports*, *4*:145–163.

Naumann, G., Alfieri, L., Wyser, K., Mentaschi, L., Betts, R.A., Carrao, H., Spinoni, J., Vogt, J. and Feyen, L., 2018. Global changes in drought conditions under different levels of warming. *Geophysical Research Letters*, *45*:3285–3296.

Naylor, D. and Coleman-Derr, D., 2018. Drought stress and root-associated bacterial communities. *Frontiers in Plant Science*, *8*:2223. doi: 10.3389/fpls.2017.02223.

Nocker, A., Fernández, P.S., Montijn, R. and Schuren, F., 2012. Effect of air drying on bacterial viability: A multiparameter viability assessment. *Journal of Microbiological Methods*, *90*:86–95.

Osakabe, Y., Osakabe, K., Shinozaki, K. and Tran, L.S.P., 2014. Response of plants to water stress. *Frontiers in Plant Science*, *5*:86. doi: 10.3389/fpls.2014.00086.

Pascual, I., Antolín, M.C., García, C., Polo, A. and Sánchez-Díaz, M., 2004. Plant availability of heavy metals in a soil amended with a high dose of sewage sludge under drought conditions. *Biology and Fertility of Soils*, *40*:291–299.

Payne, A.E., Demory, M.E., Leung, L.R., Ramos, A.M., Shields, C.A., Rutz, J.J., Siler, N., Villarini, G., Hall, A. and Ralph, F.M., 2020. Responses and impacts of atmospheric rivers to climate change. *Nature Reviews Earth and Environment*, *1*:143–157.

Raskin, I. and Ensley, B.D., 2000. *Phytoremediation of Toxic Metals Using Plants to Clean Up the Environment*. John Wiley & Sons, Inc., New York, USA.

Rejeb, I.B., Pastor, V. and Mauch-Mani, B., 2014. Plant responses to simultaneous biotic and abiotic stress: Molecular mechanisms. *Plants*, *3*:458–475.

Rizvi, A., Zaidi, A., Ameen, F., Ahmed, B., AlKahtani, M.D. and Khan, M.S., 2020. Heavy metal induced stress on wheat: Phytotoxicity and microbiological management. *RSC Advances*, *10*:38379–38403.

Sakakibara, M., Watanabe, A., Inoue, M., Sano, S. and Kaise, T., 2010. Phytoextraction and phytovolatilization of arsenic from as-contaminated soils by Pteris vittata. In *Proceedings of the Annual International Conference on Soils, Sediments, Water and Energy*, 12: Article 26. https://scholarworks.umass.edu/soilsproceedings/vol12/iss1/26

Salt, D.E., Smith, R.D. and Raskin, I., 1998. Phytoremediation. *Annual Review of Plant Biology*, *49*:643–668.

Samuilov, S., Lang, F., Djukic, M., Djunisijevic-Bojovic, D. and Rennenberg, H., 2016. Lead uptake increases drought tolerance of wild type and transgenic poplar (Populus tremula x P. alba) overexpressing *gsh 1*. *Environmental Pollution*, *216*:773–785.

Sardans, J. and Peñuelas, J. 2007. Drought changes the dynamics of trace element accumulation in a Mediterranean Quercus ilex forest. *Environmental Pollution*, *147*:567–583.

Scheff, J. and Frierson, D.M., 2015. Terrestrial aridity and its response to greenhouse warming across CMIP5 climate models. *Journal of Climate*, *28*:5583–5600.

Schlaepfer, D., Bradford, J., Lauenroth, W. *et al.* 2017. Climate change reduces extent of temperate drylands and intensifies drought in deep soils. *Nature Communications*, *8*:14196. https://doi.org/10.1038/ncomms14196.

Seth, C.S., Remans, T., Keunen, E., Jozefczak, M., Gielen, H., Opdenakker, K., Weyens, N., Vangronsveld, J. and Cuypers, A., 2012. Phytoextraction of toxic metals: A central role for glutathione. *Plant, Cell and Environment*, 35:334–346.

Sharma, P. and Dubey, R.S., 2006. Cadmium uptake and its toxicity in higher plants. In Khan, N.A. and Samiullah (eds.) *Cadmium Toxicity and Tolerance in Plants* (pp. 63–86). Narosa Publishing House, New Delhi, India.

Sharma, P. and Dubey, R.S., 2007. Involvement of oxidative stress and role of antioxidative defense system in growing rice seedlings exposed to toxic concentrations of aluminum. *Plant Cell Reports*, 26:2027–2038.

Sharma, P. and Dubey, R.S., 2008. Mechanism of aluminum toxicity and tolerance in higher plants. In Hemantranjan, A. (ed.) *Advances in Plant Physiology* (pp. 145–179), Volume 10. Scientific Publishers, Jodhpur, India.

Sharma, P. and Dubey, R.S., 2010. Protein synthesis by plants under stressful conditions. In Pessarakli, M. (ed.) *Handbook of Plant and Crop Stress* (pp. 465–518), 3rd Edition. Taylor & Francis, Florida, USA.

Sharma, P. and Dubey, R.S., 2011. Abiotic stress-induced metabolic alterations in crop plants: Strategies for improving stress tolerance. In Sinha, R.P., Sharma, N.K. and Rai, A.K. (eds.) *Advances in Life Sciences* (pp. 1–54). I.K. International Publishing House Pvt. Ltd., New Delhi, India.

Sharma, P. and Dubey, R.S., 2019. Protein synthesis by plants under stressful conditions. In Pessarakli, M. (ed.) *Handbook of Plant and Crop Stress* (pp. 405–449), 4th Edition. CRC Press, Florida, USA.

Sharma, P., Jha, A.B., Bauddh, K., Korstad, J. and Dubey, R.S., 2021. Efficient utilization of plant biomass after harvesting the phytoremediator plants. In Bauddh, K., Korstad, J. and Sharma, P. (eds.) *Phytorestoration of Abandoned Mining and Oil Drilling Sites* (pp. 57–84). Elsevier, Amsterdam, Netherlands.

Sharma, P., Jha, A.B. and Dubey, R.S., 2009. Effect of abiotic stresses on growth, metabolic alterations and tolerance mechanisms in rice crop. In Danforth, A.T. (ed.) *Corn Crop Production: Growth, Fertilization and Yield* (pp. 111–186). Nova Science Publishers, New York.

Sharma, P., Jha, A.B. and Dubey, R.S., 2010. Oxidative stress and antioxidative defense system in plants growing under abiotic stresses. In Pessarakli, M. (ed.) *Handbook of Plant and Crop Stress* (pp. 89–138). 3rd edition. Taylor & Francis, Florida, USA.

Sharma, P., Jha, A.B. and Dubey, R.S., 2019. Oxidative stress and antioxidative defense system in plants growing under abiotic stresses. In Pessarakli, M. (ed.) *Handbook of Plant and Crop Stress* (pp. 93–136). 4th edition. CRC Press, Florida, USA.

Sharma, P., Jha, A.B., Dubey, R.S. and Pessarakli, M., 2012. Reactive oxygen species, oxidative damage and antioxidative defense mechanism in plants under stressful conditions. *Journal of Botany*, Article ID 217037. doi: 10.1155/2012/217037.

Sharma, S., Tiwari, S., Hasan, A., Saxena, V. and Pandey, L.M., 2018. Recent advances in conventional and contemporary methods for remediation of heavy metal-contaminated soils. *3 Biotech*, 8:1–18.

Shi, G., Xia, S., Ye, J., Huang, Y., Liu, C. and Zhang, Z., 2015. PEG-simulated drought stress decreases cadmium accumulation in castor bean by altering root morphology. *Environmental and Experimental Botany*, 111:127–134.

Singh, D.P., Singh, V., Gupta, V.K., Shukla, R., Prabha, R., Sarma, B.K. and Patel, J.S., 2020. Microbial inoculation in rice regulates antioxidative reactions and defense related genes to mitigate drought stress. *Scientific Reports*, 10:1–17.

Singh, R., Jha, A.B., Misra, A.N. and Sharma, P., 2019a. Differential responses of growth, photosynthesis, oxidative stress, metals accumulation and NRAMP genes in contrasting

Ricinus communis genotypes under arsenic stress. *Environmental Science and Pollution Research*, 26:31166–31177.

Singh, R., Jha, A.B., Misra, A.N. and Sharma, P., 2019b. Adaption mechanisms in plants under heavy metal stress conditions during phytoremediation. In Pandey, V. and Bauddh, K. (eds.) *Phytomanagement of Polluted Sites* (pp. 329–360). Elsevier, Amsterdam, Netherlands.

Singh, R., Misra, A.N. and Sharma, P., 2021a. Differential responses of thiol metabolism and genes involved in arsenic detoxification in tolerant and sensitive genotypes of bioenergy crop Ricinus communis. *Protoplasma*, 258:391–401.

Singh, R., Misra, A.N. and Sharma, P., 2021b. Effect of arsenate toxicity on antioxidant enzymes and expression of nicotianamine synthase in contrasting genotypes of bioenergy crop Ricinus communis. *Environmental Science and Pollution Research*. doi: 10.1007/s11356-021-12701-7.

Singh, R., Misra, A.N. and Sharma, P., 2021c. Safe, efficient, and economically beneficial remediation of arsenic-contaminated soil: Possible strategies for increasing arsenic tolerance and accumulation in non-edible economically important native plants. *Environmental Science and Pollution Research*, 1–17. doi: 10.1007/s11356-021-14507-z.

Sinha, R., Singh, A.K., Bauddh, K., Sharma, T.R. and Sharma, P., 2021. Phytomining: A sustainable approach for recovery and extraction of valuable metals. In Bauddh, K., Korstad, J. and Sharma, P. (eds.) *Phytorestoration of Abandoned Mining and Oil Drilling Sites* (pp. 487–506). Elsevier, Amsterdam, Netherlands.

Solomon, S., Daniel, J.S., Sanford, T.J., Murphy, D.M., Plattner, G.K., Knutti, R. and Friedlingstei, P., 2010. Persistence of climate changes due to a range of greenhouse gases. *Proceedings of the National Academy of Sciences*, 107:18354–18359.

Suman, J., Uhlik, O., Viktorova, J. and Macek, T., 2018. Phytoextraction of heavy metals: A promising tool for clean-up of polluted environment? *Frontiers in Plant Science*, 9:1476. doi: 10.3389/fpls.2018.01476.

Tang, X., Song, Y., He, X. and Yi, L., 2019. Enhancing phytoremediation efficiency using regulated deficit irrigation. Polish Journal of Environmental Studies, 28:2399–2405.

Tennant, T. and Wu, L., 2000. Effects of water stress on selenium accumulation in tall fescue (*Festuca arundinacea* schreb) from a selenium-contaminated soil. *Archives of Environmental Contamination and Toxicology*, 38:32–39.

Tiwari, J., Chakravarty, P., Sharma, P., Sinha, R., Kumar, M. and Bauddh, K., 2021. Phytoremediation: A sustainable method for cleaning up the contaminated sites. In Bauddh, K., Korstad, J. and Sharma, P. (eds.) *Phytorestoration of Abandoned Mining and Oil Drilling Sites* (pp. 3–32). Elsevier, Amsterdam, Netherlands.

Tiwari, S., Lata, C., Chauhan, P.S. and Nautiyal, C.S., 2016. Pseudomonas putida attunes morphophysiological, biochemical and molecular responses in *Cicer arietinum* L. during drought stress and recovery. *Plant Physiology and Biochemistry*, 99:108–117.

Vicente-Serrano, S.M., Quiring, S.M., Pena-Gallardo, M., Yuan, S. and Dominguez-Castro, F., 2020. A review of environmental droughts: Increased risk under global warming? *Earth-Science Reviews*, 201:102953. doi: 10.1016/j.earscirev.2019.102953.

Yan, A., Wang, Y., Tan, S.N., Yusof, M.L.M., Ghosh, S. and Chen, Z., 2020. Phytoremediation: A promising approach for revegetation of heavy metal-polluted land. *Frontiers in Plant Science*, 11. doi.org/10.3389/fpls.2020.00359.

Zarch, M.A.A., Sivakumar, B., Malekinezhad, H. and Sharma, A., 2017. Future aridity under conditions of global climate change. *Journal of Hydrology*, 554:451–469.

Zou, Y.N., Wu, Q.S. and Kuča, K., 2021. Unravelling the role of arbuscular mycorrhizal fungi in mitigating the oxidative burst of plants under drought stress. *Plant Biology*, 23:50–57.

6 The Impact of Climate Change on Crop Production and Combat Strategies

Akansha Singh, Esha Rami, Priti Upadhyay, and Ajit K. Gangawane

CONTENTS

1. Introduction 103
2. GHG Emission, Global Warming, and Agriculture..105
3. Climate Change, Crop Productivity, and Nutrition 105
4. Climate Change and Land Degradation 107
5. Tackling Climate Change Issues..107
   5.1 Agronomic Measures 108
   5.2 Conservation Agriculture...108
   5.3 Conventional and Advanced Crop Improvement Technologies...............108
6. Concluding Remarks..110
References 110

1. INTRODUCTION

Climate change is defined as an alteration in atmospheric composition that occurs over a period of time due to anthropogenic activities. Since 1850, the increase in global mean surface temperature was observed around 1°C, while projected to be increased by 2°C in the coming decade (Zhongming et al., 2021). Anthropogenic activities such as industrialization, land misuse, use of fossil fuels, deforestation causing the change in atmospheric composition leading to climate change. The Paris Agreement on Climate Change recognizes climate change as a universal concern, emphasizing the inherent relationship that climate change actions, responses, and impacts have with equitable access to sustainable development and poverty eradication and recognizes the fundamental priority of ensuring food security and ending hunger, as well as the particular vulnerabilities of food production systems to the adverse effects of climate change (Paris Agreement, 2015).

Several factors, such as a decrease in snowfall rate, floods, rise in sea levels, increase in temperature of ocean and atmosphere, increase in ratio of GHGs indicates that climate is changing. The need of the hour is to safeguard the climate by keeping the global atmospheric temperature below 1.5°C and ensuring food security through working on resolving the constraints for sustainable crop production systems. Limiting global warming to 1.5°C is predicted to significantly minimize the likelihood of extreme drought, precipitation shortfalls, and water availability problems (Hoegh-Guldberg et al., 2019; Zhongming et al., 2021). The agriculture sector is severely affected worldwide due to changing weather conditions. Global warming is responsible for heat stress, drought, irregular precipitations, heat waves, floods, typhoons, storms, and other extreme weather disasters worldwide. These natural calamities have resulted in an economic loss of US$ 268 billion worldwide in the year 2020 (Jaganmohan, 2021), where 95% of these natural catastrophes are a result of extreme weather condition, which directly or indirectly affects the agricultural sector worldwide. Crop production is getting affected severely worldwide due to biotic and abiotic stresses. The biotic and abiotic stresses antagonistically affect the plant's development, fertility, vigour, and photosynthetic ability (Pandey et al., 2017; Gull et al., 2019; Yadav et al., 2020). The world population is expected to reach 9.7 billion by the year 2050 (Roser, 2013). To ensure the health and food security for these 9.7 billion population will further magnify the pressure on agriculture crop production. The ongoing COVID-19 pandemic has given an economic shock to the countries (Sahoo, 2021). Temperature and precipitation both are necessary inputs for sustainable agriculture. Changing climatic variables, polluted air, water, and soil natural resources are creating hurdles for increased crop production to meet the global food demand. Climate change and food security for a growing population are two prime concerns of the 21st century. The crop production in developing countries will face more challenges than the developed countries due to changing climatic scenarios. The 17 SDGs are adopted by united member nations to tackle climate change, poverty, hunger, malnutrition, reduce inequality, and strategies to preserve the environment and the ocean (Ford, 2015). The occurrence of a COVID-19 pandemic, weather disasters, rain, floods are causing negative economic growth and food insecurity (Sahoo, 2021). In addition to this, crop productivity is declining due to uncertain weather challenges. This is hindering the sustainable development goals (SDGs) to eradicate hunger by 2030. As per the Indian economic survey 2020–2021, agriculture contributes 19.9% to the GDP (Economic Survey, 2021). The arable land in India stands at 156 million hectare in 2018. Out of that 54% land is rainfed, where farming depends on the rainfall. Moreover, 42% of the total cultivated area lies in the drought-affected states. As agriculture is the economic source of 60% rural population of India, changing climatic conditions are adversely affecting the farmers' livelihood. Indian agriculture is more vulnerable to changing climate scenarios (Sathyan et al., 2018). By the year 2030, the projected mean global temperature will be in the range of 1.7 to 2.0°C, while by the year 2080 it will be 3.3–4.8. Whereas an increase in precipitation will be 5 to 6% by the 2030s and 6 to 14% by 2080s (Chaturvedi et al., 2012). This chapter highlights the GHG emission and climate change, the impact of climate change on crop productivity, and biotic and abiotic stresses, strategies to deal with climate change, and conventional and advanced crop improvement technologies to develop better crops for the future.

2. GHG EMISSION, GLOBAL WARMING, AND AGRICULTURE

The rise in greenhouse gas (GHG) emissions in the atmosphere affecting adversely to the climate. Deforestation, increased anthropogenic activities, urbanization, and industrialization are the major cause of increased GHG emissions in the atmosphere and thereby polluting the air, soil, and water bodies and contributing towards global warming. The GHGs such as carbon dioxide (CO_2), nitrous oxide (NO_2), methane (CH_4), sulfur hexafluoride (SF_6), chlorofluorocarbons (CFCs), and hydrofluorocarbons are permeable to the solar radiation while less permeable to infrared radiation, keeping the planet Earth's surface warmer leading to global warming (UNFCCC, 2009). This effect is known as Greenhouse Effect. Agricultural activities such as ploughing, grazing, deforestation, fertilization contribute to 24% GHG emission in the environment (Smith et al., 2014). The nitrogenous chemical fertilizer used for increased crop production is the cause of 33% GHG emissions. Agricultural activities contribute 10–14% of total GHG emission, while paddy field contributes 18% of total CH4 emission. According to the 2014 IPCC assessment, "atmospheric quantities of carbon dioxide, methane, and nitrous oxide are unprecedented in at least 800,000 years." Their impacts, together with those of other anthropogenic factors, have been detected throughout the climate system and are highly likely to have been the primary cause of the observed warming since the mid-20th century (Pachauri et al., 2014). The concentration of CO_2, NO_2, and CH_4 in the atmosphere has increased substantially to 390.5 ppm, 390.5 ppb, and 1803.2 ppb, which is 40, 20, and 150% greater than the pre-industrialization period (US EPA, OA, 2017). The concentration of CO_2 increased 46% from 280 ppm in late 1700s to 410 ppm in 2019. While the concentration of methane has doubled, which is entirely due to use of fossil fuel, animal waste, agricultural waste burning, rice cultivation, on field burning, fertilization, and other agricultural activities (Denman et al., 2007). The rise in NO_2 concentration from 280 ppb to 331 ppb in 2019 is also predominantly due to agricultural activities (US EPA,OA, 2017). NO_2 can stay in the environment up to a hundred years and causes 296 times more global warming than CO_2 gas. Moreover, by the end of the century, the concentration of CO_2 in the atmosphere is expected to reach up to 1,000 ppm (Zheng et al., 2018). The global warming is changing the crop pattern across the globe due to which crop yield is reducing in tropical regions. Agricultural ecology is both the source as well as sink of GHG emission in the atmosphere. Plant captures CO_2 in the process of photosynthesis to synthesize the carbohydrate, while bacteria present in soil oxidizes atmospheric methane, thereby acting as sink. While the expansion of agricultural land through process of deforestation results into release of CO_2 stored in tree and soil, causing its emission into the atmosphere. The possible strategy for climate change mitigation is an increase in crop production and productivity and simultaneously limiting the emission of GHG in the atmosphere (Tesfahun, 2018). The GHG emission can be reduced by slowing the process of conversion of organic carbon to CO2 and agricultural waste management to limit the release of NO2 and CH4.

3. CLIMATE CHANGE, CROP PRODUCTIVITY, AND NUTRITION

Agriculture and climate change are interlinked. Change in environmental conditions affect crop production and productivity, thereby causing global food insecurity (Hatfield et al., 2011; Arora, 2019; Guntukula, 2019; Guntukula and Goyari, 2020). As per the report of World Food Programme (WFP), 2018 the increase in crop productivity per hectare is slower than the rise in population (Arora, 2019). The situation gets worsen with rising GHG emission and global warming. By the year 2070, we may experience decline in major cereal crops production, such as maize (20–45%), wheat (5–50%), and rice (20–30%) (Arora, 2019). The rising temperature, water scarcity, change in rainfall pattern, and other environmental conditions will impact crop production and productivity (Ray et al., 2019). With every 1°C rise in temperature, the global yield loss is 6.0 ± 2.9% for wheat, 3.2 ± 3.7% for rice, and 7.4 ± 4.5% for maize (Zhao et al., 2017). The reduction in crop productivity is due to an increased water pressure deficit in response to increasing global temperature (Asseng et al., 2011; Zhao et al., 2016a, 2016b). As per the estimates for wheat production, India and Russia are more vulnerable to temperature increase than the U.S. and France (Zhao et al., 2017). Impact of heat on 71 cultivars on 17 different locations in South Africa was assessed from 1998 to 2014. Heat exposure above 30°C for continuous 24 hours caused 12.5% reduction in yield (Shew et al., 2020). In dryland cropping system, heat adversely affects the crop yield; hence adaptation strategy is required to mitigate the heat stress effect.

In addition to temperature, elevated atmospheric carbon dioxide (eCO_2) also affects crop yield. The yield of C3 plants such as wheat, rice is positively affected due to the increase in photosynthetic rate in high eCO_2. Whereas C4 plants such as maize, sugarcane show little effect of high eCO_2 on the photosynthetic rate in optimal soil moisture conditions. Although in drought situations the increased eCO2 is beneficial for C4 plants in carbon assimilation (Lopes et al., 2011). Elevated eCO_2 though results in increased photosynthesis and crop production but also causes reduced nutritional quality (Dong et al., 2018; Ebi et al., 2021). The elevated eCO_2 concentrations adversely affect the nutritional component in many foods, cereal, vegetables, and fruit crops (Ebi et al., 2021). In C3 plants such as wheat and rice, increases in CO_2 causes 10% reduction in protein content, 5–10% in iron and zinc, and 30% reduction in Vitamin B (Taub et al., 2008; Myers et al., 2014; Zhu et al., 2018; Loladze et al., 2019). At an elevated concentration of CO_2 (550ppm) and 1°C rise in temperature, the yield of potato was increased by 11.12%; however, the rise in temperature to 3°C will cause 13.72% reduction in potato yield by the year 2050 (Jatav et al., 2017). In strawberry, high CO_2 (600 mol mol-1 above ambient CO_2) increased fructose, glucose, and sucrose contents while decreasing malic acid, citric acid, and quinic acid concentrations (Wang and Bunce, 2004).

Dong et al. (2018) conducted meta-analysis of 57 articles and found that eCO_2 increased the concentrations of fructose, glucose, total soluble sugar, total antioxidant capacity, total phenols, total flavonoids, ascorbic acid, and calcium in the edible part of vegetables by 14.2%, 13.2%, 17.5%, 59.0%, 8.9%, 45.5%, 9.5%, and 8.2%, respectively, but decreased the concentrations of protein, nitrate, magnesium, iron, and zinc by 9.5%, 18.0%, 9.2%, 16.0%, and 9.4%. This loss in nutritional component in food, vegetable, and fruit crops translate to nutritional deficiency and malnutrition to the millions of people worldwide, mainly Asian, Middle East, and the African residents. Additionally, increased eCO_2 also causes increased toxic elements arsenic, cadmium, and methylmercury in crop plants (Lieffering et al., 2004; Taub et al., 2008; Guo et al., 2011). Rice grown under high temperature regime showed the presence of higher percentage of arsenic contaminant (Muehe et al., 2019; Farhat et al., 2021). Hence, climate change not only affects crop production and productivity but also causes reduced macro and micronutrients in addition to elevated toxic contaminants and thus hampering the mission of sustainable development goal worldwide.

4. CLIMATE CHANGE AND LAND DEGRADATION

Globally, 1.5 billion hectare lands are contributing to crop production, accounting for only 11% of total land area (13.4 billion hectare). Increased anthropogenic climate change is leading to water scarcity and low soil moisture. Water shortage areas will face severe drought and become more drier and warmer in the coming decades, posing challenges for crop production. Whereas some areas will receive higher rainfall and floods, which will eventually result in shift in agriculture to the new areas. Soil erosion, leaching of nutrients from soil surface, increased chemical fertilizer used in agriculture caused land degradation affecting >25% (37.25 million km2) of the total land area around the globe (Noel et al., 2015). Every year 15 billion tons of fertile soil is lost due to climate change attributed to anthropogenic activities. As per the 2017 reports of United Nations Environment Programme, 500 mha million hectares farmland has been abandoned due to desertification and drought. Developing countries alone experienced 40% land degradation, and 78% dryland area expansion was projected by 2100 (Huang et al., 2016). The decline in rainfall will further cause soil degradation and reduction in crop yield. Frequent occurring of heat stress, water scarcity, and low rainfall cause nutrient immobilization accumulation of salts in soil resulting in dry, nutrient-deficient, infertile soil. According to European Academies' Science Advisory Council (EASAC) report, extreme floods have increased tremendously since past decades, causing loss of top soils, nutrient leaching, and unfit for crop production (EASAC, 2018). Rise in sea level and heavy rainfalls are causing decline in coastal region agricultural lands. In response to climate change land degradation, changes in vegetation, declining soil quality are affecting crop production globally (Webb et al., 2017). Appropriate management practices should be adopted to improve soil health, supplementing with organic fertilization and suitable agronomic practices that helps in reclamation and remediation of soil biologically without further damaging the environment.

5. TACKLING CLIMATE CHANGE ISSUES

In developing countries, agriculture supports the livelihood of 50–80% population. Immediate mitigation strategy is required to sustain the agriculture, support the farmers, and ensure food security to growing population demand. Changing weather patterns, as well as developing biotic and abiotic stressors, are all having an impact on agricultural output and productivity around the world. Various agronomic measures, expansion in irrigation agriculture, cultivation in new areas, changing planting dates, limiting the use of chemical fertilizers, improved tillage is required with immediate attention to tackling the climate change. Developing climate-resilient varieties through conventional and advanced plant breeding technologies are also helping in tackling the issue (Scheben et al., 2016; Duku et al., 2018; Zenda et al., 2021)

5.1 AGRONOMIC MEASURES

The improved agronomic and cultural practices at farm management level such as use of weather-proof farm equipment; precision agriculture; use of remote-sensing technology for weather forecasting; use of water-efficient irrigation technologies; multicropping for sustainable use of soil nutrients; shifting planting dates to avoid floods or heat stress; shifting planting season to equipment avail low evaporation (Debaeke et al., 2017); selecting adaptable varieties resistant to drought, heat, and freezing stress (Fahad et al., 2017; Rani et al., 2020; Prasanna et al., 2021); efficient nutrient management practices; use of organic fertilizers (Henderson et al., 2018), nanofertilizers (Shang et al., 2019), biofertilizers (Alori and Babalola, 2018), biocontrol agents to avoid use of chemical fertilizers, pesticides, and insecticides are recommended to deal with the changing climate and enhanced crop production.

5.2 CONSERVATION AGRICULTURE

Conservation and a climate-friendly attitude agriculture may be used all around the world to increase crop productivity and stability. Conservation agriculture employs no-tillage practices for minimal soil disturbances, covering the topsoil by cover crops, mulching, plant diversification, multicropping, use of water and nutrient efficient techniques aiming to achieve higher profitability through lower production costs (Su et al., 2021). More than 79 countries across the globe are practicing conservation agriculture on 180 million hectare land (Kassam et al., 2019). Studies reported that the 2 to 8% crop yield for wheat, rice, and maize has been improved by using the conservation agriculture approach (Zheng et al., 2014).

5.3 CONVENTIONAL AND ADVANCED CROP IMPROVEMENT TECHNOLOGIES

Variation is an important aspect while developing climate-resilient crop varieties. Plant genetic resources conserved at gene and germplasm bank serve as valuable sources for transferring resistance and are utilized in conventional breeding programmes for hybridization, selection, and subsequent crop improvement. Traditional breeding approaches are quite successful in ensuring food security to growing population in 1960s. The substantial yield improvements gained over the last two decades are now difficult to continue, probably because elite cultivars have attained their genetic potential. Reduced agricultural arable land due to deforestation, land degradation, and climate change also limits crop production (Raza et al., 2019). However, reduced genetic diversity in crop species limits their ability to adapt to exacerbate climatic situations. Stability and adaptability of crop varieties to wide range of environments along with yield parameters are evaluated while developing the biotic and abiotic stress resistant varieties. Phenotyping for different morphological traits is done in stress environment either naturally or created artificially in greenhouse or growth chambers. The use of marker assisted selection for related traits can improve selection efficiency. Quantitative trait loci (QTL) mapping or genome-wide association mapping are used to identify markers for associated phenotypic traits (GWAS). Verslues et al. (2014) performed GWAS study to elucidate the genes responsible for proline accumulation in *Arabidopsis thaliana*. Under drought condition, proline accumulation is significantly increased in crop plants. The single nucleotide polymorphic (SNP) marker was used for linkage analysis, which resulted in the identification of gene regions such as aMADS box protein, Universal Stress Protein A domain proteins, protein phosphatase 2A subunit A3, thioredoxins, ribosomal protein RPL24A, and mitochondrial protease LON1 regulating proline accumulation (Verslues et al., 2014). Using a whole-genome resequencing technique (WGRS), researchers discovered over 144,000 SNP markers associated with yield and yield-related characteristics in 132 chickpea cultivars (Li et al., 2018). The sequencing data were further used to conduct SUPER genome-wide association study (GWAS) to identify SNPs linked with drought-related traits. Significant association was observed between SNPs auxin efflux carrier protein (PIN3), p-glycoprotein, and nodulin MtN21/EamA-like transporter with yield parameter under drought-prone environment (Li et al., 2018). GWAS analysis was performed on 2,671 barley lines to analyze SNPs linked with salt tolerance gene region HKT1;5 located on chromosome 4. The research found that the HKT1;5 gene is in charge of Na+ unloading to the xylem and directing its distribution in the shoots. The study provided understanding on the salinity tolerance mechanism in barley (Hazzouri et al., 2018).

Current advances in next gen sequencing technologies further provided molecular basis of stress resistance mechanism in crop plants. The phenomics coupled with genomics, transcriptomic, metabolomics provides novel insight regarding the underlying mechanism, tissue-specific gene and protein expression under the abiotic stress at different development stages of crop plants (Garg et al., 2016; Kudapa et al., 2018). Another exciting approach Genomic selection (GS) involves screening of large number of elite lines using high-throughput phenotyping coupled with marker densities to improve quantitative traits in crops (Kumar et al., 2018). Li et al. (2019) evaluated $BC_1F_{3:4}$ population of maize in four different environments for trait days to anthesis using SNPs. The study demonstrated the efficiency of prediction accuracy (PA) of GS models by analysing genotypic and phenotypic data.

Development of transgenic crops for stress resistance is another approach to develop climate resilient crop variety. Transgenic refers to the transfer of a gene from another organism into agricultural plants, which may aid in improving crop plant abiotic stress tolerance. Proline accumulation in crop is correlated with drought tolerance in crop plants. Transgenic plants to overexpress proline in wheat (Sawahel et al., 2002), potato (*Solanum tuberosum* L.) (Hmida-Sayari et al., 2005), and tobacco (*Nicotiana tabacum*) (Kishor et al., 1995) have been developed to confer drought tolerance. Nguyen et al., (2019) transferred GmDREB6 transgene into soybean cultivar to enhance salinity and drought tolerance. The GM soybean showed increased proline accumulation and was able to tolerate high salt stress. However, transgenic crops undergo a lot of regulatory hurdles for approval.

Another approach to modify or alter the gene responsible for stress resistance is genome editing technologies. This is a site-directed mutagenesis method where only the targeted gene is altered/modified to confer the resistance. Meganuclease, zinc-finger nucleases (ZFNs), transcription activator-like effector nucleases (TALENs), and CRISPR-Cas-9 are among the genome editing technologies used in crop plants for site-directed mutagenesis. Compared to other nucleases CRISPR-Cas9 offers several advantages and is widely used for knockin/knockout of genes in crop plants. Tomato mutant lines overexpressing the *SlMAPK3* gene were developed using the CRISPR/Cas9 strategy. The mutant showed increased accumulation of proline, H_2O_2, malondialdehyde conferring the drought resistance (Wang et al., 2017). For cold tolerance, in japonica rice variety the knockout of gene OsANN3 was carried out using CRISPR/Cas9 technology. The transgenic lines demonstrated increased tolerance to cold stress, indicating the role of OsANN3 gene in cold stress (Shen et al., 2017).

6. CONCLUDING REMARKS

Climate change is unavoidable; however, adopting a climate-friendly approach, such as conservation agriculture, no-till farming, remediation and reclamation of infertile soil, nutrient management, use of biofertilizers, organic crop production, reduced GHG emission from agriculture may help in tackling the issue. However, to feed the growing population simultaneously dealing with malnutrition, the development of nutrient-rich high-yielding crop varieties with significant stress tolerance is of utmost importance. Crop production not only impacted by climate change but also causes climate change. Hence, a balanced mitigation approach is required to develop climate-resilient crop varieties.

REFERENCES

Agreement, P. (2015, December). Paris agreement. Report of the Conference of the Parties to the United Nations Framework Convention on Climate Change (21st Session, 2015: Paris). https://sustainabledevelopment.un.org/frameworks/parisagreement

Alori, E. T., & Babalola, O. O. (2018). Microbial inoculants for improving crop quality and human health in Africa. *Frontiers in Microbiology*, *9*. https://sustainabledevelopment.un.org/frameworks/parisagreement

Arora, N. K. (2019). Impact of climate change on agriculture production and its sustainable solutions. *Environmental Sustainability*, *2*(2), 95–96. https://doi.org/10.1007/s42398-019-00078-w

Asseng, S., Foster, I., & Turner, N. C. (2011). The impact of temperature variability on wheat yields. *Global Change Biology*, *17*(2), 997–1012. https://doi.org/10.1111/j.1365-2486.2010.02262.x

Chaturvedi, R., Joshi, J., Jayaraman, M., Bala, G., & Ravindranath, N. (2012). Multi-model climate change projections for India under representative concentration pathways. *Dspace.library.iitb.ac.in*, *103*(7). http://dspace.library.iitb.ac.in/jspui/handle/100/15902

Debaeke, P., Pellerin, S., & Scopel, E. (2017). Climate-smart cropping systems for temperate and tropical agriculture: Mitigation, adaptation and trade-offs. *Cahiers Agricultures*, *26*(3), 34002. https://doi.org/10.1051/cagri/2017028

Denman, K., Brasseur, G., Usa, Chidthaisong, A., Ciais, P., Cox, P., Dickinson, R., Heinze, C., Holland, E., Jacob, D., Lohmann, U., Ramachandran, S., Leite, P., Dias, S., Wofsy, S., Boonpragob, K., Heimann, M., Molina, M., Denman, K., & Brasseur, G. (2007). *7 couplings between changes in the climate system and biogeochemistry coordinating lead authors: Lead authors: Review editors: This chapter should be cited as.* www.ipcc.ch/site/assets/uploads/2018/02/ar4-wg1-chapter7-1.pdf

Dong, J., Gruda, N., Lam, S. K., Li, X., & Duan, Z. (2018). Effects of elevated CO2 on nutritional quality of vegetables: A review. *Frontiers in Plant Science*, *9*. https://doi.org/10.3389/fpls.2018.00924

Duku, C., Zwart, S. J., & Hein, L. (2018). Impacts of climate change on cropping patterns in a tropical, sub-humid watershed. *PLoS One*, *13*(3), e0192642. https://doi.org/10.1371/journal.pone.0192642

Ebi, K. L., Anderson, C. L., Hess, J. J., Kim, S.-H., Loladze, I., Neumann, R. B., Singh, D., Ziska, L., & Wood, R. (2021). Nutritional quality of crops in a high CO2 world: An agenda for research and technology development. *Environmental Research Letters*, *16*(6), 064045. https://doi.org/10.1088/1748-9326/abfcfa

Economic Survey. (2021). Indiabudget.gov.in. from www.indiabudget.gov.in/economicsurvey/

European Academies Science Advisory Council (EASAC). (2018). *Extreme weather events in Europe Extreme Weather Events March*. https://easac.eu/fileadmin/PDF_s/reports_statements/Extreme_Weather/EASAC_Press_Release_Extreme_Weather_Events_March_2018.pdf Accessed on 9 September, 2021.

Fahad, S., Bajwa, A. A., Nazir, U., Anjum, S. A., Farooq, A., Zohaib, A., Sadia, S., Nasim, W., Adkins, S., Saud, S., Ihsan, M. Z., Alharby, H., Wu, C., Wang, D., & Huang, J. (2017). Crop production under drought and heat stress: Plant responses and management options. *Frontiers in Plant Science*, *8*. https://doi.org/10.3389/fpls.2017.01147

Farhat, Y. A., Kim, S.-H., Seyfferth, A. L., Zhang, L., & Neumann, R. B. (2021). Altered arsenic availability, uptake, and allocation in rice under elevated temperature. *Science of the Total Environment*, *763*, 143049. https://doi.org/10.1016/j.scitotenv.2020.143049

Ford, L. (2015). Sustainable development goals: All you need to know. *The Guardian*, 19.

Garg, R., Shankar, R., Thakkar, B., Kudapa, H., Krishnamurthy, L., Mantri, N., Varshney, R. K., Bhatia, S., & Jain, M. (2016). Transcriptome analyses reveal genotype- and developmental stage-specific molecular responses to drought and salinity stresses in chickpea. *Scientific Reports*, *6*(1). https://doi.org/10.1038/srep19228

Gull, A., Lone, A. A., & Wani, N. U. I. (2019). Biotic and abiotic stresses in plants. *www.intechopen.com*. IntechOpen. www.intechopen.com/chapters/66714

Guntukula, R. (2019). Assessing the impact of climate change on Indian agriculture: Evidence from major crop yields. *Journal of Public Affairs*, *20*(1). https://doi.org/10.1002/pa.2040

Guntukula, R., & Goyari, P. (2020). Climate change effects on the crop yield and its variability in Telangana, India. *Studies in Microeconomics*, *8*(1), 119–148. https://doi.org/10.1177/2321022220923197

Guo, H., Zhu, J., Zhou, H., Sun, Y., Yin, Y., Pei, D., Ji, R., Wu, J., & Wang, X. (2011). Elevated CO2 levels affects the concentrations of copper and cadmium in crops grown in soil contaminated with heavy metals under fully open-air field conditions. *Environmental Science & Technology*, *45*(16), 6997–7003. https://doi.org/10.1021/es2001584

Hatfield, J. L., Boote, K. J., Kimball, B. A., Ziska, L. H., Izaurralde, R. C., Ort, D., Thomson, A. M., & Wolfe, D. (2011). Climate impacts on agriculture: Implications for crop production. *Agronomy Journal*, *103*(2), 351–370. https://doi.org/10.2134/agronj2010.0303

Hazzouri, K. M., Khraiwesh, B., Amiri, K. M. A., Pauli, D., Blake, T., Shahid, M., Mullath, S. K., Nelson, D., Mansour, A. L., Salehi-Ashtiani, K., Purugganan, M., & Masmoudi, K. (2018). Mapping of HKT1;5 gene in barley using GWAS approach and its implication in salt tolerance mechanism. *Frontiers in Plant Science*, *9*. https://doi.org/10.3389/fpls.2018.00156

Henderson, B., Cacho, O., Thornton, P., van Wijk, M., & Herrero, M. (2018). The economic potential of residue management and fertilizer use to address climate change impacts on mixed smallholder farmers in Burkina Faso. *Agricultural Systems*, *167*, 195–205. https://doi.org/10.1016/j.agsy.2018.09.012

Hmida-Sayari, A., Gargouri-Bouzid, R., Bidani, A., Jaoua, L., Savouré, A., & Jaoua, S. (2005). Overexpression of Δ1-pyrroline-5-carboxylate synthetase increases proline production and confers salt tolerance in transgenic potato plants. *Plant Science*, *169*(4), 746–752. https://doi.org/10.1016/j.plantsci.2005.05.025

Hoegh-Guldberg, O., Jacob, D., Taylor, M., Guillén Bolaños, T., Bindi, M., Brown, S., . . . Zhou, G. (2019). The human imperative of stabilizing global climate change at 1.5 C. *Science, 365*(6459), eaaw6974.

Huang, J., Yu, H., Guan, X., Wang, G., & Guo, R. (2016). Accelerated dryland expansion under climate change. *Nature Climate Change, 6*(2), 166–171. https://doi.org/10.1038/nclimate2837

Jaganmohan, M. (2021, April 21). Economic loss from natural disasters worldwide 2019. *Statista*. www.statista.com/statistics/510894/natural-disasters-globally-and-economic-losses/

Jatav, M. K., Dua, V. K., Govindakrishnan, P. M., & Sharma, R. P. (2017). Impact of climate change on potato production in India. In *Sustainable Potato Production and the Impact of Climate Change* (pp. 87–104). Londhe, S. (Ed.). Hershey, PA: IGI Global.

Kassam, A., Friedrich, T., & Derpsch, R. (2019). Global spread of conservation agriculture. *International Journal of Environmental Studies, 76*(1), 29–51. https://doi.org/10.1080/00207233.2018.1494927

Kishor, P. B. K., Hong, Z., Miao, G. H., Hu, C. A. A., & Verma, D. P. S. (1995). Overexpression of [delta]-pyrroline-5-carboxylate synthetase increases proline production and confers osmotolerance in transgenic plants. *Plant Physiology, 108*(4), 1387–1394. https://doi.org/10.1104/pp.108.4.1387

Kudapa, H., Garg, V., Chitikineni, A., & Varshney, R. K. (2018). The RNA-seq-based high resolution gene expression atlas of chickpea (Cicer arietinum L.) reveals dynamic spatiotemporal changes associated with growth and development. *Plant, Cell & Environment, 41*. https://doi.org/10.1111/pce.13210

Kumar, S., Muthusamy, S. K., Mishra, C. N., Mishra, C. N., & Venkatesh, K. (2018). *Advanced molecular plant breeding: Meeting the challenge of food security*. Boca Raton, FL: CRC Press

Li, D., Xu, Z., Gu, R., Wang, P., Lyle, D., Xu, J., Zhang, H., & Wang, G. (2019). Correction: Enhancing genomic selection by fitting large-effect SNPs as fixed effects and a genotype-by-environment effect using a maize BC1F3:4population. *PLoS One, 14*(12), e0226592. https://doi.org/10.1371/journal.pone.0226592

Li, Y., Ruperao, P., Batley, J., Edwards, D., Khan, T., Colmer, T. D., Pang, J., Siddique, K. H. M., & Sutton, T. (2018). Investigating drought tolerance in chickpea using genome-wide association mapping and genomic selection based on whole-genome resequencing data. *Frontiers in Plant Science, 9*. https://doi.org/10.3389/fpls.2018.00190

Lieffering, M., Kim, H.-Y., Kobayashi, K., & Okada, M. (2004). The impact of elevated CO2 on the elemental concentrations of field-grown rice grains. *Field Crops Research, 88*(2–3), 279–286. https://doi.org/10.1016/j.fcr.2004.01.004

Loladze, I., Nolan, J. M., Ziska, L. H., & Knobbe, A. R. (2019). Rising atmospheric CO2 lowers concentrations of plant carotenoids essential to human health: A meta-analysis. *Molecular Nutrition & Food Research, 63*(15), 1801047. https://doi.org/10.1002/mnfr.201801047

Lopes, M. S., Araus, J. L., van Heerden, P. D. R., & Foyer, C. H. (2011). Enhancing drought tolerance in C4 crops. *Journal of Experimental Botany, 62*(9), 3135–3153. https://doi.org/10.1093/jxb/err105

Muehe, E. M., Wang, T., Kerl, C. F., Planer-Friedrich, B., & Fendorf, S. (2019). Rice production threatened by coupled stresses of climate and soil arsenic. *Nature Communications, 10*(1). https://doi.org/10.1038/s41467-019-12946-4

Myers, S. S., Zanobetti, A., Kloog, I., Huybers, P., Leakey, A. D. B., Bloom, A. J., Carlisle, E., Dietterich, L. H., Fitzgerald, G., Hasegawa, T., Holbrook, N. M., Nelson, R. L., Ottman, M. J., Raboy, V., Sakai, H., Sartor, K. A., Schwartz, J., Seneweera, S., Tausz, M., & Usui, Y. (2014). Increasing CO2 threatens human nutrition. *Nature, 510*(7503), 139–142. https://doi.org/10.1038/nature13179

Nguyen, Q. H., Vu, L. T. K., Nguyen, L. T. N., Pham, N. T. T., Nguyen, Y. T. H., Le, S. V., & Chu, M. H. (2019). Overexpression of the GmDREB6 gene enhances proline accumulation and salt tolerance in genetically modified soybean plants. *Scientific Reports*, 9(1), 19663. https://doi.org/10.1038/s41598-019-55895-0

Noel, S., Mikulcak, F., Stewart, N., & Etter, H. (2015). *Reaping economic and environmental benefits from sustainable land management Economics of Land Degradation Initiative: Report for policy and decision makers*. www.eld-initiative.org/fileadmin/pdf/ELD-pm-report_05_web_300dpi.pdf

Pachauri, R. K., Gomez-Echeverri, L., & Riahi, K. (2014). *Synthesis report: Summary for policy makers*. Pure.iiasa.ac.at; Cambridge University Press, Cambridge, UK. http://pure.iiasa.ac.at/id/eprint/11055/

Pandey, P., Irulappan, V., Bagavathiannan, M. V., & Senthil-Kumar, M. (2017). Impact of combined abiotic and biotic stresses on plant growth and avenues for crop improvement by exploiting physio-morphological traits. *Frontiers in Plant Science*, 8. https://doi.org/10.3389/fpls.2017.00537

Prasanna, B. M., Cairns, J. E., Zaidi, P. H., Beyene, Y., Makumbi, D., Gowda, M., Magorokosho, C., Zaman-Allah, M., Olsen, M., Das, A., Worku, M., Gethi, J., Vivek, B. S., Nair, S. K., Rashid, Z., Vinayan, M. T., Issa, A. B., San Vicente, F., Dhliwayo, T., & Zhang, X. (2021). Beat the stress: Breeding for climate resilience in maize for the tropical rainfed environments. *Theoretical and Applied Genetics*, 134. https://doi.org/10.1007/s00122-021-03773-7

Rani, A., Devi, P., Jha, U. C., Sharma, K. D., Siddique, K. H. M., & Nayyar, H. (2020). Developing climate-resilient chickpea involving physiological and molecular approaches with a focus on temperature and drought stresses. *Frontiers in Plant Science*, 10. https://doi.org/10.3389/fpls.2019.01759

Ray, D. K., West, P. C., Clark, M., Gerber, J. S., Prishchepov, A. V., & Chatterjee, S. (2019). Climate change has likely already affected global food production. *PLoS One*, 14(5), e0217148. https://doi.org/10.1371/journal.pone.0217148

Raza, A., Razzaq, A., Mehmood, S. S., Zou, X., Zhang, X., Lv, Y., & Xu, J. (2019). Impact of climate change on crops adaptation and strategies to tackle its outcome: A review. *Plants*, 8(2). https://doi.org/10.3390/plants8020034

Roser, M. (2013). Future population growth. *Our World in Data*. Retrieved from https://ourworldindata.org/future-population-Growth. Accessed on November, 2019.

Sahoo, A. (2021). The COVID-19 pandemic: Challenges and opportunities in food environments to provide sustainable healthy foods. Proceedings of the 1st International Conference on Sustainable Management and Innovation, ICoSMI 2020, 14–16 September 2020, Bogor, West Java, Indonesia. https://doi.org/10.4108/eai.14-9-2020.2304636

Sathyan, A., Funk, C., Aenis, T., & Breuer, L. (2018). Climate vulnerability in rainfed farming: Analysis from Indian watersheds. *Sustainability*, 10(9), 3357. https://doi.org/10.3390/su10093357

Sawahel, W. A., & Hassan, A. H. (2002). Generation of transgenic wheat plants producing high levels of the osmoprotectant proline. *Biotechnology Letters*, 24(9), 721–725. https://doi.org/10.1023/a:1015294319114

Scheben, A., Yuan, Y., & Edwards, D. (2016). Advances in genomics for adapting crops to climate change. *Current Plant Biology*, 6, 2–10. https://doi.org/10.1016/j.cpb.2016.09.001

Shang, Y., Hasan, Md. K., Ahammed, G. J., Li, M., Yin, H., & Zhou, J. (2019). Applications of nanotechnology in plant growth and crop protection: A review. *Molecules*, 24(14), 2558. https://doi.org/10.3390/molecules24142558

Shen, C., Que, Z., Xia, Y., Tang, N., Li, D., He, R., & Cao, M. (2017). Knock out of the annexin gene OsAnn3 via CRISPR/Cas9-mediated genome editing decreased cold tolerance in rice. *Journal of Plant Biology*, 60(6), 539–547. https://doi.org/10.1007/s12374-016-0400-1

Shew, A. M., Tack, J. B., Nalley, L. L., & Chaminuka, P. (2020). Yield reduction under climate warming varies among wheat cultivars in South Africa. *Nature Communications*, *11*(1), 4408. https://doi.org/10.1038/s41467-020-18317-8

Smith, P., Bustamante, M., Ahammad, H., Clark, H., Dong, H., Elsiddig, E. A., Haberl, H., Harper, R., House, J. I., Jafari, M., Masera, O., Mbow, C., Ravindranath, N. H., Rice, C. W., Abad, C. R., Romanovskaya, A., Sperling, F., & Tubiello, F. N. (2014). Agriculture, Forestry and Other Land Use (AFOLU). *Bristol.ac.uk*. https://doi.org/http://mitigation2014.org/

Su, Y., Gabrielle, B., & Makowski, D. (2021). The impact of climate change on the productivity of conservation agriculture. *Nature Climate Change*, *11*(7), 628–633. https://doi.org/10.1038/s41558-021-01075-w

Taub, D. R., Miller, B., & Allen, H. (2008). Effects of elevated CO_2 on the protein concentration of food crops: A meta-analysis. *Global Change Biology*, *14*(3), 565–575. https://doi.org/10.1111/j.1365-2486.2007.01511.x

Tesfahun, W. (2018). Climate change mitigation and adaptation through biotechnology approaches: A review. *Current Investigations in Agriculture and Current Research*, *3*(1). https://doi.org/10.32474/ciacr.2018.03.000154

United Nations Conference of the Parties Serving as the Meeting of the Parties to the Kyoto Protocol (UNFCCC). (2009). https://unfccc.int/resource/docs/2008/cmp4/eng/11a02.pdf

US EPA,OA. (2017, January 23). *Climate change indicators: Atmospheric concentrations of greenhouse gases | US EPA*. US EPA. www.epa.gov/climate-indicators/climate-change-indicators-atmospheric-concentrations-greenhouse-gases

Verslues, P. E., Lasky, J. R., Juenger, T. E., Liu, T.-W., & Kumar, M. N. (2014). Genome-wide association mapping combined with reverse genetics identifies new effectors of low water potential-induced proline accumulation in arabidopsis. *Plant Physiology*, *164*(1), 144–159. https://doi.org/10.1104/pp.113.224014

Wang, L., Chen, L., Li, R., Zhao, R., Yang, M., Sheng, J., & Shen, L. (2017). Reduced drought tolerance by CRISPR/Cas9-Mediated SlMAPK3 mutagenesis in tomato plants. *Journal of Agricultural and Food Chemistry*, *65*(39), 8674–8682. https://doi.org/10.1021/acs.jafc.7b02745

Wang, S., & Bunce, J. (2004). Elevated carbon dioxide affects fruit flavor in field-grown strawberries (Fragaria×ananassa Duch). *Journal of the Science of Food and Agriculture*, *84*(12), 1464–1468. https://doi.org/10.1002/jsfa.1824

Webb, N. P., Marshall, N. A., Stringer, L. C., Reed, M. S., Chappell, A., & Herrick, J. E. (2017). Land degradation and climate change: Building climate resilience in agriculture. *Frontiers in Ecology and the Environment*, *15*(8), 450–459. https://doi.org/10.1002/fee.1530

Yadav, S., Modi, P., Dave, A., Vijapura, A., Patel, D., & Patel, M. (2020). Effect of abiotic stress on crops. *www.intechopen.com*. IntechOpen. www.intechopen.com/chapters/68945

Zenda, T., Liu, S., Anyi, D., & Duan, H. (2021). Advances in cereal crop genomics for resilience under climate change. *ProQuest*, *502*. https://doi.org/10.3390/life11060502

Zhao, C., Liu, B., Piao, S., Wang, X., Lobell, D. B., Huang, Y., . . . Asseng, S. (2017). Temperature increase reduces global yields of major crops in four independent estimates. *Proceedings of the National Academy of Sciences*, *114*(35), 9326–9331.

Zhao, C., Piao, S., Huang, Y., Wang, X., Ciais, P., Huang, M., Zeng, Z., & Peng, S. (2016a). Field warming experiments shed light on the wheat yield response to temperature in China. *Nature Communications*, *7*(1). https://doi.org/10.1038/ncomms13530

Zhao, C., Piao, S., Wang, X., Huang, Y., Ciais, P., Elliott, J., Huang, M., Janssens, I. A., Li, T., Lian, X., Liu, Y., Müller, C., Peng, S., Wang, T., Zeng, Z., & Peñuelas, J. (2016b). Plausible rice yield losses under future climate warming. *Nature Plants*, *3*(1). https://doi.org/10.1038/nplants.2016.202

Zheng, C., Jiang, Y., Chen, C., Sun, Y., Feng, J., Deng, A., Song, Z., & Zhang, W. (2014). The impacts of conservation agriculture on crop yield in China depend on specific practices, crops and cropping regions. *The Crop Journal*, *2*(5), 289–296. https://doi.org/10.1016/j.cj.2014.06.006

Zheng, Y., Li, F., Hao, L., Shedayi, A. A., Guo, L., Ma, C., Huang, B., & Xu, M. (2018). The optimal CO2 concentrations for the growth of three perennial grass species. *BMC Plant Biology*, *18*(1). https://doi.org/10.1186/s12870-018-1243-3

Zhongming, Z., Linong, L., Wangqiang, Z., & Wei, L. (2021). *AR6 climate change 2021: The physical science basis—IPCC*. Ipcc.ch; IPCC. www.ipcc.ch/report/sixth-assessment-report-working-group-i/

Zhu, C., Kobayashi, K., Loladze, I., Zhu, J., Jiang, Q., Xu, X., Liu, G., Seneweera, S., Ebi, K. L., Drewnowski, A., Fukagawa, N. K., & Ziska, L. H. (2018). Carbon dioxide (CO2) levels this century will alter the protein, micronutrients, and vitamin content of rice grains with potential health consequences for the poorest rice-dependent countries. *Science Advances*, *4*(5), eaaq1012. https://doi.org/10.1126/sciadv.aaq1012

7 Environment and Sustainable Development

Ashita Rai and M. H. Fulekar

CONTENTS

1. Introduction 117
2. Sustainable Development 118
   2.1 Sustainable Development Goals at a Glance (Source: United Nations Environment Management Group) 118
3. Sustainable Development Perspectives 119
   3.1 Climate Change 119
   3.2 Sustainable Development: Energy Perspective 121
   3.3 Climate Change and Society 122
   3.4 Sustainable Development and Education 123
4. Activities Related to Environment and Sustainable Development 123
5. Achieving Sustainable Development 125
6. Environmental Governance 126
References 126

1. INTRODUCTION

The term "environment" implies to every living and non-living occurring naturally across the globe or in a particular segment of it. It embodies all biotic and abiotic entities in environment which interact with one another. Living beings, fauna, flora, microbes, and also other living creatures constitute the biological element of the ecosystem; non-living viz. air, water, soil, and rock form the abiotic aspect. There is indeed a synergistic relation between both the environmental elements (Carnwath & Nelson, 2017). Human actions are limited mainly by 2 uncertainties enforced by the planet: (1) limited resources and (2) ecological coping capability (Walls, 2018). Nearly 1.6 billion people around the world rely on natural reserves for their survival. About 60 million of them live in agriculturally marginal or inadequate regions having fragile ecosystems (Food and Agriculture Organization, 2014). As a result, industrialized nations should undertake greater responsibility and define their ambitions to restructure their economies to reduce resource and energy demand (United Nations i, 2015). The fundamental objective in accomplishing sustainability is to integrate the ideals of sustainability in governmental laws and measures, as well as to reverse the damages to the environment (United Nations i, 2015). According to the World Summit on Sustainable Development 2002, eradicating poverty, changing consumption and production system, and assessing and controlling diversity for socioeconomic success are the primary requirements for sustainable growth.

DOI: 10.1201/9781003205548-7

2. SUSTAINABLE DEVELOPMENT

Sustainability focuses on reducing environmental stresses in order to fulfil the demands of the present generation without jeopardising the environmental quality for subsequent generations (Rankin, 2014). Sustainable development is indeed a strategy for a country's economic growth which does not endanger the environment's condition for a better future (Mensah, 2019). Land degradation, soil depletion, air and water contamination, deforestation, as well as other ecosystem destruction are being paid in the name of economic expansion (Ali & de Oliveira, 2018). This harm might outweigh the benefits of higher-quality products and services (Everett et al., 2010). The sustainable development goals (SDGs) were endorsed by the United Nations (ii) in 2015 as a fundamental order to eliminate economic inequality, preserve biodiversity, and ensure that all 17 SDGs could be achieved by 2030. They highlighted those activities in one area impose an impact on the others, so the growth should align with the social, economic, and environmental sustainability. Nations agreed to strengthen those who are the most vulnerable. SDGs aim to reduce income inequality, malnutrition, and gender discrimination (United Nations Development Programme (i) n.d.). To attain the SDGs in whatever scenario, innovation, technical expertise, technology, and economic resources are required (United Nations Development Programme (ii), n.d.). The SDGs are a roadmap for a healthier and more efficient future for everyone (United Nations Environment Management Group, n.d.). The 2030 Agenda emphasizes on addressing the global concerns such as poverty, inequality, global warming, environmental destruction, peace, and justice (United Nations iii, n.d.). The targets are interrelated, and it is imperative that we accomplish every objective by 2030 in ensuring a just transformation which spares nothing behind.

2.1 SUSTAINABLE DEVELOPMENT GOALS AT A GLANCE (SOURCE: UNITED NATIONS ENVIRONMENT MANAGEMENT GROUP)

i. **No Poverty**—All types of poverty must be eradicated.
ii. **Zero Hunger**—Eliminate hunger, strengthen food availability, and boost farming.
iii. **Good Health and Wellbeing**—Assure that every individual lives a robust life and encourage proper living.
iv. **Quality Education**—Assure high-quality, comprehensive and equitable education to every child and encourage lifetime opportunities to learn.
v. **Gender Equality**—Empowerment of female gender.
vi. **Clean Water and Sanitation**—Guarantee freshwater and sanitation is managed sustainably and every individual has that everyone has accessibility to it.
vii. **Access to Affordable Energy**—Assure everybody has access to cheap, reliable, safe, and efficient energy.
viii. **Economic Growth and Decent Labour**—Strengthen long-term, comprehensive, and enhancing economic growth, as well as considerable and adequate work opportunity for all.

Environment and Sustainable Development

ix. **Industry Innovation and Infrastructure**—Build strong mechanisms, promote inclusive and long-term industrial growth, and foster creativity.
x. **Reduced inequalities**—Reduce disparities between and within economies.
xi. **Sustainable Cities and Communities**—Create inclusive, robust, and sustainable cities and human habitation.
xii. **Responsible Consumption and Production**—Ascertain that the norms in production and trade are always in equilibrium.
xiii. **Climate Action**—Consider taking quick action to combat climatic change and its effects.
xiv. **Life below Water**—To accomplish sustainable growth, water resources must be preserved and maintained.
xv. **Life on Land**—Preserve, rehabilitate, and encourage the appropriate utilization of terrestrial ecosystems, conserve biodiversity responsibly, prevent desertification, prevent soil erosion, and manage forest.
xvi. **Peace, Justice, and Strong Institutions**—For long-term development, foster peaceful and inclusive societies, ensure universal access to justice, and construct efficient, responsible organizations at all stages.
xvii. **Partnerships for the Goals**—Enhance implementation mechanisms and rejuvenate the global collaboration for sustainability.

3. SUSTAINABLE DEVELOPMENT PERSPECTIVES

3.1 CLIMATE CHANGE

Climate change must be treated as a consumer behavioural challenge instead of a manufacturing concern. (McMichael et al., 2003). A consumption-based strategy for ecologically sustained economic development, instead of a production-based strategy, will strengthen the formulation and implementation of climate protection and other environmental issues. Furthermore, incorporation in the arena of global burden sharing, where benefits aren't really distributed equally, demands a very distinct organizational blueprint driven by political equality and technology transfer, instead of cost-benefit analysis and obligations to cut pollution based on global negotiations (Sanwal, 2008).

Identifying the perfect strategy to tackle climate change has proven to be a difficult task. FutureGen, first ever coal-fired power station in the United States to absorb CO_2 and store it underneath, showcasing carbon capture and storage technique, was reformed as FutureGen 2.0, which could incorporate oxy-combustion technology to capture CO_2. Harvesting and isolating CO_2 from other gases, compression and transport of CO_2 to the sequestration facility, and infusing CO_2 into geologic formations for prolonged storage are all part of the technology (Folger, 2014). Sadly, the U.S. Department of Energy closed the project, alleging a failure to fulfil the timeline of using one billion dollars, and withheld the remaining funds (Tollefson, 2015). As per new research, ethanol, a biofuel that was supposed to lessen reliance on imported fuels, has instead exacerbated global warming. The environmental advantages of crop-based fuels are so low due to the fuel rebound effect that they are unable to cut greenhouse gases until a radical breakthrough in technology dramatically reduces

FIGURE 7.1 The sustainable development goals.

Source: National Geographic www.nationalgeographic.org/article/sustainable-development-goals

its carbon intensity (Hill et al., 2016). Due to their robust economic development, industrialized nations must exert pressure on commitments to cut CO_2 emissions. The United States percentage of world carbon emissions, both in total and per capita, is three times more than its population, ranking it one of the greatest CO_2 emitters.

India's emission contribution, on the other hand, is lesser than its population percentage. For example, the United States consumes three times as much electricity as India (Tillman, 2018). The said unequal utilization and greenhouse gas emission raises concerns on how the responsibility of lowering the problem of climate change must be distributed between individuals and countries across the world, given that different factions bear different duties for creating the damage and are vulnerable to the damage linked to climate change.

Under this perspective, there are three issues with the way existing issue has been conceptualized:

- Primarily, long-term usage of environmental reserves is linked to economic prosperity, with the costs of deferring estimates can be far costlier than efforts taken to tackle the problem (Braat et al., 2008).
- Secondly, it emphasizes the need for international-regional frameworks to be negotiated just so emerging economies could be involved in sectors in which there are no environmental regulations.
- Finally, it aims to create a worldwide market framework to ensure productivity improvements, which corresponds to cut rates in developed nations. This methodology totally eliminates the ethical issue of industrialized nations releasing carbon emissions in excess of its due proportion of tolerable global emissions having an urgent obligation to cut those national emissions regardless of worldwide cost-benefit analyses.

Global warming and other environmental challenges should've been viewed as issues with natural resource utilization trends. One such strategy would've centred emphasis solely on a single thing and demanded a significant reduction in resource use in developed nations. As a response, the Earth Summit in 1992 and the Rio Conference on Environment and Development in 1992 both put climate change on the UN's table as a matter of manufacturing processes. As emerging economies began to modernize, this framework presented a chance to continue efforts to push a large portion of the environmental clean-up load to such nations.

3.2 Sustainable Development: Energy Perspective

Electricity generation and consumption are linked not just to climate change as well as to other environmental issues such as poor air quality, ozone layer depletion, forest degradation, and nuclear waste releases. If mankind wants to attain a brighter energy infrastructure with reduced environmental repercussions, these concerns must be addressed concurrently. There is grounds to imply that if people continue to degrade the ecosystem, the next generation will indeed be harmed. There is a strong link amongst energy, the ecosystem, and long-term growth. In order to sustain growth, a community should avoid using only energy resources that have no detrimental effect on the environment. Nevertheless, because all energy supplies have some environmental effects, it is fair to suppose that some of the constraints placed on sustainability by gas emission and their detrimental effect caused in the past could be alleviated by increased efficiency. Because for the same processes of goods, energy use and contamination are typically associated with more efficient processes. Future energy consumption trends and their environmental consequences, with an emphasis upon acid precipitation, ozone layer destruction, and carbon dioxide emission consequences, are critical from the viewpoint of ecological sustainability (Dincer & Rosen, 1998). Present environment-related challenges, such as conserving energy and renewable energy generation, must be recognized and provided significant attention and evaluation.

3.3 CLIMATE CHANGE AND SOCIETY

Human-accelerated changing climate is unquestionably among predominant critical matters of the 21st century, and comprehending changing climate—underlying causes, effects, and possible solutions—remains fundamentally a socioeconomic priority (Islam & Kieu, 2021). Both socio-political variables are widely acknowledged as contributor to climate change (Rosa et al., 2015). Through its insight of social and cultural, sociology definitely has a lot to contribute in comprehending the socioeconomic origins of rising temperatures and also how sociocultural, financial, legislative, and cultural factors likely determine climate change sensitivity. The potentially detrimental consequences of increasing average temperature, including forced migration, increased civil instability, and rising levels of distress, can be explained using sociology (Dunlap & Brulle, 2015). As a result, social science may help develop climate change preparedness and response strategies, and they should be included in future climate change investigation.

Field et al. (2014) predicted that one of the prompt and critical impacts of extreme weather events—often referred as the "climate disruption" will plunge upon the world's most sociologically marginalized people—ones who have been undergoing financial, diplomatic, and historical marginalization. Other consequences include escalating tensions over environmental assets, social instability, relocation, and significant health consequences (Zhongming et al., 2013). Even through the generation of numerous sociological research investigation on climate change, the theoretical models still haven't been mainstreamed within IPCC as well as other organizations' findings (Grundmann & Rödder, 2019). Sociology has generated a corpus of research in the last few decades which can help us better comprehend the social components of changing climate, as well as its societal, organizational, and cultural processes.

Natural scientific viewpoints have been widely recognized as unsuitable for studying global climate change and environment in general. The heightened interest has led to a considerable shift in global warming examinations toward cognizance of social science, as well as sociologists' readiness to incorporate weather and climate and other factors into these research and hypotheses (Dunlap & Brulle, 2015). As a result, more sociological study upon the fundamental implications of climate change, such as "the interactions and relationships of persons, groups, corporations, countries, and all forms of organizations," is urgently needed.

3.4 Sustainable Development and Education

Education for sustainable development (ESD) as a vital enabler of sustainability is garnering widespread attention (United Nations Educational, Scientific and Cultural Organization, n.d.). During the United Nations Conference on Sustainable Development in Rio de Janeiro, the importance of strengthening learning for sustainability and strategically embedding sustainable development into academia was underlined in Agenda 21.

UNESCO launched the United Nations Decade of Education for Sustainable Development in 2005, reinforcing the value of learning in adopting sustainability and creating adaptive lifestyles. As a follow-up to the United Nations Decade of ESD, UNESCO launched the Global Action Programme (GAP) on ESD on the same day (2005–2014).

The GAP's main function is to expand and ramp up initiatives throughout all the sectors of teaching and research in order to speed up efforts forward into achieving sustainability. With an affiliation of approximately 300 academic institutions globally, the Higher Education Sustainability Initiative (HESI) had been established in partnership among many stakeholders (United Nations Educational, Scientific and Cultural Organization, United Nations Department of Economic and Social Affairs, United Nations Environment Programme and United Nations University) striving to galvanize responsibilities from institutions of higher learning to demonstrate and conduct investigations on sustainability, green infrastructure, and supporting local sustainability practices. HESI is responsible for more than a quarter of all voluntary agreements signed at the Rio+20 Conference, offering higher academic organizations a special connection for policymaking and academics at the United Nations ii (n.d.).

4. ACTIVITIES RELATED TO ENVIRONMENT AND SUSTAINABLE DEVELOPMENT

The environmental sustainability emphasizes the incorporation of financial, societal, and environmental concerns in order to accomplish a desired comprehensive idea of sustainability, which includes the following operations:

i. **Fragile Ecosystem Management:** The world had settled on to an environmental and participatory approach to environmental management that combines societal, economical, structural, and biological principles and values to ensure healthier and more productive ecosystems.
ii. **Managing Agro-diversity:** Agriculture covers one third of the nation's landmass (Scherr & McNeely, 2008). Achieving the objectives of protecting biodiversity and enhancing agrarian lifestyle and output demands a peaceful coexistence of diversity and farming (Food and Agriculture Organization, 2018). Current knowledge of the varied aims and benefits given by various degrees and elements of diversity, as well as the link among diversity, resilience, and productivity in agro-ecosystems, is extremely restricted, and further investigation is necessary. Producers'

and indigenous population's capacities must also be strengthened urgently (Food and Agriculture Organization and International Fund for Agricultural Development, 2019). Farmers may preserve diversity and avoid environmental damage within agro-ecosystems by working alongside researchers to promote ecofriendly practices, all while enhancing their individual lives. The rapid methodology too will be remastered by regional skills training, incorporating knowledge transfer (Maas et al., 2021).

iii. **Sustainable Land Management in Dry Land:** A few of the planet's most delicate ecological systems can be found in arid areas. Over 2 billion individuals are living in arid areas, and most of those have difficulty in maintaining their daily livelihood due to scarcity of marine resources. Desertification is one of many concerns, with serious consequences for people, culture, and environment (United Nations Decade for Deserts and the Fight Against Desertification, n.d.). Multidisciplinary activity, investigation, and capacity-building elements are required to encourage knowledge and dissemination of information (Food and Agriculture Organization, Global Environment Facility, 2022).

iv. **Mountains and Forests:** The deterioration of mountainous ecosystems, that are habitat to about 6 million people as well as provide fresh water to further half of the planet's population, has exacerbated existing environmental challenges like floods, avalanche, and starvation (Ives & Uitto, 1994). Forest is characterized as critical in achieving harmony between natural and anthropogenic environment in mountain regions, as well as in a bigger context (Loyche Wilkie et al., 2003).

v. **Water Crises:** Accessibility to fresh water both qualitatively and quantitatively is a must for ecological sustainability and vital water management. These are in accordance with requests for building integrated water resources management strategies, encompassing integrated coastal region and watershed management, and also executing national water management initiatives.

vi. **International River and Lake Basins Management:** Despite the fact that the freshwater resource equilibrium is interconnected and follows the hydrological processes, river systems serve as a primary supply of water for humans due to its water transport properties and circulation. Giordano and Wolf (2002) predicted that about 263 global rivers cover 45% (231 million km2) of the Earth's land surface (minus arctic regions). Depletion of limited freshwater supplies occurs as demographic groups with per capita water usage expand, with unforeseen effects such as landslides and water depletion. Despite its significance and the mounting risks, they face insufficient consideration in world's deliberations (World Bank, 2009). Out via a scientifically rigorous awareness of the entire hydrological cycle, sustainable water resource management and integrated watershed management can be encouraged. As a result, a comprehensive strategy involving individuals and organizations, regulatory frameworks, and innovation should be embedded into the regulation of global rivers and lake basins in order to minimize difficulties and maximize values deduced from such freshwater supplies whilst also identifying fair and equal sharing of profits and obligations.

vii. **Terrestrial and Coastal Hydrosphere:** Sustaining human stability and growth requires a comprehensive measure to efficient implementation of two vital environments (land and marine hydrosphere). The regulation of the land and marine hydrosphere is split into three areas (United Nations University, n.d.):
- The potable water group conducts research studies or community-level potable water monitoring throughout developing economies utilizing slow sand filtration methodologies.
- The ocean management group conducts investigations on sustainable coastal regulation and tragedy minimization models for long-term sustainability. A research organization on marine and coastal ecology, as well as social policy science, should be properly funded.
- Using skill and monitoring practice in member nations, the chemical management cluster enhances chemical analytical capability for environmental contaminants such as persistent organic pollutants (PoPs) around the planet. The goal is to create problem-driven and policy-relevant strategies for managing of chemicals.

viii. **Sustainable Urbanization:** Urban sprawl adds to the plethora of modern impediments that cities face. In several countries dealing with urbanization challenges, sustainable urban development has emerged as a critical decision-making objective (Korah, 2021). The consequences of global climatic change are colliding in perilous ways. Over half of the world's population is concentrated in cities, and this number is anticipated to climb to two thirds in less than a decade. Without careful management, configuration, and financing in the establishment of green cities, an overwhelming number of individuals might very well keep suffering from astounding adverse repercussions, with not just global warming but also lowered economy.

So far, no nation has managed to accomplish excellent livelihoods for its population without urbanization. Despite numerous attempts, no government has managed to effectively prevent or counteract the urbanization process. Climate-friendly city planning and architecture are vital not only for the safety of a city's residents but also to preserve a nation's most valuable capital resources. Safeguarding infrastructural facilities ensures people's livelihoods and enhances economic growth (United Nations i, n.d.).

5. ACHIEVING SUSTAINABLE DEVELOPMENT

Five dimensions of sustainability must be combined to accomplish sustainable growth: (1) social sustainability, (2) environmental sustainability, (3) economic sustainability, (4) resource sustainability, and (5) energy sustainability (Dincer & Ozturk, 2021). The worldwide community has endorsed the 2030 Agenda for Sustainable Development and its 17 SDGs to sustainable future. The notion of sustainability has indeed been updated on a broader level because of the agenda's five vital aspects: people, prosperity, planet, partnership, and peace, also known as 5Ps (United Nations Department of Economic and Social Affairs, 2016). The preceding five significant initiatives could be done to expedite efforts toward the SDGs.

i. **Technology:** Suitable technique adaptive to the surrounding ecology, which is culturally viable, must be implied.
ii. **Reduce, Reuse, and Recycle Method:** The 3-R strategy, which advocates for resource minimization, reusing materials, and recycle, minimizes waste production and contamination while also reducing burden on the system.
iii. **Promoting Environmental Education and Awareness**: Placing environment education at the core among all educational processes aids in shifting public perceptions and thoughts towards the planet and the ecosystem.
iv. **Resource Utilization as per Carrying Capacity:** The carrying capacity of a system is crucial to its long-term viability. When a system's carrying capacity is exceeded, ecological deterioration begins and persists until it attains a breaking point. Utilization must not surpass revival, and system modifications must not exceed the system's endurance capability.
v. **Improving Quality of Life in Social, Cultural, and Economic Dimensions:** Growth must not be confined to a small group of already wealthy individuals. Conversely, it must involve benefit distribution among the wealthy and marginalized. Indigenous peoples, as well as their traditional culture, should be preserved. In theory and legislation, there should be a heavy emphasis on civic engagement.

6. ENVIRONMENTAL GOVERNANCE

The mechanism whereby regulations are formed and executed in relation to or in prospect of ecological issues is referred to as environmental governance. Guidelines are the foundation for sustainable growth; the government establishes these rules and regulation to equip groups and institutions with the laws they must follow to achieve sustainable development (El-Haggar, 2007). Strict environmental stewardship is essential for achieving sustainable development and combating climate change. It is a fundamental tool for reducing conflicts at the international, local, national, and municipal level, as well as for forming sound policy frameworks and framework for attaining the Sustainable Development Goals.

REFERENCES

Ali, S. H., & de Oliveira, J. A. P. (2018). Pollution and economic development: An empirical research review. *Environmental Research Letters*, *13*(12), 123003.

Braat, L. C., ten Brink, P. E., & Klok, T. C. (2008). *The Cost of Policy Inaction: The Case of Not Meeting the 2010 Biodiversity Target* (No. 1718). Alterra.

Carnwath, G., & Nelson, C. (2017). Effects of biotic and abiotic factors on resistance versus resilience of Douglas fir to drought. *Plos One*, *12*(10), e0185604.

Dincer, I., & Ozturk, M. (2021). Energy, environment, and sustainable development. In Dincer, I. & Ozturk, M. (Eds.) *Geothermal energy systems* (pp. 31–56). Amsterdam: Elsevier.

Dincer, I., & Rosen, M. A. (1998). A worldwide perspective on energy, environment and sustainable development. *International Journal of Energy Research, 22*(15), 1305–1321.

Dunlap, R. E., & Brulle, R. J. (Eds.). (2015). *Climate change and society: Sociological perspectives.* Oxford: Oxford University Press.

El-Haggar, S. M. (2007). Sustainable development and environmental reform. *Sustainable Industrial Design and Waste Management, 12*(2), 48–56.

Everett, T., Ishwaran, M., Ansaloni, G. P., & Rubin, A. (2010). *Economic growth and the environment.* Munich: University Library of Munich.

Field, C. B., Barros, V. R., Mastrandrea, M. D., Mach, K. J., Abdrabo, M. K., Adger, N., ... Yohe, G. W. (2014). Summary for policymakers. In *Climate change 2014: Impacts, adaptation, and vulnerability. Part A: Global and sectoral aspects: Contribution of working Group II to the fifth assessment report of the intergovernmental panel on climate change* (pp. 1–32). Cambridge: Cambridge University Press.

Folger, P. F. (2014). *The futureGen carbon Capo9xture and sequestration project: A brief history and issues for congress.* Congressional Research Service.

Food and Agriculture Organization. (2014). *The state of the world's forest genetic resources.* www.fao.org/policy-support/tools-and-publications/resources-details/en/c/453621/

Food and Agriculture Organization. (2018). *Sustainable agriculture for biodiversity.* www.fao.org/3/i6602e/i6602e.pdf

Food and Agriculture Organization, Global Environment Facility. (2022). *Partnering for sustainable agriculture and the environment.* www.fao.org/gef/dryland-sustainable-landscapes/en/

Food and Agriculture Organization, International Fund for Agricultural Development. (2019). *United Nations decade of family farming 2019–2028.* Global Action Plan. Rome. Licence: CC BY-NC-SA 3.0 IGO.

Giordano, M. A., & Wolf, A. T. (2002). Atlas of international freshwater agreements: The world's international freshwater agreements. In UNEP (Ed.) *Atlas of international freshwater agreements* (pp. 1–8). Nairobi: UNEP, Oregon State University and FAO.

Grundmann, R., & Rödder, S. (2019). Sociological perspectives on earth system modeling. *Journal of Advances in Modeling Earth Systems, 11*(12), 3878–3892.

Hill, J., Tajibaeva, L., & Polasky, S. (2016). Climate consequences of low-carbon fuels: The United States renewable fuel standard. *Energy Policy, 97,* 351–353.

Islam, M. S., & Kieu, E. (2021). Sociological perspectives on climate change and society: A review. *Climate, 9*(1), 7.

Ives, J. D., & Uitto, J. I. (1994). UNU monitor. *Global Environmental Change, 4*(3), 261–264.

Korah, P. I. (2021). Smart urban development strategies in Africa? An analysis of multiple rationalities for Accra's City Extension Project. In *Smart cities for technological and social innovation* (pp. 157–180). Cambridge, MA: Academic Press.

Loyche Wilkie, M., Holmgren, P., & Castaneda, F. (2003). *Sustainable forest management and the ecosystem approach: Two concepts, one goal.* Rome: Food and Agriculture Organization.

Maas, B., Fabian, Y., Kross, S. M., & Richter, A. (2021). Divergent farmer and scientist perceptions of agricultural biodiversity, ecosystem services and decision-making. *Biological Conservation, 256,* 109065.

McMichael, A. J., Campbell-Lendrum, D. H., Corvalán, C. F., Ebi, K. L., Githeko, A., Scheraga, J. D., & Woodward, A. (2003). *Climate change and human health: Risks and responses.* Geneva: World Health Organization.

Mensah, J. (2019). Sustainable development: Meaning, history, principles, pillars, and implications for human action: Literature review. *Cogent Social Sciences, 5*(1), 1653531.

Rankin, W. J. (2014). Sustainability. In *Treatise on process metallurgy* (pp. 1376–1424). Amsterdam: Elsevier.

Rosa, E. A., Rudel, T. K., York, R., Jorgenson, A. K., & Dietz, T. (2015). The human (anthropogenic) driving forces of global climate change. *Climate Change and Society: Sociological Perspectives, 2*, 32–60.

Sanwal, M. (2008). Sustainable development perspective of climate change. *Economic and Political Weekly*, 49–53.

Scherr, S. J., & McNeely, J. A. (2008). Biodiversity conservation and agricultural sustainability: Towards a new paradigm of 'ecoagriculture' landscapes. *Philosophical Transactions of the Royal Society B: Biological Sciences, 363*(1491), 477–494.

Tillman, D. A. (2018). *Coal-fired electricity and emissions control: Efficiency and effectiveness*. Oxford: Butterworth-Heinemann.

Tollefson, J. (2015). US government abandons carbon-capture demonstration. *Nature*. https://www.nature.com/articles/nature.2015.16868#rightslink

United Nations (i). (2015). *Goal 7: Ensure environmental sustainability.* www.un.org/millenniumgoals/environ.shtml

United Nations (ii). (2015). *Universal sustainable development goals: Understanding the transformational challenge for developed countries.* https://sustainabledevelopment.un.org/content/documents/1684SF_-_SDG_Universality_Report_-_May_2015.pdf

United Nations (i). (n.d.). *Addressing the sustainable urbanization challenge.* www.un.org/en/chronicle/article/addressing-sustainable-urbanization-challenge

United Nations (ii). (n.d.). *Education: In sustainable development goals.* https://sustainabledevelopment.un.org/topics/education

United Nations (iii). (n.d.). *Sustainable development goals: Take action for the sustainable development goals.* www.un.org/sustainabledevelopment/sustainable-development-goals/

United Nations Decade for Deserts and the Fight against Desertification. (n.d.). www.un.org/en/events/desertification_decade/whynow.shtml

United Nations Department of Economic and Social Affairs. (2016). *Transforming our world: The 2030 agenda for sustainable development.* https://sdgs.un.org/2030agenda

United Nations Development Programme (i). (n.d.). *The SDGs in action.* www.undp.org/sustainable-development-goals

United Nations Development Programme (ii). (n.d.). *Sustainable development goals.* www1.undp.org/content/oslo-governance-centre/en/home/sustainable-development-goals.html.

United Nations Educational, Scientific and Cultural Organization. (n.d.). *Education for sustainable development.* https://en.unesco.org/themes/education-sustainable-development

United Nations Environment Management Group. (n.d.). *The UN sustainable development goals.* https://unemg.org/our-work/supporting-the-sdgs/the-un-sustainable-development-goals/

United Nations University. (n.d.). *The environment and sustainable development programme at UNU centre.* https://archive.unu.edu/esd/ESDtext.pdf

Walls, S. C. (2018). Coping with constraints: Achieving effective conservation with limited resources. *Frontiers in Ecology and Evolution, 6*, 24.

World Bank. (2009). Managing lakes and lake basins for sustainable use. *Water P-Notes; No. 24. Washington, DC.* © World Bank. https://openknowledge.worldbank.org/handle/10986/11731

Zhongming, Z., Linong, L., Wangqiang, Z., & Wei, L. (2013). *Climate change fuelling resource-based conflicts in the Asia-Pacific.* New York: United Nations Development Programme.

8 Thermal Comfort in Informal Settlements
Case Studies in Sub-Saharan Africa

Manuel Correia Guedes, Gonçalo Araújo, and Nádia Albuquerque

CONTENTS

1. Introduction 129
    1.1 Why Bioclimatic Houses in Slums? 130
        1.1.1 1950s–1970s 131
        1.1.2 1970s–1990s 131
        1.1.3 1990s 131
2. Bioclimatic Design and Thermal Comfort Criteria 132
3. Case Study: Luanda 137
    3.1 GTRUCS Visit Report 139
    3.2 Bairro Operário Visit Report 139
    3.3 Rangel Visit Report 140
4. Case Study: Maputo 141
    4.1 Workflow 141
    4.2 Case Study: Chamanculo C 142
    4.3 Building Energy Model Inputs and Outputs 143
    4.4 Results and Discussion 144
5. Conclusions and Future Work 146
6. Acknowledgments 147
References 147

1. INTRODUCTION

Africa has the fastest-growing population of any continent on the planet. It is also one of the most vulnerable continents to climate variability and change because of multiple existing stresses and low adaptive capacity. In addition, many countries in Africa suffer from poor electrical supply, frequent power shortages, and insufficient water infrastructures. In a warming world, the confluence of these factors means that solutions to the challenge of providing safe housing for populations across the continent will prove a challenge on an enormous scale.

FIGURE 8.1 The Chamanculo C' slum, in Maputo, Mozambique.
Source: Authors

Building and urban renewal in African cities has an urgency that requires a different approach to the incorporation of sustainable design solutions than those adopted in Europe. This is due to the scarcity of resources, the pressing scale of the demand for social housing, and the need for refurbished and/or new public buildings, such as schools and hospitals. All this is additionally complicated by the difficult implementation of building and town planning regulations that are often deficient or even non-existent. Moreover, solutions applied in the Western world normally includes heavy technology methods and particular design language that are not compatible with the reality of African countries. Instead, information on low-cost, sustainable, and replicable design solutions for slum regeneration are critically necessary [1].

1.1 Why Bioclimatic Houses in Slums?

As African cities are among the poorest in the world, there are challenges to accommodate this population growth, requiring the adoption of new intervention actions in urban and housing management aimed at sustainable development. This factor, coupled with high density, often sacrifices basic housing conditions, such as overcrowded, diminished, or non-existent spaces—creating deficiencies in adequate lighting and ventilation. Roofs are also a problem because they are installed without proper structure, spacing, or insulation recommendations for a given material—causing interior overheating and accelerated degradation of building materials. Overall, building structures and materials are of poor quality and utilized or applied with improper dimensions and with incorrect proportions—causing a decrease in interior thermal comfort and compromising the robustness of the construction.

The global assessment of slums undertaken by the UN-HABITAT [2] shows that 828 million or 33% of the urban population of developing countries resides in slums. In sub-Saharan Africa, 62% of the urban population resides in such settlements [3]. Over the past 50 years one can distinguish four basic phases in the approach to slums [4]:

Thermal Comfort in Informal Settlements

1.1.1 1950s–1970s

The destruction of slums was justified by urban managers by appealing to the ideologies of modernization and decolonization. This radically destructive approach assumed that the existence of slums was only provisional, a consequence of a transitional process generated by a strong rural exodus.

1.1.2 1970s–1990s

International organizations such as the World Bank and UNICEF promoted the upgrading of slums as a strategy of developing informal settlements. This new strategy pretended to reaffirm the rights of slum dwellers to "normal" forms of citizenship. The World Bank's support for slum upgrading owes much to the work of John Turner [5], who had argued based on field observation in Peru that the solution to slums was not in their demolition but in improving the environment. If governments could improve the sanitary conditions and environmental quality of slums, then residents, given their organizational skills and resourcefulness, would gradually improve their houses, especially when encouraged by the security of tenure [5]. The adoption of slum upgrading strategies marked a radical change in official attitude towards slum and informal settlements.

1.1.3 1990s

The growing consciousness of environmental problems led to a sharper focus on extreme environmental degradation in slums and the resulting risks for their inhabitants. In 1999, the World Bank and UNCHS (Habitat) formed a new organization, Cities Alliance, aiming African country governments on the need to upgrade their informal settlements and to accommodate slum-upgrading within city developing strategies [6].

The mindset shift regarding slums allowed new approaches to emerge. For example, in 2003, the Kenyan government and UN-Habitat signed a memorandum of understanding that led to the Kenya Slum Upgrading Programme. KENSUP aims to improve the infrastructure and housing of 5.3 million slum dwellers in Kenya and in other areas of sub-Saharan Africa [7].

The African countries with a very high incidence of slums—mainly located in the Sub-Saharan area—include Angola, Benin, Chad, Ethiopia, Guinea Bissau, Madagascar, Mauritania, Niger, Rwanda, Sierra Leone, Somalia, Sudan, Tanzania, and Uganda, where between 83% and 99% of urban dwellers live in slums. The very high prevalence of slums in these countries is a reflection of their low levels of income, spiralling poverty, the rapid pace of urbanization, urban development programmes, and other factors that are not readily apparent. On the other hand, the countries experiencing a low incidence of slums—are located mainly in North Africa—include Algeria, Egypt, Libya, Morocco, South Africa, and Tunisia. Within this group of countries, the proportion of urban dwellers living in slums is less than 40%, with Tunisia and Algeria having slum proportions as low as 3.7% and 11.8% respectively. When compared to countries in the previous groups, these countries have high levels of income, more stable economies, low rates of poverty, and moderate to low urban growth rates. All these tend to mitigate the proliferation of slums. It is pertinent to note that the low prevalence of slums particularly in Tunisia, Egypt, and Morocco reflect a long-term political commitment to slum upgrading, slum prevention, and service provision for the urban poor. Indeed, besides the rapid urban growth, inequality in the distribution of income—as measured by the Gini index [3]—significantly contributes to the prevalence of slums.

2. BIOCLIMATIC DESIGN AND THERMAL COMFORT CRITERIA

The use of bioclimatic design strategies can significantly improve thermal comfort conditions in slums. It is true that the use of these techniques does not promote the kind of uniform, low-temperature environments found in air-conditioned buildings. A question must then be placed: is that kind of uniform indoor environments really necessary and desirable?

In surveys conducted throughout the world in naturally ventilated buildings, where environmental conditions vary outside the conventional thermal comfort standard, a majority of people reported feeling, in fact, comfortable with their thermal environment. Other studies, conducted in buildings with central air conditioning, showed a significant dissatisfaction with the thermal environment by the occupants. This dissatisfaction could be attributed to various causes such as lack of "naturalness" and the health problems inherent to the system or yet another very important factor: the lack of environmental controls in existing buildings with a centralized system, which inhibit the natural process of human adaptation.

There is, still today, a major controversy about which thermal comfort criteria should be adopted. The conventional standards accept only a limited temperature range as theoretically "ideal," that is, within which the vast majority of the occupants of a building would feel comfortable. These conventional comfort standards are still regarded as applicable anywhere in the world, with only a small seasonal variation for summer and winter situations, despite the existing wide variety of climates. They consider summer temperatures around 22°C as ideal, with maximum temperatures

FIGURE 8.2 Maputo, Mozambique: examples of use of vegetation in open spaces, for shading. Trees generally have the effect of reducing wind speed—however, a row of trees with bare trunks for the lower 3 m may, if the foliage is dense above, deflect and enhance the breeze at ground level.

Source: Authors

Thermal Comfort in Informal Settlements

FIGURE 8.3 Street (left) and typical house (right) in Chamanculo C, Maputo, Mozambique. Considering that about 90% of the roofs are a simple metal sheet and 30% of the houses also have single-sheet metal walls—leading to serious overheating—shading and insulation may bring significant improvements to indoor comfort.

(cf. 4.; *Source:* Authors)

of around 26°C. In warmer countries, this would require the extensive, in many cases permanent, use of air conditioning systems.

On the other hand, there is now a large body of evidence from field research that shows that people adapt to their local climate, that is, people living in countries with warmer climates are satisfied at temperatures higher than those living in countries with colder climates, and these temperatures are significantly different (upper and lower, respectively) of the temperatures considered "ideal" by conventional standards. Adaptive comfort criteria [8] provide a much more realistic approach, which supports the use of bioclimatic design.

Buildings that use passive cooling techniques can be an efficient and economic, energy-efficient and environmentally friendly alternative to air conditioning buildings. These bioclimatic buildings also offer more satisfactory thermal environments—not in its ability to meet strict standards but in improving the physiological and psychological comfort of the occupants.

In slums, low-cost strategies such as improving insulation can have a huge impact on improving thermal comfort performance—as will be shown in section 4.

For a better understanding of what might mean the internal comfort of a building, Figures 8.4 and 8.5 show the psychometric graphs for various cities, representative of the diversity of climates existing in Angola and Mozambique. The dark blue area on the chart represents the climatic characteristics (wet- and dry-bulb temperature, relative humidity, and vapour pressure), and outlined in yellow is the ASHRAE conventional comfort zone, considered by the Ecotect Weather Tool software [9].

In these graphs one can observe the overlapping zones of influence of the various passive cooling techniques, based on the research by Givoni [10], [11]. The diagram shows how the conventional comfort zone can be enhanced through the use of various passive cooling techniques. The referred strategies are the most appropriate to the performance of the building in these climatic zones. Outside these areas, the use of air conditioning would be required. It can be seen that, despite the variety in climatic profiles, the strategy with the greatest impact is the natural ventilation (2—highlight

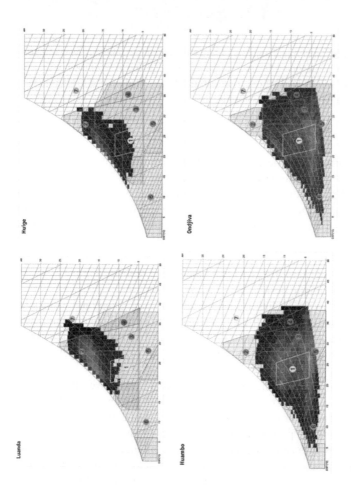

FIGURE 8.4 Psychometric diagram—for four cities in Angola—representative of the main climatic zones of the country. The dark blue area illustrates the climatic profile of the region. The diagram shows how the ASHRAE conventional summer comfort zone can be expanded through the use of various passive cooling techniques. The various areas shown on the graph were defined by Givoni (1969) and correspond to (1) ASHRAE conventional summer comfort zone, used as standard for the use of air conditioning (yellow); (2) zone of influence of daytime ventilation (light blue outline); (3) zone of influence of night ventilation (blue outline); (4) zone of influence of thermal inertia (pink contour), including zones 2 and 3; (5) zone of influence of evaporative cooling (green outline) (the evaporative cooling can also be used in zones 2, 3, and 4, for dry-bulb temperatures above 21°C); (6) passive heating zone (dark yellow) and the zone of active heating (brown outline); and (7) zone where air conditioning is required (white background).

Source: Authors

Thermal Comfort in Informal Settlements   135

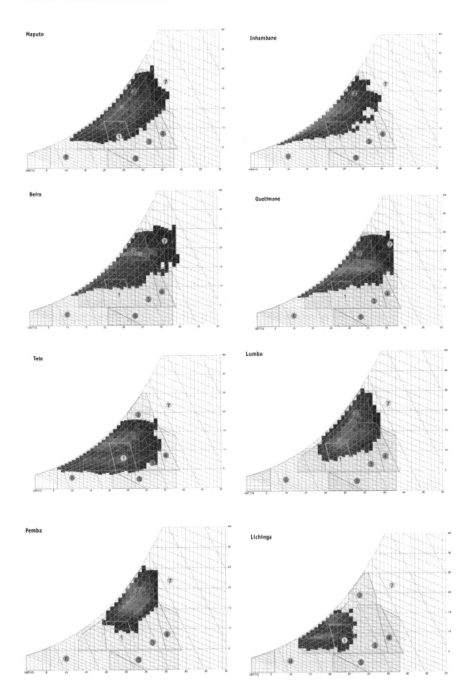

FIGURE 8.5 Psychometric diagram—for eight cities in Mozambique, representative of the main climatic zones of the country. The dark blue area illustrates the climatic profile of the region.

Source: Authors

in light blue), followed by night ventilation (3—dark blue), and especially in the dry season, thermal inertia (4—light pink) and evaporative cooling (5—green).

The need for cooling is predominant, though in some cases such as here, a small period of passive heating is also required (yellow zone) during the dry season, which can also be obtained passively (using solar energy), for example, by a proper orientation and window sizing. In very few cases, such as in Huambo and Ondjiva, in Angola, active heating (orange zone) may be required during a short period of the year—in these cases, solar thermal systems may prove useful.

Also noteworthy is that these passive strategies cover most of the climate profile (dark blue area), in a significant number of situations, such as in Uíge, Huambo, and Ondjiva in Angola, or Tete and Lichinga, in Mozambique, showing that, in theory, there is virtually no need for air conditioning active systems for cooling in these regions.

In other cases, such as in Beira and Quelimane, in Mozambique, the area which is located in the active zone (7—where artificial cooling is needed) is significant: it corresponds to the hot and rainy season, with high temperature and humidity values, surpassing the upper limits of comfort prescribed by Givoni. In these cases, one can use, for example, fans (a low-energy and economic system), or a mixed-mode system, to increase upper comfort limit—or there is now an alternative technology to conventional air conditioning, the so-called solar HVAC, air conditioning mechanical systems in which the use of electricity from fossil fuels is replaced by solar energy, a renewable source, thereby reducing the negative impact on the environment and also maintenance costs.

However, for tropical hot and humid zones like these in Quelimane, existing comfort criteria may prove rather conservative and unrealistic since they were based in empirical formulas and standards of comfort typical of cold or temperate climates. For example, field studies recently carried out in Guinea-Bissau [12] show that with external temperatures of 39–43°C, and up to 75–80% RH%, people feel comfortable

FIGURE 8.6 Luanda, Angola: the use of air conditioning can be avoided through correct use of passive design, reducing damage to the environment and operation costs.

Source: Authors

at 31°C; hence, most of the area where air conditioning would be needed would be reduced (in the presented graphs). This is an area where research is still necessary—to clarify the actual comfort requirements in hot and humid tropical regions, as in the presented cases—in order to avoid unnecessary energy consumption, with serious economic and environmental consequences.

3. CASE STUDY: LUANDA

Currently, impoverished settlements have become a dominant reality in Sub-Saharan cities, as the urban growth gains momentum, urging great scale in situ slum-upgrading programmes. There is still a significant lack of information on sustainable urban and building design for slum renewal in the African context. As environmental awareness becomes the core topic of our century, it is important to associate the refurbishment of slums with mainstream sustainability practices and policies. In addition, to avoid the recurrence of inappropriate sustained practices ignorantly considered ideal. Is it conceivable the upgrading of progressive slums in Sub-Saharan Africa that can solve its environmental and quality issues while adapting its formulation to actual and upcoming needs?

As the slum problematic has been arising, it also demands the attention and energy of African governments in implementing new policies, strategies, and interventions. The Angolan Government—for instance—is presently working in improving the slums—*musekes*—of its capital, following the 2014 Master Plan of Luanda (PDL). The Technical Office for the Urban Reconversion (GTRUCS) of Sambizanga and Cazenga *musekes* is one of the qualified and active entities in the process of implementing the PDL, which revealed the motivations and future long-term investments of the Provincial Government of Luanda and mainly seeks to solve the problems of shortage of adequate infrastructures, basic sanitation, road and pedestrian circulation, public space and housing. The irregular settlements, located on the outskirts of the city centre, are defined as the most critical areas to intervene since its representation of the highest urban density of Luanda [13].

The strategy defined by GTRUCS is very similar to the KENSUP one, which is the rehabilitation of slum areas by replacing the faulty dwellings with vertical

FIGURE 8.7 Organized Musekes (left) and Old Musekes (right) in Luanda.

Source: Authors

constructions—that can accommodate more people—in order to respond correctly to the population density. As well as providing the necessary infrastructure, services, and recreation. Moreover, GTRUCS is working on a social-housing model developed by architects *Miguel Dias* and *Acácio Manuel* that adapts to the Angolan lifestyle needs. This model also displays a sense of environmental awareness since it incorporates the concepts of sustainable building through passive design techniques, such as natural ventilation and façade shading [13].

Although measures implemented by the construction sector in recent years have somewhat improved the situation, it still falls behind expectations. The sector can only reach its true potential by the implementation of a new economic growth model based on ecologically sustainable development. In political terms, this will mean measures in such things as the promotion of usage of low-cost local materials, while simultaneously developing local typologies and construction techniques [14]. Through dialogue, both, government and community collaboration can begin to lay out their responsibilities and design programmes that communities are able to respond to positively. It is an important part of the process that these establishments understand their responsibilities and how that is linked to the success of the programme [15]. The proliferation of African slums—especially Sub-Saharan's—should be a major concern for the corresponding governments. Solutions for the slums are currently being implemented; however, they are not responding fast and effective enough in order to tackle the problem in its urgency and magnitude. The continent of Africa is in need of unconventional ideas to complement this process.

The city centre of Luanda grows vertically but is less dense than the boundary, which grows horizontally. The concerns that troubled the original *musekes*, nearest to the centre, are augmenting since these informal constructions are continuing to spread. *Musekes* vary in types, forms, size and location, subject to different land tenure, densely or sparsely occupied, with or without street patterns. Given that different contexts house a variety of slum typologies, it is clear that there is not an international feature [16]. It's undeniable the understanding of *museke*'s exclusion, since its bodily characteristics drastically differs from the planned urban centre of Luanda. The *Development Workshop* [17] classified a series of these settlements; however, we will briefly focus on *township settlements (1), organized musekes (2),* and o*ld musekes (3)*.

   i. Township Settlements—post–civil war plans, developed by the provincial government in order to build large-scale residential areas. Located on the edge of urban expansion, the buildings are predominantly vertical in order to accommodate more families.
   ii. Organized *Musekes*—social housing projects developed in the colonial period, where residential areas are built as an extension of the city centre. This plan also presented deficiencies concerning foundation infrastructures or services.
   iii. Old *Musekes*—are residential areas developed without urban planning, defined by the organic layout of the buildings, narrow streets that hinder circulation and higher densities.

Thermal Comfort in Informal Settlements

Slums started to develop decades ago but still remain a contemporary problem, even worsening because of the demography boom in urban areas. In order to solve this problem, it's necessary to embrace progressive ideologies and adapt them into the conception of new social housing programmes. The following sub-chapter present the conclusions gathered after a field trip visit to one of Luanda's main governmental entity, which is responsible for the reconstruction of local *musekes*.

3.1 GTRUCS Visit Report

A journey to the city of Luanda was prepared, with the objective of surveying the critical areas described—so as to verify its actual state—through photographic records and questionnaires. Resuming these experiences with specific reports; the first to the Rehabilitation Centre of *Sambizanga* (to make aware of the interventions been implemented in *musekes* currently by the government), the second and third subjects are visit reports of a regular—Bairro Operário—and an irregular—Rangel—*musekes*.

The Technical Office for the Urban Reconversion of Sambizanga and Cazenga *musekes* is one of the qualified and active entities in the process of implementing the Luanda Master Plan, which policies call for reconstruction of *musekes* consequently relocating residents to township settlements. Their actual system strategy relies on four important phases: 1—Delimitation; 2—Registration; 3—Construction; 4—Reintegration.

The demand of building the maximum number of dwellings at the lowest possible cost implies restraints in the decision of the minimum building areas. Accordingly, it defined the criterion of two people per room, considering that a two-bedroom apartment can accommodate up to four people. In the conception of the apartments, the accessibility adopted is by external galleries. These galleries also establish a connection with the surrounding public space and constitutes an element of shading. The three-bedroom apartment, which most meets the needs of households, is a spatial module of 3.00 x 8.00 (24.00 m2), that overlaps the structural module, which allows different responses to various programme units.

To conclude, the unplanned city—*musekes*—were built under insufficient knowledge—by people themselves—resulting in problematic areas with severe sanitary conditions. The solutions being implemented by the GTRU are motivated by relocating the people living in *musekes* to new centralities—township settlements. Finally, despite sharing many of the obstacles, the orthogonal layout of regular *musekes* facilitates the concept of in-site rehabilitation; on the opposite, the irregular *musekes*, which organic layout presents greater issues related to accessibility, circulation, and urban density, would demand a higher amount of demolition and planning in the process of rehabilitating the current structure. For that, both cases require different approaches, that are further developed in the next chapter.

3.2 Bairro Operário Visit Report

Identified by the *Development Workshop* [17] as an organized *museke*, *Bairro Operário* represents a cluster of degraded buildings with great rehabilitation potential, since its regular road system facilitates the intervention of new infrastructures.

Throughout the site's visit, it was evident that the *Bairro Operário*—although initially
intended to be regular—did not maintain the clear lines of its planning. The buildings expanded and invaded the roads organically—according to personal needs—an inevitable consequence caused by the lack of infrastructure in the foundation of the neighbourhood. Thus, the housing blocks became mutable, some resulting on the expansion of existing constructions and other annexes of new residents. The individual constructions display this diversity as the quality of the houses' materials vary between cement, wooden, and steel sheets. Through this analysis, it is possible to verify a few problematic areas within the neighbourhood, especially the ones closer to the core, where the lack of regulation is more obvious. There is also a lack of designated public spaces and services for common use, which then translates in the use of the streets—in poor sanitary conditions—for recreation and market trades spots.

During the visit, the inhabitants displayed a great distrust of strangers. Unknown people, who question and move around taking pictures, are seen as a threat to their homes. Since the government has already undergone registration processes, where several houses were demolished, this process though fell short of expectations due to budget cuts. However, the few inhabitants interviewed agreed about the urgency of new infrastructures when asked about what they would change in the neighbourhood. This would be the ideal starting point for the development of the remaining complementary structures.

3.3 RANGEL VISIT REPORT

Identified by the *Development Workshop* as an *irregular museke*—despite its mixed qualities. *Rangel*'s irregular lineage is associated with the high population density of the neighbourhood—42,097 inhabitants per km2—which encouraged the development of blocks of gigantic proportions and inhibited the introduction of sanitation and security infrastructures. Throughout the site's visit, it was possible to verify a heterogeneous structure, marked by the proximity to the organized urban centre of *Luanda*. The neighbourhood gradually becomes organic in relation to its outline neighbours—to the north, west, and south—which are regularized. The organized areas of *Rangel* cover basic sanitation infrastructure—although deficient—since the irregular area located in the east of the neighbourhood supports the scarcity of the same infrastructure.

Unlike many irregular *musekes*, *Rangel* is well-found with several services' organization, such as schools, hospitals, colleges, sport centres, supermarkets, shopping, etc. But these services are part of the regularized territory, where there is no discontinuity with the rest of the city, therefore, neglecting the irregular part of the territory. The lack of planning in the neighbourhood, as a whole, represents a great dimension that discourages urban control. In order to be able to configure and adapt to an orderly common neighbourhood, the existing division of the neighbourhood into subdivisions would have to be reinvigorated. The individual constructions are stimulated by population density since they developed rapidly close to regular buildings—with the initial aim of maintaining the same conformity—but the lack of municipal control led to the construction of extremely dense blocks with unusual dimensions and configurations, which the only access to the core is done through narrow alleys.

Quality of life is tested, and the only way to restore it is to rehabilitate the whole neighbourhood, creating new streets that regulate circulation, which also facilitate the introduction of infrastructure. The green spaces identified in the neighbourhood are of private origin, belonging to backyards and public facilities, such as the courtyard of the *Américo Boavida* Hospital and the surroundings of the *Cidadela* stadium. Due to the high density of construction, there's a lack of public open spaces [green or not] for recreation and air renovation, indispensable for *Luanda*'s tropical climate.

4. CASE STUDY: MAPUTO

In this previously researched case study [18], [19], the authors introduce a methodology that integrates algorithmic design and simulation strategies to define, study, and measure key parameters that affect the rehabilitation of the informal neighbourhood of Chamanculo C in terms of (1) environmental performance and (2) costs. Construction scenarios and design dimensions are analyzed to establish design and comfort thresholds, and alternatives are simulated and tested to identify improvements. The methodology included an optimization step integrated in the workflow that maximizes thermal comfort, minimizes costs, and ensures fairness in the rehabilitation of large sets of buildings. This step identified optimal solutions in thermal comfort for different construction scenarios, and from the obtained results we can devise a two-staged rehabilitation development process. The first stage comprises a sensitivity analysis to identify building materials regarding their improvement and cost of application, and the second defines the most suitable construction scenarios for each building from the results of the optimization process.

4.1 WORKFLOW

The workflow in this case study is divided into three phases, to structure data gathering, algorithmic processes, and sensitivity analysis (Figure 8.8). The first phase

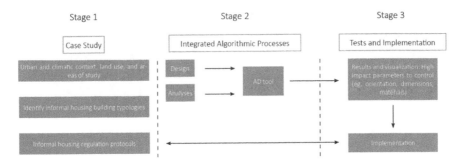

FIGURE 8.8 Chamanculo C workflow.

Source: Authors

comprises a study and definition of the case study's urban fabric and its respective building typology regarding its development and demographic situation. Phase two includes model generation and performance simulations. Finally, phase three analyzes the thermal autonomy at different scales, which promotes the understanding of how each scenario and design parameters impact indoor comfort.

4.2 Case Study: Chamanculo C

Chamanculo C is a neighbourhood in the city of Maputo, district of Nhlamankulu, which is characterized as an old suburb type A. These are mainly described as basic infrastructures composed of zinc cladding and/or cement bricks, densely distributed in non-delimited areas and showing high population density with very narrow public spaces [20]. To represent the urban fabric, we developed an algorithm to extract OpenStreetMap data and generate 3D models of the corresponding houses that match the urban landscape, covering a total of 334 building units. This allows an urban-scale analysis of different construction solutions and an evaluation of their impact on each structure of the neighbourhood. This will help to map critical areas for rehabilitation and mitigate construction and rehabilitation costs.

The most common self-made houses in the area are the "Ventoinha" houses. Landowners add units incrementally according to the family needs and their financial availability (Figure 8.9). These units usually have the same dimensions and are rotated so that the roof angles create a fan-like shape, hence the house's name. Most of these houses comprise rooms with areas ranging from 9 to 12 m^2 with exterior washrooms [21].

FIGURE 8.9 Chamanculo C satellite image and 3D model (left), Ventoinha house (right).

Source: Authors

TABLE 8.1
Construction scenarios to be tested in the neighbourhood; numbered layers go from the innermost to the outermost coating

Walls

Scenario	Layer	Material	U-value (W/m²-K)
W1	1	Zinc	5.88
W2	1	Cement brick	3.44
W3	1	Zinc	3.12
	2	Air gap	
	3	Zinc	
W4	1	Cement brick	1.78
	2	Air gap	
	3	Cement brick	
W5	1	Zinc	2.27
	2	Air gap	
	3	Cement brick	
Roof			
R1	1	Zinc	5.88
R2	1	Zinc	0.52
	2	Air gap	
	3	XPS	
	4	Zinc	
Windows			
Window1	1	Glass	1.70
	2	Air gap	
	3	Glass	

4.3 BUILDING ENERGY MODEL INPUTS AND OUTPUTS

Considering the described building and urban typology, five scenarios for wall construction materials and two scenarios for roof solutions were tested (Table 8.1). For analysis purposes, the non-existing interior walls were simulated using air wall material to ensure that the air circulates between thermal zones. A window-to-wall ratio of 0.1 was applied in each façade, and a height of 3 metres was set.

Simulation output was the percentage of time in which each house is in the comfort zone of the ASHRAE adaptive chart, a metric known as Thermal Autonomy (*TA*) [22], [23]. This analysis was made for the summer period, from 10:00 a.m. to 8:00 p.m., as it comprises the warmest hours of the year. Furthermore, results were compared with the worst-performing scenario (W1+R1—zinc cladding) to quantify and visualize the impact of each upgrade and evaluate the suitability of each scenario for each building.

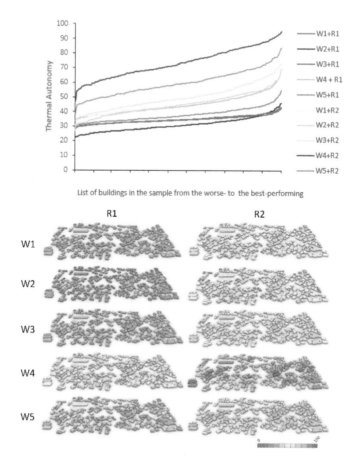

FIGURE 8.10 Chamanculo C thermal autonomy 3D model heat map for the different construction scenarios (left). Thermal autonomy from worse to best-performing house for each construction scenario (right).

Source: Authors

4.4 Results and Discussion

The urban analysis results are presented through 3D model heat maps for the TA of each building, as well as line charts comparing all construction and their TA range (Figure 8.10). While the heat maps allow the identification of areas that might benefit from modular upgrades, the line charts provide a more detailed view of the performance of each construction scenario.

By looking at the illustrated results in Figure 8.10, it is easily visible that walls W1, W2, and W3 are similar, and W4 and W5 have better performance. When looking at the same wall scenarios with roof R2, greater improvements are visible in every construction. Consequently, and regardless of the wall construction, a roof retrofit emerges as the most viable option of slum upgrade.

Thermal Comfort in Informal Settlements 145

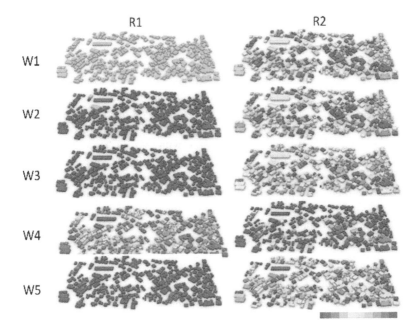

FIGURE 8.11 Heat map of increase in thermal autonomy (%), compared to the zinc scenario and roof 1 (in grey).

Source: Authors

Although most performance improvements can be identified in the heat map, a better way to visualize these results is through a line chart from worse- to best-performing buildings within the same construction scenario, allowing to observe the overall comfort spectrum (Figure 8.11).

The best-performing is W4+R2 based on a double pane of cement brick with a wall air gap and a roof composed of double zinc cladding with air space and XPS as insulation; however, it is also the most expensive solution. Scenario W5+R2, composed of one layer of zinc cladding, wall air space, and one cement brick pane, is much cheaper and also shows good improvement results with the added advantage of adaptability to the area's building typologies.

A larger performance discrepancy between walls is visible when roof R2 is applied. Buildings with W4+R1 have roughly the same performance as simple zinc walls with roof R2. Furthermore, W5, which had similar performance to scenario W1 and W3, with the first roof scenario R1, now shows a bigger improvement when the second roof R2 is applied. Consequently, roofs have shown to influence each wall construction performance and show different levels of improvement in the buildings' TA.

These improvements can be quantified by TA variation between buildings with scenario W1 and all the others with and without roof improvement. Results have shown that some houses worsen their thermal comfort up to −40%, but on average, the variation ranges from −10% up to 114%, with a maximum increase in thermal performance reaching 218%. While scenarios W4 and W5 show the biggest improvements, some buildings show a neutral or negative impact from these and other upgrades, either because of sun exposure, building density, or surface area, which motivates a spatially contextualized analysis.

Figure 8.11 shows the results of the TA variation on a scale from 0% or below (in red) to 100% and above (in green). The performance of the wall scenarios is highly sensible to the roof construction, which acts as a catalyst for comfort improvement. This is illustrated by scenarios W4 and W5, which provide little to no improvements with roof R1 and the best-performing solutions with roof R2. However, many buildings have significant TA increases with less costly walls and/or roof rehabilitation scenarios. The wide range of viable design solutions and corresponding impact factors can be hard and time-consuming to analyze and control, highlighting the need for the performed multi-objective optimization regarding the cost and TA improvement of the whole urban model [19].

Considering the presented results, we can suggest three steps towards slum rehabilitation:

- Identify buildings that critically benefit from the upgrade.
- Upgrade roof by adding a layer of insulation and zinc.
- Upgrade walls in stages, starting with the buildings that, after the roof upgrade, still have a margin to improve TA.

5. CONCLUSIONS AND FUTURE WORK

Around the world, programmes such as Africa HABITAT are addressing ways to improve people's living conditions, particularly in slums. However, most of these programmes fail to fully address important topics such as the use of bioclimatic design strategies and low-cost building materials for affordable housing rehabilitation and improvement of indoor comfort conditions.

This research highlights two case studies of informal architectural and urban practices, showing how different design and retrofit strategies affect the buildings' thermal autonomy (TA). Results show that the impact of different wall solutions can be increased through the application of alternative roof solutions. However, while some construction scenarios return little to no improvements in the building's thermal performance, others might show significant improvements. To help make this distinction, we propose the use of a heat map comparing the TA variation between the studied neighbourhood and rehabilitation scenarios. This facilitates the recognition of critical areas. Additionally, we phase the slum rehabilitation and reduce its cost, by defining strategies that gradually address hierarchical building cases and then identify the less costly upgrades that obtain acceptable levels of comfort for each building.

Although weather data and other input sources may be a cause for model uncertainty, the integration of building-performance simulation in an environmental design workflow helps architects perceive the future impact of the developed project solutions. Projects such as SURE Africa or Africa HABITAT can act as vessels for the practical application of architectural research and contribute to a more affordable and climate-friendly approach towards a comfortable and healthy environment. Future work will comprise cost analysis of the identified upgrades so that their cost-efficiency and life cycle in the urban neighbourhood as a whole can be evaluated. Additionally, we pretend to automate this workflow for any user with limited knowledge in the fields of simulation and optimization. Finally, it would be worthwhile to do an on-site validation of obtained results.

6. ACKNOWLEDGMENTS

This work was developed in the context of the Portuguese Foundation for Science and Technology (FCT) Africa HABITAT project. It was also co-financed by the ERDF—European Regional Development Fund through the Operational Program for Competitiveness and Internationalization—COMPETE 2020, the Lisbon Portugal Regional Operational Program LISBOA 2020, and by the FCT-MIT Portugal Program—refs. UIDB/50021/2020, and PTDC/ART-DAQ/31061/2017.

REFERENCES

[1] Correia Guedes, M., *Bioclimatic Architecture in Warm Climates: A Guide for Best Practices in Africa*. Cham, Switzerland: Ed. SPRINGER, 2019, ISBN 978-3-030-12035-1
[2] UN-HABITAT, *State of the World's Cities 2010/2011: Bridging the Urban Divide*. London: Earthscan, 2010.
[3] Arimah, Ben C., UN-HABITAT, "Slums as Expressions of Social Exclusion: Explaining the Prevalence of Slums in African Countries," 2015, online source: ResearchGate.
[4] Lieberherr-Gardiol, Françoise, "Slums forever? Globalisation and its consequences," *The European Journal od Development Research*, vol. 18, no. 2, 2006.
[5] Werlin, H., "The slum upgrading myth," *Urban Studies*, vol. 36, pp. 1523–1534, 1999.
[6] Huchzermeyer, Marie, *Cities With Slums: From Informal Settlement Eradication to a Right to the City in Africa*. Cape Town: University of Cape Town Press.
[7] Sebambo, Khumo, Design Indaba, "The Transformation of Kibera from Africa's Largest Slum to Promised Land," online source: www.designindaba.com/articles/point-view/transformation-kibera-africas-largest-slum-promised-land
[8] De Dear, R., & Brager, G., "Developing an adaptive model of thermal comfort and preference (Final report on ASHRAE RP—884 project)," In ASHRAE Transactions (Vol. 104, Pt. 1). Atlanta.
[9] Autodesk, "Ecotect Analysis: Sustainable Building Design Software-Autodesk," 2016. usa.autodesk.com
[10] Givoni, B., *Man, Climate and Architecture*. London: ASP, 1969.
[11] Givoni, B., *Passive and Low Energy Cooling for Buildings*. New York: Van Nostrand Reinhold, 1994.
[12] Correia Guedes, M. (Coordenador); AAVV, *Arquitectura Sustentável na Guiné-Bissau: Manual de Boas-Práticas*, ed. CPLP, Lisboa, 2011, 184pp. (ISBN 978-989-97178-0-0)
[13] Albuquerque, Nádia, MUSSUS "The guidelines for the inclusion of musekes in luanda," Dissertation to obtain the Master's Degree in Architecture, IST (Instituto Superior Técnico), Universidade Técnica de Lisboa, 2018.
[14] Correia Guedes, M. (Coordenador); AAVV, *Arquitectura Sustentável em Angola: Manual de Boas-Práticas*, ed. CPLP, Lisboa, 2011, 184pp. (ISBN 978-989-97178-3-1)

[15] Cities Alliance—available on: www.citiesalliance.org/About-slum-upgrading
[16] UN-HABITAT, *State of the World's Cities 2010/2011: Bridging the Urban Divide.* London: Earthscan, 2010.
[17] Development Workshop Angola: https://dw.angonet.org/
[18] Araújo, G., M. C. Guedes, & A. Leitão, "Integrating algorithmic processes in informal urban and architectural planning: A case study of a Maputo's neighborhood," in *Proceedings of the 35th PLEA Conference—Planning Post-Carbon Cities*, 2020, pp. 1173–1178.
[19] Araújo, G., I. Pereira, A. Leitão, & M. Correia Guedes, "Conflicts in passive building performance: Retrofit and regulation of informal neighbourhoods," *Front. Archit. Res.*, vol. 10, no. 3, pp. 625–638, 2021. doi: 10.1016/j.foar.2021.02.007.
[20] Henriques, C. D., & J. T. Ribeiro, "Habitat typology in the african city: Contribution for the characterization of the residential land use in maputo using multidimensional analysis," in *XIVth European Colloquium on Theoretical and Quantitative GeographyAt: Tomar, Portugal*, 2005, no. April.
[21] Lizancos, P., D. Otero-chans, L. Lage, & H. Vicente, *Inhabited processes Architectures where the other 90 % lives: Procesos habitados Las arquitecturas en las que vive el otro 90 %. Procesos habitados As arquitecturas nas que vive o ou . . . Procesos habitados As arquitecturas nas que vive o outro 90 %. Proc*, no. October 2014.
[22] Levitt, B., M. Ubbelohde, G. Loisos, & N. Brown, "Thermal autonomy as metric and design process," *CaGBC Natl. Conf. Expo Push. Boundary—Net Posit. Build.*, pp. 47–58, 2013.
[23] Ko, W. H., S. Schiavon, G. Brager, & B. Levitt, "Ventilation, thermal and luminous autonomy metrics for an integrated design process," *Build. Environ.*, vol. 145, no. July, pp. 153–165, 2018. doi: 10.1016/j.buildenv.2018.08.038.

9 Endorsing Scientific Hybridization of Traditional Ecological Knowledge (TEK) for Enhancing Climate Change Adaptation (CCA) Across Diverse Sectors

Suvha Lama, Shalini Dhyani, Atya Kapley, and Rakesh Kumar

CONTENTS

1. Introduction 150
2. Traditional Ecological Knowledge (TEK) as an Effective Decision-Making Mechanism 151
   2.1 Indigenous People—Who Are They? 152
   2.2 Traditional Ecological Knowledge (TEK) 153
      2.1.1 Traditional Ecological Knowledge and Biodiversity 154
      2.1.2 Traditional Ecological Knowledge and Environmental Conservation 154
      2.1.3 Traditional Ecological Knowledge and Sustainable Development 155
   2.3 Traditional Ecological Knowledge and Science 155
3. Understanding Climate Change and Traditional Ecological Knowledge (TEK) 156
   3.1 Climate Change Impact on Traditional Livelihood and Indigenous Communities 157
   3.2 Climate Change Adaptation Using Traditional Ecological Local Knowledge in Developing Countries 157
      3.2.1 Water Conservation and Management 157

       3.2.2   Forest and Argo-Management 158
       3.2.3   Transport and Infrastructure 159
       3.2.4   Sociocultural Institutions... 160
4.   Scientific Hybridization of Traditional Ecological Knowledge 160
    4.1   Need for Hybridization of TEK and Science... 161
    4.2   Scientific Hybridization of ILK 161
    4.3   Challenges with Integrations of Knowledge Systems............................. 163
5.   Conclusion... 165
References.. 165

1. INTRODUCTION

In the present century, climate change can be seen as one of the most significant threats to humankind and the overall growth and development. It is apparent that climate change is the result of the rise in greenhouse gas (GHGs) emissions (like CO_2, CH_4, N_2O, etc.) in the atmosphere of which the majority is due to anthropogenic activities (Pachauri et al., 2015). Climate variability, due to the increase of GHG emissions, affects various ecosystem services and socioeconomic sectors. These costs would be asymmetrically born by low GDP countries because of their exposure level, low incomes, and greater vulnerability to climate-sensitive sectors (Macchi et al., 2008). This is especially true for people already confronted by social and economic vulnerabilities (Olney & Viles, 2019).

    Looking at social and economic vulnerabilities, indigenous communities face a unique risk as they are at the forefront in meeting the effects of climate change and at the same time combating its effects. The socioeconomic structure of indigenous peoples is reliant on natural ecosystem services, which are, in turn, very sensitive to climate variability. These sections of people are extremely vulnerable to natural hazards and disasters caused by both climatic and non-climatic drivers (Ministry of Science Technology and Environment, 2015). Ample evidence is present in the literature that indigenous and tribal communities have been adapting to climate-induced hazards and risks for centuries (Karki et al., 2017). Often, indigenous people have their activities rooted in the belief of sustainable use of their resources. These traditional beliefs and indigenous knowledge systems are the basis of elaborate strategies to cop against any climate-induced changes. There is proven evidence that local communities are dependent on the natural resources for their daily activities, which pushed for the development of markers of local meteorological conditions and climate variability (Garteizgogeascoa et al., 2020).

    In major policy frameworks like the United Nations Framework Convention on Climate Change (UNFCC) and Kyoto Protocol, the relationship between traditional people and climate change have not been explicitly discussed (Macchi et al., 2008). The IPCC fourth assessment report (AR4) puts much-needed weightage on indigenous communities, especially in vulnerable regions and ecosystems (Macchi et al., 2008). Further IPCC AR4 emphasizes the promotion of indigenous practices. The IPCC fifth assessment report (AR5) includes the indigenous people, their experiences, knowledge, and livelihood in Working Group II (WGII). WGII portrays the indigenous people as the victims of the climate change hazards and suggests that traditional ecological knowledge (TEK) is essential in the adaptation against climate change (Ford et al., 2016).

Traditional ecological knowledge enhances resilience, reduces risks against disasters, and complements adaptive solutions for combating climate change. Yet both scientific knowledge and indigenous/traditional knowledge systems face limitations in tackling climate change impacts because of (a) knowledge uncertainty, (b) local specific applicability, and (c) exposure to global climatic shocks (Ministry of Science Technology and Environment, 2015; Karki et al., 2017). Looking at these limitations, there is a need for a paradigm shift on how these knowledge systems are approached. Traditionally, both science and traditional ecological knowledge are looked upon as separate entities. Still, there is a need to change the viewpoint, with policymakers and other stakeholders seeking to integrate science and traditional knowledge for effective adaptation against climate change.

The integration of these knowledge systems should (a) promote effective communication of hazard information, (b) improve logistic and supply chains, (c) encourage significant involvement of women in decision-making and application activities, (d) linking of traditional groups (especially women-centric) with local financial institutions, (e) dissemination of climate change knowledge (impacts and site-specific strategies) and practical skills in the local language, (f) diversification of livelihoods, and (g) new knowledge generation and situation-specific practices (Ministry of Science Technology and Environment, 2015).

The hybridization of traditional ecological knowledge for a multidimensional adaptation and resilience strategy can help developing countries to improve the realization of their climate change policies, Paris Agreement commitments, and sustainable development goals. This chapter aims to understand indigenous knowledge, its impact on climate adaptation strategies, and its limitations in the current global climatic scenario. Further, the chapter investigates the feasibility of the hybridization of traditional knowledge and applicability.

2. TRADITIONAL ECOLOGICAL KNOWLEDGE (TEK) AS AN EFFECTIVE DECISION-MAKING MECHANISM

Globally, traditional ecological knowledge (TEK) has been considered to be the rich and diverse knowledge base having beliefs, cultures, traditional practices, diverse institutions, and also worldviews that have been effectively developed and preserved across generations by diverse indigenous people and local communities (IPLC) (Berkes, 2004). Studies carried out in anthropology, systems ecology, ethnobotany, and resilience theory have supported the importance of TEK in improving livelihoods support and subsistence lifestyle of millions of IPLC across the world (Reyes-García et al., 2008). TEK supports conservation, management, and sustainable use of biodiversity and ecosystems services for human wellbeing (Gadgil et al., 1993; Reid et al., 2006; Berkes & Davidson-Hunt, 2006; Gómez-Baggethun & Reyes-García, 2013).

For combating climate change and its effects, the best available knowledge must be the centre for all stakeholders' policies decisions and actions. However, recent years have shown that scientific knowledge is deficient in tackling climate-related issues. Indigenous local knowledge is being gradually identified as an essential source of climate adaptive actions, which can be used to complement scientific knowledge in creating a robust knowledge framework. TEK has historically supported sustainable development, natural resources management, ethnomedicine, human ecology, conservation, and management of biodiversity (Nakashima et al., 2012).

To face the complex problems of the 21st century, we need to recognize the increasingly dynamic environment in which we work (Reyes-García et al., 2018). To enhance climate-adaptive action plans, natural resources management with the involvement of local stakeholders is vital. Traditional ecological knowledge is expected to play an important role in combating climate change impacts and in upgrading adaptive frameworks for climate variability and sustainability. This section gives an overview of the critical concepts of local indigenous knowledge and its interaction with science.

2.1 Indigenous People—Who Are They?

Estimated global indigenous population is of about 370 million people, which is less than 5% of the total population of the planet. Indigenous people are the treasure house of around 7,000 global languages and approximately 5,000 rich cultures. There is so far no commonly accepted definition of indigenous people. However, various international agencies have recognized that Indigenous people live in different parts of the world. It has been estimated that indigenous communities occupy 22% of the total land area, and this land-area accounts for 80% of the biological diversity of the world (Nakashima et al., 2012). They represent a large part of the planet's cultural diversity with diverse histories and languages and live in various geographical and political spectrums; establishing a common definition is a complicated matter with global implications.

However, the following characteristics of indigenous people are observed (Nakashima et al., 2012; Asian Development Bank, 2002):

- Distinct social and cultural traits in comparison to the mainstream/prevailing society
- Ancestral connection to territories and natural resources of these places
- Maintenance of these distinct cultural traits
- Self-identification and recognition
- History or prevailing situation of subjugation, dispossession, and marginalization

The United Nations acknowledges that there is no prescribed definition of indigenous peoples or communities, and generally, self-identification is the key condition (Hill et al., 2019). Looking at that, the United Nations Working Group on Indigenous People has provided a working definition for indigenous people (AFDB, 2016):

> Indigenous communities, peoples, and nations are those that, having a historical continuity with pre-invasion and pre-colonial societies that developed on their territories, consider themselves distinct from other sectors of the societies now prevailing in those territories, or part of them. They form at present non-dominant sectors of

society and are determined to preserve, develop and transmit to future generations their ancestral territories and their ethnic identity, as the basis of their continued existence as peoples, in accordance with their cultural patterns, social institutions, and legal systems.

Indigenous people face various risks and impacts due to climate variability as they are the following (Olney & Viles, 2019; Alexander et al., 2011):

- One of the poorest and marginalized section of society
- Livelihood and economic activities are dependent on natural resources
- Live in regions that are extremely vulnerable to the impacts of climate change
- Excluded from decision-making and policy formulations

While it is true that indigenous communities encounter risks and climate change will exacerbate these threats, however, indigenous people are also being looked upon as "agents of change." Most recently, the IPCC has identified indigenous people as a vital partner in the implementation of action plans for limiting global warming to 1.5°C (Olney & Viles, 2019).

2.2 Traditional Ecological Knowledge (TEK)

TEK embraces varied worldviews that include cultural, economic, religious, and practical aspects. TEK promotes the concept of sustainability through the ideas of balancing life with nature and developing deep spiritual connections (Hill et al., 2019). Although the ecological knowledge possessed by the indigenous communities is considered to be very old, it was only during the early nineties when the global community started recognizing and acknowledging them as valuable "other knowledge systems" (Roue & Nakashima, 2018).

TEK systems can be identified through several cultural and linguistic descriptions: indigenous and traditional knowledge (ITK), traditional ecological/environmental knowledge (TEK), native science, ethnoscience, indigenous science, and folk science (Karki et al., 2017). While there is no collectively recognized definition of traditional ecological knowledge (TEK), the World Intellectual Property Organization (WIPO) provides a working definition as "a broad description of subject matter, generally includes the intellectual and intangible cultural heritage, practices and knowledge systems of traditional communities, including indigenous and local communities" (Olney & Viles, 2019).

Traditional ecological knowledge (TEK) systems is a collation of diverse and dynamic, cultural and location-specific knowledge, practice and belief system. TEK is often associated with mechanical and ethnic/tribal societies (Ministry of Science Technology and Environment, 2015). These knowledge systems include spoken accounts that describe anthropological histories, cosmological occurrences, methods of communication, cropping and harvesting techniques, hunting and gathering abilities, and understanding of local socioeconomic and environmental systems (Bruchac, 2014). Generally, TEKs are communicated and recalled by subsequent generations to ensure the welfare of the community by delivering food security, health care, and strategies for coping against external fluctuations (Nakashima et al., 2012).

Houde (2007) has included TEK into six critical categories that are well interconnected and crucial for facilitating co-management viz. (1) actual observations, (2) subsistence management of resources, (3) managing lands use, (4) preserving ethical values across generations, (5) traditional identity, and (6) cosmic theories. This classification can help in understanding the various collation, validation, and finally, integration issues for co-production of knowledge. In present times, TEK has been acknowledged to be an essential supportive science that can help to find solutions to the world's major challenges, not limited to protecting and sustainably managing biodiversity, improving climate adaptive capacity, realizing sustainable development goals, post-2020 biodiversity, and restoration targets (Roue and Nakashima, 2018).

The traditional ecological knowledge systems have already been applied in various fields:

- Conservation of biodiversity and managing wildlife, natural resources management and rural development, ethno-medicine and human health, disaster risk reduction and climate change adaptations (Nakashima et al., 2012)
- Pharmacology, water engineering and conservation, ethnobotany and ethnozoology, and irrigations systems (Alexander et al., 2011)

2.1.1 Traditional Ecological Knowledge and Biodiversity

Biodiversity is an important indicator of the health of an ecosystem and the surrounding socioeconomic structure. Biodiversity and socioeconomic diversity are interdependent and go hand in hand, especially in indigenous regions. The change in consumption pattern of various resources and the environmental changes is leading to the loss of biodiversity and TEK at an alarming rate. One of the significant reasons for biodiversity and TEK loss is poverty (Mafongoya & Ajayi, 2017). The increase in poverty in indigenous regions stresses the long-established traditional knowledge systems, as TEKs are long-term and complex, and the situation demands an application of more simple and accessible technology, like chemical-fertilizer-based agriculture, mono-cropping. This shift has a twofold impact as it leads to the erosion of TEKs and has a detrimental effect on the environment.

2.1.2 Traditional Ecological Knowledge and Environmental Conservation

TEK is known to promote a Close-to-Nature approach when involved in the consumption of any resource. The TEK practices like shifting cultivation, multi-cropping systems (like mixed cropping and intercropping), and minimum tillage have been used in indigenous regions to increase the yield of crops and stimulate conservation of the environment. TEK also promotes disaster-risk and hazard reduction, especially in agriculture with the development of drought-resistant and early maturing crops, gathering of agroforestry products, and conservation and protection of sensitive ecosystems like wetlands, mangroves, and marshlands. TEK systems also are used in predicting and preparing for disasters through an array of early warning indicators, like the behaviour of certain animals, wind direction, and study of cloud shape and size.

2.1.3 Traditional Ecological Knowledge and Sustainable Development

Participatory engagement of local stakeholders in the policy and decision-making apparatus, especially in terms of adaptation and mitigation against climate change impacts, have been recognized by various agencies in the last decade. The notion that TEK is a closed, archaic, and backward knowledge system has been proved false. TEK incorporates various aspects like delineation and conservation of eco-sensitive zones, sustainable agriculture, and agroforestry for the management of the environment and socioeconomic structure. These knowledge models are based on traditions, cultures, faith, belief, and values systems, which are ecologically and socially sound (Mafongoya & Ajayi, 2017). For example, the advent of green revolution promoted the policy of mono-cropping with dependence on the external application of fertilizer, which led to the landraces loss, loss of native species of flora and fauna, loss of soil nutrition, and loss of TEKs. However, now there is a push for shifting to polyculture cropping as it has many sustainable characteristics, like low pest incidence, disaster-risk reduction, diet diversification, varied income generation, and increases production along with conservation of natural resources (Mafongoya & Ajayi, 2017).

TEK provides an all-round holistic approach by integrating various disciplines, which shows a considerable development, adaptability, and sustainability potential. This is useful in identifying proper and apt policies for climate change action. Of late, traditional ecological knowledge systems has gained considerable attention as a complementary strategy against climate change. The Paris Agreement (2015) on climate change mitigation noted indigenous local knowledge systems along with best available science as an essential tool for climate adaptation action (Olney & Viles, 2019). The authors have tried to evaluate the impact of traditional ecological knowledge for climate change adaptation.

2.3 TRADITIONAL ECOLOGICAL KNOWLEDGE AND SCIENCE

In the last decade, the traditional ecological knowledge (TEK) is emerging as a key area of interest for preventing climate change impacts. However, the interaction between science and traditional ecological knowledge dates back to centuries. Traditional ecological knowledge has been a part of humanity in one form or other, and the origins of science can be traced back to traditional knowledge (Nakashima et al., 2012; Mafongoya & Ajayi, 2017).

Traditional ecological knowledge is seen as an ancient knowledge system of gathering and analysis, which are community-specific. Some scientists argue that TEK can be deemed to be in parity to science (Weiss et al., 2013). However, others believe that TEK is pseudoscience and against conventional scientific enquiry (Mafongoya & Ajayi, 2017). TEK is neither as it is a dynamic and interdisciplinary knowledge system connecting the environment with socioeconomic and legal structures. TEK also emphasizes the relationship between humans, other species, the land, and spirits/ancestors (Weiss et al., 2013). Science-based knowledge system (SBKS) believe that for the preservation of nature, people must be excluded from it. However in indigenous views, the ecosystems and social networks are interconnected and interdependent (UNESCO, 2017). SBKS has a reductionist approach with expertise in specific domains, but complex interconnected problems like climate change present a constant test. The same cannot be said for TEK as the holders of TEK cut across various domains, and this dynamic and interdisciplinary knowledge enhances the natural resources conservation and management strategies.

The advent of global warming and the rise in incidence and intensity of climate extremes have revealed the limitation of both these knowledge systems. These drastic changes in the natural bio-geo cycles due to continuous human involvement have made TEK-based adaptation against climate change impacts non-resilient (Karki et al., 2017; Vadigi, 2016). Therefore, there is a need for co-production of knowledge using these separate knowledge systems. Combining two complex knowledge systems is a herculean task, and currently, it is limited to simple aspects of participatory roles in natural resource management practices (Vadigi, 2016). For the proper and meaningful integration of TEK and SBKS, one needs to understand that both TEK and SBKS have developed within different and distinct spheres of experience, facts, beliefs, and values (Weiss et al., 2013). TEK is often described as archaic, closed, and stagnant; however, TEK has always been central in the sustainable living in indigenous communities, which is firmly anchored in the experience of an individual, community, or place. For efficient co-production, both forms must engage in open-mindedness and learning from both sides (Chapman & Schott, 2020).

In response to the climate change–related challenges, there has been a paradigm shift in the methods of environmental management with reductionist approaches being replaced by science associated with the coupling of different knowledge systems to socio-ecological systems (Raymond et al., 2010). The integration process has many critics who point to the entrenchment by SBKS on the already disproportional relationship (Bohensky & Maru, 2011). However, this approach is vital in developing a user-inspired and user-friendly knowledge systems for environmental management (Raymond et al., 2010).

3. UNDERSTANDING CLIMATE CHANGE AND TRADITIONAL ECOLOGICAL KNOWLEDGE (TEK)

There is increasing acknowledgment of traditional ecological knowledge as a vital repository of info and practices for building resilience against climate change. Yet experimental investigations on the impact of climate change on indigenous communities, identification of appropriate adaptive options and its mobilization, which includes traditional ecological knowledge, is limited (Granderson, 2017).

Indigenous people whose livelihoods are dependent on climate-sensitive natural resources are the most vulnerable communities. These societies residing in fringe areas have been subjected to various climate-related challenges for generations, which has brought out different strategies to combat these changes (Mirjam et al., 2008). This knowledge base has helped adapt to climate change effects, but the changes in frequency and intensity of future climate extremes have pushed their adaptive capacities towards breaking point. Indigenous communities are not involved in academic, policy, and public discussions on climate change, despite these communities being the most at risk to the present and future climatic change impact (Salick & Ross, 2009).

Among many such examples, a study carried out in Mexico acknowledges that appreciating traditional ecological knowledge will improve community resilience to the effect of extreme weather events within indigenous communities (Audefroy & Sánchez, 2017).

3.1 Climate Change Impact on Traditional Livelihood and Indigenous Communities

Climate change is seen as a significant disruption influencing various meteorological parameters, especially in terms of indigenous communities and their livelihoods. Declining availability of natural resources with an introduced uncertainty due to climatic variability are threats to the sustainability of forest-dependent low external input sustainable agriculture in Indian Himalayan Region (IHR) and associated sectors (Rautela & Karki, 2015).

Study of Nepal's Tharu community concerning climate change impacts on community livelihoods have substantiated that they have a generational knowledge database of their locality and its patterns of weather and agriculture. The report further elaborates on the severe impact of climate change on their livelihoods (Devkota et al., 2011). In recent years due to shifts in seasonal progressions, the Loita Maasai pastoralists are reported to have been badly hit due to extended drought cycles that have resulted in the loss of food security because of dried local water sources, decreased crop productivity, and livestock losses (Saitabau, 2014). In a study to understand the indigenous communities' insights on climate change in the Kaduna State of Nigeria, it was seen that health, food supply, biodiversity, and fuelwood availability had a higher vulnerability to climate variability, and the marginalized poor population were most impacted by the incidence of climate change (Ishaya & Abaje, 2008).

Several adaptive measures practised by Charazani indigenous tribes in Andes Bolivia helped them to cope with climate vulnerability. These approaches are mostly traditional/indigenous adaptive practices in agriculture and risk management. These approaches are applied in complement with modern practices in agriculture, like land-use intensification, irrigation system diversification, and artificial fertilizers usage. There are a large number of possible adaptation methods that indigenous communities can implement to promote adaptive capacity, the study focused on lowering vulnerability to hazards caused by climate change, thus improving livelihood strategies (Riva et al., 2013).

3.2 Climate Change Adaptation Using Traditional Ecological Local Knowledge in Developing Countries

3.2.1 Water Conservation and Management

Various local communities manage water as a natural resource as it's considered as common property. The traditional water management system is a means to strengthen the representative constructions and satisfy community water-related demands, which is rooted in the community's traditions and faith-belief systems (Singh, 2006). Indigenous resource management systems symbiotically exist along and intermingle with modern institutional systems of state-based land and water management frameworks (Sue, 2011). Every government aims to attain sustainable water supply and sanitation in both rural and urban spheres. The design of these management mechanisms are devoid of local traditions and faith-belief systems. However, there is an enormous opportunity for integrating indigenous water management practices into conventional science-based water conservation frameworks.

Traditional ecological knowledge is often overlooked and replaced with a science-based framework when talking about water resource management (Behailu et al., 2016). Borana and Konso communities in southern Ethiopia can provide some evidence regarding the same. Boranas have the Ella (wells) and Konsos have the Harta (ponds), which are dictated by the natural hydrogeological conditions. The concepts of cost retrieval, ownership, equity, enforcement, integrity, and unity, which are highly distinct in contemporary systems, are also seen in the indigenous water managements of Borana and Konso communities. These experiences are relevant and effective for the Borana and Konso communities (Behailu et al., 2016).

In the last 100 years, the farmers of Wadi Laba, Eritrea, have developed and implemented a large number of traditional water management strategies for the (re) construction and maintenance obligations along with the requirement to impartially allocate the floodwater among the upstream and downstream needs (Haile et al., 2005). IPLC has had an important role in conserving and managing aquatic resources, and environmental flows have been considered a relevant scientific area that can help in protecting indigenous rights and interests in water conservation (Finn & Jackson, 2011).

Indigenous rights to water are not acknowledged, and the challenges faced by indigenous communities in safeguarding this right can be substantiated by the experimental water supply and sanitation data. The devaluing of the importance of this right due to cultural differences can be seen as a precursor to the bias exhibited in poor water supply and sanitation provision for indigenous communities (McLean, 2007). This bias, due to the culturally insensitive government-led engagement advances, puts forward a weak or absent political resolve to promote indigenous participation in water resource conservation and management practices. Science-based frameworks tend to presume that indigenous water interests are "just cultural" and thereby limit their viewpoints and involvement (Maclean, 2015). Non-existent documentation of indigenous knowledge, traditions, and faith-belief systems further disenfranchises the indigenous communities when discussing water-related issues.

3.2.2 Forest and Argo-Management

There is clear evidence that TEK has an essential role in forest preservation. However, peer-reviewed studies evaluating the extent of TEK involvement in modern forest conservation practices when compared with other variables are rare. There was a high overlay, reported by a study conducted in Bolivian Amazon, between traditional ecological knowledge (TEK) and modern forest preservation practices (Paneque-Gálvez et al., 2018).

Adi indigenous community in East and Upper Siang districts of Arunachal Pradesh are rich in TEK linked to bio-cultural resources, which plays a vital part in combating with climate uncertainty for sustainable livelihoods. To adapt to the future climate change, Adi communities have been establishing "community reserve forests" (CRF) within undisturbed community forest landscapes and seeking support from environmental agencies to link their CRFs with REDD projects that can support economic benefits through rewards and incentives. The future of the Adi tribe's biocultural resources and livelihood sustainability will largely depend on their TEK and their role in research, planning, and policy implementation for climate change mitigation and adaptation (Singh et al., 2011).

A study carried out, in the Congo Basin, for mapping climate vulnerability of indigenous forest communities reported that lifestyle, traditions-culture, and the livelihood approaches employed have a high impact on the vulnerability of these communities. To cite an example, for the Pygmies living within the forests, the nomadic collection of non-timber forest products (NTFPs) forest resources is a major livelihood option, whereas for the Bantus, who live on forest margins, sedentary farming is the primary livelihood option with the forest as an additional prospect. These distinctive lifestyles have major consequences on each communities' vulnerability and adaptation potential. These different and unique lifestyles and livelihood options need to be considered when preparing any climate change adaptation strategies (Nkem et al., 2013). To improve the local adaptive capacities to combat climate impacts in the forest sectors, the following parameters be to be worked on (Sonwa et al., 2012):

- Reducing poverty
- Enhancing food security
- Water availability
- Combating land degradation
- Reducing the loss of biological diversity

3.2.3 Transport and Infrastructure

For centuries, Western and other colonialisms have shaped our transport mechanisms across the world; however, there is a need for a paradigm shift to move beyond the colonial legacy (Schwanen, 2018). The utilization and deployment of indigenous transport knowledge systems is the need of the hour, which could provide a resilient alternate method to meet several rural development goals. Transport and infrastructure play a crucial role in pushing for rural socioeconomic growth and development. Looking at the present climate scenario, the integration of indigenous transport systems into mainstream rural transport options could reduce climate vulnerability and act as vanguards for improved transport service distribution (Chakwizira & Nhemachena, 2012).

It has been seen that traditional local knowledge systems can be enhanced to complement modern transportation and infrastructure systems for affordable access and mobility interventions. Traditional local knowledge-based infrastructure and transportation interventions can support various government agencies to implement its mandate for rural development schemes and service dissemination (Nhemachena & Hassan, 2007). The case study of Bucharest, Romania, supports the use of traditional local knowledge and sustainable transport to promote the development of greener cities and towns (Niţă et al., 2018; Mihai et al., 2018). Local Aboriginal design knowledge has been engaged to empower Aboriginal communities, culturally and economically, while promoting and strengthening built environment goals, which include the communities' varied knowledge systems (Hromek, 2019).

3.2.4 Sociocultural Institutions

Institutions are a significant factor explaining development outcomes. Every social institution in any given community provides the essential social needs of community members. Before industrialization era, traditional institutions were able to satisfy the various societal needs by incorporating unique mechanisms (Ukpong-Umo & Mboho, 2014). Modernization has changed every section of human society (Menhas, 2014), and to bring about socioeconomic and environmental harmony, we must recognize, identify, and study the local knowledge systems, their traditional institutions, cultures, and faith-belief systems (Kassa, 2006). Considerable studies have been conducted to analyze climate impacts and how communities react, adapt to these impacts; however, it's critical to question and evaluate the capacity of established institutions and arrangements used for community-level adaptation strategies. The success of these efforts centres on the nature of existing formal and informal sociocultural institutions (Mubaya & Mafongoya, 2017).

Review of case studies also indicates that local traditional institutions play a vital role in moulding and influencing the adaptation strategies for combating climate change: they link households to local resources and communal and supportive action, regulate the movement of external reinforcement to various social clusters, and connect local communities to national policy decisions and governance (Agrawal et al., 2008). Traditional local institutions boost cooperation as individuals expect that their aid and investment will be satisfied with some benefits or rewards (Goist & Kern, 2018). An example would be the Afoosha social networks in Ethiopian villages, which provide a local conduit for proper dissemination of technology adoption and innovation, which could help policymakers to combine various approaches for better and faster technology adoption (Desalegn et al., 2019).

4. SCIENTIFIC HYBRIDIZATION OF TRADITIONAL ECOLOGICAL KNOWLEDGE

Any knowledge system, be it TEK or science, goes through a two-step growth process. One is the fragmentation of established disciplines and the other being the recombination depending on the demand of the situation. The reintegration of these fractured specialties is the need of the hour, especially for combating climate change. The climate change impacts are far-reaching in nature and integration or hybridization of various knowledge systems is necessary to tackle and mitigate its effects on different spectrums of human life. Hybridization can be defined as a process of burrowing-lending concepts, methods, theories, and evidences (Dogan, 1996), and building these interactions between TEK and SBKS has been recognized as a pivotal opportunity to move towards sustainable ecosystem governance at multiple scales (Hill et al., 2020).

The hybridization of TEK and science is a very challenging process with various moving parts and multiple stakeholders; therefore, it requires a proper co-management approach with the distribution of power and knowledge sharing along with reconciliation and reclamation of indigenous rights (Chapman & Schott, 2020). If properly executed, the knowledge product of the integration of scientific technology and assessment with local indigenous knowledge could provide the vulnerable communities and policymakers with a robust knowledge database for decision-making on any environment-related issues (Hiwasaki et al., 2014).

4.1 Need for Hybridization of TEK and Science

Indigenous communities are adapting to climate-related risks and impacts for generations. These adaptation strategies are based on inter-generational traditional knowledge, which have developed situation-specific strategies like external hazard proof livelihood practices, traditional methods of conservation and management of resources, and overall improvement of household and community adaptive capacity. However, the current changes in climate extremes have shown limitations of indigenous knowledge in combating climate change impacts (Karki et al., 2017).

Even though the actual climate adaptation implementation takes place at microspatial level, current climate adaptation plans and policies are designed with regional or national scale in mind; the top-down approach is given high importance without understanding the local scenarios, processes, and dynamics (Srinivasan, 2004). The modern climate adaptation strategies are based on diagnostic-prescription-intervention model (Makondo & Thomas, 2018) where climate policymakers study the local problems due to climate change and propose/implement solutions based on global interaction and implications. This leads to embitterment in the local populace as the adaptation technologies prescribed falls short due to inappropriate diagnostic-prescription-intervention model implementation.

Knowledge hybridization promotes resilience, to withstand any external changes and impact, which takes cognizance when talking about climate change (Bohensky & Maru, 2011). The integration of TEK and SBKS has shown that it diminishes the weakness and shores up the strengths of the two knowledge systems. Gagnon and Berteaux (2009) and Garnett et al. (2018) have reported that the integration of TEK with SBKS has expanded the scales (spatial and temporal) of scientific knowledge, and Alexander et al. (2011) informed that indigenous narratives developed climate-related knowledge in areas without scientific documentation of climate change impact.

Therefore, it is necessary for the integration/hybridization of both these knowledge systems for proper implementation of science-based adaptation solutions as well as conservation of traditional ecological knowledge.

4.2 Scientific Hybridization of ILK

Current climate adaptation plans follow a top-down strategy, which leaves the local stakeholders as a passive participant. Therefore, to improve the implementability and adaptive capability of local people, a bottom-up approach with local participation in the early stage decision-making as well as the selection of adaptation strategies is necessary (Srinivasan, 2004). Local participation in all stages of research, technology development, implementation, dissemination, and evaluation can lead to a robust climate adaptation measure and must be kept in mind when integrating traditional ecological knowledge with science.

One of the easiest and cost-effective methods to promote local participation would be the implementation of capacity building and awareness programmes. These programmes can be used to document and preserve traditional knowledge as well as expose the local people to science and advise them on how the integration of these two knowledge systems benefits and improves their adaptive capacity. Harrison et al. (2018) describes (1) intergenerational information exchange, (2) adapting to changes in regulations, and (3) validation of traditional ecological knowledge as the critical drivers for knowledge hybridization.

Various studies have been listed in the next section (Table 9.1) that provides a conceptual or implemented knowledge hybridization strategy. These strategies have

TABLE 9.1
Various conceptual/practical strategies for TEK and science hybridization

Framework for hybridization	Authors
Utilitarian approach—a top-down management system where TEK would be seen as a supplementary information source. **Political approach**—the power relations between the two knowledge systems. **Integrative system**—a collaborative and symbiotic approach between the two knowledge systems for co-production of new knowledge.	Weiss et al. (2013)
Two-eyed seeing method: The process dictates that parties from both sides of the aisle weigh the perspectives of each knowledge system equally in terms of their importance and validity. This method can be further extended to the multi-seeing method to indicate the potential of multiple cultural perspectives.	Bartlett et al. (2012)
Knowledge coevolution framework: This framework strives to address the power and knowledge sharing dynamics and creates an environment for self-determination through a transfer of knowledge to local members using capacity building, training, and practical experience in research and governance.	Chapman & Schott (2020)
Integration model management of forest ecosystems: The model interfaces forest land-use systems (a combination of TEK and science management practices) and vegetation dynamics to promote forest ecosystem resilience.	Vadigi (2016)
Case studies on TEK integration with science: **Sustainable Uplands project (U.K.)** combines different forms of knowledge using an iterative combination of qualitative and quantitative methods. **Sustainable development in Kahua, Solomon Islands,** indigenous knowledge was used to guide question formulation and understanding of community dynamics, and Western science was used to give an epistemological perspective leading to the validation of the solution.	Raymond et al. *(2010)*

TABLE 9.1 *(Continued)*
Various conceptual/practical strategies for TEK and science hybridization

Framework for hybridization	Authors
Mapping landscape values for conservation and tourism planning in Victoria, Australia, where local place-specific perception and preference for landscape values was overlaid with land suitability assessment to develop place-specific conservation zones and management practices.	
Linking of peer-review climate impact studies with indigenous narratives within a global grid:	Alexander et al. (2011)
Complementary approach—the science-based climate impact studies and the indigenous narratives were analyzed to ascertain consistent reporting of changes in the meteorological conditions.	
Side-by-side approach—places indigenous narratives data points within 250 km of data points related to science-based climate impact studies. The authors found that indigenous narratives were complementary in defining climate impacts for regions with limited scientific records.	
Spatial framework for integration of indigenous knowledge:	Srinivasan (2004)
Prepare/compile a matrix framework of local knowledge	
Define and map homogenous spatial units related to climate change issues	
Use historical matrix framework to define a coping strategy for climate change issues	
Coping strategy scored on the frequency of usage	

had a certain degree of success, which is based on the specific area and problem in question. This shows that knowledge hybridization is local-area-specific activity and cannot be generalized (Riedlinger, 1999) The current science-based climate adaptation strategies fail to produce optimum results, especially in sensitive indigenous communities, as most of these climate adaptations strategies mainly focus on the type of problem but not the area/community where the problem occurs. This gap can be closed by the complementary addition of traditional ecological knowledge as it caters to the local community. However, there are issues/challenges relating to the hybridization of science and TEK and the implication of the hybrid knowledge produced. These issues are further discussed in section 4.3.

4.3 CHALLENGES WITH INTEGRATIONS OF KNOWLEDGE SYSTEMS

There are various definition and perspectives on what exactly constitutes a knowledge system, which creates misperception and uncertainty while striving to integrate different knowledge systems. One of the most critical challenges faced in terms of integration of TEK with science is to build trust and commitment with all participants involved. Science has to recognize the contributions of TEK and not consider it a pariah for the reduction of trust-deficit between traditional communities and scientists/external experts.

We need to stop looking into TEK systems through the prism of quantitative experimentation and validation. This could lead to the disempowerment of TEK systems, especially when compared to scientific knowledge. We need to understand that both science and traditional ecological knowledge belong to two distinct spheres of facts, beliefs, and values (Weiss et al., 2013).

Another challenge would be to integrate the opposing interpretations of empirical data due to differences in sociocultural identities and networks. Each group will try to promote their way of thinking and process by vilifying/rejecting the other knowledge sources. Non-indigenous experts will project science as objective and reliable in the public view, and similarly, indigenous experts will rely on their long cultural heritage as they are closer to home and in tune to their problems. The challenge is to build trust and use the best of both worlds to combat climate change and its impacts (Harrison et al., 2018).

Hazards occurring within a short period can be easily documented, its impact assessed and validated, but the same cannot be said for extreme natural events like earthquakes and tsunamis. Even though these cataclysmic events have a more significant impact on sensitive ecosystems and vulnerable communities, but it would be difficult to assess and validate its impact as these events occur very infrequently. Therefore, validation of integrated systems will be very specific to the type and frequency of hazards that are being investigated, which could provide a further obstacle in streamlining the process.

Hiwasaki et al. (2014), who conducted the study in villages with a population of 3,500–5,000 people with homogenous culture, ethnicity, and belief systems, suggested the size of the community where the hybridized tool is to be implemented can have an impact on the process of integration; a large sample size would require a higher number of adjustments. Raymond et al. (2010) describe three board categories challenging the integration process: (1) ontological challenges, (2) epistemological challenges, and (3) applicability challenges.

To address these challenges, experts from both knowledge systems could adopt an integrative approach mentioned by Weiss et al. (2013) based on cross-cultural interaction and cooperative approach. The integrative approach can combine both top-down legislative actions with bottoms-up action in implementation and co-management of knowledge. Another aspect for bridging the gap would be to focus on participation framework developed locally rather than having a predefined structure imposed by external institutions.

As of today, the co-production through knowledge integration is a dominant approach in environmental governance, especially in sensitive and contentious tribal and indigenous regions; however, the process of integration is often criticized for the unequal power-sharing and series of broken promises in environmental negotiations (Chapman & Schott, 2020).

The projects endeavouring to combine TEK to SBKS should have proper protocols in place that addresses the power dynamics, sharing of knowledge, and should be oriented towards understanding the problem at the indigenous level. It also should understand the impacts of the co-produced new knowledge to indigenous knowledge systems and the sociocultural systems.

5. CONCLUSION

In the past decade, the increase in greenhouse gas emission has expedited the climate change impacts all over the world. This is especially true for a vulnerable and sensitive population like indigenous communities. Indigenous people have to combat changes in the climate due to external issues for generations, and these local adaptive methods are based on generational experience and cumulative traditional knowledge. However, of late, these methods are having a limited impact as the climate extremes are increasing in frequency and intensity. Current climate adaptation plans are based on scientific knowledge and assessment. Still, they have had limited success as they look at the problem and don't assess the area where the problem arises. Therefore, it is highly imperative that policies for combating climate change also must include indigenous knowledge and perception (Ishaya & Abaje, 2008). Indigenous people are seldom considered in academic, policy, and public dialogues on climate change, even though they are greatly impacted by impending changes of climate (Berkes & Jolly, 2001).

The knowledge hybridization of TEK and science could be the answer to the climate adaptation puzzle, but this relationship comes fraught with challenges. Any attempt to integrate traditional ecological knowledge with science may reveal the history of the unsteady relationship between the non-indigenous and indigenous groups (Alexander et al., 2011). However, without the interaction between local/tribal and scientific communities and the injection of traditional ecological knowledge into any climate adaptation projects, the sustainability of the whole process is called into question (Makondo & Thomas, 2018).

This diagnostic-prescription-intervention model may have solved urgent climate issues in the past, but this model has gone past its sell date, and there is no guarantee that the target people will optimally execute these imposed solutions. Climate-related issues are interconnected with different ecosystems, economic and social institutions, so they cannot be solved with reductive-fact-based solutions alone. Indigenous communities already have the knowledge for coping, and its hybridization with science-based knowledge systems would co-produce hybridized knowledge with the potential to improve and implement climate change adaptation and conservation strategies at different scales.

REFERENCES

AFDB (2016). Development and Indigenous Peoples in Africa—Safeguards and Sustainability Series. [Online]. 2 (2). www.afdb.org.

Agrawal, Arun; McSweeney, Catherine; Perrin, Nicolas. (2008). Local Institutions and Climate Change Adaptation. *Social Development Notes*; No. 113. World Bank, Washington, DC. © World Bank. https://openknowledge.worldbank.org/handle/10986/11145 License: CC BY 3.0 IGO.

Alexander, C., Bynum, N., Johnson, E., King, U., et al. (2011). Linking Indigenous and Scientific Knowledge of Climate Change. *BioScience. [Online] 61 (6)*, 477–484. https://doi.org/10.1525/bio.2011.61.6.10.

Asian Development Bank (2002). Indigenous Peoples/Ethnic Minorities and Poverty Reduction. www.adb.org/sites/default/files/publication/28025/indigenous-peoples-philippines.

pdf%0Ahttp://beta.adb.org/publications/indigenous-people-ethnic-minorities-and-poverty-reduction-philippines.

Audefroy, Joel & Sánchez, B. (2017). Integrating Local Knowledge for Climate Change Adaptation in Yucatan, Mexico. *International Journal of Sustainable Built Environment.* 6. https://doi.org/10.1016/j.ijsbe.2017.03.007.

Bartlett, C., Marshall, M. & Marshall, A. (2012). Two-Eyed Seeing and other lessons learned within a co-learning journey of bringing together indigenous and mainstream knowledges and ways of knowing. *Journal of Environmental Studies and Sciences. [Online] 2 (4)*, 331–340. https://doi:10.1007/s13412-012-0086-8.

Behailu, B.M., Pietilä, P.E. & Katko, T.S. (2016). Indigenous Practices of Water Management for Sustainable Services: Case of Borana and Konso, Ethiopia. *SAGE Open.* https://doi.org/10.1177/2158244016682292

Berkes, F. (2004). Traditional Ecological Knowledge in perspective. In J.T. Inglis (Eds). *Traditional Ecological Knowledge: Concepts and Cases* (pp 1–6). International Program on Traditional Ecological Knowledge, Ottawa, Canada.

Berkes, F. & Davidson-Hunt, I. (2006). Biodiversity, traditional management systems, and cultural landscapes: Examples from the boreal forest of Canada. *International Social Science Journal 58*, 35–47. https://doi.org/10.1111/j.1468-2451.2006.00605.x

Berkes, F. & Jolly, D. (2001). Adapting to climate change: Socio-ecological resilience in a Canadian Western Arctic Community. *Conserv. Ecol. 5 (2)*, 18.

Bohensky, E.L. & Maru, Y. (2011). Indigenous knowledge, science, and resilience: What have we learned from a decade of international literature on 'integration'. *Ecology and Society. [Online] 16 (4)*, 1–19. https://doi.org/10.5751/ES-04342-160406.

Bruchac, M.M. (2014). Indigenous knowledge and traditional knowledge. *Encyclopedia of Global Archaeology. [Online]* 3814–3824. https://doi.org/10.1007/978-1-4419-0465-2_10.

Chakwizira, J. & Nhemachena, C. (2012). Southern African Transport Conference. Pretoria, South Africa. Ministry of Transport, South Africa.

Chapman, J.M. & Schott, S. (2020). Knowledge coevolution: Generating new understanding through bridging and strengthening distinct knowledge systems and empowering local knowledge holders. *Sustainability Science. [Online] 15 (3)*, 931–943. https://doi.org/10.1007/s11625-020-00781-2.

Nakashima, D.J., Galloway Mclean, K., Thulstrup, H.D., Ramos Castillo, A. and Rubis, J.T. (2012). *Weathering uncertainty: Traditional knowledge for climate change assessment and adaptation.* UNESCO; UNU-IAS.

Desalegn, Y.W., Belissa, T.K. & Jilito, M.F. (2019). Harnessing indigenous social institutions for technology adoption: 'Afoosha' society of Ethiopia. *Development Studies Research, 6:1*, 152–162, https://doi.org/10.1080/21665095.2019.1678187

Devkota, R., Bajracharya, B., Maraseni, T., Cockfield, G. & Upadhyay, B. (2011). The perception of Nepal's Tharu community in regard to climate change and its impacts on their livelihoods. *International Journal of Environmental Studies. 68.* 937–946. https://doi.org/10.1080/00207233.2011.587282.

Dogan, M. (1996). The hybridization of social science knowledge. *Library Trends. 45 (2)*, 296–314.

Finn, M., Jackson, S. (2011). Protecting indigenous values in water management: A challenge to conventional environmental flow assessments. *Ecosystems 14*, 1232–1248. https://doi.org/10.1007/s10021-011-9476-0

Ford, J.D., Cameron, L., Rubis, J., Maillet, M., et al. (2016). Including indigenous knowledge and experience in IPCC assessment reports. *Nature Climate Change. [Online] 6 (4)*, 349–353. https://doi.org/10.1038/nclimate2954.

Gadgil, M., Berkes, F. & Folke, C. (1993). Indigenous knowledge for biodiversity conservation. *Ambio*, 22, 151–156.

Gagnon, C.A. & Berteaux D. (2009). Integrating traditional ecological knowledge and ecological science: A question of scale. *Ecology and Society. [Online] 14 (2)*, 19. http://www.ecologyandsociety.org/vol14/iss2/art19/

Garnett, S.T., Burgess, N.D., Fa, J.E., Fernández-Llamazares, Á., Molnár, Z., Robinson, C.J., Watson, J.E.M., Zander, K.K., Austin, B., Brondizio, E.S., Collier, N.F., Duncan, T., Ellis, E., Geyle, H., Jackson, M.V., Jonas, H., Malmer, P., McGowan, B., Sivongxay, A. & Leiper, I. (2018). A spatial overview of the global importance of indigenous lands for conservation. *Nature Sustainability, 1 (7)*, 369–374. https://doi.org/10.1038/s41893-018-0100-6

Garteizgogeascoa, M., García-del-Amo, D. & Reyes-García, V. (2020). Using proverbs to study local perceptions of climate change: A case study in Sierra Nevada (Spain). *Reg Environ Change 20*, 59. https://doi.org/10.1007/s10113-020-01646-1

Goist, M. & Kern, F. (2018). Traditional institutions and social cooperation: Experimental evidence from the Buganda Kingdom. *Research & Politics.* 5. 205316801775392. https://doi.org/10.1177/2053168017753925.

Gómez-Baggethun, E. & Reyes-García V. (2013). Reinterpreting change in traditional ecological knowledge. *Human Ecology, 41*, 643–647. https://doi.org/10.1007/s10745-013-9577-9.

Granderson, A. (2017). The role of traditional knowledge in building adaptive capacity for climate change: Perspectives from Vanuatu. *Weather, Climate, and Society*, 9. https://doi.org/10.1175/WCAS-D-16-0094.1.

Harrison, H.L., Rybråten, S. & Aas, Ø. (2018). Hatching knowledge: A case study on the hybridization of local ecological knowledge and scientific knowledge in small-scale Atlantic Salmon (Salmo salar) cultivation in Norway. *Human Ecology, 46*, 449–459. https://doi.org/10.1007/s10745-018-0001-3

Hill, R., Adem, Ç., Alangui, W.V., Molnár, Z., Aumeeruddy-Thomas, Y., Bridgewater, P., Tengö, M., Thaman, R., Adou Yao, C.Y., Berkes, F., Carino, J., Carneiro da Cunha, M., Diaw, M.C., Díaz, S., Figueroa, V.E., Fisher, J., Hardison, P., Ichikawa, K., Kariuki, P., ... Xue, D. (2020). Working with Indigenous, local and scientific knowledge in assessments of nature and nature's linkages with people. *Current Opinion in Environmental Sustainability, 43*, 8–20. https://doi.org/10.1016/j.cosust.2019.12.006

Hiwasaki, L., Luna, E., Syamsidik & Shaw, R. (2014). Process for integrating local and indigenous knowledge with science for hydro-meteorological disaster risk reduction and climate change adaptation in coastal and small island communities. *International Journal of Disaster Risk Reduction, 10*, 15–27. https://doi.org/10.1016/j.ijdrr.2014.07.007.

Houde, N. (2007). The six faces of traditional ecological knowledge: Challenges and opportunities for Canadian co-management arrangements. *Ecology and Society, 12 (2)*. https://doi.org/10.5751/ES-02270-120234.

Hromek, Michael. (2019). Aboriginal design in transport infrastructure: Empowering communities through the inclusion of cultural design knowledge into project solutions. In *WEC2019: World Engineers Convention 2019* (pp 1085–1095). Melbourne: Engineers Australia.

Ishaya, S. & Abaje, I.B. (2008). Indigenous people's perception on climate change and adaptation strategies in Jema'a local government area of Kaduna state, Nigeria. *Journal of Geography and Regional Planning, 1*, 138–143.

Jackson, Sue. (2011). Indigenous water management: Priorities for the next five years. https://doi.org/10.22459/BF.05.2011.09.

Karki, M., Pokhrel, P. & Adhikari, J.R. (2017). Climate change: Integrating indigenous and local knowledge into adaptation policies and practices. In M. Cairns (Eds.). *Shifting Cultivation Policies: Balancing Environmental and Social Sustainability* (Supplementary, p. 1060). CABI, Oxfordshire, UK.

Kassa, G.N. (2006). The Role of Culture and Traditional Institutions in Peace and Conflict: Gada System of Conflict Prevention and Resolution among the Oromo-Borana, [Master's thesis]. University of Oslo. http://urn.nb.no/URN:NBN:no-17988

Macchi, M., Oviedo, G., Gotheil, S., Cross, K., et al. (2008). Indigenous and Traditional Peoples and Climate Change Issues Paper. *Indigenous and Traditional Peoples and Climate Change. [Online].* http://cmsdata.iucn.org/downloads/indigenous_peoples_climate_change.pdf.

Maclean, Kirsten & Inc, The. (2015). Crossing cultural boundaries: Integrating Indigenous water knowledge into water governance through co-research in the Queensland Wet Tropics, Australia. *Geoforum, 59*, 142–152. https://doi.org/10.1016/j.geoforum.2014.12.008.

Mafongoya, P. & Ajayi, O. (2017). Indigenous knowledge systems and climate change management in Africa. Wageningen, The Netherlands, Technical Centre for Agricultural and Rural Cooperation.

Makondo, C.C. & Thomas, D.S.G. (2018). Climate change adaptation: Linking indigenous knowledge with western science for effective adaptation. *Environmental Science and Policy, 88*, 83–91. https://doi.org/10.1016/j.envsci.2018.06.014.

McLean, J.(2007). Water injustices and potential remedies in indigenous rural contexts: A water justice analysis. *Environmentalist 27*, 25–38. https://doi.org/10.1007/s10669-007-9012-0

Mehari Haile, A., Schultz, E. & Depeweg, H. (2005). Where indigenous water management practices overcome failures of structures: The Wadi Laba spate irrigation system in Eritrea. *Irrigation and drainage, 54*. https://doi.org/10.1002/ird.151.

Menhas, R. (2014). Impact of modernization on pakistani women. *Innovare Journal of Social Sciences, 2 (3)*, 5–7 https://innovareacademics.in/journals/index.php/ijss/article/view/1055

Ministry of Science Technology and Environment. (2015). Indigenous and local knowledge and practices for climate resilence in Nepal. Kathmandu, Nepal, Government of Nepal, Minstry of Science, Technology and Environment.

Mirjam Macchi, Gonzalo Oviedo, Sarah Gotheil, Katharine Cross, Agni Boedhihartono, Caterina Wolfangel, Matthew Howell, Indigenous and Traditional Peoples and Climate Change: Issues Paper (2008). IUCN.

Mubaya, C.P. & Mafongoya, P. (2017). The role of institutions in managing local level climate change adaptation in semi-arid Zimbabwe. *Climate Risk Management, 16*, 93–105. http://doi.org/10.1016/j.crm. 2017.03.003

Singh, N. (2006). Indigenous water management systems: Interpreting symbolic dimensions in common property resource regimes. *Society & Natural Resources, 19 (4)*, 357–366, https://doi.org/10.1080/08941920500519297

Mihai, N., Badiu, D., Onose, D.A., Gavrilidis, A., Gradinaru, S., Năstase, I. & Lafortezza, R. (2018). Using local knowledge and sustainable transport to promote a greener city: The case of Bucharest, Romania. *Environmental Research, 160*, 331–338. https://doi.org/10.1016/j.envres.2017.10.007.

Nhemachena C. & Hassan R. (2007). Micro-level Analysis of Farmers' Adaptation to Climate Change in Southern Africa, IFPRI Discussion Paper No. 00714, IFPRI, Washington, DC.

Niță, M.R., Badiu, D.L., Onose, D.A., Gavrilidis, A.A., Grădinaru, S.R., Năstase, I.I. & Lafortezza, R. (2018). Using local knowledge and sustainable transport to promote a greener city: The case of Bucharest, Romania. *Environmental Research, 160*, 331–338. https://doi.org/10.1016/j.envres.2017.10.007

Nkem, J.N., Somorin, O.A., Jum, C., Idinoba, M.E., Bele, Y.M. & Sonwa, D.J. (2013). Profiling climate change vulnerability of forest indigenous communities in the Congo Basin. *Mitigation and Adaptation Strategies for Global Change, 18 (5)*, 513–533. https://doi.org/10.1007/s11027-012-9372-8

Olney S. & Viles H. (2019). *Indigenous peoples and climate change: Emerging research on traditional knowledge and livelihoods* (First Edition). ILO Publications.

Pachauri, R.K., Mayer, L. & Intergovernmental Panel on Climate Change (Eds.). (2015). Climate change 2014: Synthesis report. Intergovernmental Panel on Climate Change

Paneque-Gálvez, Jaime, Pérez-Llorente, Irene, Luz, Ana, Gueze, Maximilien, Mas, Jean, Macía, Manuel, Orta-Martinez, Marti, Reyes-García, Victoria. (2018). High overlap between traditional ecological knowledge and forest conservation found in the Bolivian Amazon. *Ambio. 47.* https://doi.org/10.1007/s13280-018-1040-0.

Rautela, Piyoosh & Karki, Bhavna. (2015). Impact of Climate Change on Life and Livelihood of Indigenous People of Higher Himalaya in Uttarakhand, India. *American Journal of Environmental Protection, 3*, 112–124. https://doi.org/10.12691/env-3-4-2.

Raymond, C.M., Fazey, I., Reed, M.S., Stringer, L.C., Robinson, G.M. & Evely, A.C. (2010). Integrating local and scientific knowledge for environmental management. *Journal of Environmental Management, 91 (8)*, 1766–1777. https://doi.org/10.1016/j.jenvman.2010.03.023

Reid, W.V., F. Berkes, T. Wilbanks, and D. Capistriano, editors. (2006). *Bridging scales and local knowledge in assessments.* Island Press, Washington, D.C.

Reyes-García, V., Mcdade, T., Vadez, V., Huanca, T., Leonard, W.R., Tanner, S., and Godoy, R. (2008). Non-market returns to traditional human capital: Nutritional status and traditional knowledge in a native Amazonian society. *Journal of Development Studies, 44*, 217–232. http://dx.doi.org/10.1080/00220380701789901

Reyes-García, V., Fernández-Llamazares, Á., McElwee, P., Molnár, Z., Öllerer, K., Wilson, S. and Brondízio, E. (2018). The contributions of indigenous peoples and local communities to ecological restoration: Indigenous *Peoples for Ecological Restoration. Restoration Ecology, 27 (1).* https://doi.org/10.1111/rec.12894

Riedlinger, D. (1999). Climate change and the Inuvialuit of Banks Island, NWT: Using traditional environmental knowledge to complement western science. *Arctic, 52 (4)*, 430–432. http://dx.doi.org/10.14430/arctic948.

Roue, M. and Nakashima, D. (2018). Indigenous and Local Knowledge and Science: From Validation to Knowledge Coproduction. In The *International Encyclopedia of Anthropology*, H. Callan (Ed.). http://dx.doi.org/10.1002/9781118924396.wbiea2215

Saitabau Henriole. (2014). Impacts of climate change on the livelihoods of Loita Maasai pastoral community and related indigenous knowledge on adaptation and mitigation. *Directorate of Research and Collections (DRC)* (pp 1–35). National Museums of Kenya.

Salick, J. and Ross, N. (2009). Traditional peoples and climate change Introduction. Global Environmental Change-human and Policy Dimensions. *Global environ change. 19.* 137–139. http://dx.doi.org/10.1016/j.gloenvcha.2009.01.004.

Schwanen, T. (2018). Towards decolonized knowledge about transport. *Palgrave Commun, 4*, 79. https://doi.org/10.1057/s41599-018-0130-8.

Singh, Ranjay K., Bhowmik, S.N., and Pandey, C.B. (2011). Biocultural diversity, climate change and livelihood security of Adi community: Grassroots conservators of eastern Himalaya Arunachal Pradesh. *Indian Journal of Traditional Knowledge 10 (1)*, 39–56.

Sonwa, D., Somorin, O., Jum, C., Mekou, Y.B., and Nkem, J. (2012). Vulnerability, forest-related sectors and climate change adaptation: The case of Cameroon. Forest Policy and Economics. *Forest policy econ, 23*, 1–9. http://dx.doi.org/10.1016/j.forpol.2012.06.009.

Srinivasan, A. (2004). Local knowledge for Facilitating Adaptation to Climate Change in Asia and the Pacific : Policy Implications. *IGES Climate Policy, 002*, 1–19.

Ukpong-Umo, R.E. & Mboho, K.S. (2014). Change in the fabrics of social institutions in Nigeria: Implications for agricultural development. *Nigerian Journal of Rural Sociology, 14 (2)*.

UNESCO. (2017). Local Knowledge, Global Goals. Local Indigenous Knowledge systems www.unesco.org/new/fileadmin/MULTIMEDIA/HQ/SC/pdf/ILK_ex_publication_ E.pdf.

Vadigi, S. (2016). Indigenous Knowledge Systems and Formal Scientific Research for Climate Change. *Journal of Human Ecology, 53 (2)*, 148–156. http://dx.doi.org/10.1080/09709 274.2016.11906967.

Vidaurre de la Riva, Marolyn & Lindner, Andre & Pretzsch, Jürgen. (2013). Assessing adaptation—Climate change and indigenous livelihood in the Andes of Bolivia. *Journal of Agriculture and Rural Development in the Tropics and Subtropics, 114*, 109–122.

Weiss, K., Hamann, M. & Marsh, H. (2013). Bridging Knowledges: Understanding and Applying Indigenous and Western Scientific Knowledge for Marine Wildlife Management. *Society and Natural Resources, 26 (3)*, 285–302. http://dx.doi.org/10.1080/08941920.2012.690065.

10 Eco-Hydrology
Conservation of Water Resources

Ashita Rai and M. H. Fulekar

CONTENTS

1. Introduction 171
   1.1 Global Water Availability—Status 172
   1.2 Water Quality and Challenges 172
2. Ecosystem Components—Role in Water Cycle 173
   2.1 Vegetation 173
   2.2 Soil 173
   2.3 Agro Forestry 174
   2.4 Wetlands 175
   2.5 Biodiversity 175
   2.6 Climate Change 175
   2.7 Ecosystem Services 176
3. India's Scenario: Case Study 176
   3.1 Landscape Restoration to Improve Water Security in Rajasthan, India 176
   3.2 Watershed Harvesting in Ralegaon Siddhi, Maharashtra 177
4. International Bodies 177
5. Global Convention and Agreement—Nature-Based Solutions 177
6. Conclusion 178
References 178

1. INTRODUCTION

The population growth, economic development, and changing consumption pattern, among other factors, water use is expected to continue increasing at the global level. Global water use has increased by a factor of 6 over the past 100 years and continuing to grow steadily at a rate of about 1% per year. Estimates at global level are complicated because of limited available observational data and the interaction of the combination of environmental, social, economic, and political factors such as global climate change, population growth, land use change, globalization and economic development, technological innovations, and the extent of international cooperation. Because of these, other economic local water management has global impact, and global development has local impacts.

- Agriculture: agriculture requires over 70% of Earth's water; large proportion is exploited for irrigation.

DOI: 10.1201/9781003205548-10

- Industry: industrial water extraction accounts for 20% (roughly) of worldwide consumption, while power generation accounts for 75%, and production harnesses the remaining 25%.
- Domestic: this represents remaining 10% of world water consumption. In all parts of the continent, it is anticipated to rise dramatically between 2010 and 2050.

Within the next couple of decades, worldwide consumption of fresh water is likely to rise dramatically. Freshwater consumption in the residential and industrial sectors is expected to increase substantially stronger over farming need.

1.1 Global Water Availability—Status

Available water resources, status highlights (early-mid 2010s), about 1.9 billion people (27% of the global population) lived in severely water-scarce areas, and in 2050 this could increase to some 2.7–3.2 billion. Water availability, if monthly taken into account, 3.6 billion people worldwide (nearly half the global population) are already living in potential water scarce areas at least one month per year, and this could increase to some 4.8–5.7 billion in 2050. The importance of current water availability challenges can only be fully understood by comparing water withdrawal to their maximum sustainable level.

1.2 Water Quality and Challenges

Water pollution has worsened in almost all water resources. The deterioration of water quality is expected to escalate over the next decades, and this will increase threats to human health, environment, and sustainable development. An estimated 80% of all industrial and municipal wastewater are released into the environment without any prior treatment, resulting in a growing deterioration of overall water quality with detrimental impact on human health and ecosystems (World Water Assessment Programme, WWAP, 2017).

Climate change will affect water quality in various ways; for example, changes in spatial and temporal patterns and variability of precipitation affect surface water flows and hence dilution effects. Increase in temperature can lead to higher evaporation from open surfaces and soil and increased transpiration by vegetation potentially, which could reduce water availability (Hipsey and Arheimer, 2013). The greatest increase in exposure to pollutants are expected to occur in low and lower-middle income, primarily because of higher population and economic growth on these countries due to the lack of wastewater management.(WWAP, 2017).

Worldwide, the challenge of water pollution and deteriorating water quality results in rise to human and ecosystem health and reducing the availability of freshwater resources for human needs as well as the ability of water-related ecosystem to provide goods and services, including natural water purification. The increasing population, urbanization, industrialization, the expansion and intensification of agriculture, and the impact of climate change, evidence of the extent of freshwater quality degradation is wide spread problem. Pollution of freshwater ecosystem and

Eco-Hydrology

ultimately coastal and marine ecosystem is of major concern. Major types of pollutants, which include chemicals and nutrients, increasing salinity level, and rising air and water temperature are having significant impacts (Zhongming et al., 2016).

2. ECOSYSTEM COMPONENTS—ROLE IN WATER CYCLE

In a landscape, ecological processes influence the water quality of water as well as soil formation, erosion, and sediment transport and deposition—all these can exert major influence on hydrology. Soil controls movement, storage, and transformation of water. Forest often receives the most attention when it comes to land cover and hydrology, but grasslands and croplands are also very important. Biodiversity has functional role. It underpins the ecosystem process functions and services. Ecosystems have important influences on precipitation. Globally up to 40% of terrestrial rainfall originates from upwind plant transpiration and often land evaporation; the remainder originates from the ocean. The physical, chemical, and biological processes of ecosystem affect hydrological pathway in water cycle. Major terrestrial, most coastal, ecosystem types or biomes including urban landscapes, vegetation, soil, and/or wetlands (river and lakes) influence water.

2.1 Vegetation

FAO/ITPS (Food and Agriculture Organisation of the United Nations/Intergovernmental Technical Panel on Soils, 2015) report highlights that plant cover is about 72% of the global land mass. Plant stem and leaves intercept precipitation (rain or snow) or cloud moisture. Plants affect water availability and climate through transpiration functions and remove water from soil and sometimes groundwater. Plant roots contribute to soil structure and health and influence soil water storage/availability, infiltration, and percolation to groundwater. However, landscapes tend to include a variety of vegetation cover categories, each of which can have different degrees of influence on water cycle. Forests play an important role in restoration and management of hydrology.

2.2 Soil

Soil is made up of intricate life forms. As well, the hydrological bioactivities that occur there are intimately tied to the functioning of ecosystems. The volume of freshwater penetration, evapotranspiration, and diffusion across soil is substantially determined by the morphology, porosity, and characteristics of soil, as well as by foliage and weather. Freshwater quality is determined by the fertility of the soil and its capacity to sustain nutrient availability (Food and Agriculture Organisation, FAO, 2011).

Primary recipient of rainfall plus heat is indeed the soil-foliage complex. Approximately 95% of the total rainfall is retained in the vadose and saturated zone of the land, with the exception of the freshwater currently held in glacier. FAO/ITPS (2015)—only 0.05% of the planet's water is held within top soil; an upwards and downwards transfer of energy and water via soil is huge and intimately associated. As a result, the primary recipient of rainfall and heat is soil-foliage complex.

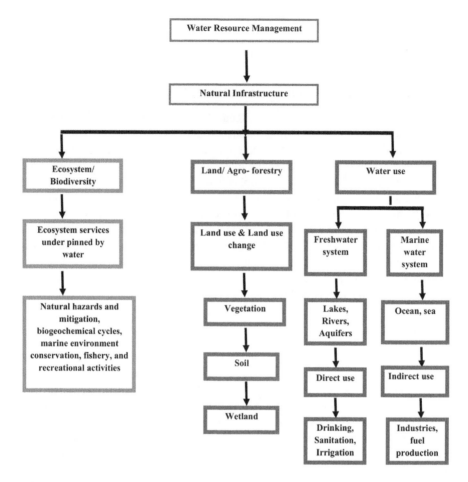

FIGURE 10.1 Nature-based solutions component for Water Resource Management.

2.3 Agro Forestry

Agro forestry describes land use systems where agricultural crops, pastures, or livestocks: which include both ecological and economic interaction between components of the system. There is a wide range of potential application that comprises two structural approaches:

i. Water harvesting: It entails collecting and storing rainwater for agricultural growth, which increases grassland and vegetation productivity and is useful in arid climates wherein water deficiency seems to be a major concern.
ii. Gully control: This monitoring method entails a series of actions that solve extreme type of soil degradation—it's useful in soil conservation and maintenance. Restoration using perennial vegetative cover is primarily dominated by structural obstacles.

Such methods are used in agricultural preservation for boosting agricultural output, that increases as well as maintains production while simultaneously providing valuable ecosystem benefits.

2.4 WETLANDS

Wetlands cover only 2.6% of the land by inland water bodies (FAO/ITPS, 2015). Wetlands include rivers and lakes and play a large role in hydrology per unit area. Wetlands conservation often receive attention in terms of hydrological processes, including groundwater recharge and discharge, flood flow alteration, sediment stabilization, and water quality. Coastal wetlands also play an important role in water-related problems; for example, mangrove ecosystem is interface between sea and land.

2.5 BIODIVERSITY

Biodiversity also plays an important role in ecological processes, system, and function, thus affects ecosystem services on land. For example, soil biota contribute important living community in the soil system, providing a wide range of essential soil services by sharing metabolic capacity and soil function. Reduction in soil biodiversity tends to be associated with negative impacts on soil organic carbon, soil moisture and infiltration, and therefore runoff, erosion, and groundwater recharge (FAO, 2011). These impacts collectively on water quality, notably in relation to nutrient load and sedimentation. Besides forests, grasslands and wetlands in their natural state tend to be more bio diverse and have different hydrological profiles and deliver better ecosystem services as compared to managed or disturbed state. Biodiversity also enhances resilience or a system's capacity to recover from external pressure such as droughts. Thus, biodiversity safeguards water quality management.

2.6 CLIMATE CHANGE

Climate change also contributes to the degradation of water quality by affecting the seasonal quantity of water available and its temperature, thus modifying its physicochemical and biological parameters (Delpla et al., 2009). More frequent and intense flooding may lead to dispersal of contaminants through runoff, and sea level rise can lead to higher salinity. Increase in water scarcity and changes to the hydrological cycle affect the spatial extent, productivity, and function of freshwater ecosystem, including their ability to provide ecosystem services, with effects often readily for downstream or into coastal areas (Parry et al., 2007). Changes to precipitation and stream flow that lower the amount or availability of water also lead directly to reduce water quality (Finlayson et al., 2006). The resulting lower water quality levels, in effect, are a form of scarcity when water is no longer directly usable for many productive uses (Aylward et al., 2005).

The degradation of water quality translates directly into environmental, social, and economic risks, impacting human health, limiting food production, reducing ecosystem functionality, and hindering economic growth (United Nations Educational,

Scientific and Cultural Organization, 2015). Thus, water quality is central to sustainable development.

2.7 ECOSYSTEM SERVICES

Water-related processes and functions of ecosystem can be managed to deliver benefits to the people as "ecosystem services." Ecosystem services that directly influence the availability and quality of water referred to as watershed services or water services as water-related ecosystem services. Water-related ecosystem services can be grouped into those that relate to the movement of water: (1) evaporation—overland flow and infiltration into the ground, (2) storage of water—in soil and groundwater, (3) transformation of water, including its quality. These three dimensions of water resources together challenge most (if not all) sectors and issues, water availability, water quality, and moderating risk and extremes, including water-related diseases risk. Ecosystem services help to manage each of these three areas and make significant contribution to key water resources management challenges, which comprises drinking water quality, sanitation, and hygiene; water security for food security and sustainable agriculture; building sustainable urban settlement; managing wastewater, land degradation, drought and desertification, and climate change adaptation and mitigation.

3. INDIA'S SCENARIO: CASE STUDY

3.1 LANDSCAPE RESTORATION TO IMPROVE WATER SECURITY IN RAJASTHAN, INDIA

In 1985–1986, usually low rainfall combined with excessive logging led to the worst drought in the history of Rajasthan. The district of Alwar, one of the poorest in the state, was severely affected. The global water table had receded below critical levels, and the state declared parts of the area "dark zones," which meant the severity of the situation warranted restrictions or any further groundwater extraction. NGO (non-governmental organization) Tarun Bharat Sangh supported local communities to undertake landscape restoration of local water cycles and water resources. With leadership provided by women, who customarily take responsibility by providing their families with safe fresh water, traditional local initiations for water were revived by bringing people together on the issue of management of forest and freshwater resources. Activities centred on the construction of small-scale water harvesting structures combined with the regeneration of forest and soils, particularly in upper catchment areas to help improve the recharge of groundwater resources.

The impact has been significant. For example, water was brought back to 1,000 villages across the state. Five rivers that used to run dry after the annual monsoon season are now flowing again and fisheries in river re-established. Groundwater level has risen by an estimated six metres. Productive farmland increased from 20% to 80% of the catchment. Crucial forest cover, including farmland, which help to maintain the integrity and water retaining capacity of the soil, has increased by 33%, and the return of wildlife such as antelope and leopard has been observed.

Everard (2015) undertook a science-based assessment of the programme confirming its socioeconomic benefits.

3.2 WATERSHED HARVESTING IN RALEGAON SIDDHI, MAHARASHTRA

Maharashtra experiences acute drought conditions, which affect agricultural production and economy every year. The village is situated in a rain-shadow zone. In a 1971 census, only 55 acres of land were irrigated as most of the rainwater was wasted as runoff, eroding top soil and lowering productivity. In 1975 Ralegaon Siddhi, Ahmednagar, Maharashtra, was struck by a poverty and water deficit. Social activist Anna Hazare contributed in the transformation of the village with idea of involving local people for water conservation and harvesting. A new initiative was taken, a project of constructing nulla bunds along with villagers. Nulla bunds reduced runoff and allowed the water to percolate and recharge the aquifers. In the first stage, 6 nulla bunds were constructed. Further villagers constructed 31 more nulla bunds of storage capacity of 282,183 cubic metres and renovated an old percolation tank of storage capacity 323,378 cubic metres built in the past. Further, plantation alongside percolation tank was done to help keep the soil permeable to water. Poor farmers (16 in number) were brought together to dig a well around the tank. By 1991 a total of 95 wells were dug.

These initiatives resolved the water scarcity and supplied water in rural areas.

4. INTERNATIONAL BODIES

International bodies, including UNESCO, have promoted eco-hydrology programme. It promotes the establishment of various demonstration sites around the world to apply systematic eco-hydrology solution in watersheds across the world. A demonstration site applies eco-hydrology in its objective of dealing with issues such as pollutant and nutrient concentration and water quality improvement, flood mitigation, and loss of retention capacity of vegetation, etc. Hydrological and ecological processes are studied from molecular (microbial processes) to catchment scales in aquatic habitats like wetlands, marshes, mangroves, and rivers from head water to plains and coastal zones, in order to find long-term solutions that integrate social component. The demonstration sites include the concept of enhanced ecosystem potential, through the application of eco-hydrological strategies to achieve ecosystem to improve IWRM. This is termed as WBSRC (W-water, B-biodiversity, S-ecosystem services, R-resilience, C-culture or social dimension), containing the five elements that should be taken into consideration to reinforce the carrying capacity or modified ecosystem.

5. GLOBAL CONVENTION AND AGREEMENT— NATURE-BASED SOLUTIONS

At the global level, nature-based solutions (NBS) offer member states a means to respond to use the various multilateral environmental agreement, especially the Convention on Biological Diversity, the United Nations Framework Convention on Climate Change, the Ramsar Convention on Wetlands, the Sendai Framework for Disaster Risk Reduction, and the Paris Agreement on Climate Change. An over-searching framework for promoting NBS is the 2030 agenda for sustainable development with its sustainable development goals.

A timeline can be traced through the research agenda with attention to NBS on similar terminology emerging around 1990 (coinciding with 1992 United Nations Conference on Sustainable Development) from which emerged the Convention on Biological Diversity (CBD, 1992), the United Nations Convention to Combat Desertification (UNCCD, 1994), and the United Nations Framework Convention on Climate Change (UNFCCC, 1992), and escalating from 2000 to 2005 onwards. A key factor was increasing attention to the concept of ecosystem services from about 2000 onwards and improved efforts to value theses enabling better management with policymaking.

6. CONCLUSION

The advancement in modernization/development correlates development with environment regardless of environmental impacts that has been considered as an acceptable cost of development. Water and environment have significantly shifted towards the direction in which the environment can be managed to protect and conserve water resources and supports human water needs. The water quality can be improved by reducing pollution, eliminating dumping, and minimizing release of hazardous chemical and material and reducing proportion of untreated wastewater and promoting reduce, reuse, and recycle.

The sustainable use of natural resources and managing the natural components (vegetation, soil, agro forestry, wetlands, biodiversity, climate change, ecosystem services) will ensure the supply of fresh water to reduce water scarcity. Implementation of IWRM will protect and restore water-related ecosystems, including aquifers, wetlands, forests, etc. In developing countries, sanitation-related activities, including water harvesting, desalination, wastewater treatment, recycle, and reuse technologies are of prime importance to support water demand and fulfil human needs for intended use in industry, agriculture, domestic, and potable by maintaining natural resources.

REFERENCES

Aylward, B., Bandyopadhyay, J. and Belausteguigotia, J. 2005. Freshwater ecosystem services. Millennium Ecosystem Assessment, Ecosystems and Human Well-being: Policy Responses. Washington, DC, Island Press.

CBD (Convention on Biological Diversity). 1992. Convention on Biological Diversity. Rio de Janeiro, Brazil, 5 June 1992.

Delpla, I., Jung, A.-V., Baures, E., Clement, M. and Thomas, O. 2009. Impacts of climate change on surface water quality in relation to drinking water production. Environment International, Vol. 35, No. 8, pp. 1225–1233.

Everard, M. 2015. Community-based groundwater and ecosystem restoration in semi-arid north Rajasthan (1); Socio-economic progress and lessons for groundwater-dependent areas. Ecosystem Services, Vol. 16, pp. 125–135.

FAO (Food and Agriculture Organisation of the United Nations). 2011. The State of the World's Land and Water Resources for Food and Agriculture: Managing Systems at Risk. Rome/London, FAO/Earth scan.

FAO/ITPS (Food and Agriculture Organisation of the United Nations/Intergovernmental Technical Panel on Soils). 2015. Status of the World's Soil Resources (SWSR)-Main Report. Rome, FAO.

Finlayson, C.M., Gitay, H., Bellio, M.G., Van Dam, R.A. and Taylor, I. 2006. Climate variability and change and other pressures on wetland and water birds: Impacts and adaptation. G.C. Boere, C. A. Galbraith and A. A. Stroud (eds.), Water birds around the world: A global overview of the conservation, management and research of the world's water birds flyways. Edinburgh, UK, The Stationery Office. pp. 88–97.

Hipsey, M.R. and Arheimer, B. 2013. Challenges for water-quality research in the new IAHS decade on: Hydrology Under Societal and Environmental Change. B. Arheimer et al. (eds.), Understanding freshwater quality problems in a changing world. Wallingford, UK, International Association of Hydrological Sciences (IAHS) Press, pp. 17–29.

Parry, M.L., Canziani, O., Palutikof, J., Van der Linden, P. and Hanson, C. (Eds.). 2007. Climate Change 2007 – Impacts, Adaptation and Vulnerability: Working Group II Contribution to the Fourth Assessment Report of the IPCC (Vol. 4). Cambridge, UK, Cambridge University Press.

UNESCO. 2015. International Initiative on Water Quality: Promoting Scientific Research, Knowledge Sharing, Effective Technology, and Policy Approaches to Improve Water Quality for Sustainable Development. Paris, UNESCO.

United Nations Convention to Combat Desertification (UNCCD). 1994. Bonn, Germany. Retrieved from https://www.unccd.int/convention/overview

United Nations Framework Convention on Climate Change (UNFCCC). 1992. Rio de Janeiro, Brazil. Retrieved from https://unfccc.int/about-us/about-the-secretariat

WWAP. United Nations World Water Development Report. 2017. Wastewater: The untapped resource. Paris, UNESCO.

Zhongming, Z., Linong, L., Xiaona, Y., Wangqiang, Z. and Wei, L. 2016. United Nations Environment Programme Frontiers: 2016 Report: Emerging Issues of Environmental Concern. Nairobi, Kenya.

11 Algae as a Biomarker Using the Free Air Carbon Dioxide Enrichment (FACE) System

Khushboo Iqbal, Sanskriti Singh, Behnam Asgari Lajayer, Smriti Shukla, Kartikeya Shukla, Ajit Varma, and Arti Mishra

CONTENTS

1. Introduction 181
2. Role of Biomarker 183
   2.1 Algae as a Biomarker 185
   2.2 Application of Algae as a Biomarker 186
3. Use of FACE System Technology as Biomarker in Algae 187
4. Environment Benefits of Algal Biomarker 188
   4.1 Wastewater Treatment 189
   4.2 Climate Change 190
   4.3 Algae Industry 191
5. Conclusion and Future Perspective 192
References 192

1. INTRODUCTION

The vast volume of pollutants spread in the environment endangers the quality of aquatic systems. The large number of pollutants distributed throughout the ecosystem puts the quality of aquatic systems at jeopardy. Metals, sewage, pesticides, prescription drugs, and other contaminants are all contributing to rising levels of pollution in the atmosphere. As predicted, global climate change and its instability are currently being debated by scientists all over the world. According to reports, air pollution, particularly the amount of greenhouse gases present in the atmosphere, is directly responsible for these difficulties (Heidari et al., 2015). Carbon dioxide (CO_2) accounts for 59% of all greenhouse gas emission, according to the World Bank's report (World

Bank Group, 2014). Massive attempts are being undertaken to find ways to comprehend why CO_2 levels in the atmosphere are so high, yet the problem remains unsolved. A variety of solutions have been proposed, one of which being the employment of microalgae. With the help of photosynthesis process, algae convert released CO_2 into organic carbon, which helps in the biomass production (Moreira and Pires, 2016). Recently, algae are being widely used as a bioindicator for controlling and monitoring the regulating pollution (Wickramasinghe et al., 2017). Algal indicators, in comparison to regularly employed animal indicators, give comparatively unique information on ecological status due to their nutritional requirements, as well as their position at the bottom of aquatic food webs. Bioindicators are organisms that can be used to detect and determine the quality of contaminants (Hertz, 1991). Biological monitors are organisms that are used to quantify pollution and are classed as either sensitive or accumulative. As algae can survive and adapt in a carbon dioxide-rich environment for a short length of time, it can be utilized to reduce air pollution and are mostly used for indicating chemical pollutant in the environment. In this context, biomarkers react to chemical stress almost instantly and also have a high toxic significance (Sinaei and Rahmanpour, 2013; Ahner and morel, 1995). Algae react quickly and consistently to a variety of contaminants, making them potential early detection of deteriorating conditions. Algal communities are among the few markers for measuring the biological status of many disrupted or marginally modified habitats and estimating prior water quality conditions (Gökçe, 2016). Algal indicators appear to be economical monitoring technique based on preliminary comparisons. The algal biomass use in the industry could help to address some of the most pressing issues confronting modern society, such as unstable water, energy security, climate crisis, food sources. The ability of aquatic species to sense environmental changes is linked to their functionality and structure, allowing them to respond quickly to climatic stimuli (Littlefield-Wyer et al., 2008). A biomarkers battery is primarily based totally on measurements of complementary traits. It is important to appropriately decide the effect of pollutants on different organisms (Sanchez and Porcher, 2009; Kim and Jung, 2016; Samanta et al., 2018).

Biomarkers are typically characterized as quantifiable indicators of biological system alterations that can be connected to environmental pollutants (WHO, 1993; Peakall and Walker, 1994). FACE is a distinctive method to assess the effects of carbon dioxide for a long term in the laboratory environments that are open. This system adjusts the carbon dioxide level according to the FACE system settings while letting the other factors prevail naturally; hence, it lets the researchers to observe the effect of carbon dioxide on living organisms without altering their pre-existing conditions. A further benefit of FACE is that it enables for the measurement of the effect of high carbon dioxide on plants that cannot be grown in compact places. It also shows environmental benefits in wastewater treatment, climate change, and algae industry. Algal assemblages are vulnerable to a variety of contaminants and can easily accumulate them. Algal metabolism is also sensitive to changes in environmental and natural disturbances (Omar, 2010). This book chapter summarizes algae as a biomarker and the potential of the terrestrial algae as a biomarker using FACE system, which is a data sensor and their role in the environment.

2. ROLE OF BIOMARKER

Chemical contaminants in environmental matrices have expanded considerably in recent years as a result of anthropogenic activity, creating hazardous conditions for living species, including people. Early warning systems for identifying, estimating, and analyzing the hazards posed by chemical pollutant discharges to the environment are becoming more common as concern about the deleterious impacts of chemical pollutants on wildlife and human health grows (Lionetto et al., 2019). The ecological importance of invertebrates with definite evidence that biochemical parameters have a significant impact on the environment. It has been recognized and so has the degree of exposure to invertebrate species. Direct interaction relationships with population change and community strength have been unsuccessfully documented. It has the ecological importance of invertebrates with definite evidence that biochemical parameters have a significant impact on the environment. Analysis of the various changes in the resistance of the progress of pesticides at population and community levels and behaviour, reproduction, and development are biochemical and expected results of the physical changes (Martinez-Haro et al., 2015). Various changes in biomarkers of stressed fish may indicate a viable method for exposing sublethal impacts of pollution presence in aquatic ecosystem. In adult females of an indigenous tribe of the Reconquista River, the response pattern of chosen biochemical and morphologically variable biomarkers was evaluated (Martinez-Haro et al., 2015). Various pollutants introduced into the aquatic environment. Toxicity is a measure of an appropriate biological response that can be easily recognized and assessed in the environment (Martinez-Haro et al., 2015). The number of organic groups represented by the bioindicator are zooplankton, benthos, phytoplankton, and fish. Small group level is a very good indicator to evaluate biomarkers, for example, molecules, pigments, lipids, fatty acids, and degree as phenolic biomarkers recognize the health of the ecosystem and anthropogenic effects (Lomartire et al., 2021). Biomarkers have been divided into two groups, first, exposure biomarkers and other effects biomarkers. Inhibition of these enzymes does not have any negative effects on the entire organism at various levels of structural organization exposure biomarker. When the activity of organophosphorus insecticides and carbamates triggers the inhibition of acetylcholinesterase, they cause substantial damage to the central nervous system of several organisms (Matsuba et al., 1998). The outgrowth of biomarker in the environmental area for the prevention and identification of harmful effect is highly needed because they are harmful for both man and the ecosystem. Biomarker and bioindicator are potential techniques for evaluating environmental quality during legal proceedings. The battery of biomarkers is not enough for the entire environmental quality monitoring. It usually permits the entire ecosystem, which is necessary to evaluate the physical integrity of all species. The toxic effects of the highest possible number of batteries of environmental contaminants can easily be assessed using biomarkers (Peakall, 1992). The increase in the number of pollution-response phytoplankton of aquatic species is detailed later. Discharge of sewage causes phytoplankton growth, increased chlorine, dissolved oxygen, turbidity, and increase in the temperature of the water. Diatoms recognized as indicators of salt water are in *Cyclotella* sp., *Surirella* sp., *Melosira* sp., *Cymbella* sp., *Campylodiscus* sp., *Campylodiscus* sp., *Cocconeis* sp.,

Bacillaria sp., especially for increasing water temperature (Saad and Antoine, 1983; Tett et al., 2007). Biomarker approach was used in many zooplankton organisms to estimate their potential applications studied with copepods *Acratia latisetosa* and *Acratia margalefi* collected from lake of Ganziri (Mesina). Mysid *Siriella armata* gathered in the lake of Faroe (Messina). *Diamysis bahirensis*, *Mysidopsis gibbosa*, and *Siriella armata* were among the mysids collected from Stagnone di Marsala.

TABLE 11.1
Biomarkers-based tools to evaluate environmental and chemical stressors in aquatic environment

Algae name	Types of stressors	Biological group	Response	Reference
1. *Cocconeis placentula*	Temperature and turbidity increase as a result of sewage discharge Pollutants	Phytoplankton	Increased diatom abundance while maintaining their natural state Excess of nitrogen or phosphorous	Saad and Antoine (1983) Tett et al. (2007)
2. *Cymbella affinis*				
3. *Cylotella meneghiniana*				
4. *Mwlosira varians, Bacillaria paradoxa*				
5. *Campylodisc biocstatus*				
6. *Campylodiscus echeneis*				
7. *Cocconeis placentula*				
8. *Phaeocystis* spp.				
9. *Pleurosigma salinarum*				
10. *Sueirella ovalis*				

Genus/Species name	Types of stressors	Biological group	Response	Reference
1. *Acartia margalefi*	Mixture of contaminants (PAHs) Heavy metal cadmium	Zooplankton	As the concentration of pollutants rises, so does the activity of enzymes Low protein intake due to the high energy expenditure required for maintenance	Minutoli et al. (2002) Aljbour et al. (2018)
2. *Acartia latisetosa*				
3. *Siriella clausi*				
4. *Diamysis bahirensis*				
5. *Siriella armata*				
6. *Mysidopsis gibbose*				
7. *Euphausia*				
8. *Crystallorophias*				
9. *Cassiopea* sp.				
10. *Pachygrapsus marmoratus*				

The Antarctic krill, *Euphausiids crystallorophias, Cassiopea* sp., *P. marmoratus* are collected after a shore along the Ionian coast of Messina (Minutoli et al., 2002; Aljbour et al., 2018). Biomarker-based tools for the evaluation of chemical stresses in the aquatic system from the environment are outlined in Table 11.1.

2.1 ALGAE AS A BIOMARKER

Microalgae are photosynthetic organisms that account for 40% of worldwide photosynthesis and produce roughly half of the oxygen in the atmosphere at any given time, making them crucial in aquatic habitats (Moreno-Garrido, 2008). The fact is that the use of biomarkers in ecotoxicology was created primarily for vertebrates. These methodologies have been excellently improved in invertebrates during the last 20 years. Biomarkers for the population and community levels can be developed using environmental evaluation and biochemical monitoring of stress responses (Adams et al., 1989). According to the report, biomarkers adequately explain the induced effect by various types of ecosystem-level environmental stress at any level of biological organization. This also implies that biomarkers are more restrictive, referring to specific biochemical sublethal changes that occur as a result of individual risk xenobiotics (Rachor and Albrecht, 1983). Even if the alga is not toxic, an algae bloom is an unacceptably harmful occurrence for aquatic life. They affect the variability of oxygen, dissolve pH, temperature, etc. In sponges and other sessile macro epifauna animals, hypoxia and anoxia form mucus, and echinoderm drape eating can come in and out. Crustaceans are abandoning their shields and congregating at the apex of ships. Based on traffic series, marine life is fully reliant on algae. Macroalgae is a multicellular species whose complex structures and organs hold the framework for understanding plants, and the photosynthesis is the rate of overall oxygen produced using algae similar to high-quality approximately 32–50% (Campbell, 1993). There are around 130 green algal species in the Mediterranean Sea. It grows at its fastest from April to August and is highly resistant to starvation circumstances such as low oxygen levels, water heating, and the presence of wastewater. Ulva is mostly utilized in biomonitoring research. *Ulva rigida* is the most widespread Ulva species on Mediterranean beaches. The pigment content of filamentous algae, sediments, and phytoplankton collected from Lake Erie throughout the summer and autumn of 2003 to 2005 was determined in a study. A thermocline forms in the eastern basin throughout the summer (Klewin and Rockwell, 2007). The phytoplanktons are the primary food source of dressiness and other invertebrates. The researchers were aiming to analyze the temporal and spatial variations in the abundance of organisms present near the shore. Lake Erie is a temperate holomictic lake that is active from autumn through the winter and into the early spring (Schertzer et al., 1987; Depew et al., 2006). Envisage of the sample is relatively shallow at the sites for collection, that is, <20 m, small adjacent, was well find mixed, non-spatial variations of class biomarkers as indicated stratified conditions. Seasonal change in algal pigments, on the other hand, was expected. The filamentous algae study objective was to access the structure and the track variations from the site of the sample, that is, in the middle of the two nearshore sites. The idea was that the sample would mainly contain *Cladophora glomerata*, a chlorophyll pigment that grew from 1995 to 2002 in a nearby area east of Lake Erie (average biomass 170 g dw/m2) (Higgins et al., 2005). Diagnostic pigments of epiphytic diatoms were expected in lesser quantity (Malkin et al., 2009), rhodophyte, imported blue-green algae from seawater (Sheath and Morison, 1982). Sediments include silica-filled diatoms, planktonic and benthic animal faeces, and digested biomass to a certain extent from cryptophytes, chlorophytes, cyanobacteria, and diatoms.

2.2 Application of Algae as a Biomarker

Heavy metals in aquatic environments have been determined and quantified using algae as a biomonitoring method (Levkov and Krstic, 2002; Shah et al., 2009). They are abundant in nature, but due to their poor solubility, they may be separated from the Earth's crust via methods consisting of erosion and weathering and are dissolved in aquatic ecosystems (Chakraborty et al., 2014), where they eventually bioaccumulate in aquatic creatures. Algal organisms are being employed to assess the pollutants present in water bodies in order to monitor and control them (Wickramasinghe et al., 2017). They are preferred as biological monitor due to their extensive distribution, presence in contaminated areas, functions at the beginning of the food chain, high heavy metal absorption, and simplicity with which metals can be tested in them (Wickramasinghe et al., 2017). They are also being used as bioindicators of chemicals contaminants as these biomarkers are sensitive and have high toxicological relevance to chemical stress (Sinaei and Rahmanpour, 2013; Tuvikene, 1995). They use a variety of biochemical processes in their cytoplasm to prevent Hg and Cd toxicity, as well as necessary trace metals and metal homeostasis (Cobbet and Goldsbrough, 2002; Hall, 2002; Szivák et al., 2009). The use of ligands that bind heavy metals, such as metallothionein (MT) and phytochelatin (PC), is one of the approaches. PC synthase enzymes are used to make phytochelatins from glutathione, cysteine, glycine, and glutamate tripeptides. Instead of a metal-specific response, phytochelatin produces induction by chemicals. Metals that do not separate work phytochelatin in detoxification of metals as inspire PC output enables a metal-phytochelatin complex that has only been evaluated in vitro and in vivo algae (Ahner and Morel, 1995; Rauser, 1999; Schmoger et al., 2000; Scarano and Morelli, 2002; Le Faucheur et al., 2006; Alberich et al., 2007; Chekmeneva et al., 2007). Metallothioneins are a protein class with a low molecular weight (6–8 kDa) with a structure that binds to metals in a unique way (Verkleij et al., 2003; Pandey et al., 2003; Sinaie et al.,2010). Due to its specificity as a detoxicant in aquatic bodies against metal stress, the synthesis of MTs and PCs has been recommended as a biomarker (Chen et al., 2007; Sinaie et al., 2010). Selected biomarkers such as metallothionein (MT) and phytochelatin (PC) were calculated in *Cystoseria indica*, that is, brown algae, taken from the Sea of Oman, in a study done by various researchers. Different approaches were used, such as chemical analysis, statistical analysis, MT analysis, PC analysis, quality control, etc., in brown algae to assess the heavy metal concentration. Highest quantity of Zn was discovered, followed by chromium > nickel > copper > lead > cadmium> mercury. The association between biomarkers and heavy metals were also discovered. Heavy metals such as Cd, Cu, Zn, Pb, Ni, and Cr had notable correlations with metallothionein, but phytochelatin and heavy metals Cd and Zn had only statistically significant correlations. The findings revealed that phytochelatin reacted with heavy metals less than metallothionein, limiting its potential as a biomarker.

3. USE OF FACE SYSTEM TECHNOLOGY AS BIOMARKER IN ALGAE

Microalgae can be found in both marine and fresh water as they are the photosynthetic microorganisms. Some microorganisms grow very quickly when biomass productivity is high, and a few species can double cell concentration in a matter of hours (Cheah et al., 2015). It has been studied that microalga removes carbon dioxide from the atmosphere (Brilman et al., 2013; Pires et al., 2012). Basically, one must employ atmospheric carbon dioxide to benefit microalgae in many ways. Transporting system of carbon dioxide are not required. Apart from carbon dioxide content, other parameters affect microalgae development such as temperature, pH, light, salinity, etc. Carbon dioxide determines rate and biomass productivity. Intensity of light and temperature are important elements in microalgae growth. The photosynthetic regulation of microalgae and carbon dioxide solubility increases as the temperature drops (Ghorbani et al., 2014). The most significant component is the intensity of the light supply and lighting. High light intensity ensures better penetration in high density culture. The free carbon dioxide enrichment method is used to determine the efficacy of a strategy that will be employed by plant biologists and ecologists in a specific area. It will increase carbon dioxide concentrations in response to increased use of plants. Researchers believe that in the future, free air carbon dioxide will become a more acceptable means of enhancing plant carbon dioxide uptake, which will be evaluated in order to determine the effect of carbon dioxide. Another benefit is that it is free to promote carbon dioxide in the air; nevertheless, it cannot be cultivated in narrow places such as trees, which permits the impacts of elevated carbon dioxide on plants. Epiphytic terrestrial algae thrive in environments with greater carbon

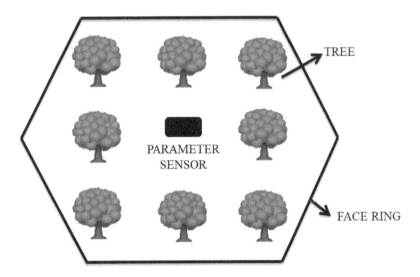

FIGURE 11.1 Quadrats placed on trees in a free air carbon dioxide enrichment (FACE) system.

dioxide levels (Bischoff, 1963). Custom designed for FACE in another study involving systems that covered the area of about a 55-metre square was used in University Kebangsaan in Malaysia that contained different species of plants (Figure 11.1).

In this method, *Barringtonia racemosa* in Southeast Asia are placed in quadrats on a tree. The FACE is a typical method for assessing the effects of carbon dioxide in a laboratory in open environment for a long term. In this method the environmental factors surrounding the area were unchanged. The recorded environmental parameters were temperature, wind direction, humidity, and wind speed. This system adjusts the carbon dioxide level according to the FACE system settings while letting the other factors prevail naturally. Hence, it allows the scientists to investigate the carbon dioxide impact on living organisms without affecting the pre-existing conditions. Components of FACE system are as follows: a sensor data sender, a sensor data timestamp, Xbee wireless sensors, a carbon dioxide scheduler, and watch, a real-time clock on the display (RTC). Xbee wireless sensors contain four nodes in which sensor nodes calculate carbon dioxide, humidity, and temperature, whereas one wind speed (WS) sensor node is present to measure wind speed. The carbon dioxide scheduler checks the functioning of valves in the area where carbon dioxide is supplied. Sensor data sends the received data by single-cell protein (SCP) to the server, which is then stored in a cloud server which is accessible by android devices and desktops. In the procedure, carbon dioxide gas is supplied at one hour interval in this system when wind speed is below 15 km/hr is present. In the system, three valves are present; in which the first valve operates for five minutes at RTC hour, the second valve also operates at RTC hour for five minutes after ten minutes, and only one valve can be activated at a time. These conditions are given by using manual push buttons as well. A buzzer goes off to indicate the ongoing process during a supply (Ghannoum et al., 2000). In this system, algal collection and quantification can be done systematically by experimental setups where algal swabs are taken from areas inside the FACE ring. The risk of carbon dioxide for 380 days with algae while quadrat control group remains in its natural conditions (Whitton et al., 1995). The density of algae can be collected and quantified as well as the total cells per ml (Ali et al., 1999).

4. ENVIRONMENT BENEFITS OF ALGAL BIOMARKER

Stress-induced alterations in ecosystems are widely acknowledged to be a major source of concern. However, such changes are frequently removed from the record of environmental stress indicators used for early detection and prediction due to their complexity (Depledge et al., 1993). At a molecular and cellular level, the effective characterization of distress signals providing early warning system of impaired performances is a possible solution to this problem (Moore et al., 2004). Biomarkers are commonly described as quantitative indications of biological system modifications that can be connected to environmental pollutants' dangerous effects (WHO, 1993; Peakall and Walker, 1994). A single biomarker may not be enough to monitor environmental quality. It is necessary to develop a group of biomarkers that can be used to assess the physiological health of all species in a particular environment (Peakall, 1992). They should be able to assess the harmful effects of as many environmental pollutants as possible. Biomarkers, in general, indicate a multiplicity of dose-response connections that are the result of all conceivable interactions of all pollutants present in the ecosystem under study, rather than a single dose-response relationship. As a result, a battery of biomarkers can be used to assess at what level of structural complexity a given ecosystem's response is to a harmful substance. Algae are seen in abundance in the aquatic environment. They are an important ecological group that has been included in ecological monitoring systems for a long time. They're ideal for measuring water quality since they reproduce quickly and have short life cycles, making them good indicators of short-term effects. Algal assemblages are vulnerable to a variety of contaminants and easily accumulate them, and changes in the environment and natural disturbances can also affect algal metabolism (Omar, 2010). Marine microalgae are particularly attractive indicator species for organic and inorganic pollutants because they are abundant in aquatic environments and occupy the bottom of the food chain (Torres et al., 2008).

4.1 Wastewater Treatment

Depending on the source, most of the utilized water is transformed to wastewater, which has a wide range of chemical compositions. The content of ammonium and organic nitrogen can be high in wastewater, for example, from animal farms and, on the other hand, wastewater from power plants and municipal wastewater, where phosphorous and nitrogen content is low, but heavy metals are present in high amount. Before wastewater may be released or reused, hazardous metal ions and nutrients must be extracted (Liu et al., 2016; Luo et al., 2017) (Figure 11.2.).

The current process of extracting metal ions from wastewater and other inorganic compounds aims not only to recover by-products of high-value but also to reduce health concerns and pollutants associated with their disposal (WWAP, 2017). To meet the sustainable development goals, water quality must be improved, and the quantity of untreated effluent must be reduced (World Bank, 2016). Biological treatment, in which toxins are broken down with the help of microorganisms and evaporate the

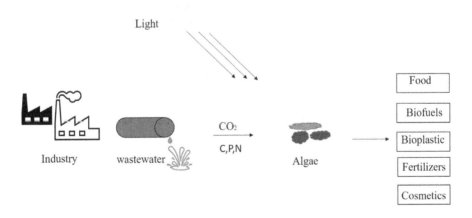

FIGURE 11.2 Cultivation of algae.

remains through the formation of value-added compounds, has been the lowest cost process for wastewater treatment as well as it is environmental friendly (Rawat et al., 2011; Bhattacharjee and Siemann, 2015). Harvesting and isolating the biomass at the conclusion of the process is one of the challenges in building microalgae-based wastewater treatment systems due to the microalgae's tiny size and the cultures' considerable dilution. Algae harvesting techniques presently need a significant amount of energy and chemicals, limiting the application in large-scale algae cultivation. Microalgae are used as an alternative for the wastewater treatment as it has a very high potential for inorganic nutrient uptake. It has been proven that in the absence of an organic source, microalgae are capable of successfully accumulating nutrients as well as metal ions (Abdel-Raouf et al., 2012; Ruiz-Marin et al., 2010). After thermal conversion, biomass can be converted to produce a variety of value-added products such as bioethanol, biohydrogen, bio-methanol, or fuel (Rawat et al., 2011).

4.2 CLIMATE CHANGE

As proof of exposure to specific contaminants, biomarkers can be assessed objectively and statistically. Single biomarkers, when assessed in isolation, usually provide enough data or knowledge to completely analyze a specific exposure hypothesis (Forbes et al., 2006). At various levels of biological structure, a well-chosen panel of biomarkers should be used to create profile of biomarkers and fingerprint. These profiles can be linked to single substances and environmental influences with caution and then generalized to population level effects (Calow and Forbes, 2003; Kidd et al., 2007; Schmolke et al., 2010). Toxins almost always have biochemical effects before they are demonstrated to affect entire populations; biomarkers can provide risk prediction values that are pre-emptive or conservative. Another benefit is the opportunity to customize a biomarker set to examine the unique problems of the pollutant or ecosystem under study. Ectotherms are marine invertebrates due to which the influence of rising temperatures on their physiology will almost certainly amplify species' responses to the change in climate (Ruppert et al., 2004). Similarly, changes in salinity have also been observed to impact functioning of detoxifying and antioxidant systems in numerous invertebrates (Zanette et al., 2011; Tu et al., 2012). Salinity has little or no effect on estuarine mussel species, according to studies of DNA damage indicators (Singh and Hartl, 2012). Several research have examined how change in salinity affects the growth and reproduction of commercially important species in estuarine environments, with high salinity fluctuations used (Pfeifer et al., 2005; Cailleaud et al., 2007; Rodrigues et al., 2012). While this research showed considerable changes in enzyme activity in response to salinity increases, they were based on short-term salt shock loads on organisms, not the continuous and chronic rise that change in climate is expected to be over many generations. According to a study, *Trebouxia* sp., a type of epiphytic terrestrial algae that can be used as a biomarker for rising the levels of CO_2. When the surrounding region has a high CO_2 content, it promotes a significant increase in algal population and the development of algae (Ismail et al., 2017). Moreira and Pires used microalgae to absorb CO_2 from the atmosphere in their investigation (Moreira and Pires, 2016). This is due to the ability of algae to convert the released CO_2 into organic carbon through photosynthesis, producing enormous amounts of biomass (Farrelly et al., 2013). Although, algae could be used to improve the air quality, there is a lack of research into the effects of algae in the presence of CO_2, such as whether they can evolve and thrive in an environment rich in CO_2 for a long time or in a short time.

4.3 ALGAE INDUSTRY

It is vital to determine the level of contaminants in an ecosystem in order to assess their potential toxicity at various stages of the tropic chain. Metal ion detoxifying systems exist in photosynthetic species, some of which might serve as biomarkers of exposure or quantifiable indicators of alterations in the biological system caused by environmental pollutants. Algae could be used as bioindicators for ecological and functional integrity of structural components (Stancheva and Sheath, 2016). The metabolism of algae is susceptible environmental and variations that occur naturally and are affected directly due to chemical and physical factors and rapidly acquire contaminants (Omar, 2010). Algae could be beneficial for transferring the ecological response to harmful substance exposure because of their natural and extensive prevalence along the world's seashores (Torres et al., 2008). The algae reaction can be measured as a biomarker, which is a short-term indicator of environmental stress, or as a bioindicator, which is a long-term indicator of an aquatic system's health status. Biomarkers that respond quickly can be used as an early alert for monitoring environmental change, whereas bioindicators can study the samples at any time after they are collected from the environment (Bellinger and Sigee, 2015). Diatoms are employed to generate a multitude of indicators that determine eutrophication, salinity, acidification, or acidity of water in algae indication systems (Fetscher et al., 2014; Bielczyńska, 2015). Lake environmental quality is assessed using the multimeric Diatom Index in Poland, which is based on phytobenthic diatoms (Bielczyńska, 2015). In a short time, *Ulva australis* can accumulate arsenic, lead, zinc, and copper, according to Farias (DR et al., 2017) and can be a valuable tool for metal pollution monitoring and control. Algae can also be used to detect pollution levels in the atmosphere. *Trebouxia* sp. studies have found it to be a good biomarker of elevated CO_2 levels. In comparison to the control location, this alga had a much higher density inside the FACE system, where CO_2 gas was supplied. Microalgae are one of the most potential sources for novel goods and uses due to their great biodiversity, metabolic and genetic engineering advancement, and introduction of advanced processes of culture and screening (Harun et al., 2010). They are rapidly rising in popularity as a food source, biochemical production and bioenergy generation, feed and climate change mitigation due to their sustainability and versatility for a longer period in applications (Ratnapuram et al., 2018; Vu et al., 2018). It is a source of bioactive chemicals with potential in the pharmaceutical, biomedical, and nutraceutical industries (Veena et al., 2007). Microalgae can produce polyunsaturated fatty acids, pigments, antioxidants, drugs for animal feed, and beneficial foods such as biomass, fertilizers, and energy crops and are becoming increasingly popular as therapeutics for a variety of diseases. They have the potential applications in the industries such as food and biofuel; fatty acids produced by microalgae are gaining popularity (Apt and Behrens, 1999; Christian et al., 2009). It has been studied that, in microalgae, fatty acids are stress-responsive biomarkers (Lu et al., 2012).

5. CONCLUSION AND FUTURE PERSPECTIVE

From this chapter it emerges that biological tools are being widely studied by the scientists over the years. Biomarkers are often defined as quantitative indicators of changes in biological systems that may be associated with hazardous exposure to environmental pollutants. Recently, algae are being widely used as a bioindicator for controlling and monitoring the regulating pollution. Algae react quickly and consistently to a variety of contaminants, making them potentially helpful early warning indicators of deteriorating conditions and their causes. Algae as a biomarker are mostly used for indicating chemical pollutant in the environment. FACE is a distinctive method to assess the long-term effects of carbon dioxide in the open laboratory environments, which is the potential of epigenetic terrestrial algae as data sensors and mid- to long-term biomarkers. Algae as a biomarker can also be used in wastewater treatment and algal industry.

The main objective of this book chapter is to intentionally regulate biomarkers at the sub-organism or organismal level to predict the effects of exposure at the population and community level (Giesy and Graney, 1989). As current research identifies, develops, and validates biomarkers that are highly sensitive, inexpensive, and easy to use, the most important growth is the evaluation of the biomarker in the field of environmental restoration. With the screening report for the bioremediation or environmental restoration, biomarker is very useful (Fossi M.C., 1998). The specific terrestrial algae *Trebouxia* sp. can be regarded as a good biomarker of long-term central to the emerging carbon dioxide concentrations as mentioned previously. If the surrounding area contained high amounts of carbon dioxide concentration, then we can see a carbon dioxide seriously trigger higher algal density. Brown algae, *C. indica*, activity of metallothioneins and phytochelatins in the Gulf of Oman's north shore because of the significant relationship with heavy metals and biomarkers, they can be utilized as proof of the substantial sensitivity of phytochelatin production in *C. indica*. They recommended examining heavy metal effects in seaweed, considering the ease of analysis of the parameter when using different biomarkers in a particular way.

REFERENCES

Abdel-Raouf, N., Al-Homaidan, A. A., & Ibraheem, I. (2012). Microalgae and wastewater treatment. *Saudi Journal of Biological Sciences, 19*(3), 257–275.

Adams, S. M., Shepard, K. L., Greeley Jr, M. S., Jimenez, B. D., Ryon, M. G., Shugart, L. R., ... & Hinton, D. E. (1989). The use of bioindicators for assessing the effects of pollutant stress on fish. *Marine Environmental Research, 28*(1–4), 459–464.

Ahner, B. A., & Morel, F. M. (1995). Phytochelatin production in marine algae. 2. Induction by various metals. *Limnology and Oceanography, 40*(4), 658–665.

Alberich, A., Ariño, C., Díaz-Cruz, J. M., & Esteban, M. (2007). Multivariate curve resolution applied to the simultaneous analysis of electrochemical and spectroscopic data: Study of the Cd (II)/glutathione-fragment system by voltammetry and circular dichroism spectroscopy. *Analytica chimica acta, 584*(2), 403–409.

Ali, M. B., Tripathi, R. D., Rai, U. N., Pal, A., & Singh, S. P. (1999). Physico-chemical characteristics and pollution level of lake Nainital (UP, India): Role of macrophytes

and phytoplankton in biomonitoring and phytoremediation of toxic metal ions. *Chemosphere, 39*(12), 2171–2182.
Aljbour, S. M., Al-Horani, F. A., & Kunzmann, A. (2018). Metabolic and oxidative stress responses of the jellyfish Cassiopea to pollution in the Gulf of Aqaba, Jordan. *Marine Pollution Bulletin, 130*, 271–278.
Apt, K. E., & Behrens, P. W. (1999). Commercial developments in microalgal biotechnology. *Journal of Phycology, 35*(2), 215–226.
Bellinger, E. G., & Sigee, D. C. (2015). *Freshwater algae: Identification, enumeration and use as bioindicators*. John Wiley & Sons.
Bhattacharjee, M., & Siemann, E. (2015). Low algal diversity systems are a promising method for biodiesel production in wastewater fed open reactors. *Algae, 30*(1), 67–79.
Bielczyńska, A. (2015). Bioindication on the basis of benthic diatoms: Advantages and disadvantages of the Polish phytobenthos lake assessment method (IOJ—the Diatom Index for Lakes)/Bioindykacja na podstawie okrzemek bentosowych: Mocne i słabe strony polskiej metody oceny jezior na podstawie fitobentosu (IOJ—Indeks Okrzemkowy Jezior). *Environmental Protection and Natural Resources/Ochrona Środowiska i Zasobów Naturalnych, 26*(4), 48–55.
Bischoff, H. C. (1963). Some soil algae from enchanted rock and related algal species. *Phycological Studies IV. University of Texas Publ. No. 6318, 6318*, 1–95.
Brilman, W., Alba, L. G., & Veneman, R. (2013). Capturing atmospheric CO2 using supported amine sorbents for microalgae cultivation. *Biomass and Bioenergy, 53*, 39–47.
Cailleaud, K., Maillet, G., Budzinski, H., Souissi, S., & Forget-Leray, J. (2007). Effects of salinity and temperature on the expression of enzymatic biomarkers in Eurytemora affinis (Calanoida, Copepoda). *Comparative Biochemistry and Physiology Part A: Molecular & Integrative Physiology, 147*(4), 841–849.
Calow, P., & Forbes, V. E. (2003). Peer reviewed: Does ecotoxicology inform ecological risk assessment?.
Campbell, N. A. (1993). *Tracing phylogeny: Macroevolution, the fossil record, and systematics*. Biology [3rd edition]. The Benjamin/Cummings Publishing Company, Inc, 474–499.
Chakraborty, S., Bhattacharya, T., Singh, G., & Maity, J. P. (2014). Benthic macroalgae as biological indicators of heavy metal pollution in the marine environments: A biomonitoring approach for pollution assessment. *Ecotoxicology and Environmental Safety, 100*, 61–68.
Cheah, W. Y., Show, P. L., Chang, J. S., Ling, T. C., & Juan, J. C. (2015). Biosequestration of atmospheric CO2 and flue gas-containing CO2 by microalgae. *Bioresource Technology, 184*, 190–201.
Chekmeneva, E., Díaz-Cruz, J. M., Arino, C., & Esteban, M. (2007). Binding of Cd2+ and Zn2+ with the phytochelatin (γ-Glu-Cys) 4-Gly: A voltammetric study assisted by multivariate curve resolution and electrospray ionization mass spectrometry. *Electroanalysis: An International Journal Devoted to Fundamental and Practical Aspects of Electroanalysis, 19*(2-3), 310–317.
Chen, L., Guo, Y., Yang, L., & Wang, Q. (2007). SEC-ICP-MS and ESI-MS/MS for analyzing in vitro and in vivo Cd-phytochelatin complexes in a Cd-hyperaccumulator Brassica chinensis. *Journal of Analytical Atomic Spectrometry, 22*(11), 1403–1408.
Christian, B., Lichti, B., Pulz, O., Grewe, C., & Luckas, B. (2009). Fast and unambiguous determination of EPA and DHA content in oil of selected strains of algae and cyanobacteria. *Acta Agronomica Hungarica, 57*(2), 249–253.
Cobbett, C., & Goldsbrough, P. (2002). Phytochelatins and metallothioneins: Roles in heavy metal detoxification and homeostasis. *Annual Review of Plant Biology, 53*(1), 159–182.

Depew, D. C., Guildford, S. J., & Smith, R. E. (2006). Nearshore offshore comparison of chlorophyll a and phytoplankton production in the dreissenid-colonized eastern basin of Lake Erie. *Canadian Journal of Fisheries and Aquatic Sciences*, 63(5), 1115–1129.

Depledge, M. H., Amaral-Mendes, J. J., Daniel, B. R. S. H., Halbrook, R. S., Kloepper-Sams, P., Moore, M. N., & Peakall, D. B. (1993). The conceptual basis of the biomarker approach. In *Biomarkers* (pp. 15–29). Springer, Berlin, Heidelberg.

DR, F., Hurd, C. L., Eriksen, R. S., & Macleod, C. K. (2017). Ulva australis as a tool for monitoring zinc in the Derwent Estuary and implications for environmental assessment.

Farrelly, D. J., Everard, C. D., Fagan, C. C., & McDonnell, K. P. (2013). Carbon sequestration and the role of biological carbon mitigation: A review. *Renewable and Sustainable Energy Reviews*, 21, 712–727.

Fetscher, A. E., Stancheva, R., Kociolek, J. P., Sheath, R. G., Stein, E. D., Mazor, R. D., ... & Busse, L. B. (2014). Development and comparison of stream indices of biotic integrity using diatoms vs. non-diatom algae vs. a combination. *Journal of Applied Phycology*, 26(1), 433–450.

Forbes, V. E., Palmqvist, A., & Bach, L. (2006). The use and misuse of biomarkers in ecotoxicology. *Environmental Toxicology and Chemistry: An International Journal*, 25(1), 272–280.

Fossi, M. C. (1998). Biomakers: Strumenti diagnostici e prognostici di salute ambientale. *Ecotossicologia (UTET) Ed. Vighi e Bacci*, 237.

Ghannoum, O., Caemmerer, S. V., Ziska, L. H., & Conroy, J. P. (2000). The growth response of C4 plants to rising atmospheric CO2 partial pressure: A reassessment. *Plant, Cell & Environment*, 23(9), 931–942.

Ghorbani, A., Rahimpour, H. R., Ghasemi, Y., Zoughi, S., & Rahimpour, M. R. (2014). A review of carbon capture and sequestration in Iran: Microalgal biofixation potential in Iran. *Renewable and Sustainable Energy Reviews*, 35, 73–100.

Giesy, J. P., & Graney, R. L. (1989). Recent developments in and intercomparisons of acute and chronic bioassays and bioindicators. In *Environmental Bioassay Techniques and their Application* (pp. 21–60). Springer, Dordrecht.

Gökçe, D. (2016). Algae as an Indicator of Water Quality, Algae-Organisms for Imminent Biotechnology.In Thajuddin, N., & Dhanasekaran, D. (Eds.). (2016). *Algae: Organisms for Imminent Biotechnology*. IntechOpen, London.

Hall, J. Á. (2002). Cellular mechanisms for heavy metal detoxification and tolerance. *Journal of Experimental Botany*, 53(366), 1–11.

Harun, R., Singh, M., Forde, G. M., & Danquah, M. K. (2010). Bioprocess engineering of microalgae to produce a variety of consumer products. *Renewable and Sustainable Energy Reviews*, 14(3), 1037–1047.

Heidari, H., Katircioğlu, S. T., & Saeidpour, L. (2015). Economic growth, CO2 emissions, and energy consumption in the five ASEAN countries. *International Journal of Electrical Power & Energy Systems*, 64, 785–791.

Hertz, J. (1991). 'Bioindicators for monitoring heavy metals in the environment', in Merian, E. (Editor) *Metals and their Compounds in the Environment*, pp. 221–231. VCH Verlagsges, Weinheim.

Higgins, S. N., Howell, E. T., Hecky, R. E., Guildford, S. J., & Smith, R. E. (2005). The wall of green: The status of Cladophora glomerata on the northern shores of Lake Erie's eastern basin, 1995–2002. *Journal of Great Lakes Research*, 31(4), 547–563.

Ismail, A., Marzuki, S. D., Mohd Yusof, N. B., Buyong, F., Mohd Said, M. N., Sigh, H. R., & Zulkifli, A. R. (2017). Epiphytic terrestrial algae (Trebouxia sp.) as a biomarker using the free-air-carbon dioxide-enrichment (FACE) system. *Biology*, 6(1), 19.

Kidd, K. A., Blanchfield, P. J., Mills, K. H., Palace, V. P., Evans, R. E., Lazorchak, J. M., & Flick, R. W. (2007). Collapse of a fish population after exposure to a synthetic estrogen. *Proceedings of the National Academy of Sciences*, *104*(21), 8897–8901.

Kim, W. K., & Jung, J. (2016). In situ impact assessment of wastewater effluents by integrating multi-level biomarker responses in the pale chub (Zacco platypus). *Ecotoxicology and environmental safety*, *128*, 246–251.

Klewin, K. & Rockwell, D. (2007). Lake Guardian temperatures for August and April 2003 to 2005, at stations ER 9, 10, 15 M and 63 in the eastern basin of Lake Erie. US EPA GLNPO, Chicago, IL. Oct 30

Le Faucheur, S., Schildknecht, F., Behra, R., & Sigg, L. (2006). Thiols in Scenedesmus vacuolatus upon exposure to metals and metalloids. *Aquatic toxicology*, *80*(4), 355–361.

Levkov, Z., & Krstic, S. (2002). Use of algae for monitoring of heavy metals in the River Vardar, Macedonia. *Mediterranean Marine Science*, *3*(1), 99–102.

Lionetto, M. G., Caricato, R., & Giordano, M. E. (2019). Pollution biomarkers in environmental and human biomonitoring. *The Open Biomarkers Journal*, *9*(1).

Littlefield-Wyer, J. G., Brooks, P., & Katouli, M. (2008). Application of biochemical fingerprinting and fatty acid methyl ester profiling to assess the effect of the pesticide Atradex on aquatic microbial communities. *Environmental Pollution*, *153*(2), 393–400.

Liu, J., Danneels, B., Vanormelingen, P., & Vyverman, W. (2016). Nutrient removal from horticultural wastewater by benthic filamentous algae Klebsormidium sp., Stigeoclonium spp. and their communities: From laboratory flask to outdoor Algal Turf Scrubber (ATS). *Water Research*, *92*, 61–68.

Lomartire, S., Marques, J. C., & Gonçalves, A. M. (2021). Biomarkers based tools to assess environmental and chemical stressors in aquatic systems. *Ecological Indicators*, *122*, 107207.

Lu, N., Wei, D., Jiang, X. L., Chen, F., & Yang, S. T. (2012). Fatty acids profiling and biomarker identification in snow alga Chlamydomonas nivalis by NaCl stress using GC/MS and multivariate statistical analysis. *Analytical letters*, *45*(10), 1172–1183.

Luo, S., Berges, J. A., He, Z., & Young, E. B. (2017). Algal-microbial community collaboration for energy recovery and nutrient remediation from wastewater in integrated photo-bioelectrochemical systems. *Algal Research*, *24*, 527–539.

Malkin, S. Y., Sorichetti, R. J., Wiklund, J. A., & Hecky, R. E. (2009). Seasonal abundance, community composition, and silica content of diatoms epiphytic on Cladophora glomerata. *Journal of Great Lakes Research*, *35*(2), 199–205.

Martinez-Haro, M., Beiras, R., Bellas, J., Capela, R., Coelho, J. P., Lopes, I., . . . & Marques, J. C. (2015). A review on the ecological quality status assessment in aquatic systems using community based indicators and ecotoxicological tools: What might be the added value of their combination?. *Ecological Indicators*, *48*, 8–16.

Matsuba, T., Keicho, N., Higashimoto, Y., Granleese, S., Hogg, J. C., Hayashi, S., & Bondy, G. P. (1998). Identification of glucocorticoid-and adenovirus E1A-regulated genes in lung epithelial cells by differential display. *American Journal of Respiratory Cell and Molecular Biology*, *18*(2), 243–254.

Minutoli, R., Fossi, M. C., & Guglielmo, L. (2002). Potential use of biomarkers in zooplankton as early warning signals of ecotoxicological risk in the marine food chain. *Marine Ecology*, *23*, 291–296.

Moore, M. N., Depledge, M. H., Readman, J. W., & Leonard, D. P. (2004). An integrated biomarker-based strategy for ecotoxicological evaluation of risk in environmental management. *Mutation Research/Fundamental and Molecular Mechanisms of Mutagenesis*, *552*(1–2), 247–268.

Moreira, D., & Pires, J. C. (2016). Atmospheric CO2 capture by algae: Negative carbon dioxide emission path. *Bioresource Technology*, *215*, 371–379.

Moreno-Garrido, I. (2008). Microalgae immobilization: Current techniques and uses. *Bioresource Technology*, *99*(10), 3949–3964.

Omar, W. M. W. (2010). Perspectives on the use of algae as biological indicators for monitoring and protecting aquatic environments, with special reference to Malaysian freshwater ecosystems. *Tropical life sciences research*, *21*(2), 51.

Pandey, S., Parvez, S., Sayeed, I., Haque, R., Bin-Hafeez, B., & Raisuddin, S. (2003). Biomarkers of oxidative stress: A comparative study of river Yamuna fish Wallago attu (Bl. & Schn.). *Science of the Total Environment*, *309*(1–3), 105–115.

Peakall, D. (1992). Biomarkers of the nervous system. In *Animal Biomarkers as Pollution Indicators* (pp. 19–45). Springer, Dordrecht.

Peakall, D. B., & Walker, C. H. (1994). The role of biomarkers in environmental assessment (3). Vertebrates. *Ecotoxicology*, *3*(3), 173–179.

Pfeifer, S., Schiedek, D., & Dippner, J. W. (2005). Effect of temperature and salinity on acetylcholinesterase activity, a common pollution biomarker, in Mytilus sp. from the south-western Baltic Sea. *Journal of Experimental Marine Biology and Ecology*, *320*(1), 93–103.

Pires, J. C. M., Alvim-Ferraz, M. C. M., Martins, F. G., & Simões, M. (2012). Carbon dioxide capture from flue gases using microalgae: Engineering aspects and biorefinery concept. *Renewable and Sustainable Energy Reviews*, *16*(5), 3043–3053.

Rachor, E., & Albrecht, H. (1983). Sauerstoff-Mangel im Bodenwasser der Deutschen Bucht. *Veröff. Inst. Meeresforsch. Bremerh*, *19*, 209–227.

Ratnapuram, H. P., Vutukuru, S. S., & Yadavalli, R. (2018). Mixotrophic transition induced lipid productivity in Chlorella pyrenoidosa under stress conditions for biodiesel production. *Heliyon*, *4*(1), e00496.

Rauser, W. E. (1999). Structure and function of metal chelators produced by plants. *Cell Biochemistry and Biophysics*, *31*(1), 19–48.

Rawat, I., Kumar, R. R., Mutanda, T., & Bux, F. (2011). Dual role of microalgae: Phycoremediation of domestic wastewater and biomass production for sustainable biofuels production. *Applied Energy*, *88*(10), 3411–3424.

Rodrigues, A. P., Oliveira, P. C., Guilhermino, L., & Guimaraes, L. (2012). Effects of salinity stress on neurotransmission, energy metabolism, and anti-oxidant biomarkers of Carcinus maenas from two estuaries of the NW Iberian Peninsula. *Marine Biology*, *159*(9), 2061–2074.

Ruiz-Marin, A., Mendoza-Espinosa, L. G., & Stephenson, T. (2010). Growth and nutrient removal in free and immobilized green algae in batch and semi-continuous cultures treating real wastewater. *Bioresource Technology*, *101*(1), 58–64.

Ruppert, E. E., Barnes, R. D., & Fox, R. S. (2004). *Invertebrate zoology: A functional evolutionary approach* (No. 592 RUPi).

Saad, M. A., & Antoine, S. E. (1983). Effect of pollution on phytoplankton in the Ashar Canal, a highly polluted canal of the Shatt al-Arab Estuary at Basrah, Iraq. *Hydrobiologia*, *99*(3), 189–196.

Samanta, P., Im, H., Na, J., & Jung, J. (2018). Ecological risk assessment of a contaminated stream using multi-level integrated biomarker response in Carassius auratus. *Environmental Pollution*, *233*, 429–438.

Sanchez, W., & Porcher, J. M. (2009). Fish biomarkers for environmental monitoring within the Water Framework Directive of the European Union. *TrAC Trends in Analytical Chemistry*, *28*(2), 150–158.

Scarano, G., & Morelli, E. (2002). Characterization of cadmium-and lead-phytochelatin complexes formed in a marine microalga in response to metal exposure. *Biometals, 15*(2), 145–151.

Schertzer, W. M., Saylor, J. H., Boyce, F. M., Robertson, D. G., & Rosa, F. (1987). Seasonal thermal cycle of Lake Erie. *Journal of Great Lakes Research, 13*(4), 468–486.

Schmoger, M. E., Oven, M., & Grill, E. (2000). Detoxification of arsenic by phytochelatins in plants. *Plant Physiology, 122*(3), 793–802.

Schmolke, A., Thorbek, P., Chapman, P., & Grimm, V. (2010). Ecological models and pesticide risk assessment: Current modeling practice. *Environmental Toxicology and Chemistry: An International Journal, 29*(4), 1006–1012.

Shah, B. A., Shah, A. V., & Singh, R. R. (2009). Sorption isotherms and kinetics of chromium uptake from wastewater using natural sorbent material. *International Journal of Environmental Science & Technology, 6*(1), 77–90.

Sheath, R. G., & Morison, M. O. (1982). Epiphytes on cladophora glomerata in the great lakes and st. Lawrence seaway with particular reference to the red alga chroodactylon ramosum (= asterocytis smargdina) 1. *Journal of Phycology, 18*(3), 385–391.

Sinaei, M., & Rahmanpour, S. (2013). Evaluation of glutathione S-transferase activity as a biomarker of PAH pollution in mudskipper, Boleophthalmus dussumieri, Persian Gulf. *Bulletin of Environmental Contamination and Toxicology, 90*(3), 369–374.

Sinaie, M., Bastami, K. D., Ghorbanpour, M., Najafzadeh, H., Shekari, M., & Haghparast, S. (2010). Metallothionein biosynthesis as a detoxification mechanism in mercury exposure in fish, spotted scat (Scatophagus argus). *Fish Physiology and Biochemistry, 36*(4), 1235–1242.

Singh, R., & Hartl, M. G. (2012). Fluctuating estuarine conditions are not confounding factors for the Comet assay assessment of DNA damage in the mussel Mytilus edulis. *Ecotoxicology, 21*(7), 1998–2003.

Stancheva, R., & Sheath, R. G. (2016). Benthic soft-bodied algae as bioindicators of stream water quality. *Knowledge and Management of Aquatic Ecosystems,* (417), 15.

Szivák, I., Behra, R., & Sigg, L. (2009). Metal-induced reactive oxygen species production in Chlamydomonas reinhardtii (chlorophyceae) 1. *Journal of Phycology, 45*(2), 427–435.

Tett, P., Gowen, R., Mills, D., Fernandes, T., Gilpin, L., Huxham, M., ... & Malcolm, S. (2007). Defining and detecting undesirable disturbance in the context of marine eutrophication. *Marine Pollution Bulletin, 55*(1–6), 282–297.

Torres, M. A., Barros, M. P., Campos, S. C., Pinto, E., Rajamani, S., Sayre, R. T., & Colepicolo, P. (2008). Biochemical biomarkers in algae and marine pollution: A review. *Ecotoxicology and Environmental Safety, 71*(1), 1–15.

Tu, H. T., Silvestre, F., De Meulder, B., Thome, J. P., Phuong, N. T., & Kestemont, P. (2012). Combined effects of deltamethrin, temperature and salinity on oxidative stress biomarkers and acetylcholinesterase activity in the black tiger shrimp (Penaeus monodon). *Chemosphere, 86*(1), 83–91.

Tuvikene, A. (1995, January). Responses of fish to polycyclic aromatic hydrocarbons (PAHs). In *Annales Zoologici Fennici* (pp. 295–309). Finnish Zoological and Botanical Publishing Board.

Veena, C. K., Josephine, A., Preetha, S. P., & Varalakshmi, P. (2007). Beneficial role of sulfated polysaccharides from edible seaweed Fucus vesiculosus in experimental hyperoxaluria. *Food Chemistry, 100*(4), 1552–1559.

Verkleij, J. A. C., Sneller, F. E. C., & Schat, H. (2003). Metallothioneins and phytochelatins: Ecophysiological aspects. In *Sulphur in plants* (pp. 163–176). Springer, Dordrecht.

Vu, C. H. T., Lee, H. G., Chang, Y. K., & Oh, H. M. (2018). Axenic cultures for microalgal biotechnology: Establishment, assessment, maintenance, and applications. *Biotechnology Advances*, *36*(2), 380–396.

Whitton, B. A., & Kelly, M. G. (1995). Use of algae and other plants for monitoring rivers. *Australian Journal of Ecology*, *20*(1), 45–56.

Wickramasinghe, W. A. D., Mubiana, V. K., & Blust, R. (2017). The effects of heavy metal concentration on bio-accumulation, productivity and pigment content of two species of marine macro algae. *Sri Lanka Journal of Aquatic Sciences*, *22*(1).

World Bank Group. (2016). *World development indicators 2016*. World Bank Group.

World Bank Group.(2014). *The Little Green Data*. World Bank Publications, Washington, DC.

World Health Organization (WHO). (1993). International Programme on Chemical Safety (IPCS) biomarkers and risk assessment: Concepts and principles. *World Health Organization: Geneva, Switzerland*, *57*.

WWAP, U. (2017). WWAP (United Nations World Water Assessment Programme).

Zanette, J., de Almeida, E. A., da Silva, A. Z., Guzenski, J., Ferreira, J. F., Di Mascio, P., . . . & Bainy, A. C. D. (2011). Salinity influences glutathione S-transferase activity and lipid peroxidation responses in the Crassostrea gigas oyster exposed to diesel oil. *Science of the Total Environment*, *409*(10), 1976–1983.

12 Wind Power

Dr. Anwesha M. Bhaduri

CONTENTS

1. Introduction 199
   1.1 What Are Greenhouse Gases (GHGs) 199
   1.2 How to Save the Planet 201
2. What Is Renewable Energy? 201
   2.1 The Most Common Renewable Power Technologies 201
3. What Is Wind Power? 201
   3.1 How a Wind Turbine Works 202
   3.2 Different Parts Wind Turbine 203
       3.2.1 Gear Box 203
       3.2.2 Generator 203
       3.2.3 Brake 203
       3.2.4 Controller 204
       3.2.5 Anemometer 204
       3.2.6 Drive Train 204
4. Offshore Wind Turbines 204
   4.1 Spar-Buoy 204
   4.2 Tension Leg 204
5. Factors Needed for Installing a Wind Turbine 204
6. Advantages and Disadvantages 207
   6.1 Advantages 207
   6.2 Limitations 209
7. Conclusions 209
References 210

1. INTRODUCTION

Continuous demand for resources such as food, clothing, water, housing, infrastructure, and other aspects stemmed an increasing demand for extraction and processing of materials, fuels, and food contributing to half of total global greenhouse gas emissions and over 90% of biodiversity loss and water stress. As the global population grows resulting in a need for more and more natural resources to sustain the current lifestyle. This has resulted in fuels in resource extraction, which has more than tripled since 1970, including a 45% increase in fossil fuel use *(Nations, 2021)*.

1.1 What Are Greenhouse Gases (GHGs)

GHGs warm the Earth by absorbing energy and slowing the rate at which the energy escapes to space, therefore, making a blanket insulating the Earth. Different GHGs

DOI: 10.1201/9781003205548-12

FIGURE 12.1 Photo courtesy: Chris LEBoutillier from Pixels.

can have different effects on the Earth's warming *(Overview of Greenhouse Gases | US EPA, 2021)*. The main GHGs in the Earth's atmosphere are water vapour, carbon dioxide (CO_2), methane (CH_4), nitrous oxide (N_2O), and ozone.

The use of fossil fuel results in a vast majority of greenhouse gas emissions like carbon dioxide (CO_2). But smaller amounts of methane (CH_4) and nitrous oxide (N_2O) are also emitted. These gases are released during the combustion of fossil fuels, such as coal, oil, and natural gas, to produce electricity. As greenhouse gases

Wind Power

trap heat in the atmosphere that would otherwise escape into space *(Overview of Greenhouse Gases | US EPA, 2021)*, resulting in global warming and increasing average temperatures on the surface.

Climate change refers to long-term shifts in temperatures and weather patterns. This temperature change is one symptom of climate change, and it is the term scientists now prefer to describe the complex shifts affecting our planet's weather and climate systems. Climate change encompasses not only rising average temperatures but also extreme weather events, shifting wildlife populations and habitats, rising seas, and a range of other impacts (Renewable energy, facts and information, 2021).

The Paris Agreement that aims to limit climate change in the 21st century to 1.5–2°C above pre-industrial levels requires the phasing out of fossil fuels *(Ipcc.ch. 2021)*.

1.2 How to Save the Planet

Scientists are trying to make any possible change to save this beautiful Earth of ours and looking for alternatives like greener sources of energy while steering away from fossil fuel. The alternative the world is heading towards is a renewable source of energy. Although it will not be the thing that reverses all the damage we have caused as a society blindly taking advantage of the common luxury, it is certainly a step in the right direction.

2. WHAT IS RENEWABLE ENERGY?

Renewable energy means that energy is generated from sustainable, 100% renewable sources like wind, sun, and water. Sun, wind, waves, rivers, tides, and the heat from radioactive decay in the Earth's mantle, as well as biomass, are all abundant and ongoing; hence the term "renewables" is available in infinite amounts because it can renew itself and won't run out like fossil fuels (Costa & Seixas, 2014).

2.1 The Most Common Renewable Power Technologies

- Solar (photovoltaic, solar thermal)
- Wind
- Biogas (e.g., landfill gas/wastewater treatment digester gas)
- Geothermal
- Biomass
- Low-impact hydroelectricity
- Emerging technologies—wave and tidal power *(Local Renewable Energy Benefits and Resources | US EPA, 2021)*.

3. WHAT IS WIND POWER?

Wind, simply stated, is the movement of air, and it all begins with the sun. Therefore it is not incorrect to say wind energy is a form of solar energy. As the sun starts

FIGURE 12.2 Photo by Kervin Edward Lara from Pexels.

warming the Earth's surface, the heat gets unevenly distributed because of the irregular nature of the Earth's surface. Warm air, which weighs less than cold air, rises, causing low pressure near the Earth's surface. The gradual rise in warm air and the void filled with cold air causes high pressure—and wind. If it weren't for this rising and sinking motion in our atmosphere, then not only would we have no wind, but we'd have no weather at all *(Wind Energy Guide: How it works, advantages and disadvantages—OVO Energy | OVO Energy, 2021)*.

3.1 How a Wind Turbine Works

Wind turbines are a machine for capturing wind energy that are usually comprised of rotors attached to a tall tower, as shown in Figure 12.3. As the rotors turn, kinetic energy is formed, which is the generation of energy through the motion of an object or particle *(How a Wind Turbine Works—Text Version, 2021).* Kinetic energy will then be converted into electricity (Tong, 2010).

Let's explain the working of wind turbines from KE to electric energy in more detail.

As the wind blows, the force is caught by the blades of wind turbines to capture its kinetic energy and make the turbine rotate and therefore changing the energy from KE to mechanical energy. Wind turbine shafts are connected to a gearbox which helps to increase the speed massively—typically 100 times more. This spinning is connected to a generator, which produces electricity.

Wind turbines have three blades, which produce the best compromise between rotational speed and mechanical reliability. Wind causes the three-bladed turbine to spin as the force of lift is greater than the force of drag.

Wind Power

There is a rotor connected to a generator through a series of gears so that the rotational speed is increased in the order of 100 times. This enables the generator to produce electricity. Computers control the pitch of the blades, and the direction they point to produces maximum power *(101 and Produce? 2021)*.

3.2 Different Parts Wind Turbine

Today's wind turbines are much more complex machines than the conventional prairie windmill. A wind turbine has more than 8,000 different parts, and 90% of the wind turbine components are recyclable. That 10% contains the blades. When they reach the end of their usefulness, most of them are sawed into smaller pieces and dragged to landfills, where they never break down.

Wind turbines are enormous. The blades average around 70 metres long, and turbine towers average 90 metres tall—it's about the height of the Statue of Liberty *(Top 10 Things You Didn't Know About Wind Power, 2021)*.

About 85% of turbine component materials—such as steel, copper wire, electronics, and gearing—can be recycled or reused. The blades of the turbines need to be lightweight for efficiency and yet durable enough to withstand storms so are made of fiberglass (a composite material) *(Wind Energy can now be 'all' clean, new tech ends wind blade waste—The Indian Wire, 2021)*.

3.2.1 Gear Box

Every type of gearbox looks different depending on what type it is. Usually, wind turbine gearboxes are made of steel, brass, or aluminium. A gearbox is usually used in a wind turbine to surge rotational speed from a low-speed rotor to a higher-speed electrical generator. A common ratio is about 90:1, with a rate of 16.7 rpm input from the rotor to 1,500 rpm output for the generator. The generator rotor turns at the same speed as the turbine rotor (Zipp, 2012).

All kinds of wind turbine gearboxes have their special features. Each gearbox type has its advantages and disadvantages, for example, the planetary gear, which has strong resistance to shock and an excessive torque to weight ratio. However, it's made of steel, so it can be very noisy and prone to wear *(Wind Turbine Gearbox Types—GlobeCore. Oil Purification Systems, 2021)*.

3.2.2 Generator

Wind energy describes the process by which the wind is used to generate mechanical energy, and a generator in a wind turbine is to convert this mechanical energy to electrical energy. Wind turbine generators are a bit unusual as compared to other generating units normally found attached to the electrical grid. One reason is that the generator has to work with a power source (the wind turbine rotor), which supplies very fluctuating mechanical power (torque) *(Wind Turbine Generators, 2021)*.

3.2.3 Brake

The braking system of a wind turbine ensures that it automatically stops when it detects that one of its critical components does not work properly. The components of a wind turbine are designed so that with proper maintenance, they can last at least 20 years *(Wind turbine braking system—iZanda, 2021)*.

3.2.4 Controller

To continuously monitor the condition of the wind turbine and collect statistics on its operation, wind turbine controller is connected to several computers. As the name implies, the controller also controls a large number of switches, hydraulic pumps, valves, and motors within the wind turbine *(The Electronic Wind Turbine Controller, 2021)*.

3.2.5 Anemometer

Anemometer is an instrument to determine the speed of the airflow in the atmosphere, and in wind flow tunnels and to check the total velocity magnitude of fluids on a horizontal plane or in a specific direction, an instrument called an anemometer is used (Froese, 2019).

To protect the assembly of all the generating components in a wind turbine, including the generator, gearbox, drive train, and brake assembly, they are encapsulated in a single cover called Nacelle cover *(How Do Wind Turbines Work? 2021)*.

3.2.6 Drive Train

The drivetrain is the group of components of a motor vehicle that deliver power to the drive wheels. This excludes the engine or motor that generates the power (Bosch, 1993).

4. OFFSHORE WIND TURBINES

Offshore wind turbines can float. Many companies are evolving floating offshore wind platforms for use in deep waters. Three kinds of floating platforms mentioned in the next section are spar-buoy, tension leg platform, and semi-submersible.

4.1 SPAR-BUOY

As shown in Figure 12.3, it is a thin *buoy* that floats upright in the water and is characterized by a small waterplane area and a large mass.

4.2 TENSION LEG

A tension leg platform (TLP) or extended tension leg platform (ETLP) shown in Figure 12.4 is a vertically moored floating structure that is mainly suited for water depths greater than 300 metres (about 1,000 ft) and less than 1,500 metres (about 4,900 ft).

5. FACTORS NEEDED FOR INSTALLING A WIND TURBINE

Wind energy is the 2030 sustainable development agenda, which is focusing on green growth, sustainable development.

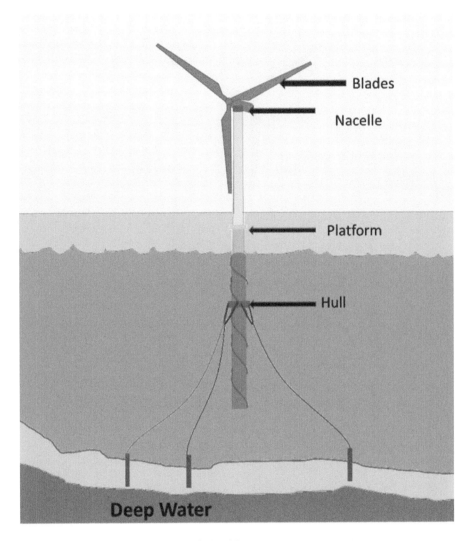

FIGURE 12.3 Spar-buoy offshore wind turbine.

Factors such as positioning of wind turbines and wind farms, wind direction, and strength are continuously changing, meaning wind farms need to be accurately positioned to maximize the amount of energy they can generate. These need to be considered for efficient production of energy from wind.

For example, land-based wind farms, the higher the altitude, the stronger the wind will be. At lower altitudes, obstructions like vegetation and urbanization cause dissipation of the wind. Additionally, when looking at sea-based wind farms, relief features can affect wind velocity. Ridges near the sea can significantly improve the wind velocity, with measures recording anything from 40–80% increase. Similarly, hills and cliffs show increases but slightly lower at 20–40%. However, when looking

FIGURE 12.4 Tension leg offshore wind turbine structure.

at relief features, turbulence must be considered as it could damage the turbines due to increased stresses placed on vulnerable joints (Le Gourieres, 2014).

Not only to generate maximum energy by positioning on the ideal location, but wind turbines should also be positioned in such a way to minimize the impact on the natural ecosystem. Due to wind turbines being so large and prominent, they alter the flight pattern of birds, especially birds of prey. Over time this will cause changes in behaviour, physiology, and morphology in animals. With fewer birds of prey flying in an area with turbines, the population of prey in that area could increase substantially with the reduction in predators. Although this may not be a significant concern, it could increase the number of vermin in towns or cities neighbouring large areas of open land. In turn, this could increase the risk of diseases spreading amongst human populations, especially in more underdeveloped regions (Thaker et al., 2018).

FIGURE 12.5 Semi-submersible: Floating wind turbine.

6. ADVANTAGES AND DISADVANTAGES

6.1 Advantages

The use of fossil fuels and nuclear power to create energy is exceptionally harmful to the environment due to the emissions of harmful gases radioactive waste (Manwell et al., 2010). With the concerning increase in global warming, such methods of energy production could be detrimental to the planet and those living on it. Additionally, fossil fuels will also run out as they are nonrenewable, meaning they do not renew quickly enough to meet demand, or they do not renew at all. This means these energy sources will eventually run out, and it is predicted that it will happen in this century (Manwell et al., 2010). In a situation like this, renewable energy is one of them, and wind power will play a significant role as it is practically a never-ending free source of energy.

Electricity is produced when wind speed reaches 6–9 miles per hour (mph) by a modern wind turbine begins. It shuts down if the speed exceeds 55 mph, when its mechanism would be in danger of sustaining damage. So while they can generate electricity for much of the time, there are other times they have to be shut down. It is estimated that an average onshore wind turbine rated at 2.5–3 megawatts can produce more than 6 million kWh every year. A 3.6 MW offshore turbine may double that *(101 and Produce?, 2021)*.

Unlike nonrenewable energy sources, wind power is a clean and renewable energy source, meaning no harmful waste products are emitted (Manwell et al., 2010). This means it will be able to support and meet the increasing demand for energy and electricity. Furthermore, as no harmful waste products are produced, they will have no detrimental impact on the environment and not catalyze the rate of climate change. A study conducted in 2010 states that the cost of a wind turbine is only marginally the cost of running a fossil fuel power station. The upfront cost of construction and instalment of a wind turbine is roughly one million dollars; however, as much as this is a high cost initially, over time the maintenance of the turbine is marginal to that of maintaining fossil fuel or nuclear power plants. For example, according to the newest Lazard, which has been following energy costs for years, wind power was 71% cheaper in 2020 than in 2009 (Office of Energy Efficiency & Renewable Energy, n.d.).

The study also supports that as technology improves over time, the cost of wind power has dropped by 80%, further supporting the use of wind-generated electricity (Cullen, 2013).

As offshore oil and gas rigs start to come down, an increase in wind-based power plants would improve socioeconomic status by increasing jobs, in turn, improving the financial state of an economy by reducing unemployment rates (Cullen, 2013). Wind energy has many effects on society. It creates jobs. For example, the U.S. wind sector employs over 100,000 employees. Also, wind turbine technician is one of the fastest-growing jobs in the U.S. (Office of Energy Efficiency & Renewable Energy, n.d.).

Additionally, for every 1% increase in the use of renewable energy to generate electricity, there is roughly a 0.53% decrease in the generation of carbon dioxide and other harmful gases. Over time as the percentage of energy generated from renewable energy is increasing, a lesser amount of greenhouse gases is emitted, benefitting the economy as it won't have to withstand the costs of damage caused by climate change (Hartono et al., 2020).

Wind turbines can be expensive to install; however, when it's installed and running, the maintenance costs are relatively low. The fuel (wind) is free, and the turbines don't need too much maintenance.

Wind power can also be harnessed by individuals as well as in an industrial atmosphere as even a small turbine can be used to power an average home, as stated by a major energy company that states, "A small turbine in the back yard can easily power a small business or a home. . . . Smaller wind turbines can be used to charge batteries or as backup power" (***13 little-known facts about wind power, 2021***). Both of these facts compliment the idea that turbines don't have to be strictly commercial. They can also be owned by people as a source of personal power or to power their own business and also to generate power to be sold.

6.2 LIMITATIONS

The main disadvantage of wind power includes initial cost and technology immaturity. Firstly, constructing turbines and wind facilities is extremely expensive (Musial & Ram, 2010).

Though offshore wind energy produces more energy than onshore wind energy, installation is expensive and needs more technology reliability. The primary costs of wind turbines include construction and maintenance (Musial & Ram, 2010).

There is a reduction caused by the unavoidable inefficiencies involved in the mechanism. Most wind turbines operate at around 30–40% efficiency though this may rise to 50% in ideal wind conditions *(101 and Produce?, 2021)*.

Due to the uncontrollable nature of wind and atmospheric pressure, it becomes increasingly difficult to meet the energy demand. A source of storing the energy would be needed to meet the demand; however, this does not yet exist, and therefore only 10% of the demand from society can be met, and as the population increases by number, the percentage of demand that can be met will be lower (Ferguson, 2008).

When the wind is at its strongest is when the demand is at its lowest, and when demand is at its highest throughout the day, the wind power is at its lowest. This is due to wind patterns fluctuating constantly, and in this particular study, the wind is more powerful in the evenings and night, meaning the most energy is available when it is least needed (Spilsbury & Spilsbury, 2007). This is one of the concerns when opting for wind energy as there may not be enough energy created during the day when demand is at its highest.

Wind turbines can have an impact on wildlife. Birds, bats, and other flying animals have slight chances of surviving when taking a hit from a spinning wind turbine blade.

Studies have appraised that between 140,000 and 500,000 birds die from wind turbines each year (Hartono et al., 2020).

7. CONCLUSIONS

In conclusion, wind power, along with other renewable energy sources is substantially more economically and environmentally friendly than the use of fossil fuels and nuclear-based power. However, there are still limitations in the research regarding how much more beneficial for the environment and how effectively renewable energy sources would be used in coming years. There needs to be more research into the impact of both land-based and sea-based wind farms, to identify which would produce the most energy while maintaining a low risk to the environment and economy. To make it a sustainable energy source, the primary disadvantage is cost of instalment. Wind turbines should be supported by new technology to lower costs of installation. Innovations and research are needed to increase reliability and energy production, expand the resource area, advance manufacturing, and infrastructure services, and alleviate known environmental impacts, as stated earlier.

REFERENCES

Bosch, R. (1993). Drivetrain. In *Automotive Handbook* (3rd ed.), p. 536. Retrieved from http://randolphtoom.com/ENSAIS/Automotive%20Handbook-Bosch.pdf

Costa, E., & Seixas, J. (2014). Contribution of electric cars to the mitigation of CO2 emissions in the city of Sao Paulo. In *2014 IEEE Vehicle Power and Propulsion Conference (VPPC)* (pp. 1–5). IEEE.

Cullen, J. (2013). Measuring the environmental benefits of wind-generated electricity. *American Economic Journal: Economic Policy*, 5(4), 107–133.

Ferguson, A. R. (2008). Wind power: Benefits and limitations. In *Biofuels, Solar and Wind as Renewable Energy Systems* (pp. 133–151). Springer, Dordrecht.

Froese, M. (2019). *Increase in Wind-power Projects Fueling Anemometer Demands*. Windpower Engineering & Development. Retrieved from https://www.windpowerengineering.com/increase-in-wind-power-projects-fueling-anemometer-demands/

Hartono, D., Hastuti, S. H., Halimatussadiah, A., Saraswati, A., Mita, A. F., & Indriani, V. (2020). Comparing the impacts of fossil and renewable energy investments in Indonesia: A simple general equilibrium analysis. *Heliyon*, 6(6), e04120.

Le Gourieres, D. (2014). *Wind Power Plants: Theory and Design*. Elsevier, Amsterdam.

Manwell, J. F., McGowan, J. G., & Rogers, A. L. (2010). *Wind Energy Explained: Theory, Design and Application*. John Wiley & Sons, Hoboken, NJ.

Musial, W., & Ram, B. (2010). *Large-scale Offshore Wind Power in the United States: Assessment of Opportunities and Barriers* (No. NREL/TP-500-40745). National Renewable Energy Lab.(NREL), Golden, CO (United States).

Office of Energy Efficiency & Renewable Energy (n.d.). *Advantages and Challenges of Wind Energy*. Wind Energy Technologies Office. Retrieved from https://www.energy.gov/eere/wind/advantages-and-challenges-wind-energy

Spilsbury, L., & Spilsbury, R. (2007). *The Pros and Cons of Wind Power*. The Rosen Publishing Group, Inc., New York City.

Thaker, M., Zambre, A., & Bhosale, H. (2018). Wind farms have cascading impacts on ecosystems across trophic levels. *Nature Ecology & Evolution*, 2(12), 1854–1858.

Tong, W. (2010). *Wind Power Generation and Wind Turbine Design*. WIT Press Ashurst, Southampton.

Zipp, K. (2012). *Gears & Gearboxes 101*. Windpower Engineering & Development. Retrieved from https://www.windpowerengineering.com/gears-gearboxes-101/

13 Climate Change– International Policies

Ashita Rai, M. H. Fulekar, and Rama Shankar Dubey

CONTENTS

1. Introduction 211
2. Intergovernmental Panel on Climate Change (IPCC) 213
3. United Nations Framework Convention on Climate Change 213
4. Kyoto Protocol 214
    4.1 Overview 214
    4.2 Emission Targets and Initial Assigned Amounts 214
    4.3 Mechanism 215
5. UNFCCC: Conference of the Parties 216
    5.1 Meetings of the Conference of the Parties (COP 1–COP 26) 216
6. The Paris Agreement 219
    6.1 Background 219
    6.2 Key Aspects of the Agreement 220
References 221

1. INTRODUCTION

The implications of climate change indicate that immediate measures must be taken to cut back greenhouse gas (GHG) emissions in the upcoming years. The advantages of taking appropriate and timely efforts to limit carbon emission is progressively being evidenced to surpass the expenditure. However, if humans want to have a meaningful opportunity to avoid severe climate change, they must lower emissions at the lowest feasible expenditure. As per the Organization for Economic Co-operation and Development (2007), a gradual decrease in GHG emissions can be accomplished at a better price if adequate measures are implemented. It further typically involves comprehensive utilization of market-based mechanisms around the world to establish a global price for GHG emissions, as well as proper integration of climate change goals into specific areas of policy, like power generation, public transit, architecture, farming, and forest management to ramp up technology advancement and dissemination. Several developed countries, along with many emerging economies, have embraced legislation ever since early nineties. By its analysis and research on the formulation and construction of appropriate climate policies, and also peer assessments of policy performance in specific nations, the OECD has made significant contribution towards the issue.

DOI: 10.1201/9781003205548-13

Climatic change itself is being experienced across many regions of the globe, and previous and recent GHG emissions have also factored in certain climatic variability. Climate change resilience must be integrated in appropriate policies. It is a lengthy procedure that encompasses educating people, embedding this into sector-specific plans, and establishing particular adaptive systems and procedures. Incorporating climate change uncertainties will necessitate more versatile, proactive, efficient, and fast strategies, as well as modifications in legal, organizational, and regulation is further required. For instance, increasing application of market-based mechanisms such as effective freshwater valuation and trading, as well as hazard insurance on property, flooding, and drought, could assist with adapting to climate change (Organization for Economic Co-operation and Development, 2007). In the following years and during the centuries, new approaches to reduce GHG emissions will be necessary. This would necessitate more legislative emphasis in order to hasten the adoption of present ecofriendly technology and approaches, such as regulations encouraging significant energy savings. Business-oriented techniques generate meaningful incentives and opportunities, although they must not be sustainable. Organizations may underfund in research and development should it anticipate; they might not be able to accomplish an appropriate return from the product design.

Business-oriented techniques can perhaps be strengthened by R&D initiatives, legislation (e.g., architectural standards and guidelines), and information instruments (e.g., eco-labelling of energy appliances). They might also facilitate in overcoming few businesses and information inefficiencies, which hamper the progress and dissemination of environmentally friendly solutions. Policies must be oriented on accomplishing specific objectives instead of defining the techniques or mechanisms to be implemented to accomplish those objectives. Furthermore, while selecting mechanisms for a framework, consideration must be made to ensure that they are compatible and eliminate excessive overlapping, including being economical. Incorporation of economic climate change adaptation in all fields is a real issue for all nations. Development assistance, as well as the United Nations Framework Convention on Climate Change's finance structures, contribute significantly in assisting emerging economies in their attempts to climate-proof major development capital, particularly regarding supporting private sector funding (United Nations Framework Convention on Climate Change i, n.d.). The introduction of a system to give monetary assistance to promote lower emissions from deforestation and forest degradation, which is a significant source of emissions in many emerging economies, would also be critical.

Towards frugal reductions in GHG emissions, a worldwide carbon price must also be established (The World Bank, n.d.). To develop the norms for carbon pricing and the prerequisites for its formation, multinational participation is essential (Stavins et al., 2014). It comprises emissions reduction surveillance, tracking, and regulatory mechanisms (Peterson, 2003). Ongoing global and regional programmes, such as emissions trading and carbon pricing, must be strengthened and integrated (Elkins & Baker, 2001). Additional measures, such as legislation and offsetting structures, may be required to strengthen GHG limits to a large number of low and diffused pollution sources, particularly wherever sector obstacles make price controls ineffective (OECD, 2007). To achieve adequate worldwide emissions reductions whilst limiting overall expenditures, every significant polluter must participate (Liu & Raftery, 2021). The smaller the economic burden of intervention, the broader the scope of mitigation activities throughout industries and countries (Watkiss, 2007). Cooperation in abatement initiatives on a worldwide platform can however assist to create a level playing field and solve competition challenges. Developed nations have an obligation to offer guidance in tackling climate change on a global scale, according to the notion of common but differentiated responsibility (Josephson, 2017).

2. INTERGOVERNMENTAL PANEL ON CLIMATE CHANGE (IPCC)

The Intergovernmental Panel on Climate Change is a non-profit organization established by the World Meteorological Organization and the United Nations Environment Programme. It evaluates scientific publications and offers crucial scientific evidence to the climate change processes (United Nations Climate Change Programme, n.d.). Renowned climate experts and scientists inspect climate change investigations for the IPCC, that is then subjected to a verification process extended to all 195 signatory countries of the United Nations (IPCC, 2021). Three working groups (WG) and a task force constitute the IPCC. Physical science of climate change is dealt by WG I; climate change implications, resilience, and susceptibility by WG II; whereas climate change mitigation is looked by WG III. Task force on national greenhouse gas inventories plays a major role in the development and refinement of a framework for calculating and documenting national greenhouse gas emissions and reductions. IPCC has produced five assessment reports (Table 13.1), as well as numerous technological and supplementary studies, for the United Nations Framework Convention on Climate Change since 1988.

3. UNITED NATIONS FRAMEWORK CONVENTION ON CLIMATE CHANGE

The United Nations Framework Convention on Climate Change, also known as "the convention," was negotiated at the United Nations Conference on Environment and

TABLE 13.1
IPCC and the assessment reports

IPCC Assessment Reports	Year	Remarks
First Assessment Report (FAR)	1990	Climate change is a global problem that requires worldwide cooperation to solve. To tackle climate change, the United Nations Framework Convention on Climate Change was constituted.
Second Assessment Report (SAR)	1995	Governments were aided in adopting the Kyoto Protocol in 1997.
Third Assessment Report (TAR)	2001	The implications of global warming and the necessity of adaptability were discussed.
Fourth Assessment Report (AR 4)	2007	Set the foundation for a post-Kyoto deal, with an emphasis on keeping global warming below 2°C.
Fifth Assessment Report (AR 5)	2013–2014	Offered scientific knowledge to the Paris Agreement.

Source: Intergovernmental Panel on Climate Change (n.d.), retrieved from www.ipcc.ch/about/history/

Development in Rio de Janeiro in 1992 (United Nations Conference on Environment and Development, 1992). Primary goal of the convention was controlling GHG levels at a point which might drastically reduce human interference with the climate process (Tian & Xiang, 2018). The UNFCCC recognizes the importance of biological systems in assessing when climate change must be stopped. The convention benchmark of "dangerous interference" is measured against three arenas of impact—sustainable development, agricultural productivity, and ecosystem response. Climate change must be maintained in a timespan that permits nature to "respond gradually" to changing climate, would not obstruct environmental sustainability, and sustains crop yields, as per the agreement (Hannah, 2011). Members must also create, manage, evaluate, and increase accessibility to their individual inventory of man-made sources of all GHGs not included by International Agreement to the Conference of the Parties (Pulselli & Marchi, 2015). The UNFCCC, which took effect on 21 March 1994, followed by the first Conference of Parties (COP1) in Berlin, Germany, in 1995, managed to bring the member states together for a panel discussion to enhance dedication to tackle climate change. Whilst also trying to stabilize GHGs at a point that'd help deter human interference with the climate system, it laid the groundwork for strong climate policy to help launch global, federal, and regional approach to mitigate global warming. It resulted in the announcement of the Berlin Mandate, that required major economies to cut GHG emissions by legally enforceable commitments whilst excluding poorer nations from the very same requirement. The mandate resulted in the establishment of the Kyoto Protocol at the 1997 United Nations Conference on Climate Change (COP3) (Keong, 2020).

4. KYOTO PROTOCOL

4.1 Overview

The Kyoto Protocol is the only accord to come out of the UNFCCC framework that sets enforceable limitations on GHG emissions (Kuh, 2018). The protocol was ratified on 11 December 1997 and came into effect on 16 February 2005. It divides the planet's territories into two groups: Annex I countries, which are mostly developed nations which have previously caused so much to changing climate, and non-Annex-I countries, which are mainly developing nations (UNFCCC, 1998). Underneath the protocol, 37 industrialized nations and the European Group pledged to reduce GHG emissions by at least 5% from 1990 levels during the first compliance period from 2008 to 2012. This included carbon dioxide, methane, nitrous oxide, hydrofluorocarbons, perfluorocarbons, and hexafluoride sulphur (Poulopoulos, 2016). The "Marrakesh Accords" are the comprehensive guidelines for implementing the protocol, which were signed at COP 7 in Marrakesh, Morocco, in 2001 (Poulopoulos, 2016).

4.2 Emission Targets and Initial Assigned Amounts

The allowable level of emissions of GHGs from the energy, industrial processes, solvent and other product use, agriculture and waste sectors is called the party's assigned amount. Every Annex I country has a specific emissions target, which is set relative to its emissions of GHGs in its base year. The Annex B emissions target and the party's emissions of GHGs in the base year determine the party's initial assigned amount for the Kyoto Protocol's five-year first commitment period (2008–2012). The quantified emission limitation or reduction targets as contained in Annex B to the Kyoto Protocol to be achieved by the Annex I countries during first commitment period is mentioned in Table 13.2.

4.3 Mechanism

The Annex I countries and non-Annex-I countries were given an option to meet their targets through one of the following three mechanisms provided under Kyoto Protocol (Kuh, 2018).

i. **Joint Implementation (JI)** is a project-based approach wherein any Annex I country invests in a project which either lowers emissions or enhances sequestration in other Annex I country in return of credits for reducing emissions or reductions accomplished (Article 6).
ii. **International Emissions Trading (IET)**—Annex I parties may trade Kyoto credits to or receive unit from the other Annex I member under Article 17 of the agreement. It does not influence the Annex I members' total assigned amount; rather, it redistributes the allocated portion between members.
iii. **Clean Development Mechanism (CDM)**—The CDM is a project-based approach. Non-Annex-I party can earn CDM points through emission reduction initiatives or plantation and reforestation programmes (Article 12).

The Kyoto Protocol was amended on 8 December 2012 in order to include new commitments to the parties for the period of 2013–2020 and revised lists of greenhouse

TABLE 13.2
Annex I countries and their emission limitation target during first commitment period of Kyoto Protocol

Annex I	Emission limitation target
Austria, Belgium, Bulgaria, Czech Republic, Denmark, Estonia, European Community, Finland, France, Germany, Greece, Ireland, Italy, Latvia, Liechtenstein, Lithuania, Luxembourg, Monaco, Netherlands, Portugal, Romania, Slovakia, Slovenia, Spain, Sweden, Switzerland, United Kingdom of Great Britain, and Northern Ireland	8%
United States of America	7%
Canada, Hungary, Japan, Poland	6%
Croatia	5%
New Zealand, Russian Federation, Ukraine	0%
Norway	1%
Australia	8%
Iceland	10%

Source: UNFCCC, 2009

gases to be reported. During the second commitment period, parties committed to reduce the GHG emissions by at least 18% below 1990 levels. However, it has not entered into force, and the most recent instrument negotiated under the UNFCCC, the Paris Agreement, is independent of the Kyoto Protocol. Therefore, the protocol represents a milestone in international environmental protection and has succeeded in making climate change a top issue for cooperation, development, and trade.

5. UNFCCC: CONFERENCE OF THE PARTIES

The UNFCCC has provided the basic institutional structure for the negotiation and adoption of a series of protocols, modifications, and agreements related to the convention's mandate (United Nations Framework Convention on Climate Change, 2020). The convention established a Conference of the Parties, a secretariat, and subsidiary bodies that reviews the implementation of the convention and related instruments within its mandate (Kuh, 2018). COP members have been meeting every year since 1995, and the first conference (COP1) was held in 1995 in Berlin.

5.1 Meetings of the Conference of the Parties (COP 1–COP 26)

TABLE 13.3
Highlights of the COP1-26

Conference of the Parties (Year)	Venue	Remarks
COP 1 (1995)	Berlin, Germany	To assess the efficiency of the convention's accords in mitigating climate change. Developing a legislative agreement under the convention is required.
COP 2 (1996)	Geneva, Switzerland	Endorsement of the second Assessment Report of the Intergovernmental Panel on Climate Change (IPCC).
COP 3 (1997)	Kyoto, Japan	Endorsement of the Kyoto Protocol on Climate Change.
COP 4 (1998)	Buenos Aires, Argentina	At the earliest, by the sixth meeting of the Conference of the Parties, a consensus on the detailed structure of the Kyoto Protocol should be reached.
COP 5 (1999)	Bonn, Germany	Issues connected to the surveillance of the Kyoto procedures were discussed.
COP 6 (2000)	The Hague, Netherlands	The Kyoto Protocol was clearly stated. The umbrella group (the United States, Australia, Canada, Japan, and Russia), poor countries, and the European Union were unable to reach an agreement.
COP 7 (2001)	Marrakech, Morocco	Endorsement of the Marrakech Accords, a set of 15 resolutions on how to structure and execute the Kyoto Protocol.

TABLE 13.3 *(Continued)*
Highlights of the COP1-26

Conference of the Parties (Year)	Venue	Remarks
COP 8 (2002)	New Delhi, India	The Kyoto Protocol's provisions have been essentially finalized in negotiation. The Clean Development Mechanism's concept and the utilization of funding granted by developed nations for tackling climate change in developing economies were decided.
COP 9 (2003)	Milan, Italy	The two-year deliberations on standards for plantation and forestry initiatives in developing economies came to a satisfactory end, bridging the very last loophole in the Kyoto Protocol's regulations of enforcement.
COP 10 (2004)	Buenos Aires, Argentina	At the session, concerns such as financing, regulatory reforms, building capacity, and technology acquisition were discussed in order to enhance the adoption of the Framework Convention on Climate Change in poor nations.
COP 11 (2005)	Montreal, Canada	Endorsement of the Montreal Action Plan, a route for an intergovernmental system after 2012. The Kyoto Protocol was executed, with a strong monitoring mechanism and greater financing bolstering its management design.
COP 12 (2006)	Nairobi, Kenya	The focus of the session was on African challenges, such as infrastructure building and aid in the development of infrastructure projects, as well as involvement in the Clean Development Mechanism.
COP 13 (2007)	Bali, Indonesia	Parties negotiated primary purpose and pledges to emissions reductions (including deforestation control), resilience, innovation, and funding up to and after 2012 in order to embrace the Bali Action Plan.
COP 14 (2008)	Poznań, Poland	The necessity of national greenhouse gas reduction goals and economic assistance for tackling climate change in third world countries were identified as primary elements of a new climate paradigm.

(Continued)

**TABLE 13.3 *(Continued)*
Highlights of the COP1-26**

Conference of the Parties (Year)	Venue	Remarks
COP 15 (2009)	Copenhagen, Denmark	A considerable lot of advanced and emerging economies concurred on a "1.5 or 2.0°C" limitation norm in the Copenhagen Accord, that specified certain fundamental elements of future international climate policy. A Technology System and a REDD+ Technique was contemplated, with the goal of assisting poor nations with innovative solutions and decreasing emissions from deforestation and forest destruction.
COP 16 (2010)	Cancún, Mexico	The Copenhagen Agreements was transformed into formal resolutions, refined extensively, and formalized with the ratification of the Cancun Agreements. Formal acknowledgment of the 2°C aim, forest conservation (REDD+ Mechanism), technology partnership, and capacity-building in emerging economies are among such initiatives. By 2020, developed economies have publicly endorsed climate action initiatives in undeveloped nations with $100 billion annually.
COP 17 (2011)	Durban, South Africa	The Kyoto Protocol will be extended for a phase 2 commencing in 2013. The meeting also approved the Green Climate Fund, which would provide additional funding to both developed and underdeveloped nations in its efforts to combat climate change. The ADP provided a timeframe for drafting a new international agreement to substitute the Kyoto Protocol when it expires in 2012. It also outlined the rationale, guidelines, and procedure for doing so.
COP 18 (2012)	Doha, Qatar	The meeting pushed for yet more rapid climate measures in order to reach the Copenhagen Accord's 2 degrees target. By 2020, the Doha Amendment to the Kyoto Protocol must have reduced GHG emission by at least 18% lower than 1990 levels during phase 2 period, that is, 2013–2020.

Climate Change — International Policies

TABLE 13.3 *(Continued)*
Highlights of the COP1-26

Conference of the Parties (Year)	Venue	Remarks
COP 19 (2013)	Warsaw, Poland	Initiated negotiations for a global climate deal in anticipation of the 2015 Climate Change Conference in Paris on themes such as abatement, resilience, funding, innovation, accessibility, and capacity-building.
COP 20 (2014)	Lima, Peru	Prepared the ground for deliberations on a globalized climate accord, which will be ratified at the 2015 Climate Change Conference in Paris.
COP 21 (2015)	Paris, France	Enforcement of the Paris Agreement.
COP 22 (2016)	Marrakech, Morocco	Maintaining progress on climate action and boosting the unified approach to the challenge of climate change is the major goal.
COP 23 (2017)	Bonn, Germany	The primary objective seems to be to expedite climate action further towards the accomplishment of the Paris Climate Change Agreement's work programme.
COP 24 (2018)	Katowice, Poland	The primary objective is to complete the Paris Rulebook, which will assist the 197 signatories to the Treaty in fully implementing the Paris Agreement, which aims to keep global climate change well below 2°C, preferably 1.5°C, by the end of the 21st century.
COP 25 (2019)	Madrid, Spain	The fundamental goal is to define the procedures for implementing the Paris Agreements and to hasten the implementation of the Accord's carbon reduction commitments.
COP 26 (2021)	Glasgow, Scotland	Parties agreed to work together to keep planetary temperature increases to 1.5°C.

Source: United Nations Framework Convention on Climate Change (n.d.); Keong, C. Y. (2021)

6. THE PARIS AGREEMENT

6.1 BACKGROUND

The UNFCCC's primary goal is to accomplish "stabilisation of GHGs in the environment at a threshold that'd preclude catastrophic human obtrusion with the climate process" (Gao, Gao & Zhang, 2017). To enable stable growth, one such threshold must be reached in a timeline that allows ecosystem to gradually adjust to climatic changes (United Nations Framework Convention on Climate Change, 1992). Following the Copenhagen Climate Change Conference in 2009 and the Cancun Climate Change Conference in 2010, the international community agreed that global temperature rises should be kept at 2°C above pre-industrial levels (The White House, 2009). Despite the fact that the Copenhagen Accord was not officially recognized by all signatories, it served as the foundation for the Paris Agreement. Nonetheless, the IPCC's AR5 highly encouraged judgement on the 2°C global temperature limit, bolstering the scientific foundation for international agreement. The Paris Agreement entered into force in December 2015 as a result of these studies. The United States, on the other hand, was an early signatory to the Paris Agreement. On 4 November 2020, regrettably, President Donald Trump removed the U.S. from the plan. Only when Biden government assumed office did they reaffirm their pledge.

6.2 Key Aspects of the Agreement

To tackle climate change and its negative impacts, world leaders at the UN Climate Change Conference (COP 21) in Paris reached a breakthrough: the historic Paris Agreement (United Nations, n.d.). The Paris Agreement is a legally binding international treaty on climate change. It was adopted by 196 parties at COP 21 in Paris on 12 December 2015 and entered into force on 4 November 2016. The agreement has the following key aspects and long-term goals (United Nations Framework Convention on Climate Change, 2016).

   i. Significantly decrease Earth's temperature to below 2°C over pre-industrial times, with attempts to curb temperature rise to 1.5°C above pre-industrial levels (Article 2).
   ii. Developed economies must facilitate financial, technological, and capacity-building assistance to emerging economies. The pact also establishes the Convention's Financial Mechanisms, which include the Green Climate Fund (Article 9, 10, 11).
   iii. All Signatories to the Paris Agreement are obliged to make greater attempts via Nationally Determined Contributions. The Paris Agreement (Article 4, paragraph 2) requires each party to prepare, communicate, and maintain successive NDCs that it intends to communicate every five years thereafter regardless of their respective implementation timeframes (United Nations Framework Convention on Climate Change ii & iii, n.d.). Developed countries were emphasized to take the lead by undertaking absolute economy-wide reduction targets, while developing countries should continue enhancing their mitigation efforts and are encouraged to move toward economy-wide targets over time in light of different national circumstances.
   iv. After every five years, the parties must disclose a nationally determined contribution.

    v. The accord emphasizes need for preventing, reducing, and eliminating the suffering and destruction caused by climate change (Article 8).
  vi. The pact also urges members to protect and improve GHG sinks and repositories, as necessary (Article 5).
 vii. Climate change curriculum, training, awareness campaigns, involvement, and knowledge exchange (Article 12).
viii. To give clarification on taking appropriate actions by members, the Paris Agreement focuses on a comprehensive accountability and reporting mechanism, with leeway for members with different capabilities (Article 13).

Besides, the regulations for implementing the Paris Agreement, as outlined in the Paris Rulebook, were adopted at the 24th COP in Katowice, Poland, and will be concluded at the COP 26 in Glasgow, Scotland, in November 2021.

REFERENCES

Elkins, P., & Baker, T. (2001). Carbon taxes and carbon emissions trading. *Journal of Economic Surveys, 15*(3), 325–376.

Gao, Y., Gao, X., & Zhang, X. (2017). The 2 C global temperature target and the evolution of the long-term goal of addressing climate change—from the United Nations framework convention on climate change to the Paris agreement. *Engineering, 3*(2), 272–278.

Hannah, L. (2011). The Climate System and Climate Change. In *Climate Change Biology* (pp. 13–52). Cambridge, MA: Academic Press.

Intergovernmental Panel on Climate Change (IPCC). (2021). *IPCC FACTSHEET. What is the IPCC?* Geneva, Switzerland. Retrieved from https://www.ipcc.ch/site/assets/uploads/2021/07/AR6_FS_What_is_IPCC.pdf

Josephson, P. (2017). *Common but Differentiated Responsibilities in the Climate Change Regime: Historic Evaluation and Future Outlooks.* Stockholm: Stockholm University.

Keong, C. Y. (2020). *Global Environmental Sustainability: Case Studies and Analysis of the United Nations' Journey toward Sustainable Development.* Amsterdam: Elsevier.

Kuh, K. F. (2018). *The Law of Climate Change Mitigation: An Overview.* Amsterdam: Elsevier.

Liu, P. R., & Raftery, A. E. (2021). Country-based rate of emissions reductions should increase by 80% beyond nationally determined contributions to meet the 2 °C target. *Commun Earth Environ, 2*, 29.

Organization for Economic Co-operation and Development. (2007). *Climate Change Policies: Policy Brief.* pp. 1–8. Retrieved from www.oecd.org/env/cc/39111309.pdf

Peterson, S. (2003). Monitoring, accounting and enforcement in emissions trading regimes. *Greenhouse Gas Emissions Trading and Project-based Mechanisms*, 189.

Poulopoulos, S. G. (2016). Atmospheric Environment. In *Environment and Development* (pp. 45–136). Amsterdam: Elsevier.

Pulselli, F. M., & Marchi, M. (2015). *Global Warming Potential and the Net Carbon Balance.* Cambridge, MA: Academic Press.

Stavins, R., Zou, J., Brewer, T., Conte Grand, M., den Elzen, M., Finus, M., . . . & Winkler, H. (2014). International cooperation: Agreements and instruments. *Climate change, 7*(5), 1001–1082.

Tian, W. A. N. G., & Xiang, G. A. O. (2018). Reflection and operationalization of the common but differentiated responsibilities and respective capabilities principle in the transparency framework under the international climate change regime. *Advances in Climate Change Research, 9*(4), 253–263.

United Nations Climate Change Programme. (n.d.). *Background-Cooperation with the IPCC*. Retrieved from https://unfccc.int/topics/science/workstreams/cooperation-with-the-ipcc/background-cooperation-with-the-ipcc

United Nations Conference on Environment and Development (UNCED). (1992). Report of the United Nations conference on environment and development. Rio de Janeiro, Brazil. Retrieved from https://www.un.org/en/development/desa/population/migration/general-assembly/docs/globalcompact/A_CONF.151_26_Vol.I_Declaration.pdfUnited Nations Framework Convention on Climate Change. (1992). New York. Retrieved from https://unfccc.int/process-and-meetings/the-convention/history-of-the-convention/convention-documents?gclid=CjwKCAiAnZCdBhBmEiwA8nDQxRJgdAHR3PfZzgRnSHITqP2CobHc9iUbMCNCJbHBfgipJ0HUooVoMBoC2okQAvD_BwE

United Nations Framework Convention on Climate Change. (1998). Text of Kyoto protocol to UNFCCC. *United Nations Framework Convention on Climate Change*. Bonn, Germany.

United Nations Framework Convention on Climate Change. (2009). *Kyoto Protocol Reference Manual on Accounting of Emissions and Assigned Amount*. Rio de Janeiro, Brazil.

United Nations Framework Convention on Climate Change. (2016). *Report of the Conference of the Parties on Its Twenty-First Session, Held in Paris from 30 November to 13 December 2015*. Retrieved from https://unfccc.int/resource/docs/2015/cop21/eng/10a01.pdf#page=2

United Nations Framework Convention on Climate Change. (2020). *Conference of the Parties (COP) (2020)*. Retrieved from https://unfccc.int/process/bodies/supreme-bodies/conference-of-the-parties-cop

United Nations Framework Convention on Climate Change i. (n.d.). *Fact Sheet: Why Climate Change Requires an Internationally Coordinated Financial Response*. pp. 1–4. Retrieved from https://unfccc.int/files/press/backgrounders/application/pdf/press_factsh_financing.pdf

United Nations Framework Convention on Climate Change ii. (n.d.). *Nationally Determined Contributions (NDCs)*. Retrieved from https://unfccc.int/process-and-meetings/the-paris-agreement/nationally-determined-contributions-ndcs/nationally-determined-contributions-ndcs

United Nations Framework Convention on Climate Change iii. (n.d.). *The Paris Agreement*. Retrieved from https://unfccc.int/process-and-meetings/the-paris-agreement/the-paris-agreement

United Nations. (n.d.). *The Paris Agreement*. Retrieved from www.un.org/en/climatechange/paris-agreement

Watkiss, P. (2007). *Climate Change: The Cost of Inaction and the Cost of Adaptation*. Copenhagen, Denmark.

The White House. (2009). *Declaration of the Leaders the Major Economies Forum on Energy and Climate*. United States Government, Washington, DC. Retrieved from www.whitehouse.gov/the-press-office/declaration-leaders-major-economies-forum-energy-and-climate

The World Bank. (n.d.). What is carbon pricing? *Carbon Pricing Dashboard*. Retrieved from https://carbonpricingdashboard.worldbank.org/what-carbon-pricing

14 Climate Change— National Action Plan

Ashita Rai and M. H. Fulekar

CONTENTS

1. Introduction to the Geography of India 224
2. National Action Plan on Climate Change (NAPCC) 224
3. Principles of NAPCC 225
4. Missions in NAPCC 225
    - 4.1 National Solar Mission 226
        - 4.1.1 Solar Thermal Power Generation 226
        - 4.1.2 Solar Photovoltaic Generation 226
        - 4.1.3 R&D Collaboration, Technology Transfer, and Capacity Building 226
    - 4.2 National Mission for Enhanced Energy Efficiency in Industry 227
        - 4.2.1 GHG Mitigation Options in the Industry Sector 227
        - 4.2.2 Potential for Emissions Reduction 228
    - 4.3 National Mission on Sustainable Habitat 228
        - 4.3.1 Promoting Energy Efficiency in the Residential and Commercial Sector 228
        - 4.3.2 Research and Development 229
        - 4.3.3 Management of Municipal Solid Waste (MSW) 229
        - 4.3.4 R&D Needs 229
        - 4.3.5 Promotion on Urban Public Transportation 230
    - 4.4 National Water Mission 230
        - 4.4.1 Water Resources 230
        - 4.4.2 Management of Surface Water Resources-Studies 230
        - 4.4.3 Management and Regulation of Groundwater Resources 231
        - 4.4.4 Upgrading Storage Structure for Rainwater and Drainage Systems for Wastewater 231
        - 4.4.5 Confirmation of Wetlands 231
        - 4.4.6 Development of Desalination Technologies 232
    - 4.5 National Mission for Sustaining the Himalayan Ecosystem 232
    - 4.6 National Mission for a Green India 233
        - 4.6.1 Conserving Biodiversity 233
    - 4.7 National Mission for Sustainable Agriculture 233
        - 4.7.1 Dryland Agriculture 234
        - 4.7.2 Risk Management 234

        4.7.3   Use of Biotechnology 234
        4.7.4   Priority Areas Include 234
    4.8   National Mission on Strategic Knowledge for Climate Chance 235
5. Implementation of Mission 235
References 237

1. INTRODUCTION TO THE GEOGRAPHY OF INDIA

India is a very large country with a land area of 2,973,190 square (The World Bank, 2022). The country is the second most populous nation in the world, housing 1,380 million people in 2020 or 17.5% of the world's population. Approximately 35% of the total population forms urban community (The World Bank, 2020). Despite the fact that India's economy has escalated significantly in recent years, yet around 58% of the total population relies upon agriculture for its livelihood (India Brand Equity Foundation, 2021). Agricultural and industrial sectors contribute roughly 21.82% and 25.92% respectively to the country's gross domestic product in line with the Ministry of Statistics and Programme Implementation, Government of India (2021). The country is already affected with the implications of climate change that has affected critical national development goals connected with habitats, health, energy, and infrastructure (Bisht & Shaikh, 2015). India's distinctive geographics yields a spectrum of climate making it a biologically and culturally rich nation (Islam, Hove, & Parry, 2011). Outsized variation in land use and rainfall pattern has been observed across the country. Land use pattern is governed by several factors like population density, urban growth, industrial settlements, agriculture, irrigation, and natural disasters like floods and droughts (Mbow, Reisinger, Canadell, & O'Brien, 2017).

India promptly endorsed climate change adaptation and awareness strategies and encouraged debates on global warming at the international level. During the conference of the signatory members of the United Nations Framework Convention on Climate Change hosted by India in 2002, the country promoted a joint declaration on the consequences of global warming. The report also emphasized on assessing vulnerabilities to climate change and its adaptation measures (Meister, Kröger, Richwien, Rickerson, & Laurent, 2009). India played a keystone role at the international level in climate negotiations, whereas it promoted actively climate policy at the national and sub-national level (Atteridge, Shrivastava, Pahuja, & Upadhyay, 2012). It is necessary to recognize prospects of international and national actions and negotiations for combating global climate change. Recently India has accelerated mitigation approaches and negotiations within the UNFCCC, as well as launched a programme called national action plan on climate change at a domestic level.

2. NATIONAL ACTION PLAN ON CLIMATE CHANGE (NAPCC)

The Indian government introduced the National Action Plan on Climate Change (NAPCC) on 30 June 2008, with the goal of raising insight and understanding amongst members of the public, administration, researchers, enterprises, and marginalized people. It also fosters preparedness and response strategies that support long-term development (Thokchom, 2020). The NAPCC is composed of eight national missions that embody multifaceted, long-term, and sustainable strategies to attain core climate change mitigation and adaptation agendas. These are the following:

  i. National Solar Mission
  ii. National Mission for Enhanced Energy Efficiency
  iii. National Mission on Sustainable Habitat
  iv. National Water Mission
  v. National Mission for Sustaining the Himalayan Ecosystem
  vi. National Mission for a Green India
  vii. National Mission for Sustainable Agriculture
  viii. National Mission on Strategic Knowledge for Climate Change

3. PRINCIPLES OF NAPCC

(Source: https://archivepmo.nic.in/drmanmohansingh/climate_change_english.pdf)

- These underlying principles regulate the NAPCC:
- Safeguards both the poor and marginalized section through a holistic climate change–related sustainable development agenda.
- Achieving national sustainability targets whilst fostering a significant shift in strategy which boosts environmental protection that reduces carbon emissions.
- Strengthening comprehensive and cost-effective demand side management techniques for end users.
- Deploying modern techniques that respond to and limit carbon dioxide emissions.
- Setting up alternative mandatory and legislative measures to facilitate in long-term development.
- Formulating and maintaining effective interventions in conjunction between civic society and local governmental entities and also fostering public-private alliances.
- Promoting global and regional R&D activities, the copyright framework, and transfer of technology through funding.

4. MISSIONS IN NAPCC

Technological innovation and its use is crucial to the National Action Plan. The enforcement of the programme would take place through appropriate institutional mechanisms designed to achieve the objectives of each mission and incorporate public-private partnerships and civil society interaction. An emphasis will be placed on helping the community to understand climate change adaptation and mitigation, as well as energy efficiency and natural resource conservation. Eight national missions embodies fundamentals of the national action plan and represent long-term, multi-layered, and consolidated strategies to achieve major goals while mitigating climate change. Programmes that are being designed/developed are part of precise efforts which require direction, amplification of scope, and time-oriented implementation.

4.1 NATIONAL SOLAR MISSION

National Solar Mission inaugurated on 10 January 2010 aims to enhance the share of solar energy in the total energy mix while expanding the use of other renewable and non-fossil options, namely, nuclear energy, wind energy, and biomass. As a tropical country, India is blessed with plenty of sunshine for long periods of time and at extreme intensity. Consequently, solar energy is a promising source of future energy (Srivastava & Srivastava, 2013). Additionally, it facilitates decentralized distribution of energy, thus empowering the grassroots. The National Solar Mission seeks to promote solar energy use for power generation and other purposes. By 2022, the mission aims to install 100 GW of grid-connected solar power plants. This is in accordance with the country's Intentional Nationally Determined Contributions (INDCs) to create approximately 40% of installed energy capacity from non-fossil-fuel-based sources by 2030, along with emission reduction of its GDP up to 35% GDP from 2005 levels (Ministry of New and Renewable Energy, Government of India, 2022).

4.1.1 Solar Thermal Power Generation

Concentrated solar power (CSP) or solar thermal power excavating (STPG) are methods of harnessing concentrated solar radiation to generate electricity at high-temperature (greater than 500°C). In principle, solar thermal power plants operate on a similar principle to traditional thermal plants. STPG is now poised for significant commercialization on a huge scale. It is estimated that the cost of a standalone solar thermal power plant (i.e., without hybridization) would be around 20 to 22 Cr/MW. Generally, it comprises of the cost of the solar concentrator's balance of system, the turbine, generator, and control equipment. R&D should focus on minimizing production and maintenance costs encompassing production design and fabrication/assembly techniques. Moreover, it should resolve issues in balance of systems with biomass combustion-based systems and/or shorten salt, thermal storage.

4.1.2 Solar Photovoltaic Generation

In photovoltaic generation, solar output is typically transformed into electrical energy using a semi-conductor, frequently a silicon diode. While there are other semiconductors that can be explored for energy production, however most of these are already in the process of being developed. Photovoltaic energy sources range between Rs.30 and Rs.35 crore every megawatt hour. This encompasses overall cost of solar arrays and the overall balance of the system (BoS). Even though the basic cost of electricity remained in the Rs.15–20 KWh level, thin-filter-based devices are witnessing cost reductions. In the near and medium term, envisaged R&D activities for photovoltaic solar generations involve enhancing solar cell performance to 15% at industrial level, updating photovoltaic modules devices to relatively high packing density and applicability for solar roots, and constructing compressed modules for use in solar lamps.

4.1.3 R&D Collaboration, Technology Transfer, and Capacity Building

Technology transfer including both solar thermal and photovoltaic systems will be essential for producing economical and practical measures suitable to be used in India. The National Solar Mission would be command of the following:

i. Innovating commercial technology for sola-based energy generation
ii. Establishing a solar research facility within an existing framework to organize multiple research, innovation, and demonstration activities
iii. Establishing a commercial solar manufacturing capabilities which encompasses solar components, hardware, and devices
iv. Integrating Indian investigation with international organizations with the aim of promoting cooperative endeavours as well as sourcing technology and making adjustments to Indian scenario
v. Providing funding for the initiatives

In the course of time, the policy should promote Indian solar scientific studies to generate potentially game-changing discoveries that cut across multiple techniques or methods.

4.2 National Mission for Enhanced Energy Efficiency in Industry

The industries in India is the biggest consumer of electricity, accounting for 42.7% of overall consumption during 2011–2020 (Jaganmohan, 2021). India's industrial sectors, that include giant, mid, and micro enterprises, grew by 10.6% between April to December 2006. The manufacturing sector has continued to make a big difference in India's high economy because it is regarded as fundamental to economic progress. Through financing agreements established in the nation's consecutive five-year plan, the industrial development efforts have assisted in the development of numerous power-oriented core production units, notably iron and steel, concrete, fertilizer, and refinery. As per the countrywide GHG inventories, primary CO_2 emissions at industrial plants accounted for roughly 31% of overall CO_2 emissions. Process-related CO_2 emissions and emissions from industrial fuel burning are the two types of CO_2 emissions produced by enterprise. In 1954, energy consumption represented for over 60% of the overall predicted 250 million tonnes of direct CO_2 emissions from industries.

4.2.1 GHG Mitigation Options in the Industry Sector

The industrial unit's emissions reduction measures have been classified into three categories:

i. Sector-Specific Technological Options

In the chlor-alkali, concrete, aluminium, fertilizers, iron and steel, pulp and paper, and clothing sectors, many emission abatement technological techniques are presently being investigated.

ii. Cross-Cutting Technologies Options

Aside from sector-specific alternatives, a middle range of industries have integrated certain cross-cutting energy-efficient innovative possibilities. In the industry, cross-cutting technologies account for almost half of all energy use.

iii. Fuel Switch Options

Organizations have been anticipated to switch from nonrenewable to renewable power generation as natural gas becomes more readily available throughout the country, whether as imported LNG (liquefied natural gas) or local natural gas. Switching to natural gas has a number of benefits, including increased energy efficiency. Switching from biomass fuels to producer gas is another possibility for thermal improvements.

4.2.2 Potential for Emissions Reduction

Owing to the fact that almost all big manufacturing firms substantially upgraded their productivity along with some of the nation's top establishments' offer to reduce energy consumption, CO_2 emissions through fuels and electricity use in sector are expected to be reduced again by 605 million tonnes by 2031. Besides the technological transfer, it will entail significant additional instruments expenses along with large financial investments altogether.

Energy Conservation Act of 2001 sets a legislative foundation for its central administration's Bureau of Energy Efficiency (BEE) and permitted provincial bodies to implement fuel efficiency initiatives. Several projects and efforts were developed, with the goal of saving 10,000 megawatts before the expiration of the eleventh five-year plan in 2012.

Significant steps are being implemented to improve resource efficiency. Which would constitute the following:

i. A business-oriented strategy for maximising fuel cost saving and efficiency by certifying and trading energy efficiency.
ii. Using new techniques to make products more affordable, accelerating the transfer of efficient appliance in fined industries.
iii. Techniques to aid in the funding of demand-side measures throughout all domains by supporting future fuel savings are being developed.
iv. Encouraging fuel efficiency through monetary incentives.

4.3 NATIONAL MISSION ON SUSTAINABLE HABITAT

National Mission on Sustainable Habitat was established in 2010 with the intent of enhancing energy efficiency, solid waste management, and paradigm shift to public transit in order to make habitats more viable. It also promotes energy savings as a critical component of urban planning and renovation. The mission is classified into three categories: fostering fuel efficiency within residential and commercial sectors, municipal waste management, and encouragement of urban public transport (Gupta & Sathaye, 2009).

4.3.1 Promoting Energy Efficiency in the Residential and Commercial Sector

In India, household power demand equates to roughly 13.3% of energy demand. Power usage in the commercial world increased at a 7.4% annualized rate from 1990 to 2003. Furthermore, energy usage in residential and commercial structures varies greatly depending upon economic classes, architectural design, geography, and a host of other issues. According to studies, significant energy reductions can be fostered in the residential and non-residential domains, leading to an improvement of interior and exterior air quality and, as a response, improved health and welfare.

Climate Change—National Action Plan

4.3.2 Research and Development

R&D in the domestic and industrial sectors is mostly focused on power alternatives. It must place a strong emphasis on the use of energy-efficient techniques for the following purposes:

   i. Buildings and components that are energy-efficient.
  ii. Manufacture of energy-efficient windows.
 iii. Insulation material development at a minimal cost.
  iv. Software development.
   v. Ceiling designs that are more energy efficient to be developed.
  vi. Development of a stand-by power circuit that consumes relatively less energy.
 vii. Lamps based on low-cost emitting diode (LED) technology will be developed for use in spacecraft lighting.
viii. Architects and designers must be educated and informed on the various energy-saving options available in new facility.
  ix. Professionally coordinated curriculum at colleges as well as other specialized organizations is necessary to impact such training for the construction of low-energy structures.

4.3.3 Management of Municipal Solid Waste (MSW)

Solid waste generation has increased from 6 million tonnes in 1947 to 69 million tonnes in 2006. The MSW Rules, Environmental Protection Act has highlighted on specific treatment alternatives, such as collection, transportation, and disposal techniques. Following are some broad factors for theoretical reform in the MSW sector:

- In the case of smaller cities and towns within an area, dumping services must be established as a broadly shared infrastructure.
- A well-coordinated framework must include systems for pickup, transportation, transport, processing, and burial.

4.3.4 R&D Needs

The underlying methodological needs must be acknowledged by the research and development domain:

   i. Biomechanization waste-to-energy technology and its widespread application for sorting trash resources such kitchen waste, butcher wastes, and dairy waste.
  ii. Minimize the product's total price and build native gas engines for waste-to-energy operations.
 iii. To lower occupational and environmental dangers, enhancing the efficiency of waste plastic recycling technology.
  iv. Formulation of recycling and reuse techniques for construction and demolition debris and e-waste.

4.3.5 Promotion on Urban Public Transportation

Considering economic expansion and population growth, an increase in demand for passenger and goods transportation services is unavoidable. Research studies suggest regulatory and technological reforms in the transportation industry can save considerable amounts of energy and hence reduce emissions. Extending the use of railway and enhancing the effectiveness of many other methods of travel, as per the planning commission, could save 115 mtoe (million tonnes of oil equivalent) by 2031/32. In contrast to the existing norms, TERI projects, including productivity improvements across transport systems, as well as increasing usage of public vehicles and rail-based running on bio-diesel, will result in a 144 mtoe energy reduction by 2031.

4.4 NATIONAL WATER MISSION

National Water Mission was developed with the intention of achieving holistic management of water resources that will assist in conserving water, waste minimization, and equal sharing within and between regions. The mission additionally includes the National Water Policy's requirements and provides a surveillance system for water use as well as a 20% increase in water utilization effectiveness. In partnership with jurisdictions, the National Water Policy will also address basin-level regulation in responding to fluctuations in precipitation and waterways. This will incorporate increased above- and below-ground reservoirs, as well as rainwater collection and its equitable and inclusive management.

4.4.1 Water Resources

India receives 1197 mm of precipitation per year on average. That's a cumulative rainfall of 4,000 billion m3. Moreover, 3,000 billion m3 is dissipated due to runoff, leaving just 1,000 billion m3 available as surface and groundwater sources, yielding in a per capita freshwater resources of 1,000 m3 per year. This is around a fifth to a tenth of what many developed countries have. Many sections of India are currently water-stressed, and by 2050, India is likely to face water scarcity. Climate change impacts may exacerbate the situation. In a nutshell, it's necessary to boost water efficiency, look for ways to supplement water supply in critical areas, and ensure better water management.

4.4.2 Management of Surface Water Resources-Studies

Waterways, which are common sources of fresh water, often represent a healthier environment than other indices. In the form of hydroelectric power, as well as significant agricultural supplies in the form of cultivation, such resources are commercially useful. The hereunder are some of the most important aspects of surface water analyses:

i. Assessment of stream flow in steep areas.
ii. Responding to the effects of global warming.
iii. For local river basin, modelling is used.
iv. Measurement of river basin discharge using isotopic tracers.

Climate Change—National Action Plan

v. Creating digital elevation models for flood risk assessment in flood-prone areas.
vi. Flood-prone locations will be examined, and a flood-control scheme will be developed.
vii. Monitoring glacial and periodic snow cover in order to assess the importance of snowmelt in Himalayan rivers in India.
viii. Developing a more extensive network of automated meteorological stations and rain gauges.
ix. Strategies for watershed management in the montane ecology.

4.4.3 Management and Regulation of Groundwater Resources

Fresh water contributes about 40% of surface water, fulfilling roughly 55% of irrigation needs, 85% of rural and urban demand, respectively. Overuse of supplies, on the other hand, has resulted in a major decline in aquifer levels in various portions of the country, eventually contributing to climatic changes. The following are some of the programme's prospective major aspects:

- Water conservation and artificial replenishment must be made compulsory in major metropolitan areas.
- Accelerated recharge of groundwater aquifers and water basins.
- Water evaluations and audits is required to ensure proper industrial waste disposal.
- Irrigational power tariffs must be regulated.

4.4.4 Upgrading Storage Structure for Rainwater and Drainage Systems for Wastewater

It is necessary to improve storage capacity and modernize drainage channels in order to conform to the difficulties of severe weather events caused by weather phenomena. Drainage is required for recovering marshy and high salinity land, as well as for limiting the deterioration of fertile land.

4.4.5 Confirmation of Wetlands

Wetlands offer a variety of hydrological functions, including water conservation, groundwater recharge, and the preservation of biodiversity, including endangered species, and also a means of livelihood for many communities. Wetlands are under potential danger of being transformed to many other purposes, causing the loss of ecosystem functions and putting the lives of those who ultimately depend on them at jeopardy. The following are some of the measures that have been suggested to help preserve wetlands:

i. Environmental impact evaluation and analysis of projects and approaches.
ii. Creating a list of strategies, particularly those with unique characteristics.
iii. Surveying and assessing land-use patterns, as well as tracing catchments.
iv. Drainage, silting vegetation cover, invasion, mangrove conversion, human settlements, and human activity, as well as their effects on reserves, must all be considered.

v. Creating awareness among local community regarding the significance of wetlands.
vi. Developing and executing a regulatory structure at the national, state, and district levels to determine the proper use of approaches.

4.4.6 Development of Desalination Technologies

Desalinating water has indeed been proposed as a viable strategy for addressing water supply through environmental assets in India, in response to increasing needs for fresh water resulting from the country's booming population and modernization. Desalination was highlighted as an important broad technical field of technology for R&D in the Eleventh Plan. The following technologies are currently being investigated and established: reverse osmosis and multistage flash dispersion are used to desalinate seawater.

4.5 National Mission for Sustaining the Himalayan Ecosystem

The Himalayan environment is vital to India's environmental protection because it supplies forest resources, sustains perennial streams that supply fresh drinking water, agriculture, and hydroelectric power, conserves habitats, and creates a strong foundation for high-value farming and landscape for successful technology. Changing climate, on contrary, may have a deleterious effect on the mountainous environment as a result of increased temperatures, shifting patterns of precipitation and droughts. Various national scientific institutions have looked into the extent of glacial mass change and whether climate change is a major factor. The Himalayan ecosystem must be reviewed and managed, particularly the state of its glacier and the consequences of variations in glacial mass on river flows. Because the Himalayan ecosystem is inhabited by several South Asian countries, important analytical interaction and information exchange may well be evaluated in order to have a proper overview of environmental factors and their consequences (Khanna, 2018).

The Himalayan Ecosystem Conversation's goal is to inspire indigenous residents to make more effort for environmental resource monitoring. The National Environmental Policy of 2006 includes, following relevant actions for alpine ecosystem conservation:

i. Adopt proper land and watershed management strategies to ensure the viability of alpine ecosystems.
ii. Promote the cultivation of traditional crop and horticultural varieties through organic agriculture, which allows farmers to profit from premium price.
iii. Encourage the adoption of best-practice norms for tourism and promote sustainable tourism.
iv. Take steps to control tourist inflows into mountain areas so that sustains the mountain ecosystem's carrying capacity.
v. Recognize characteristic mountainous scapers as objects with "incomparable values" while developing preservation plans.

4.6 NATIONAL MISSION FOR A GREEN INDIA

Green India is a centrally sponsored scheme aimed at enhancing ecosystem roles, such as carbon sequestration. Trees are essential to preserving environmental integrity and complexity. Woods are also among the nation's leading carbon sinks. They are an important source of genetic diversity and provide a number of significant benefits that contribute to maintaining natural equilibrium. Forests provide around 40% of the country's total energy needs, including over 80% in remote regions, and are at the core of forest-based populations. Trees absorb billions of tonnes of carbon dioxide equivalents in terms of biomass and soil carbon.

Green India's purpose will be accomplished on damaged forest land by participatory residents, managed by joint forest management committees, and regulated by state governments' Department of Forests. The Green India Initiative is already underway. Under the scheme, 6 million hectares of disturbed forest will be reclaimed with the support of Joint Forest Management Committees (JFMCS).

The following are some of the components of this programme:

i. Plants that are quick growing and climate-adaptable are being planted.
ii. Providing pathways for species migration, to reduce forest fragmentation.
iii. Increasing public-private investments in order to increase forest cover and density.
iv. Community-based initiatives are being revitalised and scaled up.
v. The Green India Plan is being implemented.

4.6.1 Conserving Biodiversity

Safeguarding of biodiversity at heritage sites, such as sacred grooves and protected areas, is critical for ecological processes. The following strict steps will be taken as part of the campaign: in situ and ex situ biological resource management, with a focus on fragile diversity. Development of biodiversity registers (at federal, regional, and municipal level) for the purpose of cataloguing species variability and indigenous practices.

Proper implementation of the Wildlife Conservation and Biodiversity Conservation Acts.

4.7 NATIONAL MISSION FOR SUSTAINABLE AGRICULTURE

The mission's target is to come up with ways to assure that agriculture is climate-resilient. It would explore and cultivate novel crops, specifically thermally resilient species and innovative farming techniques, which could endure weather extremes, protracted drought, inundation, and fluctuating moisture levels. Agriculture might require to acclimatize to climate change gradually, and agricultural research shall focus on monitoring and evaluating climate change and recommend modifications in farming methods as appropriate. The consolidation and incorporation of traditional education and skill, information and technology, geospatial technological advances, and biotechnology will facilitate this. The emphasis would be on increasing rainfed agricultural productivity. India will contribute greatly towards global attempts to achieve environmentally sustainable agriculture. The envisioned national mission should emphasize on four priority areas for agriculture to become climate-resilient: dryland farming, risk mitigation, information availability, and biotechnological application.

4.7.1 Dryland Agriculture

The following are the top priorities for farming systems with an emphasis on adaptation:

  i. Crop species that are drought and pest tolerant shall be developed.
  ii. Soil and water conservation technologies are being strengthened.
  iii. Discussions with stakeholders, training courses, and demonstrative events for farming areas to exchange and transmit agro-climatic data.
  iv. Financial assistance must be extended to farmers to facilitate them in investing and adapting appropriate agricultural approaches to combat climate change.

4.7.2 Risk Management

Extreme climate events may push agriculture at threat. The following are the priority areas:

  i. Existing farming and insurance strategies must be strengthened.
  ii. Climate-derived models need to be developed and evaluated.
  iii. Development of digital, localized vernacular tools that enables weather-based insurance more inclusive.
  iv. At the basin or stream catchment level, GIS and remote sensing techniques are being explored for comprehensive soil resource evaluation and land-use planning.
  v. Environmentally vulnerable areas as well as pest disease clusters are being investigated.
  vi. Assessing the level of susceptibility and vulnerability, executing localized emergency plans.

4.7.3 Use of Biotechnology

Biotechnological approaches in farming facilitates in suggesting drought- and flood-resilient cropping pattern, utilization of elevated CO_2 concentrations to increase the productivity of crops, and increasing the resistance of the crop from diseases and pests.

4.7.4 Priority Areas Include

Genetic engineering is being explored to link G3 crops to carbon-responsive G4 crops in order to enhance multi-synthetic quality and competitiveness.

Crops having enhanced carbon and nitrogen utilization capabilities which lowers the emission of GHGs and also are less prone to natural weather extremities shall be developed.

Nutritional techniques for managing extreme heat in milk production are indeed being explored in place to evade nutritional inadequacies that result in reduced dairy production and yield.

4.8 NATIONAL MISSION ON STRATEGIC KNOWLEDGE FOR CLIMATE CHANGE

To counteract climate change, the national mission anticipates the following initiatives:

i. There is a desire to increase information of essential occurrences in the aspects of meteorology, such as rainfall cycles and natural services.
ii. To enhance the effectiveness and specificity of global warming projections over the subcontinent, particularly variations in the water cycle, scientists shall practice global and regional climate modelling.
iii. Improvements in observation methods, information gathering, and integration, along with attempts to increase accessibility and availability of valuable data.
iv. Significant study facilities, such as high-performance computers and wide-bandwidth networks, will be constructed to aid investigators in accessing important computing and data discoveries.
v. Climate change's repercussions, such as their impact on health, demographic trends, migration paths, and marine communities subsistence, will also be on the mission's action plan.
vi. It will also stimulate the establishment of extreme weather events research institutes in higher learning institutions around the country.
vii. Under the mandate to promote research, a climate science research fund will also be established. Venture capital investments will be facilitated to promote private sector for developing novel technology to combat climate change.
viii. Identifying institutes to undertake research for policymaking and implementation. The mission will also emphasize upon disseminating latest scientific research and information.

5. IMPLEMENTATION OF MISSION

These national missions, which are backed up by evidence and recent and updated programmes, would not only help the economy adapt to changing climate but would also put the world on a path that will progressively and significantly reduce global warming.

These missions will be carried out by respective ministries and managed by intersectoral groups made up of industrial, academic, and societal specialists. Based on the mission's goal, the organizational framework may vary, but it will include the power to negotiate a stronger strategic approach.

The government has established a climate change steering committee, which is chaired by the prime minister, in order to effectively address the concerns of changing climate. Delegates from a diverse number of prominent groups, including government, corporate, and civilized society, serve on the committee, which sets basic

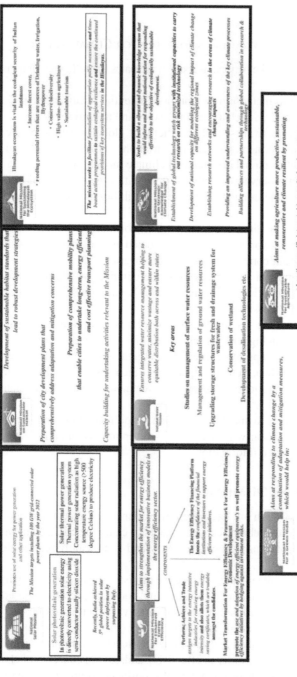

FIGURE 14.1 NAPCC: At Glance.

criteria for nationwide climate action. The council will also provide guidance on matters linked to domestic policy coordination, as well as assess the efficacy of the National Action Plan on Climate Change, together with its research and development policy.

REFERENCES

Atteridge, A., Shrivastava, M. K., Pahuja, N., & Upadhyay, H. (2012). Climate policy in India: What shapes international, national and state policy?. *Ambio*, *41*(1), 68–77.

Bisht, H., & Shaikh, G. G. (2015). Climate resilient development in Bundelkhand region of Madhya Pradesh: Mainstreaming climate change adaptation in policy and planning. *Development Alternatives*, New Delhi, p. 1.

Gupta, A. P., & Sathaye, J. (2009). Electrifying India. *IEEE Power and Energy Magazine*, *7*(5), 59–61. Retrieved from www.statista.com/statistics/1130112/india-electricity-consumption-share-by-sector/

India Brand Equity Foundation. (2021). *Agriculture in India: Information about Indian Agriculture & Its Importance*. Retrieved from www.ibef.org/industry/agriculture-india.aspx

Islam, F., Hove, H., & Parry, J. E. (2011). Review of current and planned adaptation action: South Asia. *Adaptation Partnership*. Retrieved from: https://www.iisd.org/system/files/publications/idl-55866-india.pdf

Jaganmohan, M. (2021). *Share of Electricity Consumption FY 2020, by Sector*. Statista. Retrieved from https://www.statista.com/statistics/1130112/india-electricity-consumption-share-by-sector/

Khanna, B. K. (2018). Indian national strategy for climate change adaptation and mitigation. In *Climate Change and Environmental Concerns: Breakthroughs in Research and Practice* (pp. 541–572). Hershey, PA: IGI Global.

Mbow, H. O. P., Reisinger, A., Canadell, J., & O'Brien, P. (2017). Special Report on climate change, desertification, land degradation, sustainable land management, food security, and greenhouse gas fluxes in terrestrial ecosystems (SR2). Ginevra, IPCC.

Meister, H. P., Kröger, I., Richwien, M., Rickerson, W., & Laurent, C. (2009). *Floating Houses and Mosquito Nets: Emerging Climate Change Adaptation Strategies Around the World*. Boston, MA: Meister Consultants Group.

Ministry of New and Renewable Energy, Government of India. (2022). *Solar Energy*. Retrieved from https://mnre.gov.in/solar/current-status/

Ministry of Statistics and Programme Implementation. (2021). *Press Note on Provisional Estimates of Annual National Income 2020–21 and Quarterly Estimates of Gross Domestic Product for the Fourth Quarter (Q4) of 2020–21*. Retrieved from https://mospi.gov.in/documents/213904/416359//Press%20Note_31-05-2021_m1622547951213.pdf/7140019f-69b7-974b-2d2d-7630c3b0768d

Srivastava, S. P., & Srivastava, S. P. (2013). Solar energy and its future role in Indian economy. *International Journal of Environmental Science: Development and Monitoring*, *4*(3), 81–88.

Thokchom, B. (2020). Water-related problem with special reference to global climate change in India. In *Water Conservation and Wastewater Treatment in BRICS Nations* (pp. 37–60). Amsterdam: Elsevier.

The World Bank. (2020). *Data Catalog. Population in India*. Retrieved from https://datacatalog.worldbank.org/search/dataset/0037712

The World Bank. (2022). *Land Area-India*. Retrieved from https://data.worldbank.org/indicator/AG.LND.TOTL.K2?end=2020&locations=IN&start=2020&view=map

Glossary

A

Abatement: Minimization in the concentration of greenhouse gases.

Absolute Risk: Quantifiable or subjective assessment of the probability and intensity of a given occurrence.

Acceptable Risk: Level of significant distress that a community or population finds reasonable given the existing socioeconomic, ideological, philosophical, technological, and environmental factors.

Acclimatization: Process through which a person adjusts to a variation in its surroundings (such as a rise in temperature, moisture, season), enabling it to sustain efficiency under a variety of circumstances.

Adaptation: Adaptation to natural or anthropogenic conditions that contribute to present or anticipated meteorological stimulus and associated impacts that negates damage or maximizes benefits.

Adaptation Fund: The Adaptation Fund was created to provide funding for specific adaptation programmes and initiatives in developing economies which are potentially vulnerable and are Kyoto Protocol signatories. The fund will be funded primarily through revenues of clean development mechanism (CDM) projects and will also receive funding from other avenues too.

ADP (Ad hoc Working Group on the Durban Platform for Enhanced Action): The ADP is an auxiliary organization set up at the 17th Conference of the Parties in Durban in 2011 to establish a protocol, alternative binding agreement, or an agreeable resolution having legal significance underneath the convention that binds to all members.

Agflation: Increase in food prices that happened as a result of increasing population.

Agrichar: It's been postulated that the black carbon by-product of pyrolysis can boost soil's capability of storing carbon.

Amendment: Formal change in the content of the convention by the conference of parties. Convention. When no agreement could be established, an amendment must receive three quarters of all total votes by all parties present and voting.

Annex I Parties: The developed economies included in Annex I of the convention, who agreed to reduce its global emissions to 1990 levels by the year 2000 in accordance with Article 4.2(a) and (b). They've additionally agreed to Kyoto Protocol Article 3 and Annex B emission limits for the years 2008 to 2012.

Annex II Parties: The countries mentioned in Annex II of the convention that have a specific responsibility to contribute monetary resources and assist technology transfer to emerging economies.

Assigned Amount Unit: 1 metric tonne of CO_2 is equivalent to a Kyoto Protocol unit. Every Annex I country produces AAUs close to the standards of its designated quantity, as determined by the Protocol's Article 3, paragraphs 7 and 8. Emission trading facilitates the exchange of assigned amount units.

Atmospheric Lifetime: The estimated duration a molecule remains in the environment before being eliminated by chemical process or deposition.

B

Benefit Cost Ratio (B/C Ratio): The ratio between the current value of benefits to the net present cost.

Bio-Carbon: Carbon captured and contained organically in the planet's forests, vegetation, sediments, and waterways.

Biodegradable Municipal Waste (BMW): Waste which can be broken down into simpler form biologically.

Biomass Fuels or Biofuels: A fuel generated from dried plant debris or plant-produced flammable hydrocarbons. These fuels, including timber, ethanol distilled using sugars, and flammable oil derived from soy beans, are sustainable provided the plant that produces them is preserved or restored. Since the vegetation that serve as fuel sources trap carbon from the atmosphere, utilizing them instead of fossil energy protects the environment.

Biogeochemical Cycle: Important organic elements needed for civilization, including carbon, nitrogen, oxygen, and phosphorus, circulate through ecological systems.

Biomass: Substances with a natural origin can be degraded biologically, such as forests, grains, grass, debris, animal manure.

Biosphere: All habitats and biological species in the environment, on land (terrestrial biosphere), or in the water (marine biosphere), along with derived decaying organic matter like litter, humus, and marine debris.

Biodiversity: Amount and relative proportions of diverse genes, species, and ecosystem in a particular region.

Black water, brown water, foul water, or sewage: Water that contains human excreta.

C

Cap and trade: Limit imposed upon the permitted emission level of GHGs which is distributed among emitters, as well as establishment of a market system wherein it can also be traded among each other.

Capacity Building: Capacity building in connection with climate change is the act of creating technical expertise as well as organizational proficiency in emerging economies so that they can play an active role throughout all facets of climate adaptation, countermeasures, and investigations, and also the execution of the Kyoto Protocol.

Carbon (Dioxide) Capture and Storage (CCS): It is a technique that requires separating atmospheric CO_2 from manufacturing and energy-related resources, transporting it to a storage facility, and isolating it from the atmosphere for a long time.

Carbon Dioxide Fertilization: The acceleration in plant growth and size due to the elevated CO_2 levels in the atmosphere. Several varieties of crops are much more sensitive to variation in carbon dioxide in the atmosphere than others, based on their photosynthetic process.

Carbon Finance: It looks into the financial consequences of residing in a carbon-limited environment, where the release of GHGs bear a cost. The phrase refers to both investing in emissions reduction initiatives and the formation of market-tradable financial instruments for carbon.

Carbon Footprint: The term refers to the entire amount of GHG emissions produced by a company, activity, or commodity.

Carbon Labelling: Used to determine the quantity of carbon contained in a material for purchasers.

Carbon Offset: Technique that allows people and corporations to counteract instead of lowering their GHGs by obtaining the right to claim another's emission units for their own.

Carbon Pools: Carbon repository which has the capacity to store or release carbon over time.

Carbon Sequestration: Method of separating carbon from the air and storing it in a repository.

Carbon Sink: Something which captures more carbon from the air than what it emits is referred to as a carbon sink.

Carbon Stock: The term refers to the amount of carbon contained within a reservoir.

Carrying Capacity: The maximum population density that the environment can support perpetually, based on the food availability, shelter, fresh water, and other demands.

Certified Emission Reductions (CERs): A form of emission credit given under Clean Development Mechanism for emission reduction accomplished in CDM projects and validated by a Department of Energy underneath the legislation of Kyoto Protocol.

Climate Change: Substantial shift either in weather pattern or variation that lasts for a long time.

Climate Model: Algorithmic description of the Earth's climate depending on the spatial and biochemical aspects of its constituents, as well as associated linkages and responses, accounting for some or all of the system's known attributes.

Climate Sensitivity: The measurement of how reactive the temperature of the Earth's climate system is to changes in radiative forcing.

Cloud Albedo Effect or Twomey Effect: Radiative forcing resulting from an increase in man-made air pollutants that produces apparent increase in droplet number and reduction in sizes for fixed liquid water content, resulting in a greater cloud albedo.

Circular Economy: A circular economy is characterized by marketplaces which encourage people to reuse things instead of discarding it and reusing them. All types of garbage, such as clothing, metal products, and outdated technology, are reintroduced to the economy or utilized more effectively.

Conscious Capitalism: A type of capitalism aimed at benefiting both communities and the planet.

Conscious Consumerism: Consumers contribute with their monetary investment by choosing ethical goods and products.

Convention: An assembly of individuals who express a mutual interest.

Cradle to Grave: The life of a product, from creation to end use.

Cradle to Cradle: Using an end-use product for the source of a new product.

Cost-Benefit Analysis (CBA): A structured process of arranging evidence of a significant and detrimental consequences of projects and programmes. A CBA may be used to determine whether or not to move forward with the project or to determine whether the benefits outweigh the costs.

D

Decent Work: The International Labour Organization promotes the notion of decent work as a rights-based strategy for achieving meaningful work for women and men in circumstances of liberty, equality, safety, and integrity.

Deforestation: Activities that result in densely forested lands being converted to barren lands for other activities.

Degradation: Changes that have a detrimental impact on the location's design or operation, reducing the location's capability to offer goods and/or services.

Desertification: Deterioration of land in arid, semi-arid, and dry sub-humid areas caused by a variety of reasons such as weather fluctuations and anthropogenic.

Discrimination: Underrepresentation of an individual that can be observed at all levels.

E

Early Warning System: The set of capabilities required to produce and distribute timely and accurate data in order to alert individuals, societies, and institutions impacted by a potential danger to prepare and act accordingly in time to reduce the potential harm or damage.

Eco-footprint: The ecological footprint compares how quickly humans utilize resources and generate waste to how quickly environment can assimilate and generate resources.

Ecological or Nature Restoration: Process of aiding in the rehabilitation of a deteriorated, ruined, or destructed ecosystem.

Ecological Footprint: The ecological footprint is a measurement of human influence on the biosphere. It analyzes human depletion of natural resources with the planet's ability to replenish them ecologically.

Ecological Resilience: System's ability to handle disturbances without crossing a limit that causes the system to change its form.

Embedded Carbon: The word used to indicate how a product's carbon footprint, as evaluated by a complete life cycle assessment can be expressed in kilogrammes of CO_2 per kg of item.

Emission Inventory: A record that tracks the volume of harmful gases emitted into the environment by source over a specific timeframe.

Emissions Tax: Tax charged by a government on every unit of CO_2 equivalent emissions produced by a source.

Empowerment: It relates to the procedure of strengthening people who have little or restricted right to make decisions and determine their respective fates.

Energy Efficiency: Ratio of system's energy output to its energy input.

Environmental Management Systems: A framework of procedures and policies that allow a company to lessen its ecological impact.

F

Food Insecurity: A circumstance in which humans do not have reliable access to nutritionally adequate and safe food for healthy development, as well as an active lifestyle. It can be attributed to lack of nutrition, low economic stability, improper management, or limited food availability at the community scale.

Food Sufficiency: The capacity to generate enough food to feed a community.

Fossil Fuels: Carbon-based fuels derived from fossil reserves such as coal, petroleum, and natural gas.

Fuel Switching: Typically, it entails switching from one fuel type to the other. In the context of climate change, it is assumed that the replaced fuel emits less carbon per unit of energy generated than the classic fuel, such as natural gas for coal.

Fungibility Emission: In order to fulfil a commitment, one portion or amount could be substituted with another of equivalent worth. For instance, the fungibility of a tonne of carbon dioxide equivalent (CO_2e) allows for the usage of a variety of gases, such as methane. Fungibility also can enable different sorts of reduction allowances obtained through different mechanisms to be exchanged or used interchangeably.

G

Gender Equality: Gender equality is a wide notion that relates to a scenario where both men and women have equivalent chance to grow their particular personality and decide things free of gender norms and prejudices.

Gender Equity: Gender equity means both male and female are treated similarly based on their individual needs; it means that alternative tactics can be used to recompense females for their past disparities.

Global Environment Facility: The organization brings together 182 member states to solve worldwide environmental concerns in collaboration with other international agencies, non-profit groups, and the corporate sector.

Global Warming: Progressive increase in average surface temperature measured or predicted as a result of radiative forcing induced by man-made emissions.

Global Warming Potential: It is a measure that describes the radiation attributes of well-mixed GHGs and reflects the cumulative influence of the different durations such gasses persist in the air and also its respective efficacy in absorbing exiting infrared rays.

Green Economy: An alternate low carbon, ecofriendly, and socially equitable economy for the sustainable development of a country.

Greenhouse Effect: Greenhouse gases trap infrared radiations reflected by the surface of Earth, which would have otherwise escaped into the space and cause global warming.

Greenhouse Gases: The atmospheric gases responsible for causing global warming and climate change. It includes carbon dioxide (CO_2), methane (CH_4), nitrous oxide (N_2O), hydrofluorocarbons (HFCs), perfluorocarbons (PFCs), and sulphur hexafluoride (SF_6).

Greenwashing: Greenwashing is the practice of creating a wrong illusion or presenting inaccurate data about how a company's services are ecofriendly.

H

Habitat: Specific environment or location in which an individual or species prefers to exist.

Hazard: Term used to describe a harmful phenomenon, material, anthropogenic activities, or situation that has the potential to cause death, disability, and other health implications, damage to property, loss of habitat and supplies, social and economic unrest, or environmental destruction.

Hot waves: A heat wave is a spell of unusually hot climates that is often associated with high humidity.

Hydro Meteorological Hazard: Meteorological, hydrological, or oceanic event or phenomena that could result in serious injury, illness, or other health effects, vandalism, humanitarian crisis, social and economic turmoil, or ecological damage.

Human Rights: Human rights are principles that acknowledge and preserves an individual's dignity.

I

Impact: Negative and positive effects of climate change on people and ecosystems.

Indicators: Numerical or subjective variables that give a precise and efficient approach for evaluating changes.

Indigenous Peoples: Native groups representing unique sociocultural characteristics with ancestral linkage to the land and natural resources they dwell on, inhabit, or have been driven from.

ISO Standards: ISO is an autonomous, non-governmental agency that works together with the delegates from 167 countries to build and maintain consensus standards for a diverse variety of technological and manufacturing activities.

L

Land Use Planning: Land use planning is the practice by which government authorities recognize, analyze, and make a decision on multiple possibilities for using land, taking into account long-term economic, social, and environmental goals, as well as the influence on various cultures and interest groups, and then formulating and promulgating plans that define the allowable or appropriate uses.

Life Cycle Assessment: Methodology for calculating a product's overall environmental implications from cradle to grave.

M

Marine Stewardship Council: Seafood certifications and eco-labelling arrangement.

Glossary

Mean Sea Level: The estimated standard sea level across a timeframe, long enough to balance out nonlinearities such as tides.

Meteorology: The multidisciplinary field of science related to the study of the atmosphere.

Micro-climate: Local atmospheric zone in which the weather varies from that of the surrounding area.

Micro-generation or Micro-energy: Small-scale energy production.

Mitigation: Anthropogenic activities that reduces the emissions or increases the repositories of GHGs.

Modern Slavery: Human trafficking, enslavement, and related activities like captivity, bonded, forced marriage, violence against children, and females are all covered underneath this single phrase.

N

Natural Disaster: Any environmental mishap viz. flood, drought cyclones, earthquakes, etc., having adverse implications on the economy and human life.

Nature-Based Solutions: Nature-inspired and enabled approaches which may have ecological, economical, and societal advantages whilst enhancing adaptability.

Nested Approach: A versatile mechanism which combines components of both sub-national and national methods to reduce emissions from deforestation and forest degradation.

No Regrets Options: Technologies that minimize greenhouse gas emissions while also providing additional rewards that makes the investment worthwhile.

Non-Annex B Countries/Parties: Countries that are not listed in Annex B of the Kyoto Protocol.

O

Ozone Layer: Stratospheric layer that stretches from 15–50 kms above the Earth's surface and has the highest level of ozone gas which filters ultraviolet radiation from the sun.

Ozone Layer Depletion: Slow, consistent drop of around 4% per decade in the overall volume of ozone in the stratosphere due to human activities (release of halogens from human-related operations and activities).

P

Packaging Waste Recovery Notes (PRN) and Packaging Waste Export Recovery Notes (PERN): Official documents which verify that manufacturer has completed the desired amount of recycling and reuse.

Pollution: Any changes in physical, chemical, and biological characteristics of the ecosystem caused by natural or anthropogenic activities.

Protocol: Protocol is a distinct and supplementary international agreement connected to a pre-existing convention that must be officially adopted by the signatory countries. Protocols usually introduce additional, more comprehensive obligations to a convention, making it stronger.

R

Radiative Forcing: Whenever a climatic element is altered whilst other factors stay unchanged, it leads to a change in the planet's energy balance between incoming radiant energy and thermal radiation.

Rainforest Alliance: Non-profit organization dedicated to changing land-use practices, corporate practices, and consumption patterns in order to protect ecosystems and promote long term sustainability.

Rainwater Harvesting: Precipitation that falls on rooftops and therefore would flow directly to the drainage system is collected and used for a wide range of purposes.

Ratification: Official endorsement of a treaty, agreement, or contract by a legislature or other national body, allowing a government to become a member.

Rehabilitation: Combination of procedures meant to help people return to their pre-injury, pre-illness, or pre-disease state as quickly as feasible.

Resilience: It refers to a system's, community's, or society's capacity to adjust to threats by preventing or altering in establishing and sustaining an acceptable degree of functioning.

Resistance: The environment's ability to process disruptions while remaining substantially unchanged.

Response: The provision of immediate facilities and better aid during or shortly after a tragedy in order to preserve life, protect the public, and meet the minimum survival needs of those impacted.

Risk: Likelihood of an incident combined with its adverse implications.

Risk Assessment: A strategy for determining the type and amount of risk by identifying and evaluating current vulnerabilities that could negatively affect vulnerable individuals, properties, commodities, livelihood, as well as the surroundings over which they rely.

S

Sensitivity: The intensity to which a system is impacted to climate-related events, either negatively or positively.

Sink: The term refers to any activity, mechanism (photosynthesis), or system (ocean and forests) that eliminates a greenhouse gas, from the environment.

T

Technology Transfer: A comprehensive range of procedures that include the exchange of information, funds, and commodities among many stakeholders in order to perpetuate technologies for responding to or tackling climate change.

Threatened Species: Living organisms that are at risk of extinction in the foreseeable future.

U

Umbrella Group: An alliance of non-European Union industrialized nations that was established after the ratification of Kyoto Protocol.

UN REDD Programme: United Nations' collaborative initiative on Reducing Emissions from Deforestation and Forest Degradation (REDD) in emerging economies.

V

Vector: A living entity which spreads an infection from one host to another.
Vector-borne Disease: Disease transmitted between hosts by a vector.
Vulnerability: A combination of physical, sociological, economical, and ecological conditions and processes that raise the probability of a population being adversely affected by a climatic catastrophe or transition.

W

Water Scarcity: A situation in which consumption of water surpasses availability.
Weather: The condition of the atmosphere at a specific time and location.

Z

Zero Carbon: A word that is occasionally used to characterize a product which emits no CO_2 or GHGs during its manufacture and/or processing.
Zero Waste: All resources are conserved by responsible production, consumption, recycling, and reclamation of items, materials, and resources without combustion or releases to land, waters, or atmosphere, which jeopardize the environment and public health.

Index

abiotic stress 70, 104, 109
aboriginal 160
acetic acid 41
acetylcholinesterase 183
adaptation 8, 32, 88, 239
adaptations strategies 163
adaptive actions 152
adaptive capability 161
advanced modelling 80
affordable energy 118
agenda 2030 24, 25
agricultural commodities 77
agriculture 5, 18, 26, 62, 64, 65, 66, 74, 77, 104, 105, 108, 123, 171, 173, 224, 232, 233, 234
agroforestry 154
algal biomass 182
algal indicators 182
algorithmic design 141
allothermal 44
anemometer 204
Annex B 215
Annex I Countries 214, 215
anthropogenic 1, 7, 32, 89, 103, 107, 183, 245
antioxidants 95
aquifers 177, 178
arbuscular mycorrhizal fungi 94, 95
aromatics 41

bioclimatic design 132
biodiesel 32, 34, 41
biodiversity 7, 16, 154, 173, 175, 233, 240
bioethanol 190
biofuel 19, 49, 55, 119, 240
biogas 49, 54
biohydrogen 190
bioindicator 182, 183, 191
biological treatment 189
biomarker 182, 183, 184, 185, 186, 188, 190, 191
biomass 37, 44, 49, 54, 64, 65, 91, 92, 182, 187, 190, 240
biomechanization 229
bio-methanol 190
biomonitoring 185, 186
biosphere reserve 17, 20
biota 175
biotic stress 63, 104, 107
blue hydrogen 37, 39
Bp energy 34
brake 203

Bureau of Energy Efficiency (BEE) 228
business-oriented techniques 212
butane 46

C1 chemistry 35
cadmium 94, 184, 186
capacity building 22, 124, 162, 219, 226, 240
carbon capture 33, 34, 52, 119, 240
carbon dioxide (CO_2) 32, 33, 49, 181, 233
carbon dioxide scheduler 188
carbon footprint 22, 23, 32, 50, 55, 241
carbon nanotubes (CNT) 43
carbon pricing 212
carbon tetrachloride 3
carrying capacity 126, 177, 232, 241
catalysis 35
chemical fertilizers 108
chemical recycling 51
chlorofluorocarbons (CFCs) 2, 61, 105
Clean Development Mechanism (CDM) 215, 217, 239, 241
clean water 118
climate action 15, 23, 119, 218, 219
climate change 1, 5, 12, 19, 61, 87, 103, 107, 119, 175, 190, 224
climate crisis 14, 24, 25, 182
climate disruption 67, 122
climate emergency 14
climate justice 23, 24
climate literacy 22
climate protection 119
climate-friendly city 125
CO_2 capture and storage (CCS) 34, 52, 240
CO_2 sequestration 34, 233, 241
coevolution 162
co-management 154
compliance period 214
concentrated solar power (CSP) 226
Conference of Parties (COP) 15, 218
conservation 17, 20, 21, 108, 154, 157, 174, 228, 232
conservation strategies 165
consumption-based strategy 119
controller 204
Copenhagen Accord 218, 220
co-production 162, 164
credit constraints 79
CRISPR-Cas-9 109
crop-based fuels 119
crop productivity 63, 68, 70, 80, 105
crop yield 5, 63, 75

249

cross-cutting technologies 227
crustaceans 185

dangerous interference 214
dark zones 176
decarbonization 25, 36, 52
decent labour 118
deforestation 65, 103, 108, 242, 247
desalination 232
diatoms 183, 185, 191
diesel 46
dilution effects 172
dimethyl carbonate (DMC) 41
dimethyl ether 39, 44, 45, 47, 48
disaster-risk 154
dissolved oxygen 183
drive train 204
drought 6, 12, 13, 65, 67, 71, 88, 89, 90, 92, 93, 94, 104, 109, 245
dryland agriculture 234

Earth Summit 14, 17, 121
ecofriendly 88, 243, 244
eco-hydrology 171, 177
eco-labelling 244
ecological 124, 151, 153, 154, 173, 175, 177, 182, 183, 189, 191, 242
economic development 119, 121
economic growth 104, 118, 125, 159, 175
economic prosperity 121
economic shock 104
economic sustainability 125
ecosystem 17, 19, 20, 117, 124, 150, 154, 165, 173, 175, 183, 186, 188, 191, 206, 231, 232, 245
ecosystem services 17, 18, 19, 22, 150, 175, 176
ectotherms 190
emerging economies 121, 212, 218, 220, 239, 247
emerging technologies 41
Emission Gap Report 16
emission limitation target 215
Energy Conservation Act 228
energy consumption 50, 122, 227, 228
energy efficiency 227
energy sustainability 125
environmental destruction 118, 244
environmental education 23, 126
environmental governance 126, 164
Environmental Protection Act 229
environmental services 1
environmental stresses 70, 87, 118
environmental sustainability 123
ethylene 41, 50
evaporation 66, 76, 89, 172, 173, 176
evaporative cooling 134
extended tension leg platform (ETLP) 204
extinction 16, 17, 18, 246

fertilization 105, 240
Fifth Assessment Report (AR 5) 213
First Assessment Report (FAR) 213
flue gas 35
food access 77
food availability 76
food crisis 79
food crops 63, 65, 68, 69
food safety 63, 66
food security 5, 73, 79
food utilization 78
forest cover 17, 176
forest degradation 212, 247
formaldehyde 41
fossil fuels 1, 33, 37, 89, 200, 207, 243
fourth assessment report (AR 4) 213
Fragile Ecosystem Management 123
frameworks 150, 158
free air carbon dioxide enrichment (FACE) 181, 187
fuel rebound effect 119
fuel switch 227, 243

gearbox 202, 203
gender discrimination 118
gender equality 118, 243
generator 203
genetic engineering 234
geothermal 201
GHG 51, 68, 87
Gini index 132
Global Action Programme (GAP) 123
Global Environment Facility (GEF) 243
Global Geopark 21
global sea level 4
global warming 1, 2, 15, 18, 32, 34, 64, 105
global warming potential 3, 243
good health 118
Green Climate Fund (GCF) 218
greenhouse effect 2, 33, 105, 243
Green House Gas (GHG) 12, 32, 51, 68, 87, 105, 199, 214, 227, 241
green hydrogen 37, 54
Green India 233
green jobs 23, 26
green spaces 141
grey hydrogen 37
gross domestic product 224
Gully control 174

Halon-1301 3
hazardous waste 3
hazards 5, 150, 164, 183
HCFC-21 3
heat 2, 4, 6, 18, 35, 43, 49, 64, 104, 144, 185, 201, 202, 244
heavy metal 88, 91, 92, 184, 186

Index

Higher Education Sustainability Initiative (HESI) 123
Himalayan ecosystem 232
holistic 21, 155, 230
human-induced greenhouse effect 2
hunger 75, 80, 104, 118
hybridization 108, 151, 153, 160, 161, 163
hydrocarbon 35, 49, 240
hydroelectric power 230
hydroelectricity 201
hydrogen 35, 36, 37, 38, 39, 42, 46, 51, 54
hydrogen economy 37, 52
hydrogeological 158
hydrology 173, 175

ICT-OEC 37, 54
immobilization 92, 107
Indian monsoon 6
indigenous 150, 152, 154, 156, 157, 158, 159, 164, 165, 244
indigenous knowledge 18, 150, 158, 161, 162, 163
indigenous tribe 157, 183
industry 32, 39, 44, 52, 53, 54, 63, 172, 191, 227
inequality 104, 118, 132
infrastructure 8, 20, 37, 39, 40, 53, 119, 159
innovation 24, 32, 119, 124, 209, 227
institutions 119, 123, 126, 160, 232
Integrated Water Resource Management (IWRM) 177, 178
Intentional Nationally Determined Contributions (INDCS) 226
Intergovernmental Panel on Climate Change (IPCC) 11, 14, 213, 216
International Emissions Trading (IET) 215
International Fund for Agricultural Development (IFAD) 2019 124
International Union for Conservation of Nature 4
invasive species 21

Joint Forest Management Committees (JFMCS) 233
Joint Implementation (JI) 15, 215
justice 23, 119

Kenya Slum Upgrading Programme (KENSUP) 131
kinetic energy 202
Kyoto Protocol 214, 216, 217, 218, 239

land degradation 107
leaching 107
life below water 119
life on land 119
limitations 40, 62, 80, 151, 161, 209, 214
long-wavelength infrared radiation 2
low carbon development 18
low-cost emitting diode (LED) 229
low-cost strategies 133

malondialdehyde 95, 110
mechanical energy 203
metallothionein 92, 186, 192
meteorological 150, 157, 244
methane (CH_4) 3, 16, 32, 37, 46, 49, 105, 200, 243
methanol 39, 41, 42, 43, 47, 53, 54
methanol to gasoline (MTG) 41
methyl tertiary butyl ether (MTBE) 41
microalgae 182, 185, 187, 189, 191
microbe-assisted phytoremediation 94
mission innovation (MI) 32
mitigation 80, 107, 155, 213, 224, 225, 227, 245
morphology 173
MSW rules 229
municipal waste management 229

Nation Action Plan on Climate Change (NAPCC) 224, 225, 236
National Environmental Policy 232
national mission for a Green India 233
national mission for enhanced energy efficiency 227
national mission for sustainable agriculture 233
national mission for sustaining the Himalayan ecosystem 232
national mission on sustainable habitat 228
National Oceanic and Atmospheric Administration (NOAA) 4
National Solar Mission 226
National Water Mission 230
National Water Policy 230
Nationally Determined Contribution (NDC) 15, 16, 25, 32, 226
natural greenhouse effect 2
natural Resource 53, 74, 150, 152, 153, 155, 157, 178, 225, 242
natural resources management 152
natural ventilation 133, 138
nature-based solution 18, 26, 174, 177, 245
net zero goal 33, 39
night ventilation 134, 136
nitrous oxide (N_2O) 3, 105, 200
non-Annex-I countries 214, 215
non-governmental organization (NGO) 176
nuclear power 207
nulla bunds 177
nutrition transition 78

ocean acidification 4
ocean warming 4
Organization for Economic Co-Operation and Development (OECD) 211
oxy-combustion technology 119
ozone layer depletion 1, 245

paradigm 156
Paris agreement 2015 103

partnership 119, 123, 126, 218, 225, 230
peace 118, 119, 126
people 62, 75, 76, 117, 121, 124, 150, 152, 156, 172, 224, 242
percolation 173, 177
phenology 18
photosynthesis 2, 64, 105, 182, 185, 190, 246
photovoltaic 226
photovoltaic systems 226
phytochelatins 186, 192
phytodegradation 91
phytoextraction 91
phytohormones 94
phytoplankton growth 183
phytoremediation 88, 91, 94
phytostabilization 92
phytovolatilization 92
plastic refining 50
policy 123, 126, 150, 214, 218, 224, 227, 230, 232
polyamine 95
porosity 173
poverty 15, 24, 74, 104, 117, 118, 154
prairie windmill 203
precipitation 5, 6, 62, 63, 64, 67, 68, 91, 92, 104, 230, 246
pre-industrial times 220
producer gas 228
productivity 6, 42, 63, 67, 69, 74, 123, 174, 177, 187, 234
proline 95, 109
propane 45, 46
prosperity 121
protocol 15, 214, 245
pseudoscience 155
public distribution system 76
public health 7
public transportation 230, 26
PVC 50

Ramsar Convention 21, 178
reactive oxygen species 67
reclamation 107, 110, 161
recycle 126
reductionist 156
reference gas 2
rehabilitation 246
relative water content 95
relocation 74
remediation 88, 90, 91, 94, 96, 107, 110
renewable energy 19, 34, 35, 36, 38, 39, 54, 201, 208
resource sustainability 125
resource utilization 121, 126
responsible consumption and production 119
restoration 17, 176, 242
reuse 126, 178, 189, 203, 229, 241

Rio+20 123
risk management 234
risks 153, 175

salinity 66, 109, 173, 190
sanitation 118
Second Assessment Report (SAR) 213
second commitment period 216
sequestration 23, 233, 241
silicon diode 226
simulation 142, 143, 146
single-cell protein (SCP) 188
sink 19, 21, 246, 221, 233, 241
slum regeneration 130
social instability 122
social sustainability 125
sociologically marginalized 122
soil 64, 66, 88, 89, 91, 92, 94, 95, 173
soil drought 89, 93, 95
soil erosion 19, 107, 119
soil fertility 65, 66
soil-foliage complex 173
solar energy 54, 89, 136, 226
solar photovoltaic generation 226
solar thermal power excavating (STPG) 226
solid waste management 228
spar-buoy 204, 205
stress resistance 109
strong institutions 119
subjugation 152
supply limitations 20
surface temperature 1, 2, 4, 12, 15, 103, 243
sustainability 80, 117, 118, 119, 122, 123, 125, 137, 153
sustainable agriculture 104, 157, 233
sustainable cities and communities 119
Sustainable Development Goals (SDGs) 17, 18, 76, 104, 118
sustainable land management 124

Tarun Bharat Sangh 176
task force 213
technology transfer 226, 239, 246
TEK 151, 152, 153, 154, 155, 156, 158, 159, 160, 161, 162, 163, 164
tension leg platform (TLP) 204
thermal autonomy (TA) 146
thermal comfort 130, 132, 133, 135, 137, 141, 145
thermal inertia 134
Third Assessment Report (TAR) 213
tidal power 201
tolerance mechanism 109
tolerant plant 89
top-down 161, 162, 164
transgenic crops 109

Index

transport 26, 37, 42, 44, 49, 88, 89, 109, 119, 124, 159, 173, 228, 229, 230

uncertainty 63, 73, 74, 78, 79, 146, 157, 159
unemployment 208
urban planning 228, 138
urbanization 105, 125, 205

value-added products 36, 52, 190
variability 65, 68, 129, 150, 153, 157, 172, 185, 212, 233
visible spectrum 2

waste-to-energy 229
wastewater treatment digester gas 201
water conservation 157, 231
water crises 124
water cycle 6, 173
water harvesting 174, 176, 246
water management 124, 157
water quality 172, 173, 175, 178, 189
water quality management 175
water scarcity 92, 107, 175, 178, 230, 247
watershed management 232
water supply 80, 232
water vapour 2
wellbeing 11, 78, 118, 151
wetlands 17, 21, 154, 175, 178, 231
wind turbines 202, 203, 204, 206, 208, 209
working groups (WG) 213
World Bank 131, 181
World Heritage site 20
World Resource Institute 3
World Summit on Sustainable Development 2002 117
World Water Assessment Programme 172

Xbee wireless sensors 188

Zero Hunger 118

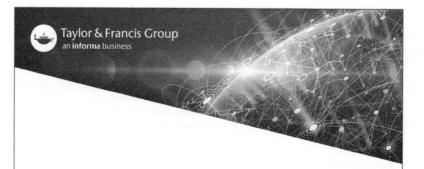